Horses and Mules
in the Civil War

IN MEMORY OF
THE ONE AND ONE HALF MILLION HORSES AND MULES
OF THE CONFEDERATE AND UNION ARMIES WHO WERE KILLED
WERE WOUNDED, OR DIED FROM DISEASE IN THE CIVIL
MANY PERISHED WITHIN TWENTY MILES OF MIDDLEBURG
IN THE BATTLES OF ALDIE, MIDDLEBURG AND UPPERVILLE
IN JUNE OF 1863

Horses and Mules in the Civil War

*A Complete History
with a Roster of More
Than 700 War Horses*

GENE C. ARMISTEAD

McFarland & Company, Inc., Publishers
Jefferson, North Carolina, and London

Frontispiece: "The War Horse" by Tessa Pullan at Middleburg, Virginia, the first memorial to the horses and mules of the Civil War (courtesy National Sporting Library & Museum, Middleburg, Virginia).

LIBRARY OF CONGRESS CATALOGUING-IN-PUBLICATION DATA

Armistead, Gene C., 1947–
Horses and mules in the Civil War : a complete history
with a roster of more than 700 war horses / Gene C. Armistead.
p.   cm
Includes bibliographical references and index.

ISBN 978-0-7864-7363-2
softcover : acid free paper ∞

1. United States—History—Civil War, 1861–1865—Cavalry operations.
2. War horses—United States—History—19th century.
3. United States. Army. Cavalry—History—Civil War, 1861–1865.
4. Confederate States of America. Army. Cavalry—History.
5. Horses—United States—History—19th century.
6. Mules—United States—History—19th century.   I. Title.
E470.A72 2013   973.7'42—dc23   2013029776

BRITISH LIBRARY CATALOGUING DATA ARE AVAILABLE

On the cover: Thomas Jonathan Jackson, full-length portrait, on
horseback, facing left, holding up hat in his right hand,
photomechanical print, David Bendann, ca. 1913
(Library of Congress); leathercraft background (Hemera/Thinkstock)

Manufactured in the United States of America

*McFarland & Company, Inc., Publishers
Box 611, Jefferson, North Carolina 28640
www.mcfarlandpub.com*

Dedicated to my grandchildren...
Elizabeth Rose ("Ellie") Tucker
Emma Rose Jacobson
Phillip John ("Philly") Jacobson

Table of Contents

Preface and Acknowledgments 1

Introduction 3

1. For Want of a Horse (or Mule) 5
2. Recruiting the Equines 14
3. Costs, Preferences, Transportation and Training 26
4. Lost on the Field of Battle 39
5. Lack of Feed, Bad Roads and Poor Care 49
6. Runaways, Stampedes and Wauhatchie 67
7. The Lightning Mule Brigade 72
8. Hippophagy 82
9. Equines and Morale 87
10. War's End and Remembrance 95
11. The Naming of Civil War Equines 103
12. Roster of Civil War Equine Veterans 107

Appendices
    A. Equine Colors and Marks 187
    B. "Charge of the Mule Brigade" 189
    C. "General Sheridan's Horse" by Bill Nye 190
    D. "Here's Your Mule" 192
    E. Locations of Civil War Equine Artifacts 194

Chapter Notes 196

Bibliography 217

Index 236

Preface and Acknowledgments

To grow up in Alabama during the 1950s was to grow up with the Civil War. Even then reference to "the War" meant that war and not World War II or the Korean War, which had only recently ended. The interest thereby engendered has followed me ever since. In the 1980s I found (or made) time to study the war more fully and gradually collected hundreds of books and articles about it. My main areas of interest became the "forgotten" or "unrecognized" people of the war — white Southern Unionists, black Confederates, and Californians — and I eventually published articles or essays on all of them.

It was in or around 2008 that I noticed that the equines of the war were generally relegated to passing mentions in the literature of the war. My curiosity, and my then 2-year-old granddaughter Ellie's love of horses (particularly Rainbow Dash, Pinkie Pie and others of the "My Little Pony" series), led me to examine this forgotten group of Civil War participants. By May 2009 I had collected enough about them to make a presentation on Civil War equines to the San Diego Civil War Round Table. This book is an outgrowth of that study and presentation. It has been a real pleasure to be able to write a book about the Civil War that involves no controversy.

The research for this book involved reading and rereading more than 3,000 books and articles, and scanning and reading portions of at least that many more. There remains much more research that could be done. Published and unpublished memoirs and diaries of the human participants would yield further incidents involving equines and the names of probably many more horses used during the war. The records of the Quartermaster Department and at the Cavalry Museum in Kansas would provide greater detail regarding recruiting and replacement of equines and their costs. This work can therefore be only an introduction to the subject. Yet, it has been an enlightening and interesting study of a neglected aspect of the war. I can only hope that the reader will find it likewise.

No book can be the work solely of the author. There are many who have contributed in various forms completing this work and to whom recognition and thanks are due. Firstly, my wife, Darlene Armistead, who has been patient and understanding of my work on this project. Then there is Ellie Tucker, my granddaughter, whose love of horses inspired me throughout. Matt and Leah Tucker, my son-in-law and daughter, respectively, provided much help with computer-related problems. I certainly might not have done this work without the encouragement of Dave Tooley, president of the San Diego Civil War Round Table, or completed it without the many helpful suggestions and encouragement of J.H. "Hank" Segars of Madison, Georgia. Good friends are always essential in a work of this type.

Many others were generous with their time and assisted me with information or with obtaining photographs for use in the book. These wonderful people include Shaun Aigner-Lee of Dementi Studios, Richmond, Virginia; Stephen Cochran of the New Harmony Working Men's Institute, New Harmony, Indiana; Mark R. Eby, Thrall, Texas; Col. Keith E. Gibson of the VMI Museum, Lexington, Virginia: Maureen Gustafson of the National Sporting Library and Museum, Middleburg, Virginia: Richard Jankowski, president of the Old Baldy Civil War Round Table of Philadelphia, Pennsylvania: Jennifer L. Jones and David Miller of the Smithsonian Institution, Washington, D.C.; P. Michael Jones of the General John A. Logan Museum of Murphysboro, Illinois; Lisa McCown and Katie Gardner of Washington and Lee University, Lexington, Virginia; David Rowland, president of the Old York Road Historical Society, Jankintown, Pennsylvania; Esther F. Simms of the Texas Civil War Museum, Fort Worth, Texas; Elizabeth Scott-Whipkey, Hodgenville, Kentucky: J.E.B. Stuart IV, of Richmond, Virginia: Don Wiles, Mount Laurel, New Jersey; and Drury Wellford and Cathy Wright of the Museum of the Confederacy, Richmond, Virginia.

To one and all, thank you!

Introduction

The Civil War has been considered the defining great event (after Independence) in the history of our nation. It has often been noted that this war was "the first modern war," with the introduction of large-scale use of rifled weapons, railroads, the submarine, ironclad vessels, the telegraph and other innovations. It was also the last of the old-style wars — especially in its heavy reliance upon equines.

When the Civil War began, mechanized vehicles were forty years in the future and powered aircraft more than fifty. Railroads had only recently begun to link the principal cities — especially in the South, where most of the war was fought. Navigable rivers were fairly abundant in the South, but could not serve all areas — especially during times of low water. Though the Southern coastlines were long, the access they made into the interior was limited to the rivers and railroads. More than a few hundred yards from the coast, a navigable river, or a railroad, soldiers had either to limit food, clothing and supplies to what they could haul or to rely on equines. Even then, a wagon was limited to about 100 miles; beyond that distance, the fodder needed for the team animals exceeded the load a wagon could carry.[1] For this reason, horses and mules were extensively used by both the Union and Confederate armies. At the beginning of his 1864 campaign to Atlanta, Union General William T. Sherman limited his trains to lessen demands for forage, only to find that reduced wagon transport even further tied his armies to railroads.[2] Almost at the war's end, Confederate General Joseph E. Johnston complained that the elements of the Army of Tennessee which joined him in North Carolina "were without artillery and baggage-wagons, and consequently were not in condition to operate far from railroads."[3]

According to best calculations, 2,213,000 soldiers served in the Northern and Southern armies combined. In contrast, at least 3,000,000 equines — 36 percent more — participated as part of the armies. The total casualties of the men was about 646,000 for a rate of about 29 percent. This rate included killed, wounded and died of disease. The comparable rate for equines, excluding wounded but recovered, was about 1,500,000, or roughly 50 percent. Obviously, they were integrally involved in all activities of the armies, including those on the battlefields. And this involvement was freely acknowledged by the commanders like Sherman and Johnston, who complained of shortages of equines, and by the veterans who wrote home and, after the war, wrote reminiscences and unit histories. There is virtually no account of the Civil War that does not include references to horses or mules. Sometimes veterans expressed genuine affection for their animals, and at other times horror at the grievous woundings and deaths of equines, similar to what they expressed for their fellow soldiers.

There are extremely few accounts of generals and commanders that do not include some reference like "his horse was shot out from beneath him."

The horse was important to the individual soldiers of the Civil War as well as to armies. It is almost impossible to find a memoir of a Civil War soldier who had a horse but doesn't mention it in some way at least in passing. A veteran of the Confederacy's 2nd Creek Mounted Volunteers, George W. Grayson, wrote: "One becomes greatly attached to any horse that he has had the exclusive use of for any considerable time, but especially fond and friendly becomes this attachment when he feels that his horse has on occasion been the means of helping him through, probably saved his life in many thrilling junctures and hair raising escapades."[4]

The Civil War could not have been fought for so long a period over so extensive an area without horses and mules. Their experiences must have been equally compelling as those of the men. This is their story.

1

For Want of a Horse (or Mule)

In order to appreciate the numbers of horses and mules used during the Civil War it is necessary to examine the many roles for which they were required.

The first image called to mind of equines when we think of the Civil War — or any pre–1900 war — is the dashing **cavalry** charge. The prominence in history and the romance of cavalry commanders such as George A. Custer, Nathan Bedford Forrest, Phil Sheridan, "Jeb" Stuart, "Fighting Joe" Wheeler and others has emphasized this role. According to Union Major General James H. Wilson, who commanded the largest cavalry force in United States history, "The horse is the prime factor in cavalry. Through him the cavalryman moves faster, gets there quicker, covers longer distances in less time, finds weaker places in the enemy's lines, strikes him in the flank or rear, or breaks his means of communication and supply."[1] It is not surprising that the Civil War cavalryman is more often thought of as "horse and rider" than as simply the cavalryman. Since a cavalryman without a horse could not fulfill his cavalry function, it is obvious that each and every cavalryman required a horse. Actually, more horses than men were required in order to ensure that remounts were available to replace steeds lost in action or tired out on the march. Cavalry required a lot of replacement horses. For example, during the first eight months of 1864, the cavalry of the Union Army of the Potomac was remounted twice (requiring 40,000 horses).[2]

Ideally a cavalry regiment consisted of ten companies of 116 men each.[3] To this number must be added horses for regimental officers, a sergeant major, quartermaster and commissary sergeants, a saddler, a chief farrier, a regimental wagon master, two hospital stewards,[4] and teams for the regimental wagons. Cavalry lieutenants were allowed to keep two horses and all other officers, three.[5] At full strength (which was exceedingly rare), a cavalry regiment required a minimum of around 1,200 horses. For the entire war, 350 men would not be too conservative a regimental average. With 137 Union and 206 Confederate full-time regiments,[6] the total minimum would be 120,050 horses. When the average four-month life for a cavalry horse[7] is calculated in, the probable total requirement for cavalry horses would be 1,440,600.

The next most prominent Civil War usage of horses and mules is in the **artillery**. Artillery batteries consisted of four to eight guns per battery (2 guns per section) with, as attrition set in, four the more common number — especially in the Confederacy. Each gun was attached to a caisson pulled by six horses and was accompanied by a limber (carrying ammunition), also attached to a caisson pulled by six horses. There was also a battery wagon

Battery M, 2nd U.S. Artillery at Fair Oaks, Virginia, 1862. Note that there are many horses in addition to those in the teams (photograph by James F. Gibson, Library of Congress).

carrying equipment and a traveling forge.[8] The men rode on the left-side horses of a team or on caissons, but the battery's officers and staff needed separate, individual horses. Most accounts of field artillery batteries seem to indicate about 120 horses as the usual complement.[9] Horse artillery (sometimes referred to as "flying artillery") which accompanied cavalry units had to be able to move faster than field artillery, so loads on teams were reduced by mounting all except a driver on separate, additional horses. Also to be mounted were two extra men who served as horse holders when artillerymen went into action.[10] Mountain howitzers were another story. These small, light, indirect-fire guns could be pulled by one mule when assembled, but were transported over distances disassembled and packed on two mules with a third to carry ammunition.[11] These types of batteries typically had thirty-three mules.[12] Excluding heavy artillery units which served in garrison or as infantry, there were 636 full-time Union and Confederate batteries. At an average of 120 horses per battery the minimum requirement would be 76,320 animals. When the average 7.5-month life of an artillery animal[13] is factored in, Civil War artillery units would have needed 488,448 horses.

Perhaps surprisingly, the **infantry** also needed large numbers of equines. Field officers needed horses to enable them to supervise lines of march and to move about the battlefield observing and directing their regiments in battle. Both Union and Confederate officers had to provide their own mounts,[14] and, especially as forage became limited, most company grade officers other than the adjutant[15] and chaplain[16] did not use horses. In the Confederate armies but not those of the Union, regimental headquarters clerks had a horse for their use.[17] At the beginning of the war, infantry regiments often had the equivalent of their own "train." William Watson described the regimental train of the Confederate 3rd Louisiana Infantry when the war began as consisting of ten company wagons, one officer wagon, one staff wagon, one commissary wagon, and one quartermaster wagon. Each of these fourteen wagons was pulled by four to six mules.[18] Company wagons relieved the load that the man had to carry, with tents and other gear being carried in them.[19] The company wagons soon disappeared since they slowed movement of units and clogged the roads, and obtaining fodder for the teams became too difficult. The infantryman "shucked" tents, overcoats, and other — to him — nonessential items. In the Union army, each infantry company usually came to have a mule which carried on a pack-saddle the equipments of the unit's cookhouse.[20] During Sherman's "March to the Sea" each company was allowed a pack mule, but the men carried their own cooking utensils.[21]

It would be almost impossible to calculate accurately the numbers of horses and mules used by Civil War infantry units. If it is assumed that each regimental headquarters and staff had about thirty horses (which is surely not a high estimate) and that there were 1,151 Union and 541 Confederate full-time infantry regiments, the result would be 50,760 horses. No average life span for infantry animals is available, but if a high guess of one year is used, then the 203,040 result does not seem at all high.

The **headquarters** of the many brigades, divisions, corps and armies of both the Union and the Confederacy required mounts in the same manner as infantry regiments and for the same reasons — only more so. Generals had an even greater need to have a fresh steed available to move about the battlefield to observe and direct affairs. Each general had his staff, the size of which increased with the size of his command. Staff organization during the Civil War was not nearly so advanced as we are accustomed to in modern times and there was much variation in the composition and size of staffs. A staff could include one to three or more assistant adjutant generals, a chief quartermaster, a chief commissary, a chief engineer,

Horses of U.S. Grant, June 1864, near Cold Harbor, Virginia. Held by unknown hostlers, left to right are Egypt, Cincinnati, and Jeff Davis. Commanders needed multiple horses in order to exercise the command and control of their units (Library of Congress).

a chief surgeon, a number of volunteer aides-de-camp, clerks, servants and couriers. Generals themselves were allowed four houses[22] but often had more available for their own use. There is no average life span information available for the horses of generals or their headquarters staffs, but there is every indication that their mounts received greater care and more feed than other horses used during the war. Major Campbell Brown of Ewell's staff in Richmond, after an inspection of government stables, noted that the horses of generals were "excessively fat — cared for by Gov't negroes."[23] The 425 Confederate and 583 Union generals[24] would have required an absolute minimum (if there were no equine deaths of disablements) of 4,032 mounts. Their staff members also each needed more than one horse available for their use, and the total staff requirement was probably ten times that of the total requirements of generals — about 40,000. If the average lifespan of such horses is guessed at as a full year, the result would be 176,128 mounts.

The greatest requirement for equines — particularly mules — during the Civil War was in the "trains" of the **quartermasters** and **commissaries**. Both sides utilized railroads or boats to move indispensable supplies to the furthest extent possible, but at some point loads had to be unloaded and then reloaded on wagons or pack animals for delivery to the units in the field. At first there were entirely too many wagons and animals to haul them. General W.T. Sherman noted in his memoirs that prior to the Battle of 1st Manassas, the soldiers were so loaded down that "it took from twenty-five to fifty wagons to move the camp of a regiment from one place to another."[25] Initially wagons were pulled by four horses, but soon after the war began a change was made to six mules per wagon.[26] Rectifications to the

Pack mules. Loads could be attached to the frames as shown or, alternatively, panniers (large wicker baskets) could be used (sketch from Josh Billings's *Hardtack and Coffee*).

Large wagon park at Brandy Station, Virginia. This photograph, taken in May of 1863, shows only a portion of the wagon train of the Union VI Corps. Examination shows 217 vehicles with the 1,902 mules necessary to pull them (photograph by Timothy O'Sullivan, Library of Congress).

number of wagons allowable followed. In October 1861, Union Major General George B. McClellan issued an order that forbade soldiers riding in wagons and soldiers' knapsacks or tent floors being carried in wagons.[27] During the 1862 Peninsula Campaign it was discovered that there were still too many wagons, and since they were seriously impeding marches, further reductions were necessary. McClellan's General Orders No. 153, issued August 10, 1862, from Harrison's Landing, made further limitations on what could be carried in Army wagons and specified the numbers of wagons allowable. The order allocated headquarters units wagons as follows: four for a corps, three per division or brigade, three per battery or cavalry squadron, and six for a full infantry regiment. One of the wagons allowed an infantry regiment was to be used exclusively for the hospital stores of the regimental surgeon. Another would carry only grain for officers' horses, with half of the wagons of batteries and squadrons limited to the same purpose.[28]

Further reductions were needed in the Union Army of the Potomac. On August 21, 1863, Maj. Gen. George Meade issued General Orders No. 83 "in order that the amount of transportation in this Army shall not in any instance exceed the maximum allowance proscribed in General Order No. 274 of August 7, 1863 from the War Department, and to further modify and reduce baggage and supply trains..." In accordance with this order no baggage or equipment of officers or men could be carried in wagons assigned by the order to the quartermaster or commissary. Meade specified limitations on the number of wagons for corps, division and brigade headquarters, upon regiments based upon their size, on batteries and on supply trains. Each wagon had to carry forage for its own team as part of its load. The final statement of the order read, "It is expected that each ambulance, and each wagon, whether in the baggage, supply or ammunition train, will carry the necessary forage for its own team."[29]

The situation of wagons was also an issue in the West. Gen. W.T. Sherman wished to increase the mobility of the three armies under his command in the Military Division of the Mississippi. In April 1864, prior to beginning the campaign to Atlanta, he limited each regiment to one wagon and one ambulance and "to the officers of each company one pack-horse or mule."[30] He further limited the loads which supply trains could carry to food, ammunition, and clothing.[31] Later, before commencing his famous "March to the Sea," he issued Special Field Orders No. 120 with even more restrictions. This order specified that there would be no "general train of supplies" and reiterated the number of allowable wagons and pack animals.[32] Pack trains of mules with panniers for the carrying of burdens were sometimes used in mountainous areas. The equines could carry approximately one-third of their own body weight.

With less capacity and slower movement, the number of wagons needed was greater than the number of trucks used by a modern army.[33] The Emperor Napoleon had specified that 12 wagons were needed to support each 1,000 men — but this applied in developed countryside with good roads.[34] On macadamized roads such as found in Pennsylvania and in parts of Virginia's Shenandoah Valley, a team could pull 1,900 pounds, but on the poorer roads and rough terrain that prevailed elsewhere, only 1,000 pounds could be pulled.[35] Actual team requirements in America were therefore more than double Napoleon's rule. The Army of the Potomac never solved the problem of too many wagons and teams. Just after the 1862 Seven Days Battles its ratio was 26 wagons per 1,000. This increased to 29 per 1,000 after Antietam and to 33 per 1,000 just prior to the Wilderness. By 1864 the entire Union Army had 222,000 horses and mules for 426,00 men — one animal for every two men.[36]

There are no similar statistics available for Confederate armies, but their requirements were certainly of the same proportions. The early-war train of a single Louisiana infantry regiment of fourteen wagons has already been cited. During "Stonewall" Jackson's 1862 campaign in the Shenandoah Valley, 250 trains were making a round trip between Winchester and Strasburg every twelve hours.[37] Later during the same campaign, he had a 200-wagon, double-column train of eight miles in length.[38] During the retreat from Antietam, the reserve ordnance train of Longstreet's Corps was about eighty wagons — forty-five of which were captured by Gregg's Union cavalry.[39] A considerable train was taken north on the Gettysburg campaign. This train was later trimmed down, with all wagons sent to Chambersburg except one medical wagon, one ordnance wagon, one wagon with cooking utensils and fifteen empty wagons for getting supplies for each regiment.[40] Major J.G. Paxton, transportation officer of the Confederate Quartermaster Post at Lynchburg, Virginia, claimed that the Army of Northern Virginia needed 7,000 horses and 14,000 mules every fifteen months.[41] Assuming only the mules were for quartermaster and commissary transport, for four years of war this would be 44,800 for Lee's army alone. The total number of horses and mules used by the quartermasters and commissaries of the Union and Confederate armies is impossible to accurately calculate. A million animals is likely too low an estimate.

Medical departments were another segment of the armies that used numerous equines. The ambulances of a Union corps were under the control of its medical director,[42] but the ambulances and medical supply trains were controlled by the Quartermaster Corps.[43] There were two types of ambulances. Until two years before the war, the U.S. Army had never provided ambulances. At that time, Secretary of War Isaac Toucey appointed a board to experiment with both 2-wheeled and 4-wheeled ambulances. The 4-wheel version received a favorable report after use during an expedition in New Mexico. The 2-wheel version never was tested but, for some reason, the board thought it would be best for badly wounded men, so it was adopted.[44] Nevertheless, the Quartermaster Corps in 1861 decided to issue some 4-wheel ambulances in a ratio of one for each of the 2-wheel version.[45] The smaller 2-wheel ambulance was pulled by one horse and the 4-wheel ambulance by 4 horses.[46] Once in use, the 2-wheel ambulance soon earned the nickname "avalanche," since it provided a very uncomfortable ride for sick or wounded soldiers.[47] Another alternative for transporting wounded men was the "cacolet." This was a frame usually mounted on a mule which could transport either one or two wounded. The cacolet proved to be extremely uncomfortable for wounded men — they felt every motion of the animal — so were not used very much.[48]

The Union Army never determined or arrived at the proper number of ambulances needed, and those available were inadequate for the numbers of wounded needing transport. An assumption was made that 4-wheelers would be best for the slightly wounded and the 2-wheeler for the seriously wounded (the reverse would seem to have been more accurate), and each regiment was initially supplied with one of the larger and five of the smaller. The Union's medical director, Dr. Charles S. Tripler, thought that this was too many and would result in a train twenty-five miles long consisting of 600 ambulances for an army of 100,000.[49] He asked for only 250 ambulances. The Quartermaster Department could not even provide that number, however, so the Army of the Potomac began the Peninsula Campaign in 1862 with only 177 of both types. The number of ambulances authorized for the Army of the Potomac after the Gettysburg campaign was 3 per infantry regiment, 2 per cavalry regiment and only 1 per artillery battery.[50] There were also pharmacy wagons pulled by four horses. On March 11, 1864, the Ambulance Corps Act went into effect. It included determination of the number of ambulances allowed each regiment based upon the size of the regiment; unfortunately, the result was to lower the number authorized for the army as a whole.[51] After the Battle of the Wilderness there were only enough ambulances to transport 10 percent of those who needed it.[52] Appeals from the commanders got the total number raised to 800 in time for the movement to Cold Harbor, but many of the ambulances issued were defective or old.[53] If the situation in the Union Army of the Potomac was an insufficiency of ambulances, it was more so for the Union's western armies, and especially so for the Confederates, who had to "make do" with whatever vehicle types might be the center. Assistant surgeons in the Confederate Army were supposed to receive two horses at the government's expense[54] — about the only advantage they had over their Union counterparts. A conservative estimate would be 30,000 horses needed by the medical departments.

Compared to other uses, the **signal corps** didn't use many horses or mules since it was a small organization. There are pictures of signalers at signal towers with a few horses at the tower's base. In Virginia, the Union had telegraphic trains for telegraph lines to keep the Army of the Potomac and others in the area in contact with Washington. Once a line was laid there were "battery wagons" containing wet-cell batteries to power transmissions over the lines.[55] The telegraph units had additional wagons to carry supplies. Large wire had to be carried on flat wagons pulled by up to four animals, which were used during the war's first year or so. Once flexible, insulated wire became available, it could be uncoiled from a moving mule.[56]

The Union's corps of **aeronauts** was a small unit was organized by Professor Thaddeus Lowe, who was given the "rank" of chief aeronaut. Its balloons were used to observe Confederate lines, camps and movements from after the Battle of First Manassas (an effort to get a balloon there failed) until after the Battle of Chancellorsville, when the corps was disestablished. Initially tanks of gas with which to fill the balloons were built atop two regular army wagons.[57] They were replaced by two hydrogen gas generator wagons to inflate each balloon.[58] There were additional wagons to carry the bags and to provide other support.[59] An uninflated balloon could be carried in one wagon.[60] A Philadelphia inventor named England in January 1863 offered proposals to reduce the costs of the balloon corps. He claimed to have a different method for gas generation that would reduce the number of wagons needed from twelve or fourteen to only two with consequent reduction of the number of horses needed from about fifty to eight or ten.[61] There were never more than six balloons in use at one time, so only 72 to 84 horses were ever needed by this small Civil War "air force."

Engineers used mules to haul their pontoons (portable bridges). The typical pontoon train needed thirty-four wagons to transport the boats. Other wagons were needed to move the timbers and cross planks to where they were needed. Six mules per wagon was normal but in mountainous areas eight were needed.[62] **Bureaus** in Washington and Richmond needed horses to carry messages. Horses and mules in lesser numbers were also needed for various purposes at **arsenals, hospitals, navy yards,** and **prisoner of war camps.** In the Union army, each corps had a **mail** wagon pulled by two horses.

A review of the calculations for equine requirements by the major military functions and estimates for some of the other functions reveals:

Cavalry	1,440,600
Artillery	76,320
Infantry	203,040
HQs & staffs	176,128
QMs & commissaries	1,000,000
Medical depts	30,000
Engineers	20,000
Signal corps (Union)	5,000
Aeronauts corps (Union)	84
Bureaus, POW camps, etc.	20,000
Total	2,971,172

This total is obviously low, so it would not be amiss to round the Civil War's total requirement for military purposes up to 3,000,000 horses and mules. The actual need for equines in the war would probably exceed the estimated 3,213,363 soldiers who served in the war.

Certain civilian activities associated with the armies also used horses. Each regiment of the Union Army was authorized (but not all had) a **sutler** whose wagon was pulled by a two-horse team.[63] Mathew Brady and other **photographers** followed the Northern armies (mostly the Army of the Potomac) with their "whatsit" wagons (portable darkrooms) pulled by two horses.[64] **News vendors** who supplied newspapers to the troops used one-horse carts.[65] The **Sanitary** and **Christian Commissions** of the North also used wagons to move their supplies and personnel during their commendable efforts to improve soldier life.

In addition to being needed for the armies, horses or mules continued to be needed for strictly civilian pursuits. Fields still had to be plowed and crops gathered. Foodstuffs and manufactured goods — and mail — still had to be delivered. People still had to travel within and between cities. Were there enough horses and mules? The 1860 Federal Census which preceded the war had revealed that there were slightly over five million horses and just over one million mules in the United States.[66] The total number was slightly more than double the white male population between the ages of fifteen and thirty who would be available for service.[67] The breakdown was:

	UNION STATES	CONF. STATES	Kentucky and Missouri
White Males, 15–30	2,582,000	791,000	300,000
Horses	3,400,000	1,700,000	800,000
Mules	100,000	800,000	200,000

Like manpower, equine numbers were heavily weighted in favor of the Union. For both sides, it was a matter of mobilizing them for service in the armies.

2

Recruiting the Equines

Few on either side really went into the war with much thought toward the massive amounts of material that would be needed for conduct of the war. After all, both sides initially thought it would be a quick war. It took time for proper realization of just what and how much, including equine requirements, would be needed for the war. Once realization of what would be required set it, there was an initial rush to locate animals. Then, with few exceptions, both sides would throughout the war be engaged in a constant struggle to round up sufficient horses and mules. There were persistent complaints by commanders of the need to "recruit our horses." In order for these horses and mules to be useful to the armies, they had to be collected in some manner. The methods for collecting equines for army use were varied: (1) purchase by the Quartermaster Departments — much less extensively in the Confederacy than in the Union; (2) private provisioning by the soldiers — the principal source for Confederate cavalry; (3) formal impressments of animals by both armies, but throughout the war by the Confederates; (4) capture from the enemy; and (5) appropriation by commands during campaigns and raids.

When the war began, the United States Army had an existing **Quartermaster Department**, which had the responsibility to purchase and supply the army with horses and mules. Soon after the war began, on June 13, 1861, Montgomery C. Meigs was appointed Quartermaster General with the rank of brigadier general.[1] Despite the huge numbers of equines needed and many obstacles, he was to perform an exceptional job in this position. One of the first problems he had to address upon assuming the job was to provide enough horses and wagons for transportation so that the army assembled around Washington, D.C., could advance, as was demanded by the loud outcry of "On to Richmond."[2] Somehow, he managed. The great demand in 1861 presented a splendid opportunity for purveyors, and the unscrupulous did not fail to take advantage of it. Initially there were too few purchasing agents and fewer qualified inspectors — one problem that Meigs was never able to completely resolve.[3] The Department of the West, commanded by Maj. Gen. John C. Frémont, early became a center of complaints about extravagant prices paid for unserviceable animals. Frémont believed there was a shortage of horses in the United States and proposed that purchases be made in Canada. By telegraph, the War Department forbade such purchases. In fact, horses were available within Frémont's departmental command as close as Quincy, Illinois, at thirty dollars a head less than Frémont sought to buy them in Canada.[4] The culpability, aside from Frémont's inattention, rested largely with his chief quartermaster, Major Justus McKinstry, who had occupied that position since before Frémont's assumption of command of the department and had been give broad power from the War Department.[5] Many of the worst complaints about Frémont were from the family of Union Postmaster General Montgomery Blair, who had in fact exerted pressure upon McKinstry and Frémont to favor their friends when purchasing horses. Blair had even recommended a Mr. Farrar to Gen. Meigs for this purpose. It transpired that this Farrar was the one who had supplied the greatest number of defective animals. McKinstry didn't need any help. Under Frémont he was promoted to brigadier general in September 1861 and commanded a division in Frémont's expedition to Springfield, Missouri. McKinstry's activities as quartermaster were investigated after Frémont was relieved of command. Among the discoveries was that on one occasion he had extorted from a contractor a $3,000 silver service for his wife. Contractors would bill other contractors at huge prices and then sell horses to the army at the greatly inflated prices.

On January 28, 1863, McKinstry was cashiered (dishonorably discharged) from the service — the only Civil War general so tainted.[6] Though Frémont and

Justus McKinstry. McKinstry's corruption in transactions involving the purchase of horses for the Union forces in Missouri earned him the distinction of becoming the only Civil War general who was cashiered (dishonorably discharged) (Library of Congress).

McKinstry were highly visible, maladroit and venal administration of the War Department by Secretary Simon Cameron was also responsible for much fraud upon the government in its purchases of equines. The original contracts for purchases were not given to breeders and traders of horses, but instead to politically connected middlemen who then sublet the contracts to professionals, garnering huge profits for themselves. Horse contracts circulated in Washington almost like money. Cameron used the contracts to repay political debts and displayed favoritism to Pennsylvanians. The result was that the army received unserviceable horses at extravagant prices.[7] Even when there was no fraud involved, the pressures upon Meigs over the purchase of horses was great. President Lincoln's wife, Mary, wrote to him on Oct. 4, 1861, to request that 500 to 1,000 horses be purchased from a friend in Kentucky.[8]

Meigs was informed in August 1861 by prominent Chicago citizens that agents there were paying $75 to $80 per horse and then charging the government $105 to $110.[9] In September 1861, Major D.H. Rucker of the Washington Quartermaster Depot dismissed all of its horse inspectors, as he had good evidence they had been taking bribes to pass unserviceable animals.[10] Henry S. Olcott, an Assistant U.S. Marshal, was detailed to the War Department to investigate fraud in supplying the army. He found that animals, forage and transportation were the principal areas of fraud in the west and southwest of the country (in the east and north it involved manufactured goods). On August 5, 1863, he was ordered to inspect the quartermaster and commissary departments of the Department of the Ohio. Within forty-eight hours he discovered a conspiracy involving a contractor, an inspector, a horse dealer, and a Republican politician. During the past year they had stolen through their frauds $1,000,000 on horse purchases at the corral in Cincinnati. They received fines and imprisonment for their crimes.[11]

The House of Representatives established a special committee headed by Congressman Charles H. Van Wyck of New York to investigate frauds against the government in horse purchases. The committee held hearings from July 1861 through April 1862. The Van Wyck Committee's report was issued in July 1862. Testimony revealed horses accepted and paid for that had distemper or spavined limbs. They heard of contractors who "shopped around" until they found an inspector who would pass their animals. One witness described observing an inspection of horses and hearing a neighbor remark that he had known one horse (that was passed) for twenty-nine years.[12] Even field commanders could be involved. At one time, Gen. Judson Kilpatrick had been implicated in "a scheme to extort bribes from brokers wishing to sell horses to his brigade."[13]

When Henry W. Halleck assumed command of Frémont's old department, he reassigned the quartermaster of Gen. Samuel Curtis's command to a "roving commission to purchase horses." This officer, Philip H. Sheridan, traveled to Madison and Racine, Wisconsin, where he bought 200 horses. He then went to Chicago, where he bought another 200 at a better price and thenceforth made that city the center of his activities.[14] Sheridan's experience illustrated the effect of using capable officers to select horses. Though there were

Barns at the Giesboro Cavalry Depot (Library of Congress).

many corrupt inspectors, most were simply not qualified to inspect horses and mules. From the beginning of the war, Meigs had continually pleaded with field commanders to assign him cavalry and artillery officers unfit for other duty for service as inspectors. His pleas went unheeded until the middle of 1863 when the Cavalry Bureau was established. The Quartermaster Department continued to purchase all horses but turned them over to the bureau, which had the responsibility to equip all the cavalry forces of the Union Army. This bureau was a separate office of the War Department with six depots: St. Louis, Missouri; Greenville, Louisiana; Nashville, Tennessee; Harrisburg, Pennsylvania; Wilmington, Delaware; and Giesboro, Maryland. With 500 men working on it, the Giesboro depot was completed in 1863 and by early 1864 could care for up to 30,000 animals at a time. Most of the animals were kept in sheds or corrals but the depot had stables for 6,000 and a hospital for 2,650. The cavalry bureau reorganized the remount service and used experienced horsemen as inspectors.[15] Purchases in the field also began to use qualified inspectors. When the 4th Kentucky Infantry (Union) was mounted in February 1864, it received "fine mounts" as they were purchased at Lexington, Kentucky, by inspectors selected by cavalry commander Col. John T. Croxton.[16] The Union quartermasters became quite proficient in obtaining animals. In December 1864, Maj. Gen. George Thomas's quartermaster, James L. Donaldson, was ordered to obtain "as many" mules as he could. He was somewhat worried that he had exceeded his discretion when his agents collected about 20,000 mules — but Thomas was elated.[17]

There has been no definitive study regarding the Confederate Quartermaster Department. It did maintain a system of posts (equivalent to the Union's depots) scattered through the military departments to service the field armies. For the Army of Northern Virginia there were four general depots which were supplemented by advance and temporary depots.[18] Government stables under superintendents supplemented this system. Horse supply was, by 1862, a problem for the Confederate quartermasters since the horse-breeding areas of western Virginia, Kentucky, Missouri, and middle Tennessee had fallen under Union control early in the war.[19] The posts could not provide enough animals for military and essential civilian needs,[20] and by the winter of 1863–64 the shortage of horses and mules reduced the mobility of the armies and restricted artillery use.[21] Lt. Gen. William Hardee, temporary commander of the Army of Tennessee, reported on Dec. 17, 1863, to the Confederate Adjutant General that it was "a source of infinite trouble" to obtain horses.[22] When Gen. Joseph E. Johnston took command of that same army the following January, he immediately observed the same problem, and on February 2 wrote President Jefferson Davis that his army was deficient 400 artillery horses — a number that was 500 the next week, and 600 in two weeks.[23] As the area under control of the Confederacy shrank further, the problem only got worse.

Private provisioning of horses was the norm for generals and other officers. There are numerous references in the letters, diaries and memoirs of generals and officers about purchases of their own horses or to receiving them as gifts from admirers who had made the purchases. The possession of multiple mounts was the practice for higher-ranking officers. Maj. Gen. Benjamin F. Butler, in the fall of 1861, had nine of his own horses sent to him at Fortress Monroe from his home in Lowell, Massachusetts.[24] Lt. Col. John Singleton Mosby of the 43rd Virginia Cavalry Battalion had as many as a half dozen at a single time.[25] When a captured horse was desired by an officer, the practice was to have it appraised by the quartermaster and then pay that amount to the government. In the Confederacy there were some artillery units that went to war after supplying themselves with horses to pull their pieces. In these cases, it seems that the method was to solicit donations from owners in the area where the battery was organized.[26] April 1862 found Semple's Battery so critically short of animals for its teams that a "Horses Wanted" advertisement was placed in newspapers.[27] Artillery units providing their own teams was the exception, however.

The Confederate cavalryman had to provide his own horse. H.B. McClellan, a staff officer in J.E.B. Stuart's command, explained that "at the beginning of the war, the Confederate government ... felt itself unable to provide horses for the numerous cavalry companies which offered their services." This was undoubtedly the case, as the Confederacy had to create an entire army and a system for finding and supplying it with all types of war materials. The result was that, for cavalry units accepted, the cavalrymen would provide the horses; each animal would then be appraised (or valuated) by the government, which would pay the soldier a per diem of forty cents for use of the animal and provide food and horseshoes. If the horse was killed in battle, the owner would be paid the amount at which the horse was valued when the unit was mustered. If the horse was lost by any other reason — captured, disabled, or worn out — the soldier received no reimbursement and had to replace it from his own means if he wished to remain in the cavalry. Would-be cavalrymen who preferred a mount whose traits and abilities they knew cheerfully accepted this policy.[28]

Problems with this system soon arose. According to Capt. Charles Minor Blackford of the 2nd Virginia Cavalry, the difficulty was particularly acute for companies originating from the cities. He wrote to his wife, "My men do not have farms from whom they can draw when their horses get killed or disabled." As a result, his company was becoming smaller and smaller. He summed up the situation by writing, "To lose a horse is to lose a man, as they cannot afford a remount and new recruits with horses of their own are almost nil."[29] Purchase of replacement horses was beyond the means of most of the men, and often families had to furnish money to buy needed remounts.[30] Cavalrymen who lost their mounts, due to inflation and low appraisals of the value of their horses, had greater difficulty in replacing their horses as the war progressed.[31]

Dismounted cavalrymen had to be given furloughs to go home to somehow obtain a remount. Sometimes even a thirty- to sixty-day furlough was not enough time to find a replacement. Some of Stuart's cavalry had to travel as far as the Carolinas, Georgia or Mississippi to find one.[32] In the west, during the relatively peaceful winters, Generals Nathan Bedford Forrest and John Hunt Morgan even gave permission for their troopers to return to homes behind Union lines to acquire horses.[33] During Forrest's 1864 raid into Kentucky, Brig. Gen. Abraham Buford even temporarily disbanded his entire command to visit their homes and obtain better mounts. This effort was largely unsuccessful, since horses and mules in the Paducah area had been too well hidden.[34] Furloughs of this type often deprived Confederate cavalry of more than half of its strength.[35] The March 17, 1863, Battle of Kelly's Ford found Gen. Fitzhugh Lee's brigade with fewer than 800 of its 2500 men available.[36]

Even when he had a horse, the Confederate cavalryman was frequently constrained to seek a better one. Due to a leg wound, Pvt. William A. Fletcher transferred from Hood's Texas (Infantry) Brigade to the 8th Texas Cavalry after the Battle of Chickamauga. His 1905 account of his service from that point thereafter records a near-constant searching for and swapping of horses to keep himself adequately mounted.[37] Many Texas units denominated as "cavalry" served dismounted as much as from a lack of horses as for the need for infantry. It was a rare instance when organization of a cavalry unit was ordered by the Confederate government. In September 1864, the Kentucky Infantry Brigade (often remembered as the "Orphan Brigade") received orders to become mounted infantry.[38] Upon arrival at their designated reorganization point at Barnesville, Georgia, they found only 200 horses ready — and very poor ones at that. The units of the brigade had to scour the countryside for the balance needed. They were never completely successful at this, and the brigade was ultimately able to mount only about 700 of its more than 900 men.[39]

Not so well known is that a few Union cavalry regiments organized early in the war were allowed to mount themselves and were paid forty cents per day for the use of the horse and $120 if the animal was killed in battle. Among these were the 2nd Illinois, 3rd Indiana, 1st Iowa, 1st Kentucky, 1st New York and 22nd Pennsylvania regiments.[40] Others were the 3rd Pennsylvania[41] and the 1st Indiana.[42] When a unit's term of service was completed and it was to be mustered out, the custom was for the government to buy these cavalrymen's mounts (given limitations on transport home, the soldier was usually constrained to sell) for the $120.[43] Nearing the end of its term of service, the 7th Kansas Cavalry offered to "veteranize" (that is, reenlist) if they could do so on the same terms as the regiments listed. General W.T. Sherman declined the offer, but most of the men reenlisted anyway.[44]

One Union regiment had a completely different experience. The 1st New Mexico Infantry was raised in 1861 with four of its ten companies mounted. The officers who raised these companies supplied most or all of the horses for their men, obtaining the steeds from their own ranches or by purchase.[45] They were told that the government would reimburse them the cost, support maintenance costs, and provide replacements when needed.[46] The men were to pay the officers the difference between the cost of their animal and the government's appraisal price out of the $12 monthly they would be paid for the use of their horse.[47] This promise proved to be an effective way to obtain needed mounted men and horses. The mounted companies immediately commenced hard service against bandits and Indians even before facing Confederate invaders under Brig. Gen. Henry Hopkins Sibley. The territorial government didn't have money, so the officers were never reimbursed even at government valuations of half their real costs. The men never received their $12 per diem. The horses were never given forage even when it was plentiful and provided to the horses of regular troops in the area. By November 1861, Capt. Rafael Chacon of Co. G reported to the regiment's commanding officer (Col. "Kit" Carson), "My horses are in dying condition from a want of protection from the inclemency of the weather and from starvation." There were no replacements, and hard service in desert and mountain continued. Then, in February 1862, Col. E.R.S. Canby, commander of the Department of New Mexico, ordered that the mounted companies be reduced to two, with the best horses purchased at the government's valuation and reallocated to the remaining two companies. Horses not purchased would be condemned as unfit. Written protests by the four captains, supported by Col. Carson, were ignored and the order put into effect. The dismounted men were of course distraught over their financial loss as much as their being dismounted. Eleven men deserted from one company. Some of the captains lost over $3,000 as a result of both the reallocation of horses and payments at less than half the real value.[48] After Confederates were driven from New Mexico, the volunteer infantry was discharged due to expense, and a cavalry regiment (1st

New Mexico Cavalry) was organized. This regiment was mounted at government expense with, as noted by Capt. Chacon, "first-class horses."[49] In the case of the New Mexican mounted infantrymen, the union might as well have impressed the horses without payment. Their contribution certainly exceeded that of those Union and Confederate cavalrymen who provided their own mounts further east.

Formal **impressment** of horses and mules was extensively used by both the Union and the Confederacy. For the purpose of this work, formal impressment is defined and limited to activities of government to take animals from areas which they controlled, with other "takings" by military commands on a campaign or a raid defined as "appropriations." Official impressment of animals was, to say the least, not at all popular with the citizenry. In such cases, receipts or vouchers were supposed to be given so that the citizen could later obtain reimbursement. Those with Confederate vouchers were, of course, unable to collect when that government went out of business in April of 1865. Some Union citizens and Southern loyalists did obtain partial recompense several years after the war through an involved claims procedure.

Confederate impressments of needed horses and mules from its citizens began early in the war. When "Stonewall" Jackson assumed command at Harper's Ferry in 1861 and discovered that there were no horses to pull his artillery, he ordered Major John A. Harman, his chief quartermaster, to "buy or impress as many as we need."[50] After Little Rock and the Arkansas River Valley fell to the Federals in 1862, the Confederate commissariat impressed the wagons and teams of southwestern Arkansas farmers in order to bring in supplies to sustain the army.[51] As Middle Tennessee was progressively lost by the Confederacy during 1863, replacement animals became more and more difficult to find, and Gen. Braxton Bragg ordered the impressment of all horses in Atlanta.[52] The various quartermaster posts in Virginia were charged to impress horses and mules in that state.[53] The various Southern governors began to receive complaints from their constituents about impressment of animals. Mr. L.E. Parsons and six other citizens of Talladega, Alabama, submitted protests to Gov. Thomas H. Watts from March of 1863 through March of 1864. Their complaints indicated increasing numbers of animals being taken. The March 1863 complaint was about only five wagons and teams taken. In August they complained that "under an order, it was said, from General Wheeler, about 175 horses were impressed." March of the next year found them advising the governor that a Captain Graham, "under an order from Lieutenant-General Polk," had been in their area and impressed numerous horses and mules. They were told by the captain that he had the right to take every seventh mule.[54] Virginia staff officer Charles Minor Blackford's wife wrote him during the same month, "I had bid farewell to the grey mare as the press-gang took her from me." She was lucky, since they sent the horse back when an inspection revealed that it couldn't pull artillery. They did impress and keep the horses of two of her neighbors.[55] One regimental commander, Col. Colton Greene of the 3rd Missouri Cavalry, was in the summer of 1864 tried by court-martial for refusing to order his men to turn over their mules to the army. He was exonerated.[56] Naturally, there were consequences of all these horse and mule impressments. The previously mentioned farmers of southwest Arkansas were prevented from planting and getting in crops,[57] as were farmers in other areas. Already a problem in the Confederacy, transportation was further interfered with by the taking of draft animals by impressment officers.[58] Late in the war, appeals were even made in the press urging citizens that their horses were needed. The

Columbus (Georgia) *Sun* made such an appeal in 1864, stating that those who voluntarily loaned their horses for local defense would not have them impressed. Very few were received, and by 1865 authorities were forced to impress the animals, promising owners they would be paid at market price.[59]

Union impressment of horses and mules, with few exceptions, was limited to areas which had been in rebellion. Horses within the limits of Union occupation were theoretically deemed to belong to the United States government. Brig. Gen. Marsena Patrick, the Army of the Potomac's Provost Marshal, used this policy in the summer of 1864 to harass newspaper correspondents when he ordered his subordinates to seize all unbranded animals and branded ones in the possession of civilians.[60] The largest instances of animal impressment by Union forces occurred on the orders of Maj. General James H. Wilson at Nashville, Tennessee, in late 1864. Newly appointed to command the cavalry of Maj. General George Thomas's forces headquartered at that city, he found that the number of mounts of the cavalry was severely depleted. Thomas gave him permission to impress horses "wherever they could be found south of the Ohio River." In his reminiscences *Under the Old Flag* (1912), Wilson conceded that it was an arbitrary measure and that he enforced it ruthlessly. His quartermasters, giving vouchers for every horse taken, impressed every horse that was useable. Wilson wrote that "all street-car and livery horses, and private carriage- and saddle-horses, were seized. Even Andrew Johnson, the vice-president-elect, was forced to give up his pair. A circus then at Nashville lost everything except its ponies; ... a clean sweep was made of every animal that could carry a cavalryman." So many horses were impressed that Wilson was able to double the number of mounted men he had.[61] Another exception occurred during John Hunt Morgan's July 1863 raid north of the Ohio River. Union cavalry impressed replacement horses during their pursuit of Morgan and his Confederates. Others were taken into service by the Indiana Legion (local emergency troops). In both cases vouchers were given, but the War Department later refused to recognize the vouchers issued by the state troops.[62]

Capture from the enemy, in comparison to other methods of obtaining mounts and draft animals, seems to have provided the least number. There are numerous accounts of horses captured during battles and skirmishes and by the surrender of foes. Only two examples involving deliberate capture of very large numbers of equines will be given. Maj. General "Jeb" Stuart's capture of a Union wagon train at Rockville, Maryland, outside the District of Columbia on June 28, 1863, is well known, since the delay caused by his taking it along with him is often cited as a reason to blame Stuart for the Confederate loss at the Battle of Gettysburg. The number of mules taken — 900, with 150 wagons[63] — would have been a temptation for any commander, and were indeed much needed by the Confederacy. Lt. Col. John S. Mosby — the "Gray Ghost" — is noted for his forays in northern Virginia, disrupting Union communications and activities. In his own *Memoirs* (1917), Mosby took pains to record the numbers of horses and mules taken and sent back to the Army of Northern Virginia's posts. He recorded that during the year from July 1863 through July 1864, he had captured 1,943 and sent them back into Confederate lines.[64] At this stage of the war, this number would have sufficed to mount a full brigade.

Appropriation of civilian horses and mules during raids and invasions was a common occurrence. In these cases there was an immediate need for either replacement mounts or sometimes to prevent the enemy of a means of pursuit. Both Union and Confederate com-

Seizing horses. Raids, particularly later during the war, became a vital method for replenishing mounts (*Harper's Weekly*, December 24, 1864, p. 829).

manders had been taught at West Point that "private property can be seized only by way of military necessity for the support or benefit of the army."[65] Rarely were receipts or vouchers given, nor were on-the-spot payments made for animals taken. Those civilians who lost animals to either army in this manner usually referred to having had their horses and mules stolen. Neither guilt nor loyalty was considered — only the need for mounts. Morgan's raiders north of the Ohio were disgusted with Northern "Copperheads" (Confederate sympathizers) who did not come forth to actively assist them, and took their horses as well as those of citizens loyal to the Union.[66] Southern Unionists were treated no better by Federal cavalry. In 1865 a Tuscaloosa County, Alabama, man told a party from Brig. Gen. John Croxton's command that it "seemed hard" to take a man's property after all of the trouble he had been given by Confederate authorities because of his loyalty to the Union. The cavalry sergeant in charge of the detail gathering horses responded, "That's what all the men say when we are around." The horses were taken.[67]

The summer of 1863 saw the largest instances of Confederate appropriations in the North. According to staff officer Moxley Sorrel, one of the objectives of the Gettysburg campaign was to renew cavalry mounts and quartermaster teams.[68] By the middle of June, the advance cavalry of Brig. Gen. Albert G. Jenkins had advanced into Pennsylvania. June 16 and 17 found him in the area of Greencastle, where carriage and farm animals were taken for use as battery teams. He left with about 120 animals.[69] On June 16, Confederates made a "good haul" at the Caledonia Iron Works (owned by Senator Thaddeus Stevens) about ten miles west of Chambersburg. They took about forty horses and mules here.[70] As the infantry moved north, a member of Longstreet's staff (Blackford), wrote his wife from Williamsport, Maryland, "Horses are becoming quite plentiful as they are sent back by our vanguard."[71] But the Confederates found that there were problems with the new wealth of horseflesh. Sorrel remembered, "The animals were nearly all for farm use. Great lumbering, powerful horses, capable of enormous draughts on those hard roads, but quite impossible to do anything out of a heavy walk."[72] Blackford advised his wife similarly that the horses taken were "too heavy and too clumsy for either cavalry or artillery. Unless they are kept well shod [which was beyond Confederate capability on the march] they soon give out and go lame on these well paved roads."[73] As related to the objective of renewing cavalry mounts and artillery teams, the Gettysburg campaign was a complete failure, with Sorrel noting that only "a few were got across the river [back to Virginia]. They proved useless and were soon abandoned."[74] Since the Confederates had insisted in paying — in their own currency — for many of the horses taken, the U.S. government refused to reimburse the owners because they had been paid![75]

Morgan's July 1863 raid north of the Ohio River was the general's own idea. Braxton Bragg, his superior, had given permission only for a raid into Kentucky to recruit horses and bring back forage for his horses and supplies for the Army of Tennessee.[76] Horses appropriated in Indiana and Ohio by his cavalrymen were thus taken solely to replace their own exhausted mounts and not to replenish the animals of Bragg's army. Morgan had, unknown to Bragg, prepared for this raid by sending Capt. Thomas H. Hines with a company of sixty-two men on a quick foray into Indiana in May. Hines's objective was to gather as many fresh horses as he could. Posing as Union cavalry, Hines and his men were successful in getting a good number of excellent horses by giving vouchers on the U.S. quartermaster in Indianapolis.[77] Through Kentucky, Indiana and Ohio the raiders rode. It was similar to an earlier October 1862 raid through Kentucky, of which a veteran of his 2nd Kentucky Cavalry recalled, "Hour after hour we rode, men and horses exhausted. As soon as one horse gave out another was procured and the ride continued."[78] Some rode appropriated mounts while leading their own favored horses brought from Tennessee, changing back to their own only when battle seemed near. This method also served to somewhat prevent the leaving behind of mounts which might be used by pursuers.[79] During their long march, Morgan's men gathered in almost all healthy horses along the way. Their own broken-down horses were left behind. The Confederates considered that the Indiana and Ohio farmers were getting the better end of a trade. They felt that the farmers would have, after several weeks' rest, a finer animal than had been taken from them. Some wept when it was necessary to leave behind their own horses. (Later in the raid they would have to take even inferior farm animals.[80]) Again, Confederates found that the horses they took were not necessarily what they had hoped for. The "big-bellied, barefooted, grass-fed beasts" were usually "sway-backed" and gave out quickly, making it necessary for the raider to find and take yet another, similar horse.[81] Perhaps Morgan's men would have been gratified to find out that the farmers were unable to retain the horses left behind. They were allowed to keep them only long enough to "make a crop." The animals then had to be turned in to Union provost marshals for delivery to the Quartermaster Department, with those found to be not serviceable con-

demned and sold for the benefit of the government. Animals were not allowed to be returned
to owners even if they had proof of ownership. In some cases, farmers had to buy back their
own teams.[82] All told, Morgan's men appropriated thousands of horses — 500 in Harrison
County, Indiana, alone and another 300 tricked out of an Indiana militia unit.[83]

Union appropriations could be as well organized as the Confederate effort in Pennsylvania. Brig. Gen. Benjamin Grierson was sent in 1863 from Tennessee through the length
of Mississippi to Baton Rouge, Louisiana, on a raid to distract Confederates trying to defend
Vicksburg. At the conclusion, he reported having taken 1,000 horses and mules.[84] When
Grant and his army arrived below Vicksburg they had limited horses and transport. Grant
ordered that all horses, mules and oxen in the area be collected to pack ammunition for his
force.[85] Sherman's 1864 "March to the Sea" is probably the best known large-scale Union
appropriation of horses. His Special Field Order No. 120 of November 9, just prior to
beginning the march, was clear on the matter. Item 6 stated: "As for horses, mules, wagons,
etc., belonging to the inhabitants, the cavalry and artillery may appropriate freely and without limit; ... Foraging-parties may also take mules or horses, to replace jaded animals of
their trains, or to serve as pack mules for the regiments or brigades."[86] From near Savannah,
Georgia, he reported to Gen. Grant on December 16, 1864, "I have no doubt the State of
Georgia has lost by our operations fifteen thousand first-rate mules." Regarding the number
of horses appropriated, he averred that his cavalry under Kilpatrick had been able to collect
all his remounts, that every officer seemed to have three or four led horses, and that mounted
footsore soldiers followed every regiment. He wrote Grant, "You can estimate approximately
the number of horses collected."[87] It must have been a huge number indeed as he recalled
it in his memoirs as "a vast herd."[88]

Perhaps almost as many horses and mules as Sherman's marchers took were taken by
the war's last great raid — that of Maj. Gen. James H. Wilson through Alabama and Georgia
during March and April of 1865. During the pursuit of Hood's retreating Army of Tennessee
from Nashville in the winter of 1864–65, the area of pursuit had been stripped of forage
and the roadways were muddy. Upon arrival at the Tennessee River, Wilson had only about
7,000 horses useable for service.[89] Having already scoured the area between the Cumberland
and Ohio Rivers prior to the Battle of Nashville, he now had to scour the area between the
Tennessee and Cumberland Rivers to remount his force (the Cavalry Bureau was sending
all horses to Gen. Canby on the Gulf). Even so, he had to reallocate what horses were available in one of his divisions to the others and leave this division behind.[90] During the march
to Selma, Alabama, his command took such large numbers of horses and mules (the area
had not before been visited by invaders) that he was able to keep his entire force mounted.[91]
When he left Selma his force was accompanied by large numbers of liberated slaves —
enough to form three regiments of U.S. Colored Troops (mustered in when Wilson reached
Georgia)—all mounted.[92] There were so many animals remaining that he had about 500
horses and 500 mules killed,[93] as well as all of those found in Selma and the surrounding
area.[94] As his force marched east to Montgomery they continued to carry away or kill horses
and mules[95] and collected even more of them there.[96] The numbers of equines taken (or
killed) must have been huge.

Union appropriations of Southern horses and mules were not limited to raids and campaigns. In areas occupied by Federal forces, parties were periodically sent out to gather in
the stock. There are numerous mentions of "horse-stealing expeditions" in the letters, jour-

nals and unit histories of Union veterans. During late 1861, the 7th Kansas Cavalry took many horses and mules from Missourians to replace their mounts and draft animals that had worn out. Kansas being nearby, some of the appropriated animals were driven across the state line to their own farms or for sale. The pedigree of a fine horse in Kansas was humorously referred to afterwards as being "by Jennison — out of Missouri" (Jennison was the unit's commander).[97] Capt. Henry Ankeny of the 4th Iowa Infantry wrote his wife that during a 6-day April 1863 expedition from Greenville, Mississippi, over 1,000 animals were taken.[98] Major Charles W. Wills of the 7th Illinois Cavalry wrote several times to his wife mentioning foraging for horses. In November 1863 he wrote her from Winchester, Tennessee, that his brigade was to be remounted (all of their horses had been reallocated to Sherman's army) with "citizens along the road to furnish the stock." He said that as soon as they collected 30 horses, men were mounted on them and sent out for more.[99] In December they had to go 75 miles west of Jackson County, Alabama, to find animals. Twenty men collected 200 horses.[100] At the end of the same month, he wrote Mrs. Wills, "Foraging for horses ... has kept us in the saddle almost constantly."[101]

Of course, citizens in the path of advancing armies or hearing of approaching raiders — and Southerners knowing of impressment agents in their communities — made every effort to conceal their horse and mules. Time permitting, they would drive their animals to another area. Sometimes this was successful. Many farmers of the Chambersburg, Pennsylvania, area had driven their animals into the upper reaches of Horse Valley as Confederates moved north into Pennsylvania. Confederate cavalry did go into this valley, but not the upper reaches, where 200 to 300 horses could have been found.[102] The result could be different, however, if the enemy went into an area of presumed safety. Some farmers had sent their animals to Franklin County, Pennsylvania, but when the Confederates reached McConnellsburg, they picked up these horses anyway.[103] Others judged wrongly when it was safe to bring their stock out of hiding. When Jenkins's cavalry left Chambersburg, horses were brought back only to be taken when more Confederates passed through the town.[104]

Other citizens were more creative in hiding their animals. Pvt. Mitchell R. Houghton of the 15th Alabama Infantry and two other soldiers chanced upon a farm girl and her younger brother hiding with a horse in a cave. Fortunately for the farmer, these infantrymen did not take the horse and proceeded on their way toward Gettysburg.[105] An old woman in Ohio remembered her father and other Ohio farmers hiding their horses in coal mines and caves to keep Morgan's men from taking them in 1863.[106] John White, owner of a plantation in eastern Tuscaloosa County, Alabama, saved his mules from the Union raiders of John Croxton in March 1865 by having his slaves ride them into hiding in a nearby swamp.[107] Sometimes foresight in hiding a farm animal required a little luck also. Confederates en route to Gettysburg recalled asking a young boy where his father was, only to be told, "He's in the cellar with the horse."[108]

Whatever methods were used, the armies managed to obtain enough equines to keep on functioning for four years of war. Appropriated horses were "free" to the appropriating army, but costs by other methods could be considerable.

3

Costs, Preferences, Transportation and Training

With the exact number of horses and mules unknown, the variety of methods used for their acquisition, and the large numbers of privately purchased steeds, it would be impossible to even somewhat accurately calculate the total costs of equines used during the Civil War. This is further complicated in the case of Southern animals by the rampant inflation — almost to the point of worthlessness — of Confederate currency. Amounts paid by the U.S. Quartermaster during the war are known, but even these would be an understatement, since five years after the war the Southern Claims Commission began authorization of payments to some Southern Unionists for horses appropriated by Union forces.

The sudden demand for horses presented those who had them available with a opportunity for profits. Union Quartermaster General Meigs made every effort to keep the costs down. He advised departmental quartermasters to put notice in the papers and, as offers to provide horses came in, to take them from the lowest bidder. He advised that even lower offers would be received in the following days. By this method Meigs claimed to have been able to reduce the prices he was paying by eight dollars per head.[1] He further instructed the department quartermasters, "Leave no margin for profit in jobbing contracts. Let speculators wait." This, he felt, would prevent horse contracts from being sold by speculators with the price run up.[2] Until active campaigning began in April 1862, Meigs's methods kept costs for the purchase of horses down. Prices even fell from $125 to $100 each at times. Meigs credited this to greater availability as workers left Kentucky and Missouri farms for the armies, reducing need and security and increasing costs for feeding animals in these horse-rich areas. As war progressed, frequent demands for immediate supply or resupply of mounts and draft animals required purchases on the open market at higher prices. Prices paid by the Union therefore rose throughout the course of the war. Horses for cavalry purposes rose from $144 each to $185. Heavier animals for the artillery rose from $161 to $185 apiece. Mules went up from $170 to $195 each.[3] When Mosby's 43rd Virginia Cavalry Battalion captured Union Brig. Gen. Stoughton asleep in the Washington defenses in 1863, President Lincoln quipped, "I can make a much better Brigadier in five minutes but the horses cost a hundred and twenty-five dollars apiece."[4] Ultimately, the United States government paid close to $124,000,000 during the war for horses and mules.[5]

Prices paid for private purchases of horses by Union generals and officers varied more than those paid by the government. In September 1861, Gen. George G. Meade paid $150 for a horse ("Baldy") that had been wounded in the nose at First Manassas.[6] This was the same period during which the government was promising to pay troopers of those volunteer cavalry units that provided their own mounts $120 reimbursements if the animal was killed or captured in battle.[7] Henry G. Stratton, an officer of the 19th Ohio Infantry, claimed that, in the fall of 1863, his horse was worth $200 to him.[8] During the fall of 1864 he bought another horse which "if at home would be worth $250."[9] Stratton, who eventually rose to lieutenant colonel of the regiment, evidently did a bit of horse trading with his fellow officers. He wrote his sister in December 1864 that he "made over $600 on horses or I would have saved but little this year."[10] Lt. Francis W. Dunn of the 1st Alabama Cavalry (Union) sold a mare in November which had been bruised in a stable for $65 with the agreement that if the new owner sold the horse for $25 or more profit, the new owner would give Dunn another $20. Dunn (from Illinois and previously a member of the 64th Illinois Infantry) included in his remarks on this transaction that he "hated to sell her but am very confident that I could not get her home. I could have got 40 or 50 [dollars] more."[11] This must have been a fairly common price for horses of Union officers in the South. Lt. Col. Charles B. Haydon of the 8th Michigan Cavalry journalized on January 31, 1864, "I bought a good five year old colt today of Kentucky racing stock for $50."[12] Lt. Gen. U.S. Grant donated his horse Jack to the Chicago Sanitary Commission in 1864. It was raffled for $4,000.[13] Doubtlessly, the price was "run up" both because of the animal's association with Grant and the charitable purpose of the raffle.

When the war started, Confederate horses had about the same values as Union horses. As the war progressed, a combination of the scarcity of horses and the high rate of inflation of Confederate money drove up prices to an incredible level. When the 9th Texas Cavalry was organized in 1861 the valuation assigned for their horses ranged from $30 to $150 with an average of between $100 and $125.[14] Bargains could be had. John W. Headley of the 1st Kentucky Cavalry paid only $50 for a white horse that had fallen off a Union transport and swum ashore.[15] A large chestnut sorrel horse belonging to Brig. Gen. Bushrod Johnson which was killed during the Battle of Shiloh was then valued at $180.[16] Admitting in his memoir, "I was never good at a horse trade," Moxley Sorrel paid $275, with a big fine well-gaited bay thrown in just before the Battle of Antietam, to another officer for a big bay. After being told of the trade, Lt. Gen. James Longstreet advised Sorrel that the horse required too much food, commenting that he "would not give $275 for the horse tied to a corn crib." Longstreet was right — the horse could never get enough to eat and had to be given to the quartermaster.[17]

Bushrod Johnson, now a major general, had five horses killed during the Battle of Perryville in September 1862. A board approved his voucher for reimbursement with horses valued at $325 (a dapple gray), $300 (a sorrel), $300 (a bay mare), $325 (a bay stallion) and $200 (another bay mare). Two of his staff officers also lost horses during that battle and their vouchers were approved for $250 and $290.[18] It could take over a year for Confederates to receive their reimbursements. Gen. Stephen D. Lee lost two horses in early 1863 (with a total value of $780), and his claims were unpaid until during 1864.[19] When appointed to the staff of Longstreet in February 1863, Charles Minor Blackford sold his two horses to the quartermaster for $635.[20] After his May 1863 capture of Union Col. Abel D. Streight and his brigade in northern Alabama, the citizens of Huntsville bought for $800 and presented Gen. Nathan Bedford Forrest an "elegant bay horse, of the best Virginia stock."[21] During this same period, men of the 9th Texas Cavalry found that they could not purchase remounts of horses valued at $125 two years earlier for less than $500 or $600.[22] Brig. Gen. Richard Garnett rode to his death during Pickett's Charge at Gettysburg on a thoroughbred horse which, at $1,400, was valued the second highest in Longstreet's Corps.[23] Early 1864 found that "a decent horse was worth $1,000 and one Captain of the 9th Texas Cavalry had a bay horse valued at $2,000."[24] John W. Headley was appointed to the secret service of the Confederacy in 1864 and sold his two horses for $1,700.[25] Robert E. Lee's famous horse Traveller was appraised at $4,600 in August 1864.[26] Everyone thought his was an exceptional horse, but doubtless its association with Lee had as much to do as inflation with this horse's increase in value over the $325 Lee had paid for it in 1862.

Costs for obtaining equines would have been greatly increased if efforts to equip units with like horses had been any greater than they were. As might be expected with so many equines required for military purposes and acquired by so many different means, great variation resulted in the types of animals used. Standards existed, but they specified only **age and height** and required passing an inspection for disease and serviceability. Horses of 4 to 9 years were preferred for cavalry and of 5 to 7 years for artillery. For both purposes a height of 15 to 16 hands (5' to 5'4") was the standard.[27] As mentioned, many purveyors of horses in the Union through fraud managed to get unserviceable horses approved. Standards were often consciously ignored in the case of privately owned animals of generals, officers and Confederate cavalrymen. It was to these men only necessary that the horse be able to keep up and do the job. As one author wrote, "They left their farms and families astride any horse that was handy."[28] "Stonewall" Jackson's famous sorrel horse was old (about 12 years) and undersized (when he was mounted on it his feet almost dragged the ground). A remount of Union Maj. Gen. Winfield Scott Hancock during the Battle of Chancellorsville was also so small that his boots nearly touched the ground.[29] There are other mentions of someone riding a pony or a small horse of less than 14.2 hands. Private Leander Stillwell of the 61st Illinois Infantry got separated from his regiment during a battle but was later able to find it because "I recognized our regiment by the little gray pony the old colonel rode."[30]

Breeds were not specified. The thoroughbred is the most commonly mention breed — both the Kentucky and the Virginia thoroughbred. Other horses are mentioned as having thoroughbreds among their ancestry. The first American breed — the Morgan[31] — was the steed of a few regiments when they were first organized. These were the 1st Maine, 2nd Michigan, 3rd Michigan, and 14th Pennsylvania Cavalry Regiments.[32] By the time of the Civil War the Morgan strain had been bred into many horses. In photographs of the Civil War it is impossible to tell whether a horse is a thoroughbred of a Morgan. The Arabian horse is infrequently mentioned. A Colonel Jenifer of Virginia cavalry had bred horses before the war and rode a gray Arabian stallion. Gen. George Crittenden is said to have remarked once to a staff officer, "There is Jenifer with his horse that has more sense than Jenifer, for Jenifer has taught him everything he ever knew and he had a lot of horse-sense to begin with."[33] One of the horses of Brig. Gen. Turner Ashby was a black Arabian.[34] There are occasional mentions from Texas of the "Mexican pony." The "Indian pony" is mentioned somewhat more frequently. As might be expected, most mentions of these types of horses are found in the Trans-Mississippi area. Union Brig. Gen. Alexander S. Asboth had two Indian ponies.[35] A few were even used in the Virginia theater of the war. Pvt. Alfred Bellard of the 5th New Jersey Infantry mentioned in his memoirs that his colonel had one that had been "captured from the Indians during his frontier life with the 2nd U.S. Dragoons."[36]

Stonewall Jackson's horse Fancy in retirement at V.M.I. The small size of this horse is evident. It would not have met army standards for mounts (courtesy Virginia Military Institute Museum, Lexington, Virginia).

There is even mention — by Lt. Col. Elisha Hunt Rhodes of the 2nd Rhode Island Infantry — of a "Canadian" which he had purchased.[37]

Horse **color** was never specified. The only mention of a Confederate unit with color-coordinated steeds is the "Black Horse Cavalry." This was a prewar Virginia militia unit of company size. For some reason, after the Battle of First Manassas, the size of this unit was magnified into the thousands.[38] Col. J.H. Kidd of the 6th Michigan Cavalry in his postwar memoirs wrote that when horses (obtained in Michigan) were issued to his regiment in 1861 "the horses were sorted according to color, the intention being that each unit [that is, company] should have but one color, as near as practicable."[39] Other forming cavalry units did likewise. The 7th Kansas Cavalry was issued its horses in late October 1861. The horses were "sorted out according to color before being assigned to the different companies."[40] Some Union artillery batteries started the war with horses of the same color. Charles Morton of the 25th Missouri Infantry remembered that during the Battle of Shiloh he "saw a dun-horse battery coming."[41] Battery I of the 4th U.S. Artillery had all bay horses as late as the Chattanooga campaign in 1863.[42] Kidd stated that the arranging of horses by color to companies "did not last long. A few months service sufficed to do away with it and horses thereafter were issued indiscriminately."[43] There were apparently exceptions, however. Being marched south after his capture during the Battle of Gettysburg, John L. Collins of the 8th Pennsylvania Cavalry "saw my own regiment drawn up for a charge about five hundred yards away! ... How did I know my regiment? ... I could distinguish the companies by the color of their horses and knew the order of the squadrons in the line."[44]

The **sex** of the animal was never a consideration except solely by preference of an officer or general. The sex of a horse is mentioned almost as frequently as the color and "my mare" (a female horse) or "my stallion" (a male horse) are common references. Often a horse is simply referred to as "he" which could indicate either a stallion or a gelding (a castrated horse). There are at least two instances of mares being accompanied in war by their colts.

Gen. Robert E. Lee was sick to hear of his horse from the Mexican War, Grace Darling, being seen on the Virginia peninsula ridden by a "Yankee" with her colt following along.[45] The 3rd Richmond Howitzers of the Confederate Army had a mare whose colt followed her.[46]

The **mule** is a type of its own. Since it is less familiar than horses to most Americans, some general information about them will be useful. It is a cross between two different species: the donkey (*Equus asinus*) and the horse (*Equus caballus*), specifically a male donkey and a female horse. (The cross between a female donkey and a male horse — the whinny — is much less common.) Mules have been bred for at least 3,000 years. It takes characteristics from both of its parents. The horse parent gives it the shape of the neck and croup, its height and uniformity of its coat (usually bay or brown). Like the donkey it has a short, thick head, long ears, thin legs, small hooves, a short mane, and no hair at the root of its tail. Its voice is a bray similar to that of the donkey.[47]

Civil War soldiers believed that "mules will stand more hard work on less food than a horse."[48] They were thus deemed better suited than horses for pulling wagons.[49] Some sources of the period even avowed that an army mule could "march a horse off his legs, with less in his belly."[50] Most modern writers accept this contention.[51] Some authorities on the donkey and mule claim otherwise, saying that these beliefs have been the "torment" of these animals.[52] Perhaps so, but because it was commonly believed otherwise, Civil War mules did have harder work demanded of them on less and lower quality food.

Regardless of the purpose for which obtained, the method used to obtain them, or the cost, equines had to be transported by means other than riding or pulling them in a team to where actually needed. Little has been found regarding this aspect of horses and mules during the Civil War. The following information is therefore incomplete but will indicate some of the problems involved in transporting equines.

Shipping horses for the army. Difficulties in coaxing horses up (or down) ramps or of hoisting them by slings are evident (*Harper's Weekly*, November 2, 1861, pp. 696–697).

Leading horses was probably the most common method — especially over shorter distances. Captured horses not needed as immediate remounts were led. All of the horses captured by "Jeb" Stuart's cavalry during the Gettysburg campaign were led back to Virginia.[53] The numerous horses captured by Mosby's command in northern Virginia were led back to Confederate lines.[54] Leading horses was not easy. When the 7th Kansas Cavalry went home in early 1864 to "veteranize," many of their horses were reallocated to the 1st Alabama Cavalry (Union). Sgt. Major Francis Dunn of the 1st went to Corinth, Mississippi, to get them and recorded in his journal that he "had some trouble in leading the horses out but got them all through."[55] The method used by Texas cavalrymen (copied from cowboys and Indians[56]) was to tie the reins or halter rope of one horse to the tail of another, which strung out one behind another. The reins or rope of the lead horse was then looped around the saddlehorn with the end in the lead rider's hand. The guide rope could be released to prevent an unruly string of horses from throwing the rider or his horse.[57]

Transport of equines by ship and by boat was frequent. Transport over the seas was necessary for Burnside's North Carolina expedition, for the occupation of northeast Florida, for the Mobile campaign and other amphibious operations. Riverine transport was required in the campaigns up the Cumberland and Tennessee Rivers and along the Mississippi River to Vicksburg. The first instance of horse transport over the seas during the Civil War was the reinforcement of Ft. Pickens, Florida, in April 1861: "With difficulty a herd of horses was secured on the forward deck" of the ship *Atlantic*. Sending a herd of horses from New York to an island fort was a diversion to conceal the real purpose of the expedition. When this herd arrived off Pensacola on April 16, 1861 — after a nine days' voyage — they were lowered overboard on slings and then swum ¾ of a mile to shore in tow by small boats.[58] Only seven horses were lost.[59] At other times, the animals were simply pushed overboard. A soldier of the 45th Pennsylvania Infantry remembered, "The officers' horses were unloaded by taking away a section of the gunwale of the vessel, bringing a horse up in front of the opening and two men shoved the horse overboard. The horse would go under water, come up and swim ashore."[60] Horses, not unnaturally, were not fond of such a method. David Day of the 25th Massachusetts Infantry explained that it was "curious to observe the horses as they are led up the gangway; to see them brace themselves back and shudder to take the fearful leap. But a little encouragement from half a dozen men in the rear pushing them, over they go, and as they come up out of the water, they shake their heads and snort, and put for the nearest land, where they are rubbed dry, blanketed and led up off the island."[61] It wasn't always that simple. A veteran of the 47th Pennsylvania Infantry wrote about the "landing" of horses at Fernandina, Florida:

"In unloading, the horses were thrown overboard and mostly made for a sand bank about a quarter mile from the steamer, but in one or two cases they put to sea and had to be chased by the boat's crew in a small boat. In this way one horse drowned, and Gen. Branan's horse had its leg broken and had to be killed."[62]

Such journeys were not easy on horses. Robert Clark Knaggs, an officer of the 7th Michigan Infantry, had been left behind at Alexandria when the regiment was transported to the peninsula in 1862 to bring forward supplies. He wrote later, "I found the supplies and put them aboard a smaller steamer. It was already loaded with cavalry supplies and a hold full of horses. We had a very rough passage and the horses were not able to lie down and rest. Whenever the bow would go up the horses would sag against the sides."[63] The

Quartermaster General, Montgomery Meigs, who participated in the Pensacola expedition, had several light-draft steam ferry transports built at Philadelphia. Each of these boats could carry an artillery battery and its horses or a train of wagons with mules.[64] Special horse transports could carry 20 horses each. A shortage of such transports was one reason Gen. McClellan gave Gen. Halleck for slowness in leaving the Virginia Peninsula to reinforce Gen. Pope in 1862.[65]

Livestock had been transported on riverboats prior to the war in pens on the main deck, where space was somewhat limited by the engines. There was always difficulty in getting horses (or mules) up a gangplank onto the boat. Sometimes the distance to cross from shore to boat, or vice versa, was as much as twelve to fifteen feet.[66] Some animals had to be dragged on their haunches across the plank.[67] In March 1864, the 1st Alabama Cavalry (Union) was transferred by boat from Memphis to Nashville. Horses were put on the boat, which was "of course very much crowded," according to the regiment's sergeant major. The third day of the trip, the boat was halted and the horses taken off to be fed — and the boat cleaned.[68] The cost for this type of transport of equines could be expensive. For a January 1863 trip from Cairo, Illinois, to Helena, Arkansas, the fee was $3.20 per horse and $2.76 per mule. (The cost for humans on the same boat was $1.10 each teamster and $2.10 for each officer — including the one general aboard.[69])

Railroad movement of animals was very common. At the beginning of the war, large numbers of horses had to be shipped from the west to the Washington and Richmond areas. Many were the animals of cavalry and artillery units or officers but, in the case of the Union, many were shipped to supply units and trains forming in the capital area. When the 11th and 12th Corps of the Army of the Potomac were transferred to Chattanooga in early fall 1863, they took with them 3,402 horses and mules plus the mounts of officers, according to some sources[70]; but Van Horne, in his history of the Army of the Cumberland, averred that they arrived without transportation.[71] Railroad movement of animals meant crowded conditions and poor care during the journey. Brig. Gen. Alpheus Williams of the 11th Corps, in a letter dated October 12, 1863, from Decherd, Tennessee, noted: "My horses arrived yesterday. Old Plug Ugly has lost pretty much all his tail. His length is so great that he rubbed at both ends of the car and has bared the bones of his head and tail, besides having had his neck bitten by some indignant horse.... The stallion looks better, though he is badly rubbed on both hips by his two weeks railroad voyage."[72] When troops were sent in the spring of 1863 to Gen. Joseph E. Johnston to assist against Grant's thrust toward Vicksburg, the general complained that they brought with them neither wagons nor artillery and that it took him until June to collect the horses and mules needed from as far away as Georgia.[73] Later that year, in September, Bragg's Confederate Army of Tennessee was reinforced by most of Longstreet's Corps from the Army of Northern Virginia. Gen. John Bell Hood recalled that the men of his division did not have any wagons or even a single ambulance.[74] The horses of E.P. Alexander's artillery battalion had also been left behind in Virginia.[75] Lack of sufficient railroad capability to transport artillery horses and supply teams obviously severely diminished Confederate ability to reinforce its armies throughout the war.

Like the soldier, an equine taken into the army needed to be trained. The soldier or teamster also needed to be trained in the care and use of his animal(s). Horses and mules are herd animals, which helped in training them in cavalry operations or in pulling a gun or wagon, but much effort was still required. The herd instinct also impelled equines to flee when in danger or startled. Breaking this instinct required training both the horse and its rider to operate in concert.

The prewar regular Army considered that three years was necessary to train cavalry. Civil War cavalry leaders believed six months was necessary to achieve efficiency.[76] War did not permit such an extended period of training. At first, there was perhaps some advantage for the South, which had a good supply of younger men who rode daily since the region lacked good roads and public transportation. Contrastingly, many Northern recruits were either small farmers or city dwellers who knew horses only as a plow puller, carriage horse or dray.[77] In the east, riding had to some extent been replaced by the buggy, and many either didn't know how or had forgotten how to ride,[78] whereas in the West a greater proportion were farmers or cowboys with more skills in horsemanship.[79] One cavalryman, James Henry Avery of the Union's 5th Michigan, recalled his unit's being tested when mustered into service. He said a recruit would be mounted on an unsaddled horse and trotted around in a circle. If the man could stand it and didn't fall off, he was accepted.[80]

Many horses accepted for service were unbroken and had to be taught to take the saddle and carry a rider. Breaking horses was quite an experience for men who had never done so. William G. Stevenson of Morgan's Confederate cavalry remembered trying to break his horse and being thrown over the horse's head, run over and struck by the horse's hind feet, breaking his kneepan.[81] One Pennsylvania cavalryman characterized his unit's mounted drills as consisting of "rearing and kicking, running and jumping, lying down and falling down, men thrown by their horses, kicked and getting hurt in various ways."[82] W.G. Avery's unit got new horses in September 1864. The men were by now experienced horsemen but still had difficulties. Avery went around behind his horse, which kicked at him with both rear feet, barely missing him. He saw another horse rear up and fall back atop his rider, killing him instantly. It took the unit three days to "take the temper out of them."[83] Perhaps they followed the advice given by Robert E. Lee on how to train a high-strung horse. He told Gen. Henry Heth that the "best way to take the wiry edge off an excitable or nervous horse is to give him plenty of exercise — regular exercise, morning, noon, and night, until he quiets down."[84]

Cavalry horses had to be trained, or at least accustomed to bugle calls used in drill and in battle formations. Veteran John D. Billings observed, "In the Cavalry service they knew their places as well as did their riders, and it was a frequent occurrence to see a horse, when his rider had been dismounted by some means, resume his place in line of column without him, seemingly not wishing to be left behind. This quality was often illustrated when a poor, crippled, or generally used-up beast, which had been turned out to die, would attempt to hobble along in his misery and join a column as it passed."[85] Some artillery horses were observed to behave similarly. The horse of a Lt. Hasbrouck of the Federal Army's West Point Battery was shot three times during the Battle of First Manassas and due to loss of blood was left behind to die. While the battery was well on the way to Washington during the retreat, the lieutenant was "joined by his faithful horse, which by strong instinct, had obeyed the bugle call to retreat and found his position with the battery." This horse recovered in Washington and reentered service.[86]

The animals also had to be accustomed to many unfamiliar noises. When bugles blew, the horses of the 9th Texas Cavalry initially laid back their ears and bucked. It took a few weeks for the animals to become accustomed to this noise.[87] When the 3rd Louisiana

Infantry arrived in Little Rock, Arkansas, in 1861, their band struck up a tune, and was joined by other bands. The horses of the 1st Arkansas Mounted Rifles, commanded by Col. Thomas J. Churchill, became restive and began to plunge, threatening to unseat their riders. The infantry commander ordered the bands to cease playing, but Col. Churchill requested that the bands continue to play in order that the horses could be trained to the sound of fifes and drums.[88] One eastern Union cavalryman recalled his unit's first brigade going along smoothly until its swords were drawn in unison. The horses were frightened and confusion resulted.[89] The noise of gunfire frightened horses even more. Unused to it, the horses of the 7th Kansas Cavalry at Columbus, Missouri, on January 8, 1862, became so unmanageable that they stampeded. The regiment lost five men killed and three thrown from their horses and captured.[90] It took longer for horses to become accustomed to gunfire than to music and some never did.[91] Team animals also had to be taught to ignore noises. Some were so trained by being "led along amid a clatter of tin cans, exploding mines and firecrackers, and having rifles shot off around them."[92] Many animals never adjusted to unexpected noises. The Colonel of the 5th New Jersey Infantry was troubled on the Virginia Peninsula in 1862 by his horse's turning its tail to the enemy whenever there was firing.[93] A horse belonging to Confederate Gen. Turner Ashby was considered worthless because it would bolt and run until tired out on hearing the rattle of arms during drill.[94] Confederate Maj. Gen. John B. Gordon had a horse captured from the Union Army which behaved very well under cannonading but became uncontrollable and fled when under musket fire.[95] During the Battle of Yellow Tavern, a private soldier of the 6th Virginia Cavalry found that, when it became excited at the sound of firing, his horse suddenly stopped and refused to budge.[96]

Riders had to learn how to ride properly. Awkward riders, out of ignorance or indifference, treated horses badly, causing them to founder or go lame.[97] Confederate cavalry Captain Charles Minor Blackford noted that a great part of horses' discomfort and suffering was due to rider inexperience in marching. He noted that many horses became sore-backed and unfit for service simply because of "awkward and unskilled riding." His observation was that "a man who slouches down, rides with a swing, sits sometimes on one side then on another, and never dismounts when the company halts, will always have a sore-backed horse." The rules to be taught according to him were to always sit straight in the saddle, never sit with uneven pressure (to one side of the saddle or the other), ride with an even gait, and always dismount and loosen the saddle girth at halts. Blackford also stated that when a march was ended or the day concluded, saddles should not be removed until the animal had cooled down.[98]

Animals had to be trained in other ways as well. Mules had to be trained to accept and carry pack loads — and their muleteers how to pack and mount loads.[99] Mules were trained to ignore noises of the battlefield by being led through exploding firecrackers, rifle shots and clattering tin cans.[100] For the first two years of the war, the Union assigned privates to drive regimental wagons. Since there were few Northerners who could handle a team, men from isolated communities often got the assignment.[101] Cavalry and infantry trained together with simulated charges of cavalry. The infantrymen were pleased to learn that horses could not be driven onto fixed bayonets.[102] Longstreet had his staff train themselves and their steeds during the fall and winter of 1861–62 in jumping obstacles and ditches.[103] Union General James H. Wilson set a similar example for his cavalry command by practicing jumping over fences and ditches.[104] A wild gallop over fences, ditches and broken ground would damage both the men and the horses and only carefully trained mounts could charge in unbroken ranks.[105]

Perhaps the most important part of horsemen's training was in the care and feeding of their animals. The men had to learn that the first thing to do — prior to tending to themselves — was to take the saddle off the horse and feed it.[106] Early in the war, hundreds of horses were lost when new troopers gave overheated animals too much water.[107] To help prevent sore backs, the men had to learn to smooth out wrinkles in saddle blankets. They had to learn that after hours of riding they needed to unsaddle and cool the backs of their horses. They also had to know that when their mount was disabled they should dismount and lead it at a walk.[108] Officers had to enforce proper care of the animals in their unit. John S. Mosby remembered when he was a private in the 1st Virginia Cavalry that his company commander "took care of his horses as well as his men. There was a horse inspection every morning, and the man whose horse was not well groomed got a scolding mixed with some cursing by Captain Jones."[109] Unfortunately for the horses, conditions of war especially during a raid or prolonged campaign often prevented the necessary care even when a soldier was inclined to do so.

Regardless of the amount of training of animals or of their riders or drivers, sometimes accidents did occur. For decades motor vehicle accidents have been a leading cause of deaths in the United States. Similarly, carriage or wagon accidents and injuries caused by equines were everyday occurrences in the days before mechanization — including the period of the Civil War. Larger and stronger than men, if scared or not adequately trained or controlled, horses and mules could present a danger to their riders. Many were injured in equine accidents and others killed.

In October 1861, Varina Davis, wife of the Confederate president, and Lydia Johnston, wife of Gen. Joseph E. Johnston, were driving together. Their horse's harness broke and their carriage overturned. Mrs. Johnston was thrown from the carriage, breaking her arm. Mrs. Davis, pregnant at the time, was unharmed.[110] A similar accident happened to Mary Todd Lincoln, wife of the United States president, in July 1863. A screw fastening the coachman's seat suddenly came off, the driver was thrown from the carriage, and the horses bolted. Mrs. Lincoln either jumped or was thrown from the carriage and struck her head on a rock. Her wound turned out to be not serious.[111] On a February evening in 1864, Confederate Brig. Gen. William E. Baldwin was riding his horse when a stirrup broke. The general was violently thrown forward, falling on his right shoulder. He died about an hour afterward.[112]

Other injury accidents did not involve equine equipment or vehicle breakages. Brig. Gen. Louis Blenker of the Union Army fell from his horse during the Battle of Cross Keys. His injury prevented further service.[113] As noted earlier, Confederate William G. Stevenson, while trying to train his horse, was thrown over its head and struck by the horse's rear feet, breaking his kneepan.[114] Pvt. Lorenzo Brown of the 112th Illinois Infantry was kicked to death by a mule.[115] Brig. Gen. Michael Corcoran of an Army of the Potomac brigade was crushed to death on December 21, 1863, when his horse fell on him.[116] Surgeon Willets of the 8th Michigan Infantry, with a train traveling to Knoxville, Tennessee, in December 1864, rolled with his horse down a bank but was luckily unhurt.[117] John S. Mosby related in his *Memoirs* that while but a private in the 1st Virginia Cavalry he missed picket duty only once. This was "when I was disabled one night by my horse falling over a cow lying in the road."[118] On another occasion that year Mosby related, "My horse slipped down, fell on me, and galloped off, leaving me in a senseless condition in the road."[119] In September 1864, he had yet another injury by equine when a horse trod on his foot and bruised it so badly that he could wear only a sock and had to walk with a cane.[120]

When the 5th Michigan Cavalry received new horses in September 1864, they were "new and vicious ones," according to Sgt. James H. Avery. He went behind his horse to stand him around for feeding. The horse kicked with both feet with one passing on each side of Avery's head. Avery was lucky — the horse didn't kick again. He did see one horse rear and fall back on its rider, instantly killing the cavalryman.[121] Some horses caused injury when startled by non-battlefield events. Sgt. Maj. Francis W. Dunn of the 1st Alabama Cavalry (Union) recorded in his diary for August 21, 1864, that the headquarters group had tied their horses in a yard. One of the cavalrymen turned over a nearby beehive seeking honey. The bees swarmed out and began to sting the horses. The horses "went crazy." All of the horses "got furious" and while Dr. John Swaving of the regiment tried to calm the colonel's horse and get it out, his leg was broken below the knee when the horse kicked him.[122]

Although an excellent horseman, Gen. U.S. Grant seems also to have been particularly unlucky with falls from horses. Though sometimes alleged that he was drunk on some of these occasions, it seems to this writer that these were legitimate accidents. The first instance was the night of April 4, 1861, just prior to the Battle of Shiloh. That night he had visited Gen. W.H.L. Wallace and was returning to the riverboat he was using as headquarters. Grant described the event: "The night was one of impenetrable darkness, with rain pouring down in torrents; nothing was visible.... On the way back to the boat my horse's feet slipped from under him, and he fell with my leg under his body. The extreme softness of the ground, from the excessive rains of the few preceding days, no doubt saved me from a severe injury and protracted lameness." The boot had to be cut off his injured ankle and the general had to walk with crutches for two or three days.[123]

The general's most grievous injury by horse occurred in 1863 when he visited Maj. Gen. N.P. Banks at New Orleans after Vicksburg and Port Hudson were both captured. He had reviewed Banks's army. His own story of the accident was as follows:

> The horse I rode was vicious and but little used, and on my return to New Orleans ran away and, shying at a locomotive in the street, fell, probably on me. I was rendered insensible, and when I regained consciousness I found myself in a hotel near by with several doctors attending me. My leg was swollen from knee to the thigh, and the swelling, almost to the point of bursting, extended along the body up to the arm-pit. The pain was almost beyond endurance. I lay at the hotel something over a week without being able to turn myself in bed.

Grant was taken by litter to a steamer which returned him to Vicksburg. It was some time later before he was able to move.[124] Later that year, Grant was ordered to Chattanooga. While crossing Walden's Ridge into the city, his horse slipped and fell. Grant's injured leg was jammed.[125]

A well-known horse accident involved Gen. Robert E. Lee during the 1862 Antietam campaign. Though there are some variances in the details, the basic story is the same. According to E.P. Alexander, on August 31, "Lee, in reconnoitering Pope's lines, had dismounted, and was holding his horse by the bridle when an alarm of Federal cavalry had startled the party, and the general's horse had jerked him to the ground fracturing some of the bones of his right hand." Lee's arm was placed in a sling and he could not handle the reins.[126] The story of Lee's nephew, Gen. Fitzhugh Lee, is in basic agreement. He related that during the Battle of Antietam, Lee was most of the time afoot, "having both arms and hands injured before leaving Virginia from being thrown violently to the ground, his horse making a sudden jump when he was standing by his side with the bridle reins over his arm. Some of the bones in one hand were broken and the other arm injured. He was obliged to ride in an ambulance or let a courier lead his horse."[127] Later historian Douglas Southall Freeman wrote, "Lee was standing by Traveller, with the reins on the animal's neck. Suddenly a cry was raised, 'Yankee cavalry!' Traveller started at the sudden commotion, and Lee stepped forward to catch the bridle. He tripped and fell. He caught himself on both hands and was up in an instant, but it was soon apparent that he was hurt.... The nearest surgeon was sent for. He found a small bone broken in one hand and the other badly sprained. Both had to be put in splints."[128] A still later historian wrote that Lee "had been standing beside Traveller when the horse shied, and Lee, lunging to regain control, had fallen, sprawling," and that he afterwards had bandages and splints on both hands.[129] A history of the battle which includes the story adds that it had been raining and Lee was wearing rubber overalls and a poncho. He was preparing to mount when the horse was startled. Reaching for the reins, Lee tripped in his heavy clothing. Falling forward, he reached out with both hands to brace his fall.[130]

An almost entirely different version of this incident appeared in a note from a Mrs. Leverette of Eatonton, Georgia, in a book of reminiscences published by the Georgia Division of the United Daughters of the Confederacy in the early 1900s. Her story involved Dr. Nathaniel S. Walker, surgeon of the 44th Georgia Infantry, who was "the only surgeon to dress a wound for Robert E. Lee." The circumstances given in this story are:

> While returning from the first Maryland campaign, an admiring friend presented a very fine horse to the Confederate commander. The animal, however, was untrained to the bustle of army movements. General Lee was standing, holding the horse, as some artillery wagons rattled by. Frightened, the animal made a sudden plunge, by which the General was thrown violently to the ground and two fingers on his left hand were broken.... Dr. Walker, being near at hand, was called and dressed the wound. He gave General Lee a bottle of linament to relieve the pain."[131]

This account could fit in with the others except for two points. Dr. Walker could well have been the "nearest surgeon" called into attendance and, not having been personally present when the incident occurred, could have slightly misunderstood what caused the horse to start. After years had passed, the doctor (or Mrs. Leverette) could have mistaken the timing as being after Antietam instead of before that battle. The major difference is that most other accounts identify the horse as Lee's famous steed, Traveller, whereas the doctor identifies it as a gift horse.

Perhaps on the matter of the "gift horse," Dr. Walker confused this incident with one involving "Stonewall" Jackson during the same campaign. During most of the campaign Jackson did not have present his famous Little Sorrel, which had been lost or stolen. He was riding a cream-colored horse.[132] Biographer James A. Robertson wrote that during the retreat from Antietam to the Potomac ford, "one unusually grateful Marylander told Jackson that he had the finest horse in the state and would feel deeply blessed if the general would accept the mount as a gift. The animal was a gigantic, gray mare, heavy and awkward.... Jackson somewhat embarrassingly accepted the horse and tested her that evening."[133] One history of the battle states that when Jackson had crossed the Potomac headed north, Southern sympathizers gifted him a young mare. When "Stonewall" mounted it for the first time, it refused to move. He then dug in his spurs. The horse reared up, causing Jackson to lose his balance and fall backward to the ground. The severe jolt resulted in doctors' ordering the general to an ambulance.[134] Another who wrote of Jackson's horse accident said that the donor was an influential citizen, that the general mounted it in the public street and was immediately thrown into the mud![135] The exact facts of these two incidents will never be resolved but they illustrate the danger to riders that could be caused by suddenly startled steeds regardless of the ability of the rider or the training of the animal.

4

Lost on the Field of Battle

There are more anecdotal and passing references to horses and mules killed or wounded in battle than any other category of equine stories in Civil War literature. This seems to be because of (1) the significance of such an event to the rider, (2) the animal's association with a notable commander, or (3) the gruesome nature of the wounding or death of the animal. The essentiality of horses and mules during the Civil War made their loss in battle significant and worthy of comment. It has been estimated that one and a half million horses and mules were killed during the war — three times the number of men lost to battle deaths, disease and other causes.

There is one instance of mules themselves being used as weapons. Though it appears neither in Confederate nor Union official reports, it has widely been accepted as fact.[1] It appeared in *Battles and Leaders* in an article authored by former Federal Lt. George H. Peters. Peters was not present at the stated date of the incident (the February 20, 1862, Battle of Valverde in the New Mexico Territory) as he was then serving with Co. K of the 1st California Infantry. Later he became adjutant of the 1st New Mexico, where he served with the "hero" of the article and others who had been present at that battle. Captain James "Paddy" Graydon had been in the regular army, but at the beginning of the Civil War had been authorized to organize an independent spy (or scout) company. Nearly all of the men of the company were Mexican-Americans. The story as told by Peters was as follows:

> On the evening of February 20th, when the enemy was encamped opposite Fort Craig, Graydon was allowed to make a night attack upon them. Without explaining the details of his plan, he had prepared a couple of wooden boxes, in each of which half a dozen 24-pounder howitzer shells were placed, with the fuses cut. These boxes were securely lashed on the backs of two old mules, and the captain with three or four of his men crossed the river just below the fort and proceeded in the darkness toward the Confederate camp. Graydon's project was to get the torpedo mules within sight of the enemy's picket-line without being discovered, when he was to light the fuses, and the mules being directed toward the picket-line, would move in the direction of the animals there. He finally arrived within 150 yards of the picket-line, and everything being in readiness, the fuses of the boxes were fired, and the captain and his party commenced their retreat, when to their consternation they found that the mules, instead of going toward the enemy, were following themselves; the shells soon began to explode, the Confederate camp was quickly under arms, and Graydon's party made its way back to Fort Craig without the mules.[2]

Retellings of the story vary only very slightly. The only significant difference in any of them is a pamphlet citing *Report of the Joint Committee on the Conduct of the War*, vol. 3, from 1863. This version adds that the explosion of the two mules stampeded a herd on beef cattle into the Union lines, depriving the invading Confederates of much-needed provisions.[3] If so, then the "mule bomb" attack was successful since, following the Battle of Valverde, the Confederates were cut off from Mesilla (on the Rio Grande south of Fort Craig and north of El Paso) with only five days' rations.

This instance of mules being "exploded" was an exceptional circumstance of equine casualties on the battlefields of the war. More typically they were deliberate targets or "collateral damage." Sometimes the equines themselves were the targets, other times it was their riders, and often they were simply in the way of gunfire. One Federal cavalry veteran, Willard Glazier, a lieutenant of the 5th New York, explained it: "In battle the horse is a larger target than the man, and hence is more frequently hit, so that more than twice the number of horses fall in every engagement than men. The cavalryman is more shielded from the deadly missile than the infantryman. The horse's head and shoulders will often receive the bullet that is intended for the rider's body."[4] John D. Billings, a Massachusetts artillery veteran, wrote more extensively about horses and mules than any other Civil War writer of memoirs. He summed up their battlefield experience, writing in 1887 that "the horse was a hero in action" that behaved far better than men in under similar exposure.[5]

Horses and mules, being larger and of a different physique than men, were able to take more serious wounds than men and to continue functioning longer when wounded. Partially at least for this reason, equines seemed to suffer stoically. Union Brig. Gen. John Beatty, after the Battle of Murfreesboro, heard of a mule which had a leg blown off during the first day of the battle. Beatly wrote of it: "Next morning it was on the spot where first wounded; at night it was still standing there, not having moved an inch all day, patiently suffering, it knew not why nor for what."[6] Confederate Staff Officer G. Moxley Sorrel recollected after the war, "There is occasional talk of groans and shrieks of horses when wounded. I have seen many badly hurt, but cannot recall an instance in which the animal made any noise."[7] Pvt. William R. Houghton of the 2nd Georgia Infantry partially agreed. He remembered: "It was pathetic, too, to hear in the still hours of the night the screams of horses with one or more legs shattered by a cannon shot. Other wounds they bore in silence, but the effort to stand on shivered bones was more than the poor creatures could bear."[8] Often it was not even noticed at the time that an animal had been wounded. U.S. Grant wrote in his memoirs that during the Battle of Shiloh at one time he had been riding with his engineer staff officer James B. McPherson (later Major General) and W.T. Sherman when they came under fire. After "we arrived at a perfectly safe position we halted to take an account of the damages. McPherson's horse was panting, as if ready to drop. On examination it was found that a ball had struck him forward of the flank just back of the saddle, and had gone entirely through. In a few minutes the poor beast dropped dead; he had given no sign of injury until we came to a stop."[9] At Chancellorsville, a solid shot almost completely severed a leg of Maj. Gen. Winfield Scott Hancock's horse. It was hanging by only a small bit of skin but the horse was cropping grass as if nothing had happened. An aide was ordered to dispose of the horse.[10]

Confederate Gen. Jubal A. Early's horse had one of its eyes shot out during the 1862 Battle of Williamsburg, but Early continued to ride it while directing his brigade.[11] Nathan Bedford Forrest's first horse during the Battle of Ft. Donelson received seven bullet wounds before it fell dead.[12] Union Maj. Gen. Grenville Dodge lost three horses during the war — one of which fell with twenty musket balls in it.[13] Capt. H.C. Parsons, 1st Vermont Cavalry, was riding the horse of his bugler during Farnsworth's Charge near the end of the Battle of Gettysburg. He wrote of this horse's performance: "How he sprang into the charge! How he leaped the four walls! How he cleared Farrington's horse as it rolled over in the rocks! And how gently he carried me from the field, although blood spurted from his side at every step."[14] Knowledge of a steed's wounding and its durability could be of advantage to the rider. During a Rossville, Georgia, cavalry charge the day after Chickamauga, Gen. Forrest's horse was shot through the neck. "The blood spurted out, and Forrest, realizing that the horse would bleed to death before he could complete the attack unless the hemorrhage was stopped, leaned forward and thrust his finger into the wound, thus controlling the hemorrhage. The animal bore his rider safely through the fight, when, his rider dismounted, the hemorrhage recurred and the horse soon expired."[15]

There are similar stories regarding artillery horses. Guns of the Sherman Battery of the Union Army were saved from capture at First Manassas when brought off the field by two horses that had been shot through by Minié balls.[16] In 1892, a Medal of Honor was awarded to Private Casper Carlisle, Co. F, Independent Battery (Pennsylvania), who "saved a gun of his battery under heavy musketry fire, most of the horses being killed and the drivers wounded."[17] The criteria for Medals of Honor were much less rigorous for Civil War soldiers than they became after 1900, and this particular medal was presented long after the war. Further details about the justification for this medal would, today, more likely qualify one of the horses rather than Carlisle for the medal. It seems that on July 2, 1863, during the Battle of Gettysburg, Pvt. Carlisle was assisted by the battery commander, Capt. James Thompson, and that he used two wheel horses — one of which was mortally wounded — to remove the gun. Taking fire from three sides, they nursed the dying horse north past Bigalow's Massachusetts Battery to the Trostle farm, where the horse dropped dead.[18]

The best description by a contemporary of the specific impact of wounds on Civil War equines was penned by Billings in 1887. He wrote that he had seen bullets buried in the necks or rumps of horses who showed no more than temporary uneasiness in response. Bullets that penetrated some fleshy part of the animal created a dull thud, sounding something like a pebble thrown into mud. These wounds caused a horse only to "start for a moment or so." He saw one horse, hit by a bullet in the neck, only shake his head. Wounds in the legs were another situation entirely. These "made a hollow snapping sound and took [the animal] off his feet." One pole-horse so shot went down at once, but even encumbered with harness, scrambled up and stood on three legs. Billings saw one horse take seven bullets prior to falling and reported that companion artillerymen believed that five such wounds was the average a horse could take before falling.[19]

Artillery horses, hitched to their limbers, were kept in the rear of batteries when the guns were in action. Musketry and counterbattery fire directed at the guns often passed over the battery and fell among them. Additionally, the artillery's animals were prime targets themselves. Shooting these animals could delay or immobilize a battery, hampering its effectiveness — or even making it susceptible to capture. Pvt. "Wash" Crumpton of the 37th Mississippi Infantry recalled that during the Battle of Atlanta he observed "the [Federal] caissons were being rushed forward as fast as the horses could carry them, but we shot the horses down."[20] Billings stated that at Ream's Station on August 25, 1864, his battery's horses were "a sightly target" for Rebel sharpshooters who poured on the bullets: "Their object was to kill off our horses, and then, by charging, take the guns, if possible."[21] After

Shiloh, John A. Cockerill of the 70th Ohio Infantry wrote, "In one spot I saw an entire battery of Federal artillery which had been dismantled in Sunday's fight, every horse of which had been killed in his harness."[22] During the first day of the same battle, Polk's Tennessee Battery (Confederate) went into action next to the Corinth Road and was barely in position when all of its horses were disabled and its guns had to be abandoned. After the battle, the battery had to be disbanded and the men reassigned to other units.[23] Writing about his artillery battery at First Manassas for *Battles and Leaders* in 1887, John D. Imboden remembered that his battery had more than half of its horses killed with only one or two left for each of several teams. The remaining animals had to be divided among the guns and caissons.[24] During the October 29, 1863, Battle of Wauhatchee near Chattanooga, one battery of Geary's Union division had thirty-seven of its forty-eight horses shot.[25] During the November 7, 1861, Battle of Belmont in Missouri, only one Confederate battery — Watson's Louisiana Battery — was involved. It was overrun when forty-five of its horses were killed.[26] On January 19, 1862, McClung's Tennessee Battery lost all twelve of its guns and had forty-five horses killed at the Battle of Mill Springs, Kentucky.[27] The 116th Pennsylvania Infantry captured a battery at Spottsylvania. Daniel Chisolm of the regiment noted, "Some of the guns [were] already hitched up as if they ... [were] getting ready to move. We killed the horses and turned the guns on the retreating enemy."[28] Gen. Braxton Bragg estimated that one-third of all the Confederate artillery horses were lost at Chickamauga.[29]

The teams of trains carrying supplies for the armies were similarly targets. The immobilization of the wagons either facilitated capture or at least temporarily prevented needed munitions or supplies from reaching the enemy. Judson Kilpatrick's Union cavalry attacked the train of Gen. Richard S. Ewell at Monterey Springs while it was retreating from Gettysburg. The troopers used their sabers on the mules and horses to immobilize wagons.[30] Later during the retreat, Gen. John Imboden's cavalry's train was attacked. In addition to chopping at wagon wheels with axes, the Federals "shot up the teams."[31] The train of Charles Cruft's brigade of the Army of the Potomac, while marching to relieve and reinforce Chattanooga, had entered into Halley's Trace, where they were intercepted by sharpshooters belonging to Longstreet's Corps. The sharpshooters shot the front and rear teams to block the train at both ends. One quarter of the mules in the train were shot before the remaining animals could be cut loose by the teamsters and led out of the valley.[32] "Wash" Crumpton marched with the 37th Mississippi from Columbia toward Franklin, Tennessee. On the way he saw that "wagons had been abandoned. Some of the teams had been shot, to keep the mules from falling into our hands."[33] Chaplain John M. Garner of the 18th Missouri Infantry tried to help a cook load and evacuate supplies as Union forces retreated during the first day's fight at Shiloh. They were unsuccessful since one mule was wounded and the team could no longer be controlled.[34] The problem of Union starvation within Chattanooga, described in a previous chapter, was made worse by the raid of Gen. Joseph Wheeler's cavalry from October 1–9, 1863, of routes leading into the city. He claimed over 1,000 mules destroyed and some estimated even more.[35] Union Assistant Secretary of War Henry Dana, who was with Rosecrans in Chattanooga, in his final report to Secretary Stanton on October 18, 1863, said that there was "a stinking wall of 10,000 dead horses and mules" along the road from Bridgeport, Alabama, to Chattanooga.[36] As the 1st Alabama Cavalry (Union) marched to that city in May 1864 to reinforce Sherman's army they found that "dead mules and broken wagons were in sight most of the time."[37] Raiding south of Atlanta in the summer of 1864, Brig. Gen. Edward McCooks's cavalry destroyed about 2,000 Confederate mules.[38]

Another reason for targeting equines, in addition to immobilizing their heavy firepower or impeding their supply, was to disrupt the enemy's "command and control." This meant going after the commanders, their staffs, and their couriers. For enhanced observation and more rapid movement about a battlefield, these were invariably mounted and always considered to be prime targets — to the detriment of the horses they rode. During the second day of the Battle of Corinth, Union Colonel John Sprague saw "a man on horseback, leading the charge in a most gallant manner. Sprague jumped forward. He shook the shoulders of several of his men and shouted at them to shoot the man on horseback. They did, and horse and rider collapsed beside a large stump."[39] Confederate staff officer G. Moxley Sorrel recollected, "It was always among the soldiers, 'fire at the fellow on the white horse.'"[40] Lt. Bayard Wilkinson of the 4th U.S. Artillery was near Meade's headquarters during Gettysburg's second day directing his Battery G. Fire was directed at him by Confederate Gen. John B. Gordon and he "was brought to the ground, desperately wounded, and his horse killed."[41] Lt. Gen. "Stonewall" Jackson met Gen. John G. Walker and his staff during the afternoon at Antietam. Walker later wrote, "By this time, with staff-officers,

Rebel caisson destroyed by federal shells at Fredericksburg, May 3, 1863. Eight horses were killed. Examining the scene are, left to right, U.S. Brig. Gen. Herman J. Haupt, Col. William W. Wright (Haupt's assistant in operating the U.S. Military Railroads), and an unidentified soldier (photograph by Andrew J. Russell, Library of Congress).

couriers, etc., we were a mounted group of some ten or dozen persons, presenting so tempting a target that a Federal battery, at a distance of five hundred yards, opened fire upon us, but with no other result, strange to say, than the slaughter of the horse of one of my couriers."[42] Col. Thomas J. Morgan of the 14th U.S. Colored Infantry, while temporarily on the staff of Gen. O.O. Howard during the 1864 Battle of Adairsville, found himself with about a dozen others mounted in an open field. A Confederate shell directed their way exploded above and just in front of them, wounding 2 officers and 5 horses.[43] In December 1864, Col. Morgan was commanding a provisional brigade of U.S.C.I. during the Battle of Nashville. At one point during the first day of the battle, Morgan, "being the only horseman on that part of the field, soon became a target." His horse was wounded in the face just above the nostril.[44] The horse, being larger, always made a better target and was likely to be hit if the rider target was missed. One Union staff officer remembered that at Cedar Creek, "General Emory's horse, which was white and a tempting mark, received a fatal shot."[45]

This aspect of the war was well-known to commanders and, at times, efforts were made to avoid it — or at least to be advised about it. At Pea Ridge, Confederate Brig. Gen. Ben McCulloch, preparing to ride forward to reconnoiter on his sorrel, advised his staff, "Your gray horses will attract the fire of sharpshooters," and left them behind. McCulloch himself was mortally wounded — and the horse shot in four places — soon thereafter.[46] Wright Whitlow, a servant in the 18th Tennessee Cavalry, which fought under Forrest at Ft. Pillow, recalled in his Confederate pension application that Forrest had three horses, two of which died after being shot during the battle. Whitlow's captain suggested to Forrest that he continue a reconnaissance on foot. Forrest declined, feeling that his chances were about the same mounted or afoot and he could see better from the saddle.[47] Prior to Pickett's Charge at Gettysburg, "General Lee, knowing it would be almost certain death for an officer to go into the charge on horseback, advised all who could possibly walk to go on foot."[48] One staff officer, Capt. Robert A. Bright, later remembered, "I was sent [by Pickett] to General Kemper with this order: You and your staff and field officers are to go in dismounted."[49] Horace Porter accompanied Lt. Gen. U.S. Grant on an observation of heavy fighting in the rear of the Petersburg Crater in 1864: "After proceeding a short distance I said, 'General, you cannot go much farther on horseback, and I do not think you ought to expose yourself in this way. I hope you will dismount, as you will then be less of a target for the enemy's fire.'"[50] At Seven Pines in 1862, Confederate Gen. D.H. Hill mounted and rode across an open field between the lines. Two of his officers chided his recklessness. Hill's response was, "I did it for a purpose. I saw our men were wavering, and I wanted to give them confidence."[51] The men in the ranks also recognized this danger. The story of Gen. R.E. Lee's being impelled to the rear during the Wilderness by his men is well known and became the subject of a lengthy poem.[52] The staff of Confederate Corps commander William J. Hardee implored him to remove himself from the lines during the 1864 battle at Resaca, Georgia. The soldiers all along the line cried out, "Go back, General, go back, go back."[53] Hardee declined his troops' advice and was unscathed — but three of his horses were killed.[54]

D.H. Hill was somewhat more reckless than most. He had three horses killed beneath him during the Battle of Antietam. The circumstances of the death of the second of these has been often related in accounts of both Hill and of others who were there. Lt. Gen.

TWO SCENES FROM THE TROSTLE FARM AT GETTYSBURG

TROSTLE'S HOUSE, SCENE OF THE FIGHTING OF BIGELOW'S BATTERY.

TROSTLE'S BARN, THE SCENE OF THE FIGHTING BY BIGELOW'S NINTH MASSACHUSETTS BATTERY.

Two Scenes at the Trostle Farm, Gettysburg, Pennsylvania. Artillery batteries drew counterbattery fire to the consequent devastation of their own teams, as occurred on July 2, 1863, to the animals of Bigelow's 6th Massachusetts Battery (woodcuts from photographs by Alexander Gardner, *Battles and Leaders*, vol. 3).

James Longstreet twice reported the incident — once for the *Battles and Leaders* series in the 1880s, and then later in his memoir *From Manassas to Appomattox*. The following account is taken from *Battles and Leaders*:

> During the progress of the battle of Sharpsburg General Lee and I were riding along my line and D.H. Hill's, when we received a report of movement of the enemy and started up a ridge to make a reconnaissance. General Lee and I dismounted, but Hill declined to do so. I said to Hill, "If you insist on riding up there and drawing fire, give us a little interval so that we may not be in the line of fire when they open upon you." General Lee and I stood on the top of the crest with our glasses, looking at the movements of the Federals to the rear left. As I did so, I noticed a puff of white smoke from the mouth of a cannon. "There is a shot for you," I said to General Hill. The gunner was a mile away, and the cannon-shot came whisking through the air for three or four seconds and took off the front legs of the horse that Hill sat on and let the animal down on his stumps. The horse's head was so low and his croup so high that Hill was in a most ludicrous position. With one foot in the stirrup he made several efforts to get the other leg over the croup, but failed. Finally we prevailed upon him to try the other end of the horse, and he got down.[55]

Longstreet's staff officer, G. Moxley Sorrel, in his account of the incident, mentioned, "The poor horse did not fall immediately, and made no sound, but put his nose into the grass, nibbling at it seemingly."[56]

There are numerous generals noted as having had multiple horses wounded or killed beneath them during the Civil War — sometimes multiple animals in a single battle. Three in a single day — like those of D.H. Hill at Antietam — is not all that unusual. In his memoirs, Gen. Grant mentioned that William T. Sherman had "several" shot beneath him at Shiloh.[57] The apparent record-holder for most horses killed in a single battle is the previously mentioned Bushrod Rust Johnson (then a brigadier general), with five slain during the Battle of Perryville.[58] Sixteen horses were killed in battle under Confederate cavalryman Maj. Gen.

Dead horse on the Gettysburg battlefield (Library of Congress).

Joseph Wheeler.[59] Being ridden by yet another famous Confederate cavalry commander proved most dangerous to his horses. Lt. Gen. Nathan Bedford Forrest had a total of twenty-nine horses shot from under him.[60] A total of nineteen — perhaps more — of the general's horses were killed,[61] giving him the record for most horses killed during the war.

Only two Army commanders were killed during the Civil War — Confederate Albert Sidney Johnston at Shiloh[62] and Federal James B. McPherson at Atlanta.[63] Both were mounted at the time. Eight generals were killed or mortally wounded during the Battle of Gettysburg: Confederates Lewis A. Armistead, William Barksdale, Richard B. Garnett, and William D. Pender; and Federals Elon Farnsworth, John F. Reynolds, Stephen H. Weed, and Samuel Z. Zook. Of these, six (75 percent) — all excepting Armistead and Weed — were mounted at the time.[64] Other notable generals not previously mentioned who were slain while astride their steeds included Union generals Phil Kearny[65] at Chantilly, J.K. Mansfield at Antietam,[66] and Alexander Hays at Germania Ford.[67] Confederates included Felix Zollicoffer at Mill Spring,[68] "Jeb" Stuart at Yellow Tavern,[69] "Stonewall" Jackson at Chancellorsville (friendly fire),[70] and in the last days of the war in Virginia, A.P. Hill at Petersburg.[71] Many other generals were wounded while astride their steeds.

Bushrod Rust Johnson. This Confederate major general had five horses killed beneath him during the 1862 Battle of Perryville — the most of any general in a single battle (Library of Congress).

The wounds and deaths suffered by the animals in battle were often quite gruesome and were remembered by veterans with sorrow and horror. Explorer Henry Morton Stanley was in the Confederate Army at Shiloh. He afterwards recalled the gruesome sight of a horse "galloping between the lines, snorting with terror, while his entrails, soiled with dust, trailed behind him."[72] John Cockerill of the 70th Ohio Infantry also had his memory of Shiloh: "Here and there in the field, standing in the mud, were ... poor wounded horses, their heads drooping, their eyes glassy and gummy, waiting for the slow coming of death."[73] While placing artillery the third day of Gettysburg, Confederate E.P. Alexander saw "a 20 pr Rifle shell knocked one whole buttock off a leadhorse in making a turn."[74] Moxley Sorrel had a mare killed under him at Gettysburg when a shell burst under her, while Sorrel himself was untouched.[75] The second of Forrest's horses was instantly killed at Ft. Donelson when a cannonball passed through its belly.[76] John S. Mosby attacked a Union wagon train of 325 wagons and teams near Berryville, Virginia, in 1864. Fired from a howitzer, "a shell was sent screaming among the wagons, beheading a mule."[77] A shot knocked off the rear part of the saddle of the horse of an aide to Union Brig. Gen. Nelson at Shiloh, breaking the animal's back.[78]

Prior to the Confederate cannonade on the third day of Gettysburg, Union generals Hunt, Schurz and Howard were conferring with a battery officer on Cemetery Ridge when "one solid shot plowed into six horses standing just a few yards from the group of officers. All six animals were killed or mortally wounded on the spot."[79] After the Battle of Corinth, Sgt. Alonzo L. Brown of the 4th Minnesota Infantry examined the ground where the 11th Ohio Battery had been sited. He saw "twelve horses belonging to two caissons [that] had become tangled together and piled up like a pyramid. Some below were wounded; others dead, and above all, with his hind feet entangled down among the dead and wounded beneath him stood a noble animal with head and ears erect, his right fore leg bent over the neck of a horse beneath him, his eyes wide open and out of his nostrils there extended, like a great white beard, a foam fully a foot long and streaked with purple. He was dead."[80]

One of the most compelling stories about wounded horses was penned by Mrs. James M. Loughborough, a citizen of Vicksburg, in her diary:

> One evening I noticed one of the horses tied in the ravine writhing and struggling as if in pain. He had been very badly wounded in the flank by a Minie ball. The poor creature's agony was dreadful: he would reach his head up as far as possible into the tree to which he was tied, and cling with his mouth, while his neck and body quivered with pain. Every motion, instead of being violent as most horses' would have been when wounded, had a stately grace of eloquent suffering that is indescribable. How I wanted to go to him and pat and soothe him! His halter was taken off and he was turned free. He went to a tree, leaned his body against it and moaned, with half-closed eyes, shivering frequently throughout his huge body as if the pain were too great to bear.
>
> Then he would turn his head entirely around and gaze at the group of soldiers that stood pityingly near, as if he were looking for human sympathy. The master refused to have him shot, hoping he would recover, but the noble black was doomed. Becoming restless with pain, the poor brute staggered blindly on. My eyes filled with tears, for he fell with a weary moan, the bright intelligent eyes turned still on the men who had been his comrades in many a battle.[81]

Nathan Bedford Forrest. This famous Confederate cavalry general had at least 19 horses killed beneath him during the war (an average of almost five each year)—the most of any general (Library of Congress).

William G. Stevenson, a New Yorker in the Confederate Army who later deserted to the North, perhaps described the most gruesome death of any horse in battle (at Shiloh) in his 1863 book *Thirteen Months in the Rebel Army*:

General Hindman ... was leading his men ... when a shell from the Federal Batteries, striking his horse in the breast and passing into his body, exploded. The horse was blown to fragments, and the rider with his saddle, lifted some ten feet in the air. His staff did not doubt that their general was killed, and some one cried out, "General Hindman is blown to pieces." Scarcely was the cry uttered, when Hindman sprang to his feet and shouted, "Shut up there, I am worth two dead men yet. Get me another horse." To the amazement of every one, he was but little bruised. His heavy and strong cavalry saddle, and probably the bursting of the shell downward saved him.[82]

5

Lack of Feed, Bad
Roads and Poor Care

Battlefield losses come readily to mind when casualties are considered, but they are but the tip of the iceberg. During the Civil War many more men were lost due to disease than to actual battlefield causes. It was the same for equines. Poor or non-existent food, bad roads and inadequate care played their part.

When Civil War food is thought of, invariably the trials of the soldier come to mind. The ragged and near-starved Confederate soldier on the march, the "Beefsteak Raid" to supply meat for besieged Confederates at Petersburg, the rock-hard, often weevil-infested hardtack of the Union soldier, coffee substitutes, roasted rats — all are valid pictures of the food problems faced by Civil War soldiers. Much less realized is that the Civil War equine's food requirements were both greater and not nearly so well met as those of the men.

The daily requirement of water for each horse and mule was about ten gallons.[1] Most Civil War campaigns, fortunately for the equines, were conducted in areas well-watered by streams and rivers. Camps had to be located near good water sources and water located nearby at the end of a day's march.[2] Acid minerals in the soil caused Confederates' horses near Corinth, Mississippi, in early 1862 to almost refuse to drink the water.[3] The enemy could deny water sources. In August 1863, during Sherman's Meridian Campaign, one wagonmaster wrote that the retreating Confederates had "destroyed the efficiency of all the watering places, by driving hogs and cattle in, shooting them, leaving the carcass in the water. Of course, nothing could drink it. Consequently, from want of water, excessive heat, and hard marching, the horses and mules began to die off by dozens."[4]

Water sources determined the course of one campaign. Sibley's Confederate invasion of the New Mexico Territory in 1862 had only one route — advance up the valley of the Rio Grande. Their later retreat and the Union pursuit were likewise constrained. Federal reinforcements from California arrived only when the campaign was practically over due to insufficient water sources along their route (the Overland or Butterfield Mail Route) across the Arizona deserts. This small brigade (known as the "California Column") was rarely united, as "not over four companies could move together over the desert on account of the scarcity of water."[5] It was even worse at some places, with the commander of the column, Col. Carleton, reporting, "Now, not over one company at a time could pass a night at many of the wells, which are a march apart."[6] At some watering spots (near Apache Pass, for one), water for animals had to be dipped with cups from the springs.[7] Only a very small portion of a cavalry company sent to Fort Davis in Texas reached it since its commander left troops

Negro baggage train drivers watering their mules (Pleasanton's Cavalry Brigade, Army of the Potomac). In addition to train animals, each company of the Union army was authorized a baggage mule for its cooking equipment. After initially detailing soldiers to the task of driving the mules, the Union Army switched to hiring black men for the task. As depicted in this sketch, water sources could become very crowded — and soon fouled by the huge number of equines (*Frank Leslie's Illustrated Newspaper*, December 20, 1862, p. 206).

behind "on account of the scarcity of water."[8] With this exception, obtaining water for the horses and mules was never so difficult as feeding the animals.

The natural feed of equines is grass. Idle animals that graze large fields have fewer respiratory and digestive problems than confined animals or those that must work. A more complete diet for working animals must include grain, the protein of which is essential to produce firm muscles. Grass or hay usually provides sufficient calcium, but may lack phosphorus, which is essential for bone growth. Equines need a variety of feeds and some bulk and prefer palatable feeds. Without palatable feeds they will not consume enough for their needs. Oats are the most satisfactory grain, being palatable, bulky and nutritious for them. In order to use barley, it had to be ground or rolled. Corn, which was fed extensively, lacked protein and essential minerals.[9] Civil War equines infrequently received what they needed: twelve pounds of grain and fourteen pounds of hay each day.[10] According to H.V. Redfield, writing after the war for a *Philadelphia Times* series, Confederate cavalry horses were "usually fed on raw corn on the cob," whereas the Union's horses received baled hay, sacked corn and oats.[11] But the Civil War equine rarely received its feed in the type, variety or timing needed.

The amount of feed required by a horse or mule was much greater than that required by a soldier. The Union Quartermaster Department calculated that a soldier needed three pounds of provisions daily as opposed to an equine's twenty-six pounds of forage. More than half of all supplies forwarded daily by the department to field armies consisted of forage for the animals. Meigs' 1865 report (found in *Official Records of the Union and Confederate Armies in the War of the Rebellion*, Series 3, Vol. V, 239–40 and Series 3, Vol. V, 315–22) said that between December 8, 1862, and June 30, 1865, the department had shipped 2,787,758 bushels of corn, 20,997 bushels of oats, 43,411 bushels of barley, 269,814 tons of hay and 8,243 tons of straw. With very little wastage during transport (only ⅞ of 1 percent), the department utilized 8,567 railroad carloads, 560 canal barges, 29 barks and 20 propeller cargoes on lakes. This capacity had been made partially possible by a decrease in the transport of shelter materials for the soldiers (after the "pup tent" was introduced).[12]

Even these huge amounts of food for the animals were not enough. Sometimes there was just not the capability to transport to them what was available. The animals of Gen. John Pope's Army of Virginia in early 1862 were dying for lack of forage while seventy-eight carloads of grain were available on railroad tracks in Washington with other supplies cluttering tracks in Alexandria, Virginia. There was just too much for the quartermasters to unload.[13] The Confederacy likewise needed a large labor force to gather forage for its animals. In January 1863, the Army of Northern Virginia was serviced by 160 black teamsters delivering forage and another 40 to unload it at the depot.[14] The winter of 1864–1865 found 244 blacks, 44 whites, 39 horses and 55 mules engaged only in the collection of forage in the Virginia Piedmont and Shenandoah Valley. At other times, there was a shortage of wagons to deliver forage. In May 1864, the Union V Corps animals were shorted grain when, after a first delivery, the infantry seized the wagons for use as ambulances.[15] As late as November 24, 1864, Maj. Gen. Benjamin F. Butler, in temporary command of the Armies of the James and the Potomac during Grant's absence, telegraphed the Secretary of War: "The battery and cavalry horses are suffering for hay.... For this there can be no excuse, as there is hay enough in the country." He suspected "inexcusable remissness [*sic*] somewhere."[16] The problem of delivery did not end once the grain or forage reached a forward depot, even if wagons were available to take the feed to the field units. Union Brig. Gen. Alpheus Williams wrote from Muddy Brook, Maryland, to his daughter on November 9, 1861, about the added difficulty. He commented, "I am obliged to send the wagons of my brigade 25 miles for hay and oats. The roads are now so heavy [difficult to travel] that the mules consume much of the load before they return, or on the return. When you reflect that we have in the division about a thousand four-mule wagons, besides the horses of officers, artillery, cavalry, and various staff departments, you will comprehend somewhat the difficulty we have to feed them."[17]

It might be thought that shortages of feed deliveries could be met by grazing in the vicinity where an army was located. Grazing was never really an alternative. The foods that might be had by grazing the animals in fields was neither efficient nor particularly healthful. It took eighty pounds of pasturage to equal the optimal daily twenty-six pounds of grain and dry hay. Additionally, green grass or plants increased the danger of the animal's foundering.[18] In fact, horses needed a balanced diet. One Confederate artillery officer noted, "Corn alone will not keep the animals in condition: they will not eat rations of corn if no long forage is furnished. Horses fed on corn alone are more liable to disease."[19] Pasturage, however, was widely used — when possible. It could be used only once a year since an area was soon denuded of pasturage upon its first visit by an army. After his victory at Second Manassas, Lee had to move his army because the area was then "devoid of food for men or forage for animals."[20] Writing in his journal on June 14, 1864, while south of the Chickahominy River, Sgt. Daniel Chisolm of the 116th Pennsylvania Infantry observed, "The cattle, mules and horses have nearly destroyed all the meadow, wheat and corn."[21] When the Union Army of the Cumberland became besieged in Chattanooga in late 1863 there was little forage within the lines and "it was used up fast with pastures chewed to dirt."[22]

Lack of food for their animals was particularly detrimental to the success of Confederate armies, but was also a problem for the Union. Seeking forage supplements in the neighborhood of an army was never completely successful — nor popular with the area's denizens — even early in the war. As early as October of 1861, Union Brig. Gen. Alpheus Williams was writing his daughter, "Our horses had a little poor hay for a day or so and then a little corn, but at length we have ferreted out the resources of the land and have meat for ourselves and oats and hay for the horses." He continued with information that the people of the area did not bring in anything, few were willing to sell, and that the area was quickly eaten out. And this was in Maryland — an area not yet visited by battles.[23] Confederate artillery and cavalry were often reduced by the problem. The Army of Northern Virginia had only two cavalry brigades available for the Chancellorsville campaign, as it had to be widely dispersed from the Fredericksburg area over the winter of 1862–1863 to obtain forage. One brigade (Wade Hampton's) was south of the James River, another far to the west in the Shenandoah Valley, and a third far downstream the Rappahannock River.[24] During the winter of 1863–1864, after assuming command of the Army of Tennessee, Gen. Joseph E. Johnston directed that most of his cavalry, almost all of his mules, and about half of his artillery animals be sent thirty to forty miles south to winter along the Coosa or Etowah Rivers, where there was better pasturage and nearer supplies of grain.[25] Robert E. Lee reported to the Confederacy's Secretary of War in February 1865 that his cavalry had been dispersed for forage.[26] "Shortage of horses and forage" after the Battle of Cache River in northeastern Arkansas in 1862 led to orders dismounting three Confederate cavalry regiments. In February 1865, Parson's Brigade of Texas cavalry had to be transferred from the Mississippi Valley to Texas because of the "disturbing mortality rate among cavalry horses" due to lack of forage along the eastern border of the Confederate Trans-Mississippi Department.[27]

Mules in the armies often made use of "alternative foods" when rations of grain or long forage were not available. It was commonly believed, according to Union veteran John Billings, that "mules have a great advantage over horses in being better able to stand hard usage, bad feed, or no feed, and neglect generally ... they will eat brush, and not be very hungry to do it, either. When forage was short, the drivers were wont to cut branches and throw them before them for their refreshment. One [mule driver] tells of having his army overcoat partly eaten by one of his team — actually chewed and swallowed."[28] Capt. John Morton, commander of a Confederate battery, stated that prior to the Battle of Chickamauga he "had a new uniform packed away in a wagon which was eaten by a mule."[29] The mountains about Chattanooga were completely devoid of food, and it was not unusual to see trees with their bark chewed off for as high as a mule could reach.[30] A Union veteran, Warren Lee Goss recalled of the mule that "when provender was scarce he ate rubber blankets, rail fences, pontoon boats, shrubbery, or cow-hide boots."[31] Sgt. Major Francis Wayland Dunn of the 1st Alabama Cavalry (Union) wrote in his diary for June 15, 1864, that Gen. John Logan was "at this time unusually cross on account of mules having eat the tail of his black stallion."[32] When food was short for Burnside's army at Knoxville, mules were gnawing on the poles of wagons and even the wagons. To prevent destruction of the wagons, hoop iron was wrapped abound the poles and trees and brush dragged in front of the wagons.[33] Teamsters who slept overnight would awaken to find that their mules spent the night in harness chewing the tailgates of the wagons in front of them.[34] Horses, too, when desperate for nourishment, would eat items not generally considered feed. After the Battle of Murfreesboro at the end of 1862, a driver of Lumsden's Alabama Battery reported, "The horses hitched to the pole of one of the caissons, had eaten off about three feet of the seasoned oak pole."[35] Capt. John Rowan of a Georgia battery reported in January 1864 that his starving horses had "gnawed completely through their bridles."[36] During the Vicksburg siege, horses of Confederate officers were eating cane tops and mulberry leaves.[37] "Depraved appetite" is the technical term for equines desiring such foods unnatural for them.[38]

The worst starving times for equines were during sieges. December 1863 and January 1864 were times of food shortages for the animals of Burnside's Union force in and about Knoxville, Tennessee. Charles B. Haydon, an officer of the 2nd Michigan Infantry, journalized about the problem frequently: Dec. 23 — "forage gone"; Dec. 27 — "scant forage for morning"; Dec. 28 — "entirely out of forage"; and Jan. 19 — "There is danger that all the govt. animals will die for want of forage."[39] The worst starving time for large numbers of animals, however, was the besiegement of the Union Army of the Cumberland in Chattanooga from October 1863 through January 1864. Capt. Ankeny of the 4th Iowa Infantry wrote that by October 16 at nearby Bridgeport, Alabama, "the mules are dying by the fifties every day for the want of grain."[40] By the third week of the siege, Union soldiers were on quarter rations and their horses and mules were receiving less. It has been estimated that during the siege 10,000 horses and mules died of starvation.[41]

Though soldiers sympathized for their starving animals, they too were near starving and often worsened the problem for the equines by stealing their food for themselves. Union officers at Chattanooga had to post guards over the horses to prevent soldiers from stealing the sparse amount of corn available for them.[42] Confederates besieging Knoxville during the same period picked up and ate raw corn which had dropped from the mouths of horses and raided corn which had been given to headquarters horses.[43] It has been related that during the 1862 Valley campaign in Virginia, even Confederate Brig. Gen. Isaac Trimble was found stealing ears of corn from horses.[44] Confederate Maj. Gen. Henry Heth admitted after the war, "The ration of a general officer was double that of a private, and so meager was the double supply that frequently to appease my hunger I robbed my horse of a handful of corn, which, parched in the fire, served to allay the cravings of nature."[45]

Equines, particularly the mules of the trains and artillery horses, even if they had been sufficiently fed and were not under fire, suffered greatly through a combination of the heavy loads which they had to pull (or carry, in the case of pack mules), bad terrain, and poor roads. When the weather was dry, dust stirred up by marching men and other animals choked their breathing. Rough roads became even rougher with ruts as hundreds of vehicles passed over them. As the wagons or caissons bumped over and through ruts, the strain on the teams increased and was applied unevenly. Mountainous terrain complicated the problem. An officer of the 19th Ohio Infantry, Henry G. Stratton wrote his sister in July 1863 from Manchester, Tennessee, that "the teams were overloaded and the roads all but impassible."[46] A month later, from Pikeville, Tennessee, in the Sequatchie Valley he reported that ten to twelve mules were needed per wagon in his regiment's train.[47] A letter of Sgt. John March Cate of the 33rd Massachusetts Infantry, written in mid-May 1863 from Bridgeport,

Alabama, stated that due to bad roads over a mountain it took the train he was with from 3:00 P.M. until the next day to journey only seven miles.[48] In March 1865 the wagons carrying the canvas pontoon boats of Brig. Gen. John Thomas Croxton's cavalry through the mountains of northern Alabama had to be pulled by eight mules rather than the usual six, and at one hill, thirty were needed.[49] If a single mule fell over a precipice, it had to be cut loose before pulling the rest of the team over. John Duke of the 53rd Ohio Infantry saw one cut loose that fell 200 to 300 feet to the bottom.[50]

The fording of unbridged creeks and rivers could also create problems. Union Brig. Gen. Alpheus Williams wrote his daughter at length about his train and then cavalry fording a river during the Second Winchester Campaign. He commented that the river there was about 300 feet wide, four to five feet deep, and had a swift current. It was a night crossing: "The descent into the river from the bank is very muddy and each wagon, as it went in, stalled on the start and then the poor animals would struggle and flounder in the rapid stream, which reached nearly to their backs, till many a horse and scores of mules were drowned."[51] By dawn the river had fallen half a foot but the mule-trains were balking and mules drowning. Eventually two pieces of artillery and dozens of wagons blocked the way, increasing the difficulty. The men had to work with ropes to draw them out and open the way. "Then down came the cavalry to try the ford.... The strong current would take some away down stream. Others would ride fearlessly over and with little trouble. Several got so confused that they lost the ford and swam away down the river in the middle of the stream.... Now and then a rider would be thrown and would disappear, floundering in the water."[52] On April 2, 1865, Croxton's Union cavalry command had to cross the Black Warrior River at Black Rock Shoals in north central Alabama, where, though the river was in full flood, it could be crossed. The men crossed using some old ferryboats, leading their horses alongside by the reins. Not only was this a difficult crossing, it was dangerous and several men and a number of horses were swept downstream, with their bodies later found below Tuscaloosa.[53] The next day, his command had to ford the North River, which was also in flood. Several of his men missed the crossing place and were carried downstream where they and their horses drowned.[54] Even when not in flood, creeks could be troublesome. During July 1862, while Bragg's artillery was moving from Tupelo, Missis-

Union baggage and gun carriages of the Army of the Potomac, 1863. Winter and spring rains played havoc on the roads (*London Illustrated News*).

sippi, to Chattanooga, the artillery horses were exhausted and balked at crossing creeks.[55] During the retreat from Chattanooga, the horses of a Lt. Beauregard's South Carolina Battery lay down and refused to cross a boggy creek.[56] One Union army wagonmaster en route to Knoxville, Tennessee, in late 1863 was probably more aggravated when the mule he was riding lay down in the middle of a stream, drenching him.[57]

The greatest difficulty of teams on the roads occurred when it rained and the roads became slippery. George Lee, quartermaster of the 3rd Brigade, 3rd Division, Union XV Corps, wrote from near Bear Creek, Mississippi, of such an experience of his train:

Rappahannock mud. Burnside's early 1863 "Mud March" prompted this cartoon in *Harper's Weekly* (*Harper's Weekly*, March 21, 1863, p. 192).

Yesterday morning I started from camp with my train. We had gone but a little ways when it commenced raining, and made the roads so slippery that one of my wagons, getting in a weaving way, slipped off a bank twelve foot high, rolled over three or four times, mashed a wheel, piled seven mules up in a huddle, driver included, and stopped finally, only from exhaustion. Such a moment is the wagon master's delight! Well, after some hard work we got all right and moved on to the next bad hill, when it commenced a merciless rain, and we had another sweet time. So it was all day, now rain, now shine, but finally after considerable slipping and sliding we arrived in camp after dark, muddy and tired.[58]

If it rained enough, the roads got muddy, at which time the difficulties became multiplied. When road conditions and the weather were ideal, a mule-pulled wagon could travel about twenty miles a day, but when rainy weather made the roads into bogs of mud, five miles a day was considered lucky.[59] In January 1863, Maj. Gen. Ambrose Burnside planned to flank Lee's Confederates by mov-ing the Union Army of the Potomac westward. Heavy rains caused the complete failure of this movement, which has become known as "Burnside's Mud March." The storm which caused the mud was described to his daughter by Brig. Gen. Alpheus Williams, who had recently moved his command to the Fredericksburg area:

On the evening of the 20th a severe northeast cold storm began with wind and rain, prostrating the few tents we had, putting out camp fires, and exposing the whole command to the peltings. It was a savage night. In the morning everything looked afloat. The rain still fell heavily, and the frost was all out of the ground, and the deepest mud was substituted. We worked all day to get four miles; floundering in bottomless holes;... Many of our wagons stuck fast inextricably and many mules were drowned in the middle of the road, fairly swallowed up in the mud. It was, in places, really difficult to force a horse through the tenacious stuff.[60]

Of the "mud march" itself, Williams wrote that Burnside's army had to return or starve after two days of floundering in the mud.[61] Others later wrote of the actual march:

After making about two miles the wagons began to turn over and mules actually drowned in the mud and water.... The mud was so deep that sixteen horses could not pull one gun."

   Elisha H. Rhodes, officer, 2nd Rhode Island Infantry.[62]

The pontoon trains could not move at all. The supply trains were in the rear unable to come up, and twenty-eight horses stalled with a cannon.

   A veteran of the 2nd Pennsylvania Reserves Infantry.[63]

The wagon trains became hopelessly mired, with draft animals dying in the traces, up to their heads in the quagmire.

   A history of the 9th New Hampshire Infantry.[64]

Hundreds of horses and mules were also lost....

   Pvt. Alfred Bellard, 5th New Jersey Infantry.[65]

The usual team for one-gun light artillery is six horses. I saw ten and twelve hitched to guns, and then the horses had as mutch [sic] as they could do to move. It is said that there was killed, while on this move, over 60 horses and over 300 mules.

   Sgt. John March Cate, 33rd Massachusetts Infantry.[66]

The ground was so soft that the wagons settled to the hub, and the mules over the fetlock.

   Quartermaster Sgt. Samuel S. Partridge.[67]

The "Mud March" may be the most commented-upon mud event of the Civil War, but it was hardly the only such incident.

   McClellan's 1862 Peninsula Campaign was also, at times, plagued with mud. Confederate artillery officer E. Porter Alexander remembered that during the retreat from Yorktown to Williamsburg the roads were "a river of mud; with frequent long halts when some stalled vehicle blocked the road. The men from the nearest ranks would swarm to help the jaded horses pull the vehicle out."[68] Pvt. Robert Knox Sneden of the 40th New York Infantry noted these conditions in his diary — frequently. His entry for January 24 noted, "The roads and camps were six to eight inches deep in red mud and slush. Long lines of army wagons were stalled in it, doubling up the mule teams was necessary...."[69] On April 6 he noted that his regiment's headquarters train got mired up to the axles several times with the soldiers having to use fence rails to pry them out.[70] The night of May 4 he wrote about the Yorktown and Williamsburg Turnpike that the road was "sandy but full of sloughs of mud and water" and that every few minutes wagons got stuck in the mud.[71] Union Pvt. Warren Lee Goss, writing about this campaign in *Battles and Leaders*, recalled that the heaviest trains had to be unloaded to facilitate releasing the wagons out of the mud.[72]

   The Siege of Chattanooga was also notable for its mud. After the fall rains began in mid–October 1863, teams by the hundreds floundered and became stuck in the mud.[73] Confederate couriers reported, "From Bridgeport [Alabama] to the foot of the mountain the mud is up to the horses' bellies."[74] Sherman's armies, on reaching Savannah after marching across Georgia, were met with deep mud. On January 23, 1865, Gen. Alpheus Williams wrote, "I found some forty-odd wagons stalled, and the roads so bad that six mules could not draw through an empty wagon. Indeed, the mules themselves were nearly drowned in mud." He stated that this was a time of "regular pour-down rain."[75] Confederates and Federals alike suffered from the mud during Hood's retreat from Nashville after defeat there in December 1864. Marshall's Tennessee Battery of Hood's Army of Tennessee had to use eight or ten horses to pull each piece or caisson.[76] Gen. George Thomas wished his cavalry to vigorously pursue the retreating Confederates, but a "difficulty was the impossibility of moving the cavalry off the turnpike on the flanks of the infantry column ... on account of the softness of the soil."[77] Unseasonable rains could create similar difficulties even in summer.

Drawing up the guns. Bad roads and poor weather combined to make the tasks of teams difficult (sketch by A.R. Waud, Library of Congress).

During the June 1863 Tullahoma campaign it was noted that horses and mules became mired in mud — some even floundering up to their noses and smothering.[78]

The bad roads and their loads occasioned another form of "suffering" on equines–particularly the mules. They — if susceptible like humans — suffered much verbal abuse. This was generally accompanied by liberal application of the mule driver's whip. This abuse was occasioned by the struggling of tired, overworked mules, traffic jams on the roads, and reluctance at deep or swift fords and quagmires. Army teamsters were considered scientific for the volubility with which they swore at their animals.[79] Union veteran Warren Lee Gross felt that "profanity was considered indispensable in mule driving."[80] Another veteran who wrote about mules during the war, John D. Billings, believed that mule drivers could curse more than any other class of men in the army. In his postwar *Hardtack and Coffee* he advanced the theory that the war could have been ended in the fall of 1864 if all of the mule drivers in the trains of the Army of the Potomac could have been assembled before the Petersburg trenches and, "at a signal, set to swearing simultaneously at their level-*worst*, the Rebels would either have thrown down their arms and surrendered then and there, or have fled incontinently."[81] Billings described the language of mules as "a kind of cross between an unearthly screech and a groan."[82] Whatever language was used in cursing mules, by all accounts it was always vigorously applied among the trains of both armies.

The profanity directed at army mules has given rise to enduring stories of the originality of mule-cursers in refuting rebukes of their profanity by superiors. One account by Horace Porter states that U.S. Grant considered such swearing at mules as a waste of time. Hearing this, one teamster ceased his cursing only long enough to respond that "the old man never druv mules."[83] The mule drivers considered cursing as indispensable to the management of their animals. Responding to the admonishment of a Michigan colonel on his "unchristlike language," one teamster responded that it was "hard if a feller couldn't cuss a mule."[84] Other teamsters considered such admonishments as interruptions. One chaplain, shocked at the fierce profanity of a teamster trying to get a mule unstuck from mud, asked the man if he knew who died for sinners, only to garner the response, "Damn your conundrums. Don't you see I'm stuck in the mud?"[85]

Clinton Bowen Fisk, a notable Christian general in the Union Army, was an abolitionist who neither drank nor swore (he later founded Fisk University with his own funds and was the 1888 Prohibition Party candidate for president, gaining over 200,000 votes[86]), was the subject of one early anecdote about the swearing of teamsters. Fisk organized the 33rd Missouri Infantry as its first colonel in September 1862. As a result of a revival-type exhortation by a Presbyterian minister, the men of the regiment entered into an agreement to leave all swearing in the unit to Col. Fisk. Fisk was promoted to Brigadier General the following November. His brigade, which included his old regiment, campaigned in Arkansas. In February 1863 he heard swearing in a river bottom by a teamster whose mules had run their overloaded wagon onto a stump and snapped off the pole. The teamster directed his profanity at the mules, the mud, the Rebels and Jeff Davis. About an hour later the teamster (whom Fisk knew from the 33rd) was passing headquarters and the general called to him:

> "John, did I not hear some one swearing most terribly an hour ago down on the bottom?"
> "I think you did, General."
> "Do you know who it was?"
> "Yes, sir; it was me, General."
> "Do you not remember the covenant entered into at Benton Barracks, St. Louis, with the Rev. Dr. Nelson, that *I* should do all the swearing for our old regiment?"
> "To be sure I do, General, but then you were not there to do it, *and it had to be done right off.*"[87]

By virtually all accounts, Major John Harmon, the chief quartermaster of "Stonewall" Jackson, was the legendary curser in the Confederate Army. Staff officer Capt. Charles Minor Blackford once described Harmon as having "a powerful and sharp-sounding voice and is very profane." Many histories and near-contemporary accounts of Jackson or the Antietam Campaign relate a story of Jackson's corps crossing the Potomac River as illustrative of both Harmon's profanity and effectiveness in cursing and of Jackson's disdain for it. Blackford, who was there with Jackson, related the story in his *Letters From Lee's Army.* They found Harmon at the ford having little success in getting a team to jerk its wagon through and out of the ford. Jackson mildly inquired of Harmon, "Don't you think you would accomplish just as much without swearing so hard?" Harmon responded, "If you think anybody can make a set of damned mules pull without swearing at them, you just try it, General! Just try it! I'll stand by and see how damned quick you get tired of it!" The first wagon happened to be light and pulled out of the ford, prompting Jackson to remark, "You see, Major, how easy it is?" Harmon's retort was that Jackson should wait until an ordnance wagon came along. Soon, an ordnance wagon did come along and promptly stalled. The driver did everything but swear (he recognized Jackson) without success until Harmon advised, "Better let me damn 'em, General, nothing else will do!" Jackson didn't reply, Another heavily loaded wagon got stuck at the ford. Despite driver efforts, suggestions from the general, and pushing, the wagon remained stuck until Harmon piped up, "What do you say now, General? Try swearing at them yourself, General, since nothing else will suit a mule!" A disappointed Jackson rode off, saying, "Well, Major, I suppose you will have to have your way!" Blackford wrote that they hadn't gone more than fifty yards when Harmon's "fluent damnation" startled the mules and they pulled the wagon out.[88]

Brig. General John D. Imboden, then colonel of the 62nd Virginia Mounted Infantry of Stonewall's command, told the story somewhat differently — and probably more accurately — in an article for *Battles and Leaders.* Imboden wrote that he had never heard Jackson curse and had heard of only once that he had not rebuked cursing. Imboden said that the incident had been reported to him by "the chief actor in it" — Major Harmon. In his telling, Edwards Ferry over the Potomac was blocked by a wagon train and Major Harmon was ordered to clear the ford.

> Harman [*sic*] dashed in among the wagoners, kicking mules, ... and, in the voice of a stentor, poured out a volume of oaths that would have excited the admiration of the most scientific mule-driver. The effect was electrical. The drivers were frightened and swore as best they could, but below the major's standard. The mules caught the inspiration from a chorus of familiar words, and all at once made a break for the Maryland shore, and in five minutes the ford was cleared. Jackson witnessed and heard it all. Harman rode back to join him, expecting a lecture, and, in touching his hat, said: "The ford is clear, general! There's only one language that will make mules understand on a hot day that they must get out of the water." The general smiled, and said: "Thank you, major," and dashed into the water at the head of his staff, and rode across.[89]

Union President Abraham Lincoln had better luck. According to Noah Brooks, *Sacramento Union* correspondent and friend and confidant of the president, this occurred on April 9, 1863. Brooks had accompanied Lincoln on a visit to the Army of the Potomac. On the date named, they rode by ambulance to review the Union I Corps. Brooks later wrote of the incident:

> We rode thither in an ambulance over a rough corduroy road; as we passed over some of the more difficult portions if the jolting way, the ambulance driver, who sat well in front, occasionally let fly a volley of suppressed oaths at his wild team of six mules. Finally Mr. Lincoln, leaning forward, touched the man on the shoulder, and said: "Excuse me, my friend, are you an Episcopalian?"
> The man, greatly startled, looked around and replied: "No, Mr. President, I am a Methodist."
> "Well," said Lincoln, "I thought you must be an Episcopalian, because you swear just like Governor Seward, who is a churchwarden." The driver swore no more.[90]

On the North Anna River line in 1864, General Lee heard a teamster cursing a mule from 100 yards away. Lee did not like to see animals mistreated and inquired why. The driver responded, "Is this any of your mule?"[91] As to the matter of cursing the mules, it was obviously the opinion of the "experts" that it was both necessary and best left to those who knew how to do it. This was the very least of suffering that Civil War equines had to endure.

Road conditions — deep ruts, difficult fords and mud — combined with heavy loads and poor or insufficient forage, caused many animals to break down. They could stand hard service for but a few days but could not pull a wagon or caisson or carry a man day after day without food or rest.[92] Hard use on campaigns over rough ground, bad weather, poor or insufficient food, and wounds all contributed to large numbers of worn-out and diseased animals. Efforts to preserve the vitality and health of equines in the armies began with training the men in preventive care and attention to minor ailments. Such care was sometimes not given by neglectful or tired soldiers and they had to be reminded by their officers. One remedy for sore backs was to order a cavalry trooper to dismount and lead his disabled horse.[93] Even generals had to be reminded of the necessity for equine preventive care by higher commanders. Gen. Robert E. Lee wrote from his headquarters on November 17, 1862, to his cavalry commander "Jeb" Stuart: "I very much regret to learn of the injury to your horses by scratches & sore tongue. The former I think by proper attention on the part

Return of Kautz's Cavalry Expedition in Virginia, 1864. Long cavalry raids, as illustrated in this contemporary sketch, wore down the horses tremendously, necessitating "appropriations" of remounts along the route of the raid (*Harper's Weekly*, August 6, 1864, p. 508).

of your men can be easily remedied, & the latter is probably occasioned or aggravated by feeding on the ground. I need not recommend to you to urge upon your officers & men strickt [*sic*] attention to this matter."[94]

Quartermasters responsible for providing remounts and new teams also complained of the improper care of horses and mules. Union Quartermaster General Montgomery Meigs engaged in lengthy correspondence, both telegraphically and by letter, with Maj. Gen. William S. Rosecrans, who had been demanding thousands of animals for his army. Finally he sent a lengthy missal to Rosecrans offering advice on the subject:

> With great deference to your experience, would not the less costly mode of defending your communications from the Rebel cavalry be to give them some occupation in protecting their own?...
>
> Compel your cavalry officers to see that their horses are properly groomed. Put them in some place where they can get forage, near the Railroad, or send them to your rear to graze and eat corn. When in good order start them, 1000 at a time, for the Rebel communications, with orders never to move off a walk unless they see an enemy before or behind them; to travel only so far in a day as not to fatigue their horses: never to camp in the place at which sunset finds them; to rest in a good pasture during the heat of the day....

Meigs concluded with the comment, "We have over 126 regiments of cavalry, and they have killed ten times as many horses for us as for the Rebels."[95] Rosecrans and Meigs were evidently on friendly terms as Rosecrans's response was a note of thanks for "taking pains to write so fully."[96] The advice was excellent, but exigencies of war frequently prevented field commanders from ensuring the level of care needed by the animals.

Winters were particularly hard on horses and mules. The mud caused by hard, cold winter rains has been reviewed in the previous chapter. Mud was, however, only a part of the problems winter caused equines. January 1862 was so cold in Virginia that the manes and tails of one artillery battery's horses were reported as looking like they were made of glass instead of hair.[97] Lack of shelter was as hard on equines as on men. Brig. Gen. Alpheus Williams of the Union Army wrote his daughter from near Frederick, Maryland, on December 23, 1861: "Our hundreds of public horses are in the open air, exposed to sleet and cold rain, freezing as it falls. One such day will cost the government more than lumber to cover the whole army would. There will be hundreds of horses and mules dead tomorrow morning. The very high wind and low temperature will make sad havoc."[98] Pvt. William R. Houghton of the 2nd Georgia Infantry remembered one winter scene of cavalry horses with their lower limbs snapped, writing postwar: "At Dandridge, Tenn., the Eighth Texas Cavalry had charged up a steep hill, the surface of the frozen ground being melted by the sunshine. Their horses had broken through the frozen crust underneath the surface and many strewed the ground and in an upright position, their legs buried in the mud."[99] Lack of shoes for the animals would immobilize them on hard winter ground.[100]

Unshod horses and mules were often referred to as being "barefoot," which was a serious problem for the animals. This problem was increased during winter as frozen ground would even sooner immobilize horses and mules.[101] Barefoot animals wore out sooner. Missouri's Confederate Governor Thomas Reynolds complained to Gen. Sterling Price in October 1864 that he and his staff had had to abandon one horse and two mules which had worn out due to the lack of horseshoes.[102] H.B. McClellan of J.E.B. Stuart's staff noted that it was "not an uncommon occurrence to see a cavalryman leading his limping horse along the road, while from his saddle dangled the hoofs of a dead horse, which he had cut off for the sake of the sound shoes nailed to them."[103] Confederate staff officer Charles Minor Blackford noted that many of the horses taken by Confederates during the Gettysburg Campaign were unshod and soon gave out on paved roads.[104] The difficulty in keeping horses shod is illustrated by the experience of Britisher A.J.L. Fremantle's journey during June 1863 north from Culpepper, Virginia, to join the Army of Northern Virginia in order to observe its operations in Maryland and Pennsylvania. For June 20 he was supplied with a horse by the Quartermaster Department; it was "deficient of a shoe." The next day, the horse of his then companion on the journey (a Sgt. Norris of the Quartermaster Department), "cast a shoe" after only a few miles. The third day of the journey, Fremantle's horse threw two more shoes and Fremantle rode into Winchester, Virginia, with "my horse minus his foreshoes, showed signs of great fatigue." They reached Martinsburg on the 25th with Fremantle's horse "nearly broke down," in consequence of which he had to dismount and walk. The next morning a new companion's horse had cast a shoe and Fremantle's own horse was now "in such a miserable state that I had not the inhumanity to ride him." Fremantle finally connected with Lee's army on the 30th at Greenwood, Pennsylvania, where he recorded that he was "forced to abandon my horse here, as he was now lame in three legs."[105] Barefoot animals were — seemingly to a much lesser extent — also a difficulty in the Union army. On October 19, 1863, Sgt. Major Francis W. Dunn of the 1st Alabama Cavalry (Union) recorded in his diary that he had borrowed a horse which was not shod on one rear foot. Dunn got the horse shod. Then on October 21 he "found that one shoe was off and horse getting lame."[106]

Long hours of use under the saddle also broke down horses. Sgt. Major Dunn noted on August 15, 1864: "Started before daylight. Horses backs getting sore, saddles not been off since we left camp [on Aug. 13] longer than 15 minutes."[107] Fremantle noted that his horse (in addition to being lame in three legs) upon arrival at Greenwood after a journey of ten days, had "a very sore back."[108] Fremantle had rested his animal nightly. Prevention of sore backs was relatively simple — if conditions permitted and the master was attentive. Soldiers needed to smooth out wrinkles in saddle blankets, dismount and walk steep inclines, and unsaddle to cool the backs of their mounts after long hours in the saddle.[109] Pvt. Sneden of the 40th New York noted that after the Battle of Glendale on June 30, 1862, he found that "the saddle had galled the back of my horse badly during the forenoon. And when the wagons moved off I loosened the girths to apply a salve."[110]

Poor, insufficient or the wrong type of feed also led to broken-down or diseased animals. "Sneeze Nuratum weed" was poisonous, and if eaten by equines and caused them to have "fits" (called "the blind staggers") and even die.[111] Capt. Holman S. Melcher of the 20th Maine Infantry wrote his brother in late July 1863 that the campaign had been hard, mentioning as evidence "the protruding bones of the Artillery and Cavalry horses."[112] Sgt. Major Dunn of the Union's 1st Alabama Cavalry diarized on July 5, 1864, from near Atlanta that the supply train's mules were "about used up" due to a lack of grain, to the extent that some teams would stall pulling a wagon loaded with only five boxes of hardtack.[113] The difficulties of feeding large numbers of equines has been noted already. The poor or insufficient food combined with hard service contributed to disease among animals. The commander of Rowan's Battery of the Confederate Army of Tennessee had noted that "horses fed on corn alone are more liable to disease."[114] An inspection in February 1864 proved him correct. Disease had spread among his animals, and in three weeks' time his battery had lost eighteen; of the remaining forty-eight, ten were unserviceable.[115] Confederate General Isaac Trimble reported in his diary in February 1863, "Many horses dying daily in Div. for want of food and disease."[116]

Diseases and conditions suffered by horses and mules were many and caused more deaths of equines than battle. From October 18, 1862, through April 9, 1865, the 10th Massachusetts Battery lost 157 horses. Of these, 112 (71 percent) died of disease — 45 from glanders.[117] Among the diseases mentioned by Civil War participants are glanders (three of "Jeb" Stuart's died of this during the winter of 1863–1864[118]), black tongue (peculiar to mules[119]), strangles, lockjaw, grease-heel, and hoof-rot. In November 1862, Confederate Secretary of War George W. Randolph was advised by Robert E. Lee that the cavalry, diminished already by battle and hard service, was being further reduced by "disease among the horses, sore tongue and soft hoof."[120] Already mentioned is that during movements through mud, many animals "foundered." A better understanding of some of these conditions is helpful. Glanders is a disease of the respiratory passages which exhibits pussy nasal passages and sores in the nose lining, fever, weight loss, and sometimes cough or pneumonia. It is severe, with death occurring in a few weeks, and is contagious (particularly through inhalation in stables). Its principal cause is ingestion of a bacillus in contaminated food or water.[121] Founder is a separation of the sole of the hoof from the wall, the pain of which causes animals to refuse food, to sweat and to tremble, can be both chronic and acute. It is caused by overfeeding on grain, overwork on hard surfaces, or drinking a lot of water while hot after exercise.[122] Spavin is a disease of the hock which is characterized by swelling.[123] Lockjaw — or more properly tetanus — is produced by bacteria living in soil or manure (horses make a lot of this — about 13.5 lbs. per day each[124]) that enter the animal's body through a wound.[125] Strangles (also called distemper) is a bacteria-caused infection of the lymph nodes, usually in the head. Abscesses form, large enough to block the animal's airways. It can spread to other parts of the body and appear as lumps. It is highly contagious.[126] Grease-heel, also called mud fever, is inflammation of the heels or legs caused when mud is left on them for extended periods of time.[127] The spread of disease or other conditions could be epidemic among equines kept in close contact of necessity; conditions could multiply disease as much as contagion.

The units of the soldiers had surgeons, assistant surgeons, and hospital stewards to help the men when wounded, sick or diseased. They did not have veterinarians for the equines of the regiments. If a horse or mule was unable to be "cured" or "healed" by rest, good food or the efforts of the soldiers or farriers, its chances of recovery were not good. Sending horses away from the armies to allow them to recover was not popular with the locals. North Carolina's Governor Zebulon Vance complained that broken-down animals quartered in the northwest of the state were eating up the substance of people who were already suffering shortages. Vance threatened to use his militia to drive them out of the state. if the Richmond government did not have them removed.[128] The Union army provided more extensive and better facilities for recovery of wounded, sick or broken-down animals than the Confederacy. The Cavalry Bureau's six depots included large stables for some and hospitals for others. The hospital of the Giesboro depot in the District of Columbia could hold and treat 2,650 horses at a time.[129] The quartermaster posts of the Confederate Army had as one of their responsibilities the care of unserviceable animals. Col. John R. Chambliss Jr., in command of an Army of Northern Virginia cavalry brigade, recommended in August 1863 that veterinary hospitals be established. A "Horse Infirmary Camp" was established for the Cavalry Corps in the Tye River Valley that same month. The following December, Stuart reported that 1,210 horses had been sent back to his command by the camp.[130] Chambliss's recommendations included the hiring of blacks to care for the animals and the building of sheds or some other type of cover for the winter. The following October an infirmary for horses and mules was established at Lynchburg, Virginia. Unfortunately for the horses, most weren't sent to the infirmary until they were almost completely worn out. Many of them developed glanders and others were just too exhausted to recover. Consequently, their recovery rate was poor. From October 1863 through January 1865, the Lynchburg infirmary received 6,875 horses from the army. Of these only 1,057 horses (15.4 percent) recovered.[131] It was not without reason that some Confederates referred to such infirmaries as "dead horse camps."[132] The mules fared somewhat better, with 1,644 of 2,855 returned to service.[133] Evidently, mules were not sent unless there remained a fairly good chance of recovery.

Despite the large numbers used and their importance in every aspect of war, very little provision was made for the care and recovery of broken-down, sick or wounded equines. Even less provision was made for their disposal when they died. Burial seems to have been the least-used method for the disposal of dead animals, but it did happen. Some horses, individually owned and treasured, were buried by or at the direction of their owners. Confederate staff officer John Cheves Haskell had a horse badly wounded during the Wilderness. The horse was a popular racer and neither Haskell nor any of his men would shoot it, so a man from another regiment was called upon to do it. Then, "when it was done, the men set to work and dug a deep grave so that the buzzards could not get him. They buried him in it and put a headboard over him, though there were any number of dead men left on the ground. Thus the horse fared better than the men."[134] Decaying animals created a great stench and if not disposed of could ruin the health of soldiers. Therefore, when a unit remained in an area, it had to do something about the dead animals. After the 1862 Battle of Fair Oaks, the 7th Michigan Infantry remained near the battlefield. The adjutant of the regiment, Robert C. Knaggs, narrated the problem: "The camp at Fair Oaks was a horrible place. It was a swamp and we had to bury our men and horses, but we could not bury them deep enough because we got drinking water at the depth of a spade. Whenever it rained the bodies would rise up, both horses and men. Then we would have to go in and cover them all over again."[135] Gen. Joseph Hooker had to place his division's lines further back due to the stench of dead animals, which he ordered cremated.[136]

Frank A. Haskell, soon after the Battle of Gettysburg, wrote his brother about the battle as he experienced it. During an artillery bombardment he had noticed men seeking "to get shelter in an excavation nearby, where many dead horses, killed in yesterday's fight, had been thrown."[137] The effort to perform some removal of dead animals during a battle is notable. It is not known whether the dead horses in the pit were later covered over (buried) or cremated. Burning dead animals in piles was more prevalent than burial. Use of this method after the Battle of Shiloh was frequently commented upon. Gen. Grant estimated that after the battle there were 500 dead horses left on the field.[138] The Union Army burned these animals — apparently in some areas before the men were buried, and in other areas after. William F. Crummer of the 45th Illinois Infantry recorded that the day after the battle — after burying the men — "we burned the dead horses and mules."[139] Another report stated that the carcasses of the horses were removed as soon as possible by burning, but that it took burial details several days to clear the human casualties.[140] To take care of large numbers of dead equines, details would be formed to drag the bodies by ropes from the immediate area, heap them onto piles of logs or brush, and burn them.[141]

Burning dead horses near the Peach Orchard at Shiloh. Often the most efficient method for disposing of the carcasses of large numbers of equines after a battle was to throw them atop piles of brushwood and burn them. Numerous fires for this purpose must have raised a terrible stench (*Frank Leslie's Illustrated Newspaper, Supplement*, May 17, 1862).

If convenient for the troops, rivers could be used. During a movement by river from Memphis to Nashville by steamer, the horse of Major Cramer of the 1st Alabama Cavalry (Union) had the glanders and was thrown overboard.[142] After the Battle of Selma in 1865, Wilson's Union cavalry corps had captured numerous animals and collected hundreds of others from the area afterwards. After mounting all of his force (and "contrabands" who would accompany his columns) the general ordered that the remaining animals — about 500 horses and 500 mules — be killed. Most of them were thrown into the Alabama River.[143]

By far the most prevalent method for "disposal" of dead equines was to leave them lying. If they obstructed a road, they would be dragged out of the roadway by ropes so trains could pass,[144] but mostly they just were left where they fell. The hundreds of dead mules lining the roads into Chattanooga have already been mentioned. A month after the capture of Fort Donelson, Major James A. Connolly of Charleston, Illinois, visited the fort and described the scene in a letter to his wife: "A great many horses were lying on the field just where they fell, scattered all over the field."[145] Operating in the Manassas area in August 1862, men of the headquarters element of the 40th New York Infantry found themselves stumbling over dead mules and broken wagons that remained there from the 1861 battle of that name.[146] In April 1865, two Taliaferro brothers returned to their home plantation on the north side of the Rappahannock River twelve miles from Fredericksburg — an area occupied by the Union army from November 1862 until May 1863. It took them five years to get the plantation back in shape. Their start in this process was collecting bones of horses and mules off their property. Within two days they collected 2,000 pounds of bones which they sold in Fredericksburg for $40.00.[147]

An entry dated February 4, 1864, at Memphis, Tennessee, in the diary of the sergeant major of the Union's 1st Alabama Cavalry noted, "Dead horses are scattered all around the outskirts of the city and the coming summer can not do otherwise than bring a terrible amount of sickness to the city. If they attempt to bury them it will not be half done...."[148] Noble C. Williams was a boy when Atlanta was ordered evacuated by Gen. Sherman. Writing in 1902, he remembered: "The woods and field were strewn with the carcasses of dead and decaying animals, most of which had performed valuable service but, becoming disabled, were shot or left to die of starvation." He remembered that there was a "sickening stench" and large numbers of buzzards.[149] It was similar at Selma after Wilson left. Despite his having thrown hundreds into the river, there were hundreds left lying "in the roads, streets and dooryards where they were shot." In a few days there was a terrible stench. The citizens of the town had to send far out into the countryside for teams to drag away the dead animals.[150]

The inability to adequately dispose of large numbers of dead equines can be explained by exigencies of a campaign — the armies had to move on and had not the time. The same reason would apply to individual animal carcasses often encountered by troops on the march. During the retreat from Perryville in 1862, men of Hilliard's Alabama Legion discovered some dead horses. As one of its battalion adjutants, marching in the rear of McCown's Division, remembered, "It was a dry fall, and pure water was sometimes hard to find. On one occasion just before we reached the Cumberland River we crossed a muddy-looking stream. We all filled our canteens and took a full draught. The road ran close to the bank for some distance. We had not gone far before we discovered some dead horses lying in the stream above the ford from which we had filled our canteens."[151] Sgt. Daniel Chisolm of the 116th

Pennsylvania Infantry had a similar experience. His unit was marching to Berksville Station, Virginia, on April 13, 1865, along a railroad. He chronicled what happened: "Nice clear water was running down by the side of the ties, we took our cups and dipped up and drank it and thought it was pure and nice, and when we reached the middle [of a grade] we found that we had drunk the essence of two dead horses. The Cavalry had a fight here and threw them into the cut and they was rotten. I tried to belch it up, but it was there to stay, gag, gag was all we could do."[152]

6

Runaways, Stampedes and Wauhatchie

When startled, frightened or wounded, equines often resorted to flight — running away with their riders, or, if in groups, stampeding. Runaway steeds could carry their riders to the rear or into enemy lines. Runaway teams could damage their wagons or artillery pieces or disrupt troop formations, knocking down and injuring soldiers found in their way. One such instance impressed itself on Sgt. Cyrus F. Boyd of the 15th Iowa. He recorded his observation about the first day of the Battle of Shiloh in his diary: "Riderless horses came thundering through the woods with empty saddles and artillery horses with caissons attached ran through the squads of men and striking trees caused the percussion shells to explode blowing horses, caissons and everything around to atoms."[1] Stampeded animals could hamper unit effectiveness by time lost to recover them. As might be imagined, there were many Civil War incidents involving runaway or stampeded animals.

Confederate Maj. Gen. John B. Gordon mentioned in his *Reminiscences* a captured horse that he had acquired which "came near to disgracing me in the first and only fight in which I attempted to ride him." As the general neared the front lines, this "immense" horse wheeled and fled so fast that Gordon was unable to halt him until more than a hundred yards in the rear. Gordon believed that it was well that this incident was not the first time he was under fire with his men or they would have followed his example and also fled to the rear.[2] At Chancellorsville on the night of May 2, 1863, fire by some North Carolina troops panicked some horses of General A.P. Hill's staff. They bolted, carrying two of the group into the enemy lines.[3]

The stampeding of animals at nighttime could escalate rapidly into even further confusion. Pvt. Alfred Bellard of the 5th New Jersey Infantry in his journal noted one such incident during the 1862 Peninsula Campaign. In this account one of the regiment's pickets began firing at what he thought was an enemy cavalry charge. "It turned out to have been a horse belonging to the rebs who had broken loose, and being shot at by our men, he started on a full gallop, thus making great noise as he dashed through the woods in the dead of night. As he went tearing along, he drew the fire from one end of the line to the other. The whistling of the balls gave the rebs the impression that they were the object of attack, and they joined in the row too."[4] During the same campaign, on a night movement toward White Oak Creek, one of the wagon guard of the 4th Pennsylvania Reserves stepped into the woods. His musket was accidentally discharged and, mistaken for an enemy, he had several shots fired at him. Some of the teams became frightened and dashed among the marching men and "for a time created considerable excitement."[5]

Nellie, the Brave Battle Horse. Gunfire and other battlefield noises could cause many horses to run away, though sometimes they continued along in a charge with their companions (Frazar Kirkland's *Anecdotes of the Rebellion*, p. 501).

The 19th Massachusetts Infantry was involved in a panic caused by a runaway horse near Tennallytown, Virginia, on September 4, 1862. Some officers fired at the horse or in the air. Hearing this gunfire, some cavalry in front of the regiment charged down the road, firing away. The regiment heard the noise, and seeing a mass of men in front of them rush from the roads, and then hearing clattering horse hooves growing louder and closer, rapidly hid themselves behind trees alongside the roadway.[6]

John Smith of the 19th Maine Infantry witnessed an incident at Spotsylvania in 1864 when a pack mule carrying cookingware panicked and galloped through the night. The noise of kettles and frying pans striking trees and the loud brays of the mule panicked soldiers into believing they were being charged. Some men began to flee through the woods. No shots were fired and the stampede of the men was checked.[7] Union veteran Warren Lee Goss had a similar mule story: "One night, a mule, heavily laden and bristling with shovels, picks, and axes, broke loose from his company, and with terrible clatter and clamor went charging into the enemy's lines, undaunted and alone. The enemy, believing they were being charged by cavalry, were in considerable consternation, and hastily formed to resist. They fired in volleys and at will, when the mule, not fancying his reception, wheeled, threw up his heels, brayed, and amid shouts and laughter, came prancing back to his allegiance, unhurt."[8]

Mules gained their greatest degree of fame as the result of a stampede during the Battle of Wauhatchie which occurred on the night of October 29, 1863, near Chattanooga. This was a relatively minor battle, significant as the only night attack during the Civil War.[9] On the 28th, Joseph Hooker's command — the XI and XII Corps — was moving toward the relief of the Army of the Cumberland and camped the night in the Lookout Valley between Lookout Mountain and Raccoon Mountain. A brigade of Gen. John Geary was encamped about three miles south of the main force at the hamlet of Wauhatchie as a rear guard. Lt. Gen. James Longstreet believed that a night attack could retrieve the situation for the besieging Confederates, and his plan was approved by Gen. Braxton Bragg. Shortly after midnight Geary's position was attacked by Jenkins's brigade (under command of its senior colonel, John Bratton). Then the mules came into the picture. The actual extent and effect of the mules' participation in this battle is somewhat questionable if not controversial.

The most common version was published by Horace Porter (at the time of the battle an ordnance officer in the Army of the Cumberland but not personally present for the battle) in his 1897 book, *Campaigning with Grant*:

> The fight raged for about three hours, but Geary succeeded in holding his ground against greatly superior numbers. During the fight Geary's teamsters had become scared, and had deserted their teams, and the mules, stampeded by the sound of battle raging around them, had broken loose from their wagons and run away. Fortunately for their reputation and the safety of the command, they started toward the enemy, and with heads down and tails up, with trace-chains rattling and whiffletrees snapping over the stumps of trees, they rushed pell-mell upon Longstreet's bewildered men. Believing it to be an impetuous charge of cavalry, his line broke and fled. The quartermaster in charge of the animals, not willing to see such distinguished services unrewarded, sent in the following communication: "I respectfully request that the mules, for their gallantry in this action, may have conferred upon them the brevet rank of horses." Brevets in the army were being bestowed pretty freely at the time, and when this recommendation was reported to General Grant he laughed heartily at the humor of the suggestion.[10]

Frazar Kirkland had published a slightly different version in 1889:

> While [the troops were] engaged in the movement up the valley, ... a great stampede among the mules took place. It was the dead of night, when both armies were resting from the fatigues of the previous day, and the sentinel's tread was the only sound that disturbed the universal quiet.
>
> Rushing from the wagons, to the number of about thirty, the mules made for the enemy's lines like frightened sheep. The drivers were awakened by the noise, just in time to witness the disappearance of the animals through our advanced pickets. The enemy's pickets were not caught napping. Hearing the mule brigade tearing across the valley, they mistook them for Yankee cavalry charging, discharged their muskets at the supposed "Yanks," and fell back upon a battalion stationed a little in the rear of them, with the cry that the enemy was upon them.
>
> The battalion partaking of the alarm, sprang to arms only in time to hear the sound of the frightened mules, whose race was not checked by the volley from the pickets. They retreated also a short distance to a point where a whole rebel brigade had stacked their arms, and were calmly dreaming of home and battle scenes. In rushed the battalion, more dead than alive from fright, with the exclamation —"Hooker has surprised us; his cavalry is upon us!" The valiant sons of Mars did not wait to gather up their blankets or guns, but made the fastest pedestrian time on record back to the main force, leaving on the field, for the mule brigade, over one thousand stand of arms, among which were three hundred new Enfield rifles, blankets, small arms, knapsacks, etc. Meantime, our teamsters had given the alarm, and a force was sent out for the recovery of the mules, and in a few hours the expedition, inaugurated by the mules, returned to our lines with the valuable spoils.

The midnight charge of the mule brigade is well worthy of a place in history. Through its aid a large amount of valuable stores and arms was secured, and Hookerwas enabled to push his advance much nearer the point of ground contended for.[11]

In 1887, John D. Billings (not present — he was in the Army of the Potomac) included a sentence in a chapter about army mules in his book, *Hardtack and Coffee*, that mentioned Wauhatchie: "About two hundred mules, affrightened by the din of battle, rushed in the darkness into the midst of Wade Hampton's Rebel troops, creating something of a panic among them, and causing a portion of them to fall back, supposing that they were attacked by cavalry."[12] General Grant was also very brief in his mention of the event. In his *Personal Memoirs* (published 1885), he wrote: "In the darkness and uproar, Hooker's teamsters became frightened and deserted their teams. The mules also became frightened, and breaking loose from their fastenings stampeded directly toward the enemy. The latter, no doubt, took this for a charge, and stampeded in turn."[13] Obviously, by the 1880s the mule brigade charge was well known among Union writers about the war (it also appeared in other works of the period which are not cited).

Confederates? There were no Southern reports of an "attack by mules" at Wauhatchie. Neither Longstreet nor E.P. Alexander, his artillery chief, both of whom wrote extensively about the Chattanooga campaign during the 1880s and '90s, said a word about it when covering the Battle of Wauhatchie. For that matter, neither did Thomas B. Van Horne in his comprehensive history of the Army of the Cumberland, published in 1875. Neither Hooker nor Geary mentioned mules in their official reports of the battle. The earliest Confederate mention of the mule charge occurred in 1887 in a footnote in *Battles and Leaders*. *Century Magazine* had published as an article Gen. Grant's account from his *Personal Memoirs* and had drawn on a letter from J.L. Coker of Darlington, South Carolina, who had been present on the field of battle. Coker's response categorically denied the charge of the mules:

> The engagement of Wauhatchie, or Lookout Valley, was of minor importance; but it is well to have errors corrected. General Geary's Federal division was not attacked by Longstreet's corps, but by Jenkins's South Carolina brigade, commanded by Colonel (afterwards General) John Bratton. No other troops fired a shot at Geary's men that night. The battle lasted about one hour and a half, and was brought to a close on account of Gen. Howards's advance threatening Bratton's rear, and not by a Confederate stampede caused by a "mule-charge" in the dark. When the order to retire was received, the brigade was withdrawn in good order. The writer, acting assistant adjutant-general on Colonel Bratton's staff, was wounded and taken from the field at the close of the battle, and did not observe any disorder. General Howard was opposed by a small force, and made such progress that Jenkins's brigade was in danger of being cut off from the crossing over Lookout Creek. They were ordered out when they seemed to be getting the better of General Geary, who was surprised by the night attack, and no doubt thought himself "greatly outnumbered" and reported himself attacked by a corps instead of a brigade.[14]

The stories of the "charge of the mule brigade" seem a bit fantastic, but given other accounts of confusion caused by stampeding mules or horses in the dark, could certainly be true. The differences in numbers of mules and how their "battle" began could be attributed to faulty memories or additions to a story when repeated to others as second-hand accounts. Where, then, did the story come from? Soon after the battle, an unknown soldier of an Ohio regiment (there were no Ohio units in Geary's force) wrote a poem in the style of Tennyson's "Charge of the Light Brigade" which was published in newspapers (a common occurrence in those days). This poem (see Appendix B), evidently amused many Union veterans and from it the story grew. But was it true?

The mules with Geary's command almost certainly did something. Every legend had its basis in fact. Two days after the battle, on November 1, 1863, Henry G. Stratton of the 19th Ohio Infantry (also not present) wrote a letter to his sister. He told her that 1,000 to 1,500 stand of arms had been captured in the fight at Wauhatchie and explained:

> The large proportion of arms captured was the result of a rich joke. Hooker had forty or fifty mules in a pen during the fight they broke out and made directly for the rebel lines regardless of shot or shell. The enemy thought it was a charge of cavalry, became panic stricken and the result was their men through [*sic*] away 1000 stand of arms and ran, we capturing them and the mules also who after their success returned. It is now proposed to enlist a brigade of mules in place of our cavalry as they were never known to make so brilliant a charge....[15]

A relation of the actual events at Wauhatchie has been researched and compiled by modern historian Peter Cozzens. In his *The Shipwreck of Their Hopes* (1994) he states that as the Confederates entered Geary's lines they found the wagon train park ahead of them. The train guards were scattered by a few shots. In the dark, some of the South Carolinians slipped away to loot the wagons (Confederate soldiers were always on the alert to improve their rations and attire). Some of the mules broke loose and began running about, braying. This caused some confusion among the attackers, but they recovered quickly. However, the confusion caused by the mules and the resultant delay in pushing forward the attack provided time for the 137th New York Infantry to arrive at the point of contact and hold the Confederates. Cozzens added that the rampaging mules had also impeded the Union forces as much as they had the Confederates because some of them — the teams of several ammunition wagons — had stampeded into the path of the 149th New York Infantry, causing them to open ranks. Out-of-control horses of some mounted orderlies and three headquarters ambulances further disrupted the regiment, which needed an hour to reassemble and continue into the battle.[16]

Col. Adin B. Underwood of the 33rd Massachusetts Infantry opined similarly. In writing in 1881 of the Battle of Wauhatchie, he stated:

> The Hampton Legion outflanked Geary's men on their left, got into the wagon train and shot down some of the mules. When it fell back it was in too much of a hurry to drive any of them along and certainly retreated from them. Probably on this basis of fact was founded the funny incident, as worked up into a parody on "The Charge of the Six Hundred" by some unknown poet....[17]

The exact details of whatever the mules did at Wauhatchie will never be precisely known, but the story is too humorous and too good to abandon. If not here, the mules certainly did perform "heroically" throughout the war in performance of their arduous work.

7

The Lightning Mule Brigade

Strange as it may seem, there actually was, in the Union Army in 1863, a brigade of soldiers mounted on mules. This brigade had a brief life — from April 7 to May 3 — but it was the only brigade in either army specifically organized to be mounted on mules. Officially it was designated as the Provisional Brigade, Army of the Cumberland, but because of its purpose — conducting a quick, surprise or "lightning" strike on its unusual mounts — it was sometimes referred to as the "Lightning Mule Brigade" by its members. Their Confederate foes, also because of the mounts used, referred to it as the "Jackass Cavalry."[1] Its brief history is completely wrapped up in the Civil War story of Streight's Raid, the details of which, except for one incident, are agreed upon by both Union and Southern histories. The details for the following brief history of the brigade, its expedition and its pursuit, are principally draw from John Allan Wyeth's *That Devil Forrest: Life of General Nathan Bedford Forrest* (originally published 1899) and William R. Hartpence's *History of the Fifty-First Indiana Veteran Volunteer Infantry* (published 1894), both of which made extensive use of official records and interviews with participants.

When the spring of 1863 began, Maj. Gen. U.S. Grant was operating against Vicksburg, and Maj. Gen. William S. Rosecrans with the Army of the Cumberland was facing Gen. Braxton Bragg and the Confederate Army of Tennessee at Tullahoma, Tennessee. Col. Abel D. Streight of the 51st Indiana Infantry, realizing that Rosecrans's campaign to defeat and displace the Confederates from Tennessee would be furthered if the railroads in northern Georgia supplying Bragg's army could be cut, applied for an independent mounted brigade to engage Confederate cavalry bands under Forrest and Wheeler and cut the railroads. He submitted the plan in early march to Brig. Gen. Thomas J. Wood, commander of the XXI Corps, who forwarded it to Brig. Gen. James A. Garfield, chief of staff to Maj. Gen. Rosecrans. The future president of the United States was quite favorable to the application and secured the approval of Rosecrans.

In late March, Rosecrans issued verbal orders for formation of an "Independent Provisional Brigade" to be commanded by Streight with about 1,700 officers and men.

The elements of the brigade were designated as:

> the 51st Indiana Infantry under Lt. Col. James W. Sheets
>   from the 3rd Brigade, 1st Division, XXI Corps;
> the 73rd Indiana Infantry under Col. Gilbert Hathaway
>   also from the 3rd Brigade, 1st Division, XXI Corps;
> the 80th Illinois Infantry under Lt. Col. Andrew F. Rogers
>   from the 1st Brigade, 5th Division, XIV Corps;

the 3rd Ohio Infantry under Col. Orris A. Lawson
　　　from the 2nd Brigade, 1st Division, XIV Corps;
2 companies (I and K) of the 1st Alabama Cavalry under Capt. D.D. Smith
　　　from the Cavalry Brigade, District of Corinth, 2nd Division, XVI Corps;
and two mountain howitzers (under a Major Vananda) attached.

Most of the Alabamians added to the brigade were from the northern Alabama area, containing many Union sympathizers, in which Streight's command was to operate. Streight's own regiment also contained many North Alabamians — about 400 of them, according to many records.[2] This number is probably much inflated given the actual total strength of the regiment and the fact that only about fifty enlistments in the regiment are noted on its roster as occurring during the period before the raid.

On April 7, Garfield wrote Streight stating the verbal orders which had been given to him. "By Special Field Orders No. 94, Paragraph vii, you have been assigned to the command of an independent provisional brigade for temporary purposes." Streight was told, after fitting out his command, to proceed to a steamboat landing on the Tennessee River (which would be designated later by telegraph) not far above Fort Henry. He was to embark his command there and proceed upriver. He was to confer with Brig. Gen. Grenville M. Dodge (commander of the District of Corinth, XVI Corps, Grant's Army of Tennessee) at Hamburg, Tennessee, and join with him there (or at Eastport, Mississippi) as Dodge was en route to Iuka, Mississippi. Streight's command would march with Dodge's command to Tuscumbia. Dodge would, as a diversion, create the impression that Streight's brigade was part of his. After marching to Tuscumbia, Alabama, with Dodge's force, Streight was ordered to move south to Russellville or Moulton in Alabama.

His route from there would be governed by circumstances, but he was to get into western Georgia and cut railroads supplying Bragg's army by way of Chattanooga. Garfield emphasized this point stating, "To accomplish this, is the chief object of your expedition: you must not allow collateral nor incidental schemes, even though promising great results, to delay you so as to endanger your return." Garfield advised Streight that the quartermaster had furnished him with sufficient funds. Streight was "to draw your supplies, and keep your command well mounted, from the country through which you pass. For all property taken for the legitimate use of your command, you will make cash payments in full to men of undoubted loyalty; give the usual conditional receipts to men whose loyalty is doubtful, but to rebels nothing." Garfield was very specific in ordering, "You are particularly commanded to restrain your command from pillage and

Abel D. Streight. This Union colonel commanded the war's only mule-mounted unit (Library of Congress).

marauding." Streight was told that he could destroy all Confederate supply depots, manufactories of guns, ammunition, equipment and clothing for Confederate use if "you can without delaying you so as to endanger your return."[3]

Streight's orders as transmitted by Garfield indicate a remarkable if not surprising degree of coordination between two separate armies not under a common commander. The two Alabama cavalry companies in his command would come from the XVI Corps of the Army of the Tennessee; the command would be moving to its starting point (Tuscumbia) through the operational area of the Army of Tennessee and would be initially screened by elements of the XVI Corps. Additionally, Gen. Dodge had been ordered to assist Streight's force in mounting his command if and as needed. The facts speak well of Grant's willingness to cooperate with the commander of an army not under his command and of his subordinates — particularly Dodge — to render the necessary cooperation. Perhaps he was somewhat motivated in that Streight's raid would cause Confederate diversion from another raid planned for the same period by the Army of the Tennessee — that of Col. Benjamin G. Grierson (also of the XVI Corps) down the length of Mississippi to facilitate Grant's movements against Vicksburg. Streight's river movement to join Dodge would be tasked with escorting rations and forage from Kentucky to Dodge's force. The coordination of the 2 separate armies in launching the 2 raids — in distant areas with communication hampered by distance — would make a fascinating study in itself. The fact that, albeit indirectly, Rosecrans's Army of the Cumberland participated in the Vicksburg Campaign is surprising.

Col. Streight acknowledged Garfield's statement of his orders on April 9 from Nashville, stating that he understood them. He also requested permission to dress two of his companies "after the promiscuous Southern style." Since the Confederates operating in the area did not have standard uniforms, he felt that two companies dressed in this manner would give an advantage for his advance. There is no record of any reply to this request; in any event, none of the brigade's companies were dressed in such a manner during the raid. The colonel at the same time advised that he could move his command within three hours of receiving orders to do so. Orders were received from Garfield to embark on the 10th. Horses were in short supply in the Army of the Cumberland, and mules were believed to be better suited for operations in rugged terrain such as the Independent Provisional Brigade would operate across. For these reasons it was decided that the brigade (except for the two Alabama cavalry companies, which had their own horses) would be mounted on mules to be supplied at Nashville.

Difficulties for Streight and his brigade commenced almost immediately. It was not until late in the evening of the 10th that the mules supplied at Nashville could be loaded. The brigade arrived at Palmyra, Tennessee, on the 11th and unloaded, except for Col. Lawson (3rd Ohio) and four companies of the 51st Indiana, who would continue on the steamboats to Smithfield, Kentucky, to take on the rations and forage for Gen. Dodge. As soon as daylight arrived, the brigade began to catch and saddle mules. The sergeant major of the 51st Indiana (William R. Hartpence), in his history of the regiment, recalled the problems: "It was then discovered for the first time, that the mules were nothing but poor, wild and unbroken colts, many of them but two years old, and that a large number of them had distemper. Forty or fifty of the lot were too near dead to travel, and had to be left at the landing. Ten or twelve died before starting; and such as could be ridden at all, were so wild and unmanageable, that it took the boys all that day and the next to catch and break them."

Parties were sent out into the surrounding countryside to gather horses and mules (the number of mules provided at Nashville was insufficient to mount the entire brigade even if they'd all been in health). They collected about 150 animals described by Hartpence as "very good animals, though mostly barefooted."

On April 13, the brigade left Palmyra on a cross-country march to Fort Henry on the Tennessee River. They made fifteen miles that day. They did not find many horses or mules since the people of the country had gotten warning of the brigade's movement and had driven off most of their stock. They resumed their march early on the 14th and arrived at Fort Henry about noon on the 15th. Another 100 mules had given out and had to be left behind, but the expedition reached Fort Henry with about 1,250 animals. The boats did not arrive until the evening of the 16th. They had been delayed in getting the rations and forage for Dodge loaded. They also had to wait for two gunboats and Brig. Gen. Alfred W. Ellet's "Marine Brigade" of the Department of the Mississippi. The "fleet" of steamers with Col. Lawson's detachment and the supplies, the "Marine Brigade" and two gunboats did not arrive at Fort Henry until late in the day on the 16th. The pilots refused to continue that night, saying it was unsafe with the then low stage of the river. Orders also came to proceed as far as Eastport, Mississippi. Streight's brigade finally left Fort Henry on the morning of the 17th and arrived at Eastport during the afternoon of the 18th. Col. Lawson was left in command and Streight traveled to Bear River, twelve miles away, to meet with Gen. Dodge, whose 8,000 men were located there.

Col. Streight returned to Eastport about midnight and discovered yet another problem. While he was absent a stampede had occurred and many of the mules had escaped. Actually, the stampede had been caused by the Confederates. Brig. Gen. Phillip D. Roddy had a small brigade (Roddy's old 4th Alabama Cavalry was its principal unit) operating in the area. The braying of so many mules attracted the attention of some of Roddy's men, who then, hoping to obtain better mounts for themselves, crept into the camps and stampeded the mules. It was discovered in the morning that about 400 of the best mules had escaped. The 20th and half of the 21st was spent searching for them in the countryside. Only about 200 were recovered. Nevertheless, the brigade left Eastport on the 21st bringing up the rear of Dodge's command. A large number of the mules issued at Nashville were left behind at Eastport due to distemper; several of them died. There was some skirmishing all the way to Tuscumbia with Roddy's men. At 11:20 P.M. on the 24th, Dodge advised his immediate superior, Maj. Gen. Richard J. Oglesby, that Tuscumbia had been taken without severe fighting. He had orders to operate in the area for about two weeks in order to cover Streight's operations. Dodge pledged to "help Streight in his movement all I can."[4] Dodge indeed did much to help Streight, reporting that he "took horses and mules from my teams and mounted infantry and furnished him some six hundred head." He also gave the mule brigade 10,000 rations of hardtack.[5]

Meanwhile, on the 23rd, the famous Confederate cavalry commander, (then) Brig. Gen. Nathan Bedford Forrest, received orders at Spring Hill, Tennessee, from Gen. Braxton Bragg to force march his brigade (the 4th, 9th, 10th, and 11th Tennessee Cavalry regiments, plus Morton's Tennessee Battery) to Decatur, Alabama, where he was to join with Col. Roddy to stop the Union advance. By the 26th, Forrest had crossed the Tennessee River near Courtland, Alabama, and was positioned to resist any further advance by Dodge. That same date, Streight wrote a final communication to Garfield: "After numerous difficulties and delays, I am at last supplied with animals to mount all but 200 of my command. I have

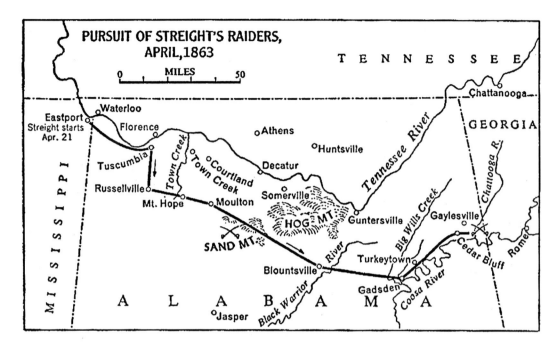

Route of the Lightning Mule Brigade across North Alabama, 1862 (John Allan Wyeth's *That Devil Forrest*).

met with a great drawback on account of mules drawn at Nashville being such poor ones." He reported that he would start at 1:00 A.M. on the 27th for Russellville, and then from there to Moulton with hopes of procuring the necessary animals along the way. "General Dodge has let me have nearly 400 animals, and has done everything in his power to aid me; but the people throughout the country here run off most of their horses and mules." Still, Streight was hopeful of success. He thought there were 1,500 to 4,000 Confederates between him and Decatur, but hoped he'd have a two- to three-day head start on them.[6]

The Lightning Mule Brigade left Dodge's lines at Tuscumbia on April 26 at about 11:00 P.M., leaving behind them with Dodge the men determined by the surgeon to be unfit. The brigade was now reduced to about 1,500 men, 150 of whom had neither mule nor horse. Other animals were too unfit to carry more than their saddles, so about 300 of the brigade were afoot. It was raining very hard and progress was made difficult by mud and darkness. After thirty-four miles they had to halt at Mount Hope for the unmounted men to catch up. Streight quartered himself with a lady of Union sentiments and had the quartermaster pay her for a fine horse taken to mount one of his men. Nashville-supplied animals continued to fail, but enough animals were gathered to mount all but about fifty men by the morning of the 28th when it left for Moulton. On the evening of the 28th, a citizen advised Gen. Forrest that about 2,000 mounted Federal troops had passed through Mount Hope headed toward Moulton. Forrest made preparations to pursue. Roddy was to take his own 4th Alabama and the 11th Tennessee and get between Streight and Dodge to prevent escape back or rescue. The rest of the command would pursue Streight's men. Three days' worth of rations were cooked and distributed along with shelled corn for two days' forage. At 1:00 A.M. on the 29th, Forrest and his men left Courtland.

Streight's brigade had entered Moulton about dark on the 28th. The advance — Smith's two companies of Alabama cavalry — drove out or captured a small group from Roddy's command and freed some jailed citizens imprisoned for their Unionist sentiments. Some of them were friends or neighbors of the Alabama Federals. About midnight, the mule brigade left Moulton headed toward Mountsville by way of Day's Gap, at the mouth of a gorge leading to the summit of Sand Mountain. After two days of rain, the roads were in terrible condition. The 29th was consumed by a 35-mile march to Day's Gap. All of the men were now mounted. Though many of the animals were poor or in poor condition, the men felt they would be able to supply all their future needs along the way. Three wagons full of supplies that had been sent to the mountains were taken and destroyed during the day's march. Streight learned nothing about any pursuit — only that small parties were in the area on conscription duty. The mule brigade encamped here at the foot of the mountain. Just after midnight on the 30th, Forrest, within four miles of the gap, learned that they were there. Having rested his command for only one hour in Moulton, they were allowed to rest until daylight.

At daylight on the 30th, Streight left camp with his wagons (Dodge had given him six) in front. Movement was slow up a rocky, narrow and winding road. When the crest was reached, the rearguard (the 73rd Indiana) was still at the campsite. From five hundred yards away the column received a cannon shot. Forrest had also moved at daylight, with two of his regiments sent by a neighboring pass to try to flank Streight in the rear. Streight decided to make a stand about two miles west of the crest. The mules were sent into a ravine to his rear where they would be safe from enemy fire. The Battle of Dug Gap commenced with an attack by the Confederate scout company of about forty men under Capt. William Forrest, the general's brother. The captain was severely wounded in the leg and several of his men killed. Confederate reinforcements arrived and advanced dismounted, soon driving in Streight's skirmishers. The 51st and 73rd Indiana charged on the left to draw the fire of the Confederate batteries. The 3rd Ohio and 80th Illinois advanced. After a short but stubborn resistance, Forrest's men retreated, leaving behind 2 pieces of artillery with caissons, forty prisoners — a large number of them wounded — and thirty dead. The losses of the mule brigade were about thirty killed and wounded, among them Lt. Col. Sheets of the 51st Indiana (he would die of his wounds on June 21 while a prisoner of war). The 4th and 9th Tennessee, having been unable to get behind Streight, rejoined Forrest. Col. Roddy was sent back with his regiment and a battalion to observe Dodge. To prevent Streight from escaping north to the Tennessee River, one regiment (Col. Edmonson's) was sent to march north of and parallel to the mule brigade.

The brigade moved out at about 11:00 A.M., leaving behind a strong, dismounted guard. After about six miles, Confederates were observed advancing to the left of the column. Sharp skirmishing began at Crooked Creek some ten miles south of Day's Gap with the 4th Tennessee driving the rearguard onto the column. Streight took a strong position at Hog Mountain about a mile south of a creek crossing. Fighting continued until about 10:00 P.M. when the two howitzers and the two captured cannon helped repulse the Confederates. The march then resumed with the 73rd Indiana again serving as rearguard and that regiment's Assistant Surgeon William Spencer left behind with the wounded in a field hospital. Several miles were made before the rear was again attacked about 4:00 P.M. Smith's cavalrymen held off Forrest's men for two hours, then Streight halted and offered battle. The

73rd Indiana was put into ambush. The countryside was open woodland and the moon was bright when the leading elements of the Confederate column were taken under fire. Several Confederate charges were repulsed, with Gen. Forrest himself having one horse killed and two others wounded in the fighting. Finally, about 10:00 P.M., a flank movement threatened the mule-holders in Streight's rear and he had to retreat after spiking the two captured cannon and destroying their caissons.

Streight accompanied the 73rd Indiana in the rearguard. Coming to a dense pine thicket on both sides of the road he dismounted the 73rd, placed them in ambush and sent the mules up the road. The horse of the leader of the most advanced Confederates stopped suddenly in the road. Volunteers were sent forward to expose the ambush. Two of Forrest's cannon soon opened up about 2:00 to 3:00 A.M. on May 1. Streight again had to withdraw. After forty-four hours without sleep — eighteen of them fighting — Forrest rested his men. The mule brigade reached Blountsville about 10:00 A.M. They took corn for their animals and collected every horse and mule that they could. After resting only two hours, they left town; Confederates entered behind them and drove off Smith's Alabamians. Streight ordered a faster pace. Ammunition and rations were issued, and the remainders put on pack mules. His wagons were burned. It was ten miles to the Black Warrior River. To secure a crossing over the swift stream, Streight had to turn and fight off his pursuers. His command crossed the rocky ford with a heavy skirmish line and the two mountain howitzers providing cover. Only two mules carrying hardtack were lost during the crossing at about 5:00 P.M. on May 1.

As Streight's brigade neared Gadsden, they found an opportunity to delay their pursuers. Black Creek was deep and unfordable with steep clay banks. The road crossed it on an uncovered, wooden bridge. There was no other crossing within two miles. Streight's men were rushed across and the bridge burned. A rear guard was set to impede Confederate efforts to replace it. This, they thought, would provide them time to reach Rome, Georgia. What then occurred here is a matter of dispute between Southern and Northern accounts. In Southern accounts, a sixteen-year-old girl, Emma Sampson, lived near the bridge with her mother. She told Gen. Forrest of a nearby forgotten ford over the creek. Mounted on his horse behind him, she led the general to the ford. Forrest's artillery drove the Federal rear guard from the other bank. His command crossed at the ford with their guns and caissons dragged under water across the creek by ropes. The Confederates were only very little delayed. Emma Sampson became the premiere Alabama heroine of the Civil War and her assistance to Forrest has passed into legend.

There is another story about Forrest's getting his command across the creek, however. The mule brigade, unable to carry them along, had immediately paroled all prisoners taken during their ride. The rule was that paroled soldiers could not take up arms or participate in any activities against their foes until exchanged. "But," according to Sgt. Major Hartpence, "among a lot of prisoners captured by our men that morning, was one named Sansom, a low-browed brute; who in common with others, as was the custom, was immediately paroled; and who, as soon as he was set at liberty, made his way direct to Forrest, and piloted him to a ford, where the whole rebel force soon crossed. Sansom, the perjured scoundrel, was with Forrest, when our command surrendered; and notwithstanding his oath of parole, was fully armed and equipped; and boasted that it was a bullet from his gun that killed Col. Hathaway, of the 73rd Indiana."[7] Regardless how he learned of the ford,

Forrest's brigade was delayed only a brief time. Streight and his men, worn out and exhausted faced another night march with their enemy still hot upon their heels.

The Lightning Mule Brigade moved on to Gadsden. Some of their ammunition was damaged in crossing the deep ford at Will's Creek. They stayed in Gadsden only long enough to destroy some arms and commissary stores found there. Many of the men and animals were so worn out that they could not keep up with the column. They gradually fell behind the rear guard and were captured. There was continual skirmishing at the rear of the column as it proceeded fifteen miles to reach Blount's Farm. It was hoped that forage for the animals could be found there, and an overnight rest was much needed. The command was dismounted and formed in line of battle on a ridge southwest of the farm. The rear guard was driven in and the main line attacked in the center. This attack, repulsed by the 73rd Indiana and Vananda's two howitzers, was followed by a turning attack on the Federal right. This attack was repulsed by the 80th Illinois assisted by two companies of the 3rd Ohio. During this three-hour engagement, Col. Hathaway of the 73rd Indiana was mortally wounded and died within minutes. Charles McWilliams, a soldier of the 51st Indiana serving with Major Vananda's small howitzer battery, had his head shot off by a cannonball. Streight realized that the only hope was to reach Rome, Georgia, and destroy behind him the bridge over the Coosa River there. Capt. Milton Russell of the 51st Indiana was sent with 200 of the best mounted men selected from the entire brigade to capture and hold that bridge. A Confederate flanking movement was discovered just in time to check it. Streight decided to pull out and push on in the direction of Rome.

By now, a large number of the men were dismounted, their animals having given out. The remaining mounts were so jaded and tender-footed that progress of the march was slow. The brigade had to leave the road for three miles to avoid a Confederate ambush. They reached the ferry of the Chattooga River at Turkeytown (five miles east of Gadsden) the night of the 2nd. About an hour earlier, Capt. Russell had ferried his detachment across, but in the meantime, locals had taken the ferryboat away and hidden it. The brigade headed seven or eight miles upriver to a bridge near Gaylesville. Near daylight on the 3rd they crossed and burned it — and a nearby iron works. It was evident that the brigade had to halt to rest and feed the animals if they were to reach Rome. Large numbers of their mules were continually giving out — they probably only had remaining about twenty of those supplied to them in Nashville — and most of those they'd collected in the countryside were barefoot and had such sore backs and tender feet that they couldn't be ridden. The men were utterly exhausted. The Lightning Mule Brigade made its last camp at 9:00 A.M. near Gaylesville, just short of the Georgia border. It was almost impossible to keep some of them awake long enough to feed the animals.

There was no hope of reaching Rome. Russell had reached the vicinity of Rome about 8:00 A.M. the day after the fight at Blount's Farm after riding badly jaded animals through the night. He found the town full of armed men and the bridge barricaded. A rural mail-carrier, John H. Wisdom, about 2:00 P.M. on the 2nd had seen Union soldiers across the river in Gadsden. He set out in his buggy for Rome, 67 miles to the east. He had to abandon his buggy and change horses several times along the way but reached Rome about four hours before Russell arrived and spread the alarm. "Wisdom's Ride," which has been compared in Alabama histories to that of Paul Revere, spelled the doom of Streight's mule brigade.

At Lawrence, near Gaylesville, Streight had formed a line of battle. His report noted, "A large portion of my best troops actually went to sleep while lying in line of battle under a severe skirmish fire."[8] The officers were unable to awaken many of them. A messenger from Russell had informed him of failure to secure the bridge at Rome. The Confederate pursuers were also tired — they had marched and skirmished 119 miles over the past three days and hadn't eaten for a full day. Forrest's command was also smaller. The two regiments sent to screen Streight off from the Tennessee River wouldn't return for another day. The gray-clad command was also shrinking. The mule brigade had been able to pick up remounts along their route, leaving none behind for Forrest's men. His command was by now probably one-third the strength of Streight's. But Streight didn't know that — in fact, he thought he was outnumbered. Forrest had his available men loudly repositioning themselves all around the Federals to create the impression that they were surrounded by a superior force. He positioned a gun from his battery where visibly commanding the Union camp. He sent in a staff officer to demand that Streight surrender.

Col. Streight held a council with his officers. Believing that they were outnumbered and surrounded, knowing there was no chance of reaching safety beyond the Coosa River at Rome, seeing their men completely exhausted and unable to fight and with their mounts unable to carry them off, they unanimously voted that the command should be surrendered. Streight surrendered at noon on May 3, 1863. The career of the Civil War's only organized force of men mounted on mules was over. Controversy was soon to follow.

Alabama Governor John Gill Shorter was enraged about the Alabamians in Streight's brigade. He thought that they had been arming slaves and inciting rebellion. He sent a letter to the Confederate Secretary of War demanding that the captured Alabama men be delivered to the state, where they would face the penalty of treason (death). From articles in captured Southern newspapers, Indiana Governor Oliver P. Morton read that Streight's captured men were to be paroled except for "four companies of renegade Alabamians." He thought this meant the Alabama men in the 51st Indiana (Shorter probably didn't even know about these men). He demanded that Union Secretary of War Edwin Stanton hold twice as many Confederate prisoners hostage for their safety. Governor Yates of Illinois also demanded instant retaliation. The Union's commissioner for exchange, E.A. Hitchcock, explained that such action would only provoke further retaliations and would be useless since, at that time, the Confederacy held more prisoners than did the Union. Confederate War Secretary James A. Sheddon advised Shorter that he had referred the matter to President Jefferson Davis but believed that the Alabama men with Streight had either escaped before the capture or had already been exchanged.[9] Sheddon was correct — the enlisted men of the Lightning Mule Brigade had indeed been speedily paroled into Northern lines. All of the officers had been interred as prisoners of war. Capt. Smith of the 1st Alabama was later to die while incarcerated at Libby Prison in Richmond. Col. Streight later organized a partially successful escape (including himself) from the same prison.

The Deep South was ecstatic over Forrest's success with his outnumbered command. The people of Rome purchased and presented him with an expensive horse for saving their town from the raiders. Citizens of Huntsville, Alabama, did likewise. Gen. Bragg gleefully reported Forrest's capture of 1,600 men with weapons and horses to Richmond. The rapid pursuit and capture of Col. Streight and his brigade was indeed a spectacular success which brought Forrest much attention and recognition. His rapid rise to fame followed. Bragg gave him the command of the western wing of his cavalry, and later that year he was promoted to major general.

The performance of Col. Streight and the Lightning Mule Brigade was also meritorious. They had destroyed some Confederate supplies and destroyed one iron forge during their journey. They had also diverted, for almost a month, more than a brigade of cavalry from operations screening and scouting for Bragg's army. They rode hard and they fought hard. Other than seizing needed horses and mules (a few of which they paid for) they neither pillaged nor devastated the regions through which they passed. Only when they were completely worn down with no hope of completing their mission did they surrender. If there had not been delays caused by the supply of poor mules in insufficient number at Nashville, getting up the Tennessee River to Eastport, and having to replace stampeded mules and find others at Tuscumbia, the brigade would have very likely "stolen the march" and Forrest would have been unable to overtake them so rapidly. The plan by Streight was a good one and without the delays may very well have disrupted the rail lines supplying Bragg. Though not in the end successful, the Independent Provisional Brigade had earned (but never received) fame for their efforts. General Lord Garnett Wolseley, for many years at the end of the century Great Britain's greatest military commander, thought both the raid and its pursuit "reads like a romance" and that interest in its exploits would endure as long as women "bring forth male children."[10] Alas, that fame was not to be for the Lightning Mule Brigade.

8

Hippophagy

Humans have used equines as a food source since Paleolithic times. The horse cultures of Central Asia, though they raided and conquered wide areas from astride their steeds, thought nothing of eating the flesh of their animals. The ancient Greeks and Romans ate them — with some preference for mules. There are numerous stories of mountain men, Indians, and others eating their horses or mules without a qualm during the American conquest of the western prairies and mountains of North America. The eating of horse meat even today is not considered with aversion in many cultures — including Europe. The Kushun breed of Russia was developed principally for meat.[1] The Breton,[2] Comtois,[3] and Percheron[4] breeds are used for meat. Because of farm mechanization, the Italian Heavy Draft horse is declining, with demand now almost limited to its meat.[5] Americans, however, possess a strong aversion to the practice. This abhorrence of the eating of horseflesh or muleflesh began with papal objections to the practice. Pope Gregory II (715–730) instructed the missionary Boniface to impose severe punishments on those who ate horseflesh "because they are mean and evil."[6] Shortly later, Pope Gregory III (731–740) issued a papal edict forbidding it.[7] The Prophet Muhammad, in the 7th century, enjoined the eating of mules and domestic donkeys. Though not specifically forbidden, the eating of horses became viewed as reprehensible by Islamic scholars,[8] a teaching that was influential in Spain after its conquest by Muslims early in the 8th century.

By the time of the Civil War there was a general, strong aversion among Americans toward the consumption of horses and mules. Therefore (in the Union army especially) it was quite common to refer to any kind of meat that was poor in taste or quality as originating from equines. Sgt. John M. Cate of the 33rd Massachusetts Infantry, in a November 1862 letter, said of his food, "Hard tack and salt horse, or 'hoss' as we call the salt meat we get."[9] (This was not a new usage of the term — the Pilgrims had referred to salt pork as "salt horse."[10]) Similarly, the soldiers referred to plug tobacco as "mule harness."[11] The *Boston Traveller* of December 14, 1861, reported that a soldier from Connecticut had written home that the commissary had issued so much mule meat that the ears of the men had grown three and one-half inches.[12] William R. Hartpence, who had been the sergeant major of the 51st Indiana Infantry, wrote postwar that while the regiment was at Bowling Green, Kentucky, in early 1862 they were issued meat rations that had been captured from the Rebels. Though the commissary issued it as beef, Hartpence recalled that it "turned out to be nothing less than *mule*." He said that one soldier ate his full ration in one meal and became very sick, with others getting sick as well, but that no one died.[13] Union prisoners of war in Castle Thunder at Richmond believed that their meat rations were mostly horse and mule and even averred that these rations were increased after cavalry battles.[14] Officers of the 36th Illinois Infantry who had been incarcerated at Libby Prison in Richmond recalled that their daily rations included "six ounces of mule meat pickled in brine."[15]

When they heard that their Confederate foemen were eating horses and mules, Union soldiers did not want to believe it. The 4th Iowa Infantry served in the siege of Vicksburg. Capt. Henry G. Ankeny wrote his wife on July 2, 1863, advising her, "It is now said they are living on mule meat, but I don't believe it, and you must not believe all that the papers say."[16] But the rumor was true. The Confederates within the Vicksburg lines — and at Port Hudson, Louisiana, as well — were eating mules (and rats and dogs, too). Both locations were completely surrounded by Federal armies and neither supplies could be gotten in nor hungry mouths out. Lt. Gen. John C. Pemberton, Confederate commander at Vicksburg, had ordered that unnecessary horses and mules be driven out where they shifted for themselves for whatever forage might be available between the lines. He kept only three teams of mules per regiment and did not interfere with private mounts belonging to civilians or officers.[17] Rations still ran low, and the expedient of eating equine flesh was perhaps first proposed by Brig. Gen. Martin L. Smith. He had seen it done on the plains and issued a circular to his brigade recommending horse meat as a way to extend supplies. That same evening, steaks cut from a dead horse between the lines were barbecued at the fire of Brig. Gen. John C. Vaughan and tried.[18]

With the stock of bacon almost exhausted (aside from a supply of fat bacon set aside for the hospitals[19]), Pemberton had a "butcher shop" for mules established at the old railroad depot. Here he had a group of about a half dozen, described by one veteran as looking like Mexicans or Indians, cutting up mules and jerking the meat over slow fires to make it "handy and lasting."[20] These men were probably teamsters from Waul's Legion.[21] The meat was to be issued "only to those who desired to use it."[22] This meat was made available to citizens as well as to soldiers. It sold for one dollar per pound with many ready purchasers, according to reporter Alexander St. Clair Abrams, who visited after the siege.[23] The situation at besieged Port Hudson was similar. Here, the period of issue began on July 1, 1863, at the request of many officers when one wounded mule was killed and butchered as an experiment. There was quickly a demand for mule meat and it was served as rations from July 5 until the surrender.[24] Whole units of infantry — the 1st Alabama, 12th Arkansas, 16th Arkansas and 18th Arkansas — petitioned that either mule or horse meat be issued to them. Their petition was annotated, "They would like to have this ration for tomorrow, this evening."[25]

The reactions to the eating of mule meat were varied. Sgt. Osborn Oldroyd of the 10th Ohio Infantry, who helped besiege Port Hudson, recalled that the Northerners asked many questions about it and were horrified at the practice.[26] Union soldiers, upon entry into Vicksburg, found the typeset for the July 2 edition of Vicksburg's newspaper, the *Daily Citizen*. They added a note at the bottom and published a souvenir edition. They pointed out that this edition would be the last printed on wallpaper, and said that General Grant had dined in the city "and he did bring his dinner with him." Their note also stated that the paper would "no more ... eulogize the luxury of mule-meat."[27] The *Chicago Tribune* issued a menu from the fictional "Hotel de Vicksburg" making fun of the situation the Confederate defenders had faced. This fictional menu featured such delicacies as mule tail soup, boiled mule bacon with poke greens, mule sirloin, mule beef jerked ala Mexicana, mule liver hashed, mule hoof soused, and mule tongue cold a la bray.[28] The reaction of Confederate mule-eaters was different. Some took a kind of pride in the fare. Capt. John W. DeForest of the 12th Connecticut Infantry, one of the conquerors of Port Hudson, noted, "They often alluded to the fact that they had held out until they were at the point of starvation, reduced to ... such rats and mule meat as the sharpest foraging might furnish."[29] Mary Ann Loughborough, a citizen of Vicksburg, pointed out that the fresh meat was a welcome change from bacon and salt rations that had become monotonous and that the fresh meat was also a welcome preventative to scurvy.[30] Gen. Pemberton was pleased that his soldiers found mule "not only nutritious, but very palatable, and in every respect preferable to poor beef."[31] It was accepted in preference to having no meat at all.[32]

The two other great sieges of the Civil War were at Chattanooga and at Petersburg. In neither case, however, were the besieged completely cut off, and there is only one story of horses or mules being eaten. The Union Army of the Cumberland came close at Chattanooga in late October and November 1863. By mid–October there were some reports that "some soldiers were skinning and eating rats,"[33] and the colonel of a relieving regiment reported that "even horse meat was scarce."[34] There are indications that at least once there was widespread resort to horse meat in the Union army. After the January 1863 Battle of Murfreesboro it was reported, "The hungry soldiers [of the Union Army of the Cumberland] cut steaks from the slain horses, and, with the scanty supplies which have come forward, gather around the fire to prepare supper...."[35] Col. John Beatty of the 3rd Ohio Infantry, commanding a brigade in the Battle of Murfreesboro, stated that during a lull of that battle, "The hungry soldiers cut steaks from the slain horses."[36] Gen. Lovell Rousseau had a similar memory: "Some of them ate horse steaks cut from the horses on the battlefield and broiled.[37] The 42nd Indiana Infantry was in reserve during the first day of battle. An officer's horse was killed by a cannonball, and "before the blood had ceased to circulate in the animal, so hungry were the boys that they cut steaks from the dead animal and broiled them for supper."[38] Capt. John Henry Otto of the 21st Wisconsin Infantry remembered that the "horse of Lt. Starkweather was killed by a cannonball on the 1st of January [1863], and being in good condition, was cut-up, and partaken by many of the soldiers." A similar meal was made of the colonel's horse.[39] Postwar, Lt. Col. Michael H. Fitch of the 21st Wisconsin Infantry noted, "Some ate horse steaks cut and broiled from horses upon the battlefield," and, like Otto, regarding one such meal, recalled, "It was a piece of Fred Starkweather's horse — a black one at that. A solid shot had struck it on the leg the day before, taking the foot of at the fetlock joint. The boys of the Twenty-fourth Illinois, Colonel Mihalotzy's German regiment, killed the horse and cut him into slices that looked like beefsteak."[40] J. Henry Haynie, a veteran of the 19th Illinois Infantry, recalled that in the evening after the first day of the battle, "Our Regiment feasted on hot coffee, hard tack, and horse steak broiled on coals."[41] Marshall P. Thatcher of the 2nd Michigan Cavalry also remembered sleeping on arms after the cutting, broiling and eating of horse steaks.[42]

There were also many scattered reports of hippophagy. As early as December 1861, Texan cavalry operating in the Indian Territory far from their supply wagons ate horse.[43] During the Peninsula Campaign of 1862 there was a shortage of foodstuffs for Union wounded in a hospital near the Chickahominy River. Brig. Gen. John Sedgewick provided two cavalry horses which were butchered by men of the 1st Minnesota Infantry for the benefit of the wounded.[44] Nearby, no other being available, a young horse belonging to

Gen. O.O. Howard (who had been wounded) was killed and butchered to make soup for the wounded, who, not knowing what it was, "greatly relished" it.[45] One who participated in Gen. Sterling Price's fall 1864 raid into Missouri reported that during the return, "Our men [are] feeding on hickory nuts, acorns, and dead horse flesh."[46] One of the sergeants of Lumsden's Alabama Battery wrote that, while in northern Alabama just prior to Hood's 1864 Nashville campaign, when they got any bacon or salt pork it was generally rancid. When a young mule had its back broken by the fall of a tree cut down in the camp, it was killed and divided among the members of the battery, who considered it an "unusual luxury in the way of food." They rendered the fat from its "innards" and saved it in bottles and cans to use as shortening. Though they carried along hunks of the mule with them on the march and enjoyed it, they did make fun of it. They would pull out a hunk, bray, bite off a mouthful and chew away.[47] Union soldiers far from the principal theaters of the war— Californians in Utah—even depended on the equine source in the late summer of 1865, when the troops ate both horse and mule meat.[48]

How did it taste? Like all meats, doubtless "preparation and presentation" had much to do with it. Presentation as mule or horse went against inclinations, but there were few "whose natural prejudices were so strong as to prevent them from cooking and eating their share."[49] As mentioned, Pemberton's commissary had the meat jerked. This was apparently not the situation at Port Hudson. One Port Hudson defender, 1st Lt. Joseph M. Bailey of the 16th Arkansas Infantry, later thought that if it had been well cooked the meat might have done well. His memory was that "having no grease of any kind, we could only boil, broil, or barbecue our meat."[50] Actual descriptions of the results are best left to those who ate it.

About horse:

> "...ate quite heartily of the meat and pronounced it good beefsteak."
> Harrison C. Hobart, Colonel, 21st Wisconsin Infantry, Murfreesboro[51]

About mule:

> "...equal to the best venison ... tender."
> Alexander St. Clair Abrams, northern correspondent who himself sampled it afterwards, Vicksburg.[52]
>
> "...fairly good though coarse grained and very poor."
> Joseph M. Bailey, 1st Lt., 16th Arkansas Infantry, Port Hudson.[53]
>
> "...a little tough and the grain coarser than [ox], but I discovered no difference in the taste."
> Washington B. Crumpton, Pvt., 37th Mississippi Infantry, Vicksburg.[54]
>
> "...coarse and nobody hungered for any more. Some of the soldiers did like it."
> Edward S. Gregory, Confederate officer, Vicksburg.[55]
>
> "The meat was very fine, much better than any beef we had gotten for a long time."
> James R. Maxwell, Sgt. Lumsden's (Alabama) Battery, in north Alabama.[56]
>
> "...coarse-grained and darker than beef, but really delicious, sweet and juicy."
> W.H. Tunnard, Major, 3rd Louisiana Infantry, Vicksburg.[57]
>
> "...treated to a new taste of meat, and the smell thereof preceded it, and it was like unto the smell of a saddle blanket after it be removed from a horse

which had been ridden hard for five hours. The meat was the meat of a mule, and we did eat it and were satisfied...."
John M. Stanyan, Captain, 8th New Hampshire Infantry and a prisoner, Port Hudson.[58]

"All those who partook of it spoke highly of the dish. The flesh of mules is of a darker color than beef, of a finer grain, quite tender and juicy, and has a flavor something between that of beef and venison."
Howard D. Wright, officer, 30th Louisiana Infantry, Port Hudson.[59]

"The mule meat was good...."
E.E. Houston, Captain, staff of Gen. Vaughan, Vicksburg.[60]

9

Equines and Morale

The great campaigns and battles consumed only a minute portion of the Civil War soldier's time. Most of his time was spent in camp or garrison with only a small portion of this occupied by camp activities, drill or picket duty. There were prolonged periods of boredom which could break down discipline and have detrimental effects upon both individual and unit morale. For the most part, Civil War soldiers — both Union and Confederate — were left to devise their own amusements and diversions to relieve the tedium. Music or song was the most common diversion among the soldiers. Other diversions included storytelling, gossip, jokes, horseplay and pranks.[1] Equines were also used in soldier diversions.

Mounted Music

Bands and concerts are frequently noted among infantry organizations during the war — but seldom in connection with mounted units. These, however, had been initially, like Union infantry regiments, authorized bands.[2] Anyone who has ever played a musical instrument can easily imagine how difficult it would be to perform in a band on horseback — especially during combat.

The 17th Pennsylvania Cavalry was organized at Harrisburg in late 1861. The unit applied for authority to possess a band but was denied. Nevertheless, continued requests resulted in a compromise. The regiment would be permitted to have a band, but the bandsmen had to be recruited from the ranks without government expense and trained as cavalrymen with combat their primary duty. Officers of the regiment paid for the purchase of the necessary instruments. They also paid the salary of a Professor J.F. Whittington to serve as bandmaster. The regimental historian, H.P. Moyer, wrote, "The band was a valuable adjunct to the regiment, especially for dress parade, guard mount, and reviews and accomplished much in relieving the monotony of camp life."[3]

In late 1862, just prior to the Battle of Fredericksburg, the 116th Pennsylvania Infantry was positioned on the north bank of the Rappahannock River. A New York cavalry regiment was in the area. Pvt. William McCarter of the 116th reported in his memoirs that the New Yorkers had a "fine band." He and his unit heard their music in the distance growing louder as they approached. First to appear was the cavalry colonel, advancing at a slow walk, and "immediately behind him was the band, likewise mounted and playing a military march." Soon, Confederate artillery was firing at them and the new regiment and its band sought cover.[4]

Some accounts have Sherman's entry into Atlanta with parades.[5] Mary Rawson, the daughter of a city councilman, remembered hearing martial music one afternoon after Sherman's occupation of the city. Looking up, she saw cavalry, infantry and wagons crowded together with "the musicians all riding on white horses." She said they rode silently until passing the headquarters of Gen. Geary, at which time they struck up "Hail, Columbia." Afterwards, they marched on silently.[6]

Brig. Gen. George A. Custer, to say the least, was one of the Union's exceedingly flamboyant generals. It is therefore not surprising that he used mounted bands in combat. A pencil sketch exists in the papers of Cleveland's Western Reserve Historical Society which is labeled "Custer Charging Near Columbia Furnace." It depicts a cavalry charge led by a mounted group of musicians.[7] Maj. Gen. Phil Sheridan was a noted lover of music. He took personal interest in his mounted bands' being supplied with good uniforms and equipment. He also had them mounted on "spirited steeds of a uniform gray color." An engraving of the period shows his band moving along at full gallop while playing their brass instruments. He liked them to play during combat and was not concerned if a "trombone — or even a trombonist — was hit."[8]

The Confederate armies had, in general, many fewer regimental bands than the Union armies and had too much difficulty keeping cavalry, artillery and trains in horses to be able to spare any for mounted bands. Maj. Gen. J.E.B. Stuart was very fond of music, so it is not surprising that his cavalry corps in the Army of Northern Virginia had the only mounted band of which record can be found. This, the only complete band, was that of the 2nd Virginia Cavalry.

Its instruments had been captured near Haymarket from a New York regiment. They were said to be "generally well mounted" and it was a source of pride to the regiment. Its musicians were:

George R. Lyman	Leader and Solo-alto
Charles H. Rau	E Flat Cornet
Thomas Walker	2nd E Flat Cornet
Frank Myering	B Flat Cornet
A.R. Edwards	First Tenor
James M. Edwards	Second Tenor
Hercy E. Carper	Second Alto
H.M. Harris	Bass
R.W. Thurman	Drum
Thomas Wilson	Cymbals[9]

It is not known if this band ever performed mounted while on march or in battle.

Also associated with Stuart was the banjo player Sam Sweeney. Stuart collected Sweeney, a virtuoso with the banjo, along with fiddlers and singers, to entertain in his camp. There are hints that Stuart liked to ride around singing and on such occasions he was accompanied by Sweeney.[10] One of the general's staff officers, William W. Blackford, said that Sweeney "always carried his instrument slung at this back on marches, and often in long night marches the life of the men was restored by its tinkle."[11] One banjo player is hardly a band, but Sweeney certainly gave musical life to the march.

Racing

There are numerous mentions of recreational riding in the letters and memoirs of Civil War officers who had horses. First Lt. Wayland Dunn of the 1st Alabama Cavalry (Union)

Music on Sheridan's line of battle. Union Maj. Gen. Phil Sheridan believed music made for good morale during battles (*Battles and Leaders*, vol. 4).

took this a step further. While his unit was part of Sherman's army during the occupation of Atlanta, upon promise of a mule, a local man gave him a sulky. In the evenings when other duties did not prevent it, Lt. Dunn would hitch one of his mares to the sulky and go out trotting. He said that this "took like fun."[12]

Sometimes equines were utilized in pranks. Sgt. John M. Cate of the 33rd Massachusetts Infantry wrote his wife on August 27, 1862, of one such incident. While in camp, one of the unit's teamsters, Pvt. James Shields, was standing on the front of a wagon buying pies from a baker's cart. Someone threw some slats on the back of the horse to startle it. Frightened, the horse kicked up and smashed one of Shields' ankles so badly that the bones stuck up through the skin. Shields was sent to hospital in Alexandria, Virginia, where he died of gangrene in October.[13] A less malicious prank was to dress up a mule in uniform and parade it through the camp. This prank was apparently fairly widespread in the armies. At the dedication of the Irish Brigade Monument at Gettysburg, Col. James J. Smith recalled men of the 69th New York Infantry "driving a mule in full uniform into the colonel's tent."[14] A very similar incident happened at Oxford, Mississippi, in November 1862. Men of the 31st Illinois Infantry "clothed an army mule in full uniform and drove the solemn looking animal through the town" accompanied by singing and shouts.[15] A vengeful prank was to cut off the tail or mane of the horse of an unpopular officer.

The favorite diversion involving equines was, however, racing. Horse racing had long been a popular entertainment for Americans both North and South. Confederate Maj. General Benjamin F. Cheatham had bred and trained thoroughbred racers prior to the war,[16] and after the war Lt. Gen. Richard S. Ewell established a farm for trotters and pacers.[17] Confederate Brig. Gen. Abraham Buford, who served under Forrest, had operated a "fine stock farm" in Kentucky before he went to war.[18] Lt. Gen. U.S. Grant had been quite a horseman during his days at West Point. An interesting and amusing anecdote from the November 7, 1861, Battle of Belmont, Missouri, illustrates the prominence of racing in those days. Capt. William M. Polk, who had been on the staff of his father, Lt. Gen. Leonidas Polk, related it in an article for the *Century Magazine* series:

General Cheatham, who was an ardent follower of the turf, discovered symptoms of a like weakness in General Grant. After they had been conversing for some time on official matters, the conversation drifted upon the subject of horses. This congenial topic was pursued to the satisfaction of each until it genially ended in a grave proposition from Cheatham to Grant that, as this thing of fighting was a troublesome affair, they had best settle the vexing questions about which they had gone to war, by a grand, international horse-over on the Missouri shore. Grant laughingly answered that he wished it might be so.[19]

This just might be in character with Gen. Cheatham, and if he did suggest such a thing, Grant would surely have laughed.

It is no wonder that horse racing in any of its forms was popular with the men. It didn't usually take a lot of preparation to arrange a race — and wagering on the results only enhanced the fun. One Confederate staff officer wrote in his memoir of a horse killed during the Wilderness that "was the fastest horse in the corps, and in the favorite amusement of saddle-horse races was never beaten."[20] Immediately prior to the commencement of the war, Texas Governor Sam Houston had to issue an order prohibiting (among other things) horse racing and gambling in the camps of frontier defense rangers.[21] A similar order had to be issued on June 18, 1861, by Col. Henry E. McCulloch to his 1st Texas Mounted Rifles.[22] None of these orders seemed to make much a difference. A Texas cavalryman stationed in Texas in 1862 wrote his wife that he had lost one hundred dollars and, as a result, had to bet his horse on a future race. The racing of horses — even while on duty — continued. It became such a nuisance that in June 1863 Col. James E. McCord of the Texas Frontier Regiment issued an order prohibiting gambling on horse races — and promised court-martial or other punishment for violation of the order.[23]

The Union army also had its problems with racing. While stationed at Germantown, Tennessee, in March 1863, the men of the 7th Kansas Cavalry — despite most of their horses being weakened, broken-down or diseased — arranged an impromptu horse race to occupy their leisure time. This practice was so further detrimental to the condition of the horses that the regiment's commander, Col. Thomas P. Herrick, had to issue an order forbidding the racing with severe penalties for disobedience.[24]

Even the sternest of commanders had difficulty in preventing the racing of horses. In an effort to preserve the quality of his command's horses, Gen. Forrest issued a General Order in February 1865 specifying: "Galloping and other unnecessary use of horses about camps, or on the march, is positively forbidden." The very next day some of his men laid out a racecourse in front of his headquarters and began loudly racing and betting on the results. Forrest joined in the merriment, but at its conclusion reminded them of the seriousness of the order and had the men arrested and put under guard. A court-martial sentenced the men to carry fence rails through the camp for a specified time.[25]

Other commanders really didn't try to ban horse races and even participated fully. "General, Field and Staff officers freely indulged in it,"[26] according to many reports. One officer of Custer's Michigan Cavalry Brigade recalled, "At division and brigade headquarters alone was there time for play. Generals Custer and Kilpatrick had a race course where they used to devote time to the sport of horse racing."[27] A Confederate staff officer of Lt. Gen. James Longstreet called "saddle-horse races" the favorite amusement in the corps — and that his own horse was never beaten.[28] Steeplechase racing was also popular.

The same staff officer wrote that while in camp near Centerville, Virginia, in 1861, a group met regularly at the headquarters of Gen. Longstreet to "practice jumping our horses." Every rider who had a fall had to pay a forfeit spent to entertain and amuse the group of which Longstreet was the leader. Longstreet was evidently good at the sport as he never had to pay a forfeit.[29] During the same period, Gen. Joseph Johnston's elder brother took a spill with the general's horse in a jumping contest.[30] Confederate General John C. Breckinridge organized a grand review of Hardee's Corps of the Army of Tennessee in mid–March 1863 which was followed by horse racing enjoyed by his entire division.[31] Although its horses were in terrible condition, the Confederate Army of Tennessee had horse races in December 1863 for the men's morale.[32] President Jefferson Davis himself once participated in a horse race using a thoroughbred chestnut mare borrowed from a staff officer. The other participants in the November 14, 1863, race were Gens. Rosewell S. Ripley and Henry A. Wise. Wise won.[33]

Union Brig. Gen. John Beatty himself was a participant in races. In 1862, when Union forces entered Murfreesboro, Tennessee, a lame horse (supposedly abandoned by Texas cavalrymen) was picked up along the road by his unit. It helped out with his brigade's hospital unit, carrying light loads until its shattered hoof was healed, at which time it was turned over to the brigade quartermaster department. The quartermaster brought it to Beatty's attention who had it appraised and purchased it for his own use. Under the care of Beatty's hostler the horse shed a shaggy brown coat and developed one of "velvety black." Gen. Beatty believed that this horse was the fastest in the Army of the Cumberland and often made or accepted challenges to race it.

On June 1, 1863, while at the headquarters of Gen. Lovell Rousseau's division, he won a race. The challengers in the race were Brig. Gen. George D. Wagner (on a long-legged white horse; Col. Arthur C. Ducat, Inspector General of the Army of the Cumberland; a Col. Harker; and a Major McDowell of Rosecrans's staff. Beatty's black won. Two days later, Brig. Gen. Thomas J. Wood, a division commander in the XXI Corps, and XXI Corps commander Maj. Gen. Thomas L. Crittenden challenged Beatty to a race which was scheduled for a few days later. This race never came off since the Army of the Cumberland moved out on its Tullahoma campaign. Beatty's fast black (for which he unfortunately never provided the name in his memoir) died during the Chattanooga siege.[34]

There were times that racing was more formal. Union soldiers on furlough or stationed in the area of Washington, D.C., could enjoy the new National Race-Course (near the insane asylum), where trotting races were held. Spectators, of whom soldiers consisted the greatest proportion, at this plank enclosure could cover ten acres. The races held here were three heats out of five with betting and wild cheering throughout.[35] The siege of Petersburg provided more opportunity for the soldiers of the Army of the Potomac to enjoy racing either as participants or spectators. One Union telegrapher noted in October 1864, "Horse racing has become quite the rage in all ranks of the army." Racecourses were laid out all along the lines — any level stretch behind the Union lines would serve. Racing on Halifax Road was conducted from September 1864 through March 1865. Another course was located on New Market Road north of the James River. There was even competition racing between the staffs of divisions and corps.[36]

St. Patrick's Day, March 17, 1863, was occasion for a grand series of races held near Falmouth, Virginia (opposite Fredericksburg), by elements of the Union Army of the

Potomac. Father William Corby, chaplain of the Irish Brigade, went into great detail of the preliminary events (including a mass conducted by himself), but regarding the racing itself, he noted only that Brig. Gen. Thomas Meagher had issued a general invitation to attend to all officers of the army the preceding day and directed the entire affair, that stands were erected which were occupied by the race judges and "the major generals," and that no one rode in the races except commissioned officers.[37] The announcement advertised a "Grand Irish Steeple Chase" over a 2.5-mile course having 4 hurdles each 4.5 feet high, and 5 ditch fences including 2 with artificial rivers. The hurdles were made of pine from nearby forests.[38] Unlike races today, heats were involved, with the winner being the horse with the best two heats of three. Two rather detailed accounts of the races were published in 1867 — unfortunately, they disagree on the names of horses, their number, their owners and their riders in the first race. Writing anonymously, Oliver Wilson Davis in his *Life of David Bell Birney, Major-General, United States Volunteers* said there were seven entrants,[39] whereas David Porter Conyngham in his *The Irish Brigade and Its Campaigns* said six.[40] The location is not precisely defined, with one source saying Meagher's Irish brigade in one place,[41] and then a page later a field near the headquarters of Gen. Joseph Hooker (commanding Army of the Potomac).[42] Another account strongly implies the site was near the headquarters of Maj. Gen. David Bell Birney, stating that between races refreshments were available and entertainment were held there.[43]

Sgt. Frederick C. Floyd of the 40th New York Infantry was very clear: "General Birney ... provided a diversion for all, consisting of horse races with hurdles, and any officer could enter. The amusement consisted, principally, of witnessing the falls of the riders, which were numerous."[44] Witnessing the racing were Major Generals Hooker, Darius Couch (commanding II Corps), O.O. Howard (commanding XI Corps), Dan Sickles

St. Patrick's Day in the Army — a hurdle race. Steeplechase was the favorite type of equine racing. The March 17, 1863, races at the Falmouth, Virginia, camp of the Army of the Potomac were widely reported (Library of Congress).

St. Patrick's Day in the Army — the mule race. After participation by officers in three races, enlisted men ran a mule race (Library of Congress).

(commanding III Corps), Hiram Berry and Winfield Scott Hancock. There were also numerous brigadiers present.[45] Accounts further disagree on which horse won, who owned them and who rode them. Col. St. Clair Augusting Mulholland, whose presence that day was agreed in both accounts, when he published his *The Story of the 116th Regiment Pennsylvania Volunteers in the War of the Rebellion: The Record of a Gallant Command* in 1903,[46] followed the account of Conyngham. The chart on the following page presents both "fields" along with owners and masters. Only Davis's account provides details of those races. The second was a steeplechase with 12 horses, won by Archy. The third race was flat-course and had only four entrants, Black Diamond, Hunter, Independence, and the winner, Rodney.[47]

Another grand race was held on St. Patrick's Day, 1865, within the Union lines about Petersburg, Virginia. Sgt. Daniel Chisolm of the 116th Pennsylvania Infantry, in his diary, recorded the event in detail. He said that the track was near the corps headquarters and was "like a Fair Ground Track," with four three-foot-high hurdles with ditches three feet deep and four feet wide between them. The racers included one colonel of a New York regiment, a lieutenant of a Zouave regiment, a captain from Chisolm's own regiment, and several others. Chaos resulted once the racing began. While some of the horses followed the course, others ran through the crowd. A sergeant of the 69th New York Infantry was trampled to death and others were badly hurt. That was just the first circuit. In the second, the horse of the New York colonel fell going over a hurdle and broke its neck and both arms of the colonel. The racing continued with "horses flying the track, running over the spectators, falling over the hurdles, into the ditches, breaking arms, legs, ect. [sic]" Chisolm left before it was over, returned to his camp and wrote, "Never did I see such a crazy time. I will have to alter [sic] my mind if I ever go to see another Irish fair."[48] The racing of equines during the war may have been crazy, but there is no doubt that it was an indispensable entertainment of both men and officers.

Entries in the "Grand Irish Steeple Chase"
of March 17, 1863 (St. Patrick's Day), at Falmouth, Virginia
The First Race

Horse	*Owner*	*Rider*
1st race according to Conyngham and Mulholland:		
Jack Hinton (gray)	Gen. Meagher	Capt. John Grisson
Kathleen Mavorneen (bay mare)	QM Capt. Martin	QM Capt. Martin
Major (chestnut)	Maj. Mulholland	QM Wade
Napper Tandy (bay)	Capt. Hogan	Lt. Ryder
Nigger Bill (black)	Capt. Langdon	Lt. Byron
Sharpsburg (bay)	QM McCormick	Lt. O'Connor

3 horses couldn't clear the first leap and 2 saddles were emptied. Jack Hinton won.

1st race according to Davis:		
Billy (bay gelding)	Col. McKnight	Lt. McHenry
Faderland (sorrel gelding)	Col. von Schaik	Col. von Schaik
Fasco (bay)	Col. zu Salm-Salm	Col. zu Salm-Salm
Kathleen Mavorneen	QM Capt. Martin	Dr. Reynolds
Napper Tandy (bay gelding)	Gen. Meagher	Capt. Whitefield
Queen	Capt. Kurshaw	Capt. von Blucher
Zella (bay mare)	Lt. Seibrie	Lt. Seibrie

During the 1st heat, Salm-Salm was thrown, and his injury prevented his continuing the race. Faderland won both of the first 2 heats, so there was no 3rd heat.

10

War's End and Remembrance

By the time the war ended in 1865, the heavy demand for horses and mules for military purposes had already created problems in the South. Animals taken off to war by their owners, Confederate impressments of equines, and the taking or slaughter of them by Union raiders and campaigning armies all had severe impacts. The number of horses and mules gone can be imagined from what happened to those from Kentucky — a "loyal" state affected by only one major campaign. There had been 338,000 horses in Kentucky in 1860. By October 1865, there were only 39,000. It was a similar story with the mules. They declined from 95,000 to only 58,000.[1] A similar large decrease in Alabama's equine populations was revealed by the 1870 Federal Census. The number of horses had declined from 127,000 to 80,000, and mules from 111,000 to 76,000.[2] On July 7, 1865, Robert G.H. Kean, who had been chief of the Bureau of War in the Confederate War Department, listed seven causes for the failure to gain Southern independence. His 5th reason was want of horses for transports and artillery, and that the "country [had been] stripped by impressments of horses."[3] The experience of the farmers of southwest Arkansas in 1862, who could neither plant nor get in crops after impressments of their animals,[4] was not uncommon throughout the war and at its end. Some Northern areas were likewise temporarily affected. Farm labor in southern Pennsylvania had come to a complete standstill after Lee's 1863 invasion.[5] There were other impacts. Attendance at churches dropped all over Mississippi because of impressments of animals.[6] John Massey wrote of his return to Tuscaloosa, Alabama, from the war in 1865, "There were no mails. There were no means of public conveyance and little private travel, for all the horses had been taken by one army of the other. I could not go anywhere. I could not hear from anywhere."[7]

If the animals of surrendered armies had been taken as captured property, the situation would have been much worse. Fortunately for all the people of the South, this did not happen. This came about largely due to the magnanimity of the Union commanders who accepted the various surrenders by Confederate armies. The story of Gen. Lee's concern for his men and Gen. Grant's response is well known but merits retelling. The details were provided by Gen. Grant in his *Personal Memoirs*:

General Lee remarked to me again that their army was organized a little differently from the Army of the United States...; that in their army the cavalrymen and artillerists owned their own horses; and he asked if he was to understand that the men who so owned their horses were to be permitted to retain them. I told him that as the terms were written they would not; that only the officers were permitted to take their private property. He then, after reading over the terms a second time, remarked that that was clear.

I then said to him that I thought this would be about the last battle of the war — I sincerely hoped so; and I said further I took it that most of the men in the ranks were small farmers. The whole country had been so raided by the two armies that it was doubtful whether they would be able to put in a crop to carry themselves and their families through the next winter without the aid of the horses they were then riding. The United States did not want them and I would therefore instruct the officers I left behind to receive the paroles of his troops to let every man of the Confederate army who claimed to own a horse or mule take the animal to his home. Lee remarked again that this would have a happy effect.[8]

Notice that it did not actually have to be a man's horse or mule — he had only to claim that it was. (Grant had been generous in this manner before. When Vicksburg had been surrendered in 1863, the terms allowed field, staff and cavalry officers to take one horse each with them.[9]) The paroles of the surrendered Confederates even noted their horses. E.P. Alexander's concluded that he had "permission to go to his home and there remain undisturbed with four private horses."[10]

The final terms of surrender given Gen. Joseph E. Johnston by Gen. Sherman in North Carolina a few weeks later were similar — officers could keep their private horses. But Sherman also liberally allowed any of the surrendered Confederates to take horses and mules away with them to go home.[11] A military convention with supplemental terms specified that artillery horses could be used for transport home and that both officers and men could keep private horses.[12] The beneficial impact was not as widespread in Johnston's army, though. Once its men began to hear about the surrender of Lee's army, thousands had begun to desert, stealing horses and mules to get home.[13] The last Confederate forces east of the Mississippi were not surrendered until May 8, 1865, at Citronelle, Alabama, when the Confederate department embracing Mississippi, Alabama and western Florida was surrendered by Lt. Gen. Richard Taylor to Maj. Gen. E.R.S. Canby. This one went a little differently. General Taylor later wrote, "It is due to the memory of General Canby to add that he was ready with suggestions to soothe our military pride. Officers retained their side arms, mounted men their horses, which in our service were private property...."[14] Canby had even specified all mounted men — not just officers. Gen. James H. Wilson had captured Confederate officers in his raid across Alabama in March and April 1865, who were not paroled and had to ride along with his cavalry division. Upon reaching Columbus, Georgia, he heard of Lee's surrender, so he then paroled the captured officers and sent them home on their own horses.[15]

The surrenders in the east resulted in thousands of defeated Confederates' being able to reach home both more easily and quickly, but also, once they got there, to be able to resume farming, as was intended by the Union commanders. Those not engaged in farming made other use of their animals. Gen. John B. Gordon, after Appomattox, sold one of his horses to a Union officer to raise sufficient funds for his journey home.[16] Lt. Gen. Richard Taylor made his way to New Orleans. He had no money at all and his estate had been confiscated and sold. He later wrote, "I felt somewhat eager to get hold of the 'greenbacks,'" and sold his own two horses. His eagerness to sell prevented his getting the best prices for them, but he garnered enough to bring his wife and children from the Red River country to New Orleans, where they began again to make their way in life.[17]

West of the Mississippi in the vast Confederate Department of the Trans-Mississippi, by the time Gen. E.K. Smith surrendered it on June 5, 1865, many of its forces had already disbanded themselves and gone home with whatever animals they had. Col. William H. Parsons had not disbanded his Texas cavalry brigade. On May 20 he heard that the Department had been surrendered — it hadn't yet, though it might as well have been. There were no Union forces nearby. He assembled his brigade, announced that he'd heard the Department was surrendered, asked his officers to divide the teams and wagons among the men and concluded, "Go home. The war is over!" His cavalrymen did just that — rode their horses home.[18]

The officers and the enlisted men of those few Union cavalry regiments permitted to provide their own horses also went home with their mounts. It wasn't easy, however. When cavalry regiments owning their own horses were mustered out during the war, it was particularly difficult. Needing horses then, the government offered to purchase those of the men. Those who declined the offer had to secure papers for their animals' transit at every change of transport along their way home.[19] Even officers traveling home at war's end with their units encountered difficulties with their horses' transport. Lt. Col. Elisha Hunt Rhodes of the 2nd Rhode Island Infantry kept a diary throughout the war and until he got home to Providence, Rhode Island. On July 16, 1865, he noted at Groton, Connecticut, "My horse *Katie* started with us, but I do not know where she is now." Two days later, at Providence, he noted, "I found much to my joy that the car containing my horse *Katie* had been attached to our train...."[20] The officers even took horses appropriated during their campaigns home with them.[21] The opportunity to purchase their horses from the government and take them home was given to Union cavalrymen. Some, who had become attached to their steeds, did so.[22]

The further lives of those equines who survived the war would be as varied as the lives of the men who rode them. And like the vast majority of the soldiers, as they died, memory of their individual services faded away. So, the horses and mules also went "home" to take up whatever occupation or use their owners had for them — pulling a plow, a dray wagon, a carriage, or a city tram, or just being ridden. Like the common soldiers, most went on into obscurity in their local communities. Those who had been associated with famous commanders became attractions to visitors in their area. Some, like Jackson's Little Sorrel, were even taken to exhibitions around the country — where hairs were plucked from his mane and tail. Other horses also became famous for their association with a notable general — Lee's Traveller most prominently, but also Grant's Cincinnati.

Because of two poems written about his 1864 ride from Winchester to Cedar Creek, one of Sheridan's horses also became legendary. Neither of the poems, Herman Melville's "Sheridan at Cedar Creek" and Thomas Buchanan Read's more famous "Sheridan's Ride," were actually about the horse. Melville's poem contained tributes to the horse, such as "Shoe the steed with silver" and "House the horse in ermine," and saying it led the charge.[23] Read's poem is more descriptive of the horse with lines like, "A steed as black as the steeds of night/Was seen to pass, as with eagle flight," and "With his wild eye full of fire;/But, lo! he is nearing his heart's desire;/He is snuffing the smoke of the roaring fray." His stanza concluded that in an "American soldier's Temple of Fame," with the general's name, "Be it said, in letters bold and bright: 'Here is the steed that saved the day/By carrying Sheridan into the fight,/From Winchester — twenty miles away!'"[24] Neither poem named the horse — probably at that time neither author knew the name. The almost constant mention of Winchester in Read's poem led to the public's identification of the horse as being named

"Winchester," and under this sobriquet it is mostly remembered today. Stories about this Civil War horse multiplied in popular imagination. Humorist Bill Nye took note, and his "General Sheridan's Horse" (see Appendix C) points out that even in that day legends of the war were multiplying, and that a lot of them were inaccurate.

Some were perhaps reminded of the role of horses and mules during the war when they recalled poems and songs from the war which mentioned them. Such mentions were mostly in passing. One little ditty, in various forms, was apparently very popular. The usual disdain for mules figured in an insult to United States President Abraham Lincoln. The following versions — the first from Virginia and the second from Mississippi — of this brief, humorous ditty illustrate its widespread popularity:

> Jeff Davis is our President,
>   Lincoln is a fool.
> Jeff Davis rides a white horse,
>   Lincoln rides a mule.[25]

> Ol' Jeff Davis, long and slim,
> Whuped ol' Abe wid a hick'ry limb.
> Jeff Davis is a wise man an' Lincoln is a fool,
> Ol' Jeff Davis rides a gray an' Lincoln rides a mule.[26]

When Union soldiers besieging Vicksburg sang "We'll Hang Jeff Davis from a Sour-Apple Tree," Confederates would respond with yet another variation:

> Jeff Davis is a President,
> Abe Lincoln is a fool;
> Jeff Davis rides a dark bay horse,
> Abe Lincoln rides a mule.[27]

One song, "Mister, Here's Your Mule," was popular in the western armies of the Confederacy. It is about a farmer who went into a camp to sell his milk and eggs and lost his mule. The gist is that the soldiers taunted him as he sought it with the comment, "Mister, here's your mule!" The actual status of the mule is perhaps related by the chorus of one version:

> Come on, come on, come on, old man, and don't be made a fool.
> I'll tell the truth as best I can,
> John Morgan's got your mule.[28]

Given Gen. Morgan's notoriety for locating horses and mules needed by his command, there is certainly an element of believability to the song's story. Another version, sung to the tune of "My Maryland," began, "Old Stonewall Jackson's in the field,/Here's your mule, Oh, here's your mule!" This song was also popular in the Confederacy's western armies.[29] A third version of the "Here's your mule" theme originated in the Trans-Mississippi. On November 3, 1863, the Texans of Brig. Gen. Thomas Green's brigade achieved a minor victory over Union General Franklin's infantry at Bayou Boubeau south of Opelousas, Louisiana, at the beginning of the Red River Campaign. An unknown member of the brigade penned a song commemorating this victory. A continuing refrain in the song is "On his mule, on his mule," or similar words, with the concluding stanza having the refrains of Gen. Franklin ordering his men, "On your mules, on your mules!" and finally, "Where's my mule! Where's my mule!"[30] (See Appendix D for the original version of this song as printed as a "Comic Camp Song & Chorus" by C.D. Benson in Nashville, Tennessee.)

A more serious poem, "The Confederate Soldier's Horse," was penned by a C. Drew of Lake City, Florida, on August 17, 1863, and published four days later in the *Savannah* (Georgia) *Republican*. The author asserted, "Take my horse home to my wife, my mother, or my aged father, is often the last request of the dying soldier." The six four-line stanzas promote this thought with but little regarding the horse of a soldier. The poet notes that his horse is "war-battered ... trusty in charge or retreat," and "true hast thou been through the peril, my steed...."[31] The poem was never well-known.

There were numerous poems written about personages and events of the war during the war itself. Many of the efforts occasionally mentioned in passing that someone was on a horse, or use terms like "the horses plunged," "clash of spur and saber," and the like. Other than the previously mentioned "Charge of the Mule Brigade" and "Mister, Here's Your Mule," there was only one poem written during the war that was specifically about a horse and, more significantly, named the horse. The Confederacy's Gen. William J. Hardee was wounded during the Battle of Shiloh and so was his horse. Soon an anonymous poem, "General Hardee at the Battle of Shiloh," appeared in the *Chattanooga Rebel*. The poem begins:

> Amidst the carnage and the crash,
> Black Auster fearless stood,
> Receiving on that field of fame,
> His baptism of blood.

Near the end it entreats garlands for Auster's mane and concludes that Hardee's and Black Auster's names are blended in immortality.[32] In 1886, a Richmond, Virginia, newspaper published a poem, "The Dying War-Horse" by "S.B.V.," about "Stonewall" Jackson's horse.[33]

The Civil War equines didn't fare any better in postwar historical writing. Articles in newspapers and journals, reminiscences and unit histories often made mention of horses as they figured in specific events or in relation to specific commanders. There were occasional poems written and published in newspapers about a horse when its master died. There was no writing addressing the roles horses played in the war. Even when a horse's death was specifically memorialized, the result could ambiguous. When the horse of Union Brig. Gen. Charles W. Tilden died some time after the war, he directed its burial. A Rev. Nathaniel Butler wrote a sixteen-stanza poem, "Death of the Old War Horse," for the occasion. In the poem, Tilden's horse is referred to as having a "hero soul" and "tireless feet," and as being "true as steel" and an "old friend." Curiously though, it is never named.[34] Mules fared somewhat better. Two Union veterans both devoted chapters to "the Army Mule." A twenty-two-page Chapter IX in John D. Billings's *Hardtack and Coffee* appeared in 1887. A similar chapter followed in 1890 in *Recollections of a Private: A Story of the Army of the Potomac* by veteran Warren Lee Goss. Both also wrote a good bit about horses during the war.

In 1901, E.P. Henderson, a veteran of the 2nd South Carolina Cavalry, published his memoir of the war, narrating it as though from the mind of his horse, Arab.[35] It was to be over half a century later before any books specifically about Civil War horses appeared. The first was a juvenile historical novel, *A Horse for General Lee*, by Fairfax Downey in 1953. He followed this up in 1959 with *Famous Horses of the Civil War*. Though written at the juvenile level, this history gave detailed information on over 50 horses as well as general commentary on the uses of equines, their care and their training. Next, in 1988 was Richard Adams's *Traveller*. Though a novel, it names the horses of major commanders (with two exceptions) correctly, and some specific incidents of the war related to horses are faithfully related. The book — supposedly narrated by Traveller with a Southern "country" accent — is a highly entertaining read. Then, in 1995, Blake A. Magner published *Traveller & Company: The Horses of Gettysburg*, which is well-researched and provides some general information about horses, in addition to relating specific horse events of that battle. It includes numerous pictures, including those of some of the equestrian monuments on the battlefield. *Fly Like the Wind*, by Bridgette Z. Savage in 2006, is written on a juvenile level but accurately tells the story of an actual Civil War horse which belonged to a private soldier of the 1st Indiana Cavalry. All of these books are well worth reading by anyone interested in equines of the Civil War.

There have never been any movies about Civil War equines, though they, of course, figure incidentally in movies about their masters or are depicted being ridden or pulling cannon or wagons in general movies about the war. The beginning of the 21st century did bring forth a television program about equines during the war. The History Channel's *Civil War Minutes* program about them was filmed in 2006 and released in May 2007 under the title *Horses of Gettysburg*. This two–DVD set of 116 minutes was directed by Mark Bussler and narrated by Ronald F. Maxwell.

The last Civil War horse — or least so it is claimed — died in 1894 at Aiken, South Carolina[36] (see Old Jim in the roster following). Nevertheless, some Civil War horses — or rather, portions of them — can still be viewed today. The largest collection of such "horse artifacts" is in the Museum of the Confederacy in Richmond, Virginia. This museum possesses souvenirs from Lee's Traveller, from Jackson's Little Sorrel, and from Gen. Turner Ashby's horse Tom Telegraph. This museum also possesses many pieces of horse equipment used by President Jefferson Davis, Generals Lee, Jackson, Sterling Price, Joseph Johnston, John Hunt Morgan, Nathan Bedford Forrest, and others.[37] The New Harmony Working Men's Institute, a small museum in New Harmony, Indiana, has on display the skeleton and part of the tail of Fly, the Civil War horse used Pvt. George M. Barrett of the 1st Indiana Cavalry.[38] The VMI Museum of the Virginia Military Institute at Lexington, Virginia, displays the mounted (on a plaster frame) hide of "Stonewall" Jackson's Little Sorrel (actual name Fancy),

Hoof of Gen. Ashby's Tom Telegraph. Even during the war, soldiers clipped hair from the mounts of commanders as souvenirs. Postwar, pieces of bone were made into jewelry and sewing needles and hooves were preserved (photography by Alan Thompson, courtesy Museum of the Confederacy, Richmond, Virginia).

said to be the oldest mounted horse in the United States.[39] Until 1997, the Institute also possessed the skeleton of this horse, but during the summer of that year, the bones were cremated and buried in front of a statue there of Gen. Jackson.[40] Since 1922, the taxidermized horse of Maj. Gen. Phil Sheridan, Rienzi (more commonly remembered as Winchester), has been on display in the Hall of Armed Forces History of the Smithsonian Institution in Washington, D.C.[41] A final horse artifact viewable today is the mounted head of Baldy, a horse used by Maj. Gen. George G. Meade, which is now displayed by the Grand Army of the Republic Museum and Library in Philadelphia, Pennsylvania.[42] Hooves of two animals are held by museums. A forehoof of Meads's Baldy is at the Old York Road Historical Society at Jenkintown, Pennsylvania, and one of Dick, a horse was used by Lt. Robert Oliver of the 24th New York Infantry, is at the Oswego County Historical Society at Oswego, New York. (See Appendix D for details about Civil War horse artifacts viewable today.)

There are numerous equestrian statues of Civil War commanders and no little confusion regarding the horses they are mounted on. There has long been a persistent legend that on the Gettysburg battlefield the number of hooves the statue horse has raised indicates what happened to the general. The story went that if one hoof was raised the rider had been wounded, and if two were raised, the rider had been killed.[43] When a statue to Confederate Lt. Gen. James Longstreet was erected on the battlefield in 1998 there was some furor over the fact that one of the horse's hooves was raised though the general was neither killed nor wounded during the battle. It turned out that previous equestrian statues on the battlefield had, by chance, followed the legendary pattern.[44]

Another confusion regarding equestrian statues is the idea that the horse on which a general rides is his "favorite" mount. In the great majority of cases however the horse depicted is simply a "generic" horse. There are some cases in which a particular horse is intended. The Virginia State Memorial at Gettysburg depicts at its apex Gen. R.E. Lee mounted on a horse. The sculptor of this monument, Frederick William Sievers, did intend the horse to be Traveller. He had visited Lexington, Virginia, to view the articulated skeleton of the horse (it was then on display at Washington and Lee University) and used a live horse closely matching the size and shape of the famous subject.[45] John Sedgewick's statue at Gettysburg is supposed to depict him astride his horse Handsome Joe, and the sculpted horse is said to be a perfect likeness of it.[46] Most assume that the statue of Union Gen. George Meade on the battlefield has him mounted on Old Baldy. In fact, however, the sculptor used as his model for the horse a portrait of an animal given by the Khedive of Egypt to President Grant.[47] The best known equestrian statue of Lee is that on Monument Avenue in Richmond. Though believed to be so, this horse is definitely not Traveller. The sculptor, a Frenchman, thought Traveller's actual dimensions were too slender and not heroic enough. He used a French hunter, which he thought more impressive.[48] Sculptor "liberties" with horses of equestrian statues can even be comical. At Lexington, Kentucky, there is a statue of Confederate Gen. John Hunt Morgan mounted on, according to the monument, his Bess. As its name indicated, this horse was a mare. The sculptor, Pompeo Coppini, didn't believe that a hero should be shown bestride a mare. He therefore added testicles to the horse! Students of the nearby University of Kentucky have been known to paint these testicles in the school colors of blue and white. This led to an anonymous poem titled "The Ballad of Black Bess," which humorously tells the story of this mare and her testicles.[49] At Greenville, Tennessee, there is a commemorative plaque about the "Death of Gen. John Hunt Morgan" at the site where he died in 1864 while trying to reach the stable where his horse Sir Oliver was. The marker, however, includes a picture of the general with another horse — Black Bess.[50] There are other commemorative plaques which mention horses. A notable one is that which is placed on the wall of the stable behind Lee's home while he was president of Washington and Lee University. It reads:

> The Last Home of Traveller
> Through War and Peace, the Faithful
> Devoted and Beloved Horse of
> General Robert E. Lee[51]

Other than this plaque and a few "grave markers" — including three of horses of the 5th New York Cavalry[52] — there were no monuments or memorials specifically dedicated to Civil War equines until 1999. In that year, the National Sporting Library and Museum dedicated a bronze statue titled *War Horse* in front its new library building in Middleburg, Virginia (for picture, see facing the title page). This bronze is three-quarters actual size of a horse. Its inscription reads:

> IN MEMORY OF
> THE ONE AND ONE HALF MILLION HORSES AND MULES
> OF THE CONFEDERATE AND UNION ARMIES WHO WERE KILLED,
> WERE WOUNDED, OR DIED FROM DISEASE IN THE CIVIL WAR.
> MANY PERISHED WITHIN TWENTY MILES OF MIDDLEBURG
> IN THE BATTLES OF ALDIE, MIDDLEBURG AND UPPERVILLE
> IN JUNE OF 1863.

A copy in dark patina was erected at the Cavalry Museum at Fort Riley, Kansas. A full-size copy has been placed at the Virginia Historical Society in Richmond.[53] More recently, a planned housing development south of Nashville, Roderick Place, was named after one of Gen. Forrest's horses which had been killed nearby and a statue representing it erected at the entrance.[54] Finally, after almost a century and a half, a few monuments specifically dedicated to equines of the war have been erected to perpetuate the memory of their service.

11

The Naming of Civil War Equines

A Kentucky cavalryman wrote, "A horse is more than a dumb brute to a soldier. It is a companion and friend."[1] James H. Stevenson, a veteran of the 1st New York Cavalry, wrote in a history of his unit that all "had pet names for their horses."[2] With a natural and proper emphasis on the war's human participants, the names of all but a very few equines have been lost to us. Equines of the war were never enumerated by name in any contemporary document. Only a few horses from the war are today readily identifiable by name. These are Lee's Traveller, Jackson's Little Sorrel and Sheridan's Winchester, and of these, two are recognized by sobriquets rather than the actual names by which their masters called them, and the name of the other is frequently misspelled.

There have been relatively few published lists of the names of Civil War equine veterans. Mark Mayo Boatner's *Civil War Dictionary* (1959) identifies 30 by name. Also from 1959, Fairfax Downey's *Famous Horses of the Civil* War named 59 and provided significant details for most of them. Webb Garrison's *Civil War Curiosities* of 1994, listed 43. Donald Cartwell's *Civil War 101* (2001) listed 32. Blake Magner's *Traveller & Company* (1995) listed 46 (and another 4 were named in the text). The advent of the World Wide Web has facilitated and brought new interest to the names of the Civil War's horses and mules. A 2009 blog to the Thoroughbred Bloggers Alliance by "Zarvona" named 43, of which all but three belonged to Confederates who mostly served in the Virginia theater of the war. Wikipedia's list (2011 update) has 80 names, of which 1 is in error. Fictitious names of equines have begun to creep into such listings, and typically no authority is cited for lists, so inaccuracies cannot easily be disproved. (All animals identified in these and other lists are included in the "Roster of Civil War Equines" provided in the following chapter.) No listing has included the names of any of the mules used during the conflict.

The greatest problem in compiling names of Civil War equines is the fact that this type of information is so scattered over thousands and thousands of published individual veteran diaries, letters and reminiscences or unit histories; where equines' names are mentioned (and often no names are provided), typically only one or two are given. Unpublished journals and letters would likely provide even more names but are significantly more difficult to access. It is particularly difficult and almost impossible to determine the names of two classes of equines of the war. These are those animals used by the artillery and in the trains as part of teams. Their work was cooperative rather than individual in nature. Though doubtless they did have names they were called by, it was their teamwork that was remembered, not their names. For this reason the roster provided in the following chapter contains extremely few names of team animals. Artillery animals identified by names are for the most part mounts used by officers and NCOs, not those that pulled the guns. The names for animals of the quartermaster and commissary teams are even scarcer — six mules.

Horses used as mounts are much more readily found, and those of animals belonging to generals, field officers and staff officers are the most frequently found. There are two reasons for this. One is that proportionately memoirs and biographies of commanders were (and, to some extent, still are) of greater interest to readers, so more attention has been given to them. The other is that their very position in the armies made them — and their mounts — more noticeable and memorable. Thus, subordinates who wrote about the war were more likely to mention the name of a general's or colonel's horse. The fact that riders invariably used multiple horses during the war, and even at the same time, complicated matters. It is even probable that many an enlisted man never even heard the name of his colonel's or general's horse.

As might be expected, more equine names are known for the two most prominent generals of the war and the two most "romantic" cavalry commanders. These are the mounts of:

> CS Maj. Gen. J.E.B. Stuart —12
> > Bullet, Chancellor, General, George, Lady Margrave, Lilly Dandridge, Lily of the Valley (probably same as Lilly Dandridge), Lucy Long, Mazeppa, My Maryland, Star of the East and Virginia.
>
> U.S. Lt. Gen. Ulysses S. Grant —10
> > Cincinnati, Claybank, Egypt, Fox, Jack, Jeff Davis, Kangaroo, Little Reb, Methuselah and Rondy.
>
> U.S. Brig. Gen. George Armstrong Custer — 8
> > Bess, Custis Lee, Dandy, Don Juan, Harry, Lancer, Roanoke and Wellington.
>
> CS Gen. Robert E. Lee — 6
> > Ajax, Brown Roan, Grace Darling, Lucy Long, Richmond and, of course, Traveller.

Only three names each were found for the horses of such notable cavalry commanders as Union Maj. Gen. Phil Sheridan, Confederate Lt. Gen. Nathan Bedford Forrest and Confederate Maj. Gen. John Hunt Morgan. In the case of Forrest this is probably because he had at least 19 killed (an average of 5 horses per year) and another 10 wounded beneath him. He simply didn't ride any horse long enough for it to gain sufficient fame. The same is perhaps true of the horses ridden by Confederate Maj. Gen. Joseph Wheeler, another famous cavalryman. He had 29 shot from beneath him during the course of the war and the name of only one is remembered. In all, some 22 percent of horses identified in the roster are those of generals and another 27 percent belonged to lower-ranking officers.

Identification of multiple horses of regimental-sized or smaller units is problematic. Only a small proportion of an infantry unit's officers — the field grade officers, adjutant and chaplain — had horses. In the artillery, as mentioned, horses were used in teams more than individually and had limited average life-spans during the war. There was a higher attrition rate among cavalry horses with a correspondingly high rate of changes of mounts. However, the unit for which the names of the most horses is known was a cavalry regiment. The roster contains the names of 20 horses used by the 5th New York Cavalry. This chanced solely because all of the original horses of its Company H were purchased by a single man (the father of the colonel). They were of a single breed (the Morgan — then concentrated in the company's upstate New York area), and, in 1899, his son compiled information from surviving members of the company still resident there and published these in a local newspaper.[3] The unit with the next highest number of horse names — 14 — was the staff of J.E.B. Stuart. He had a highly literate staff of which many left memoirs of service with him. The 1st Massachusetts Cavalry follows in third place because its Major Benjamin W. Crowninshield devoted almost a chapter to horses of the unit.[4] The fourth-place unit is the 2nd South Carolina Cavalry. A veteran of the unit named one horse of the unit's commander, his own, and six of others who served as scouts. Somewhat surprisingly, the fifth-place unit is the Confederate 9th Kentucky Infantry with six. This unit was mounted during the fall of 1864, and Pvt. John Jackman in his diary included the names of some of the horses that he had an association with.

Even though the sample provided in the roster (706 animals) is quite small in comparison with the total number of equines used, some naming patterns are apparent. "Old" is used as part of or in conjunction with the names of 69 equines (9.8 percent). It seems evident that in most cases the "Old" is more of an affectionate prefix to the actual name and often was applied postwar if the horse survived and lived to a good age. Colors were also used as part of— or additions to — names. The most frequent color used was "Black" for 15 (2.3 percent) of the animals in the roster. Other colors were less frequent — eight of gray, seven of white, five of red, with lesser occurrences of sorrel and claybank.

As to actual names, there was as great variation among the equines in the sample as among soldiers. They were named after where they came from (such as Cincinnati), from battles (Chickamauga and Manassas occur thrice each), from notable people (Confederate General P.G.T. Beauregard had six named after him and President Jefferson Davis had six horses — Union as well as Confederate — named after him), after a previous owner (Mott) from a characteristic (such as a color), with a classical allusion (like Bucephalus), after a friend (Sherman's Sam), after a previous owner from whom the animal was captured (Milroy, for an example), and other reasons not now understandable. If there is any specific naming pattern visible, it is to use common, everyday names such as are often given to people. Billy/Billie was given to 28 animals — 4.4 percent of the total and the most for any single name. Next most frequent is Bill for another 19. These and another two variants of "William" comprise 49 names (7.3 percent of the total). Next most frequent are Charlie/Charley with 19 so named (2.7 percent) and Dick with 12 (1.9 percent). No other single name occurs more than nine times, including the most frequent feminine name, Nell/Nellie/Nelly. Among other "regular" names encountered more than only once or twice are Bess, Belle, Fanny, Frank, George, Jack, Jim, Joe, John and Tom. The name Prince is found 10 times (and Princess once) and Dixie is encountered five times. Curiously, of the names found for six mules, two of them were called Simon.

Equine names were fairly frequently changed. In many cases the name used by a previous owner — this especially applies to captured animals — was unknown. According to Confederate Maj. Gen. John B. Gordon, it was a practice to name a captured horse after its previous owner, if known. In this manner, Union Brig. Gen. Alexander Shaler's Abe was captured by Confederates and called thereafter General Shaler by Gordon. It is presumed that a third owner at war's end, a Union colonel, restored the original name, since he knew the horse from before. At other times a name change was made deliberately by an owner. A horse named Jeff Davis (after a then Senator from Mississippi) was purchased by Gen. Robert E. Lee and initially renamed Greenbriar (after the place of its origin) and soon after finally Traveller (after a characteristic — because of its easy gait it was pleasant to travel upon). Other animals had "pet" or shorter versions of their names which were used by their masters. Into this case would fall J.E.B. Stuart's Lily of the Valley which he often called Lily for short. Sometimes it was others than the owner who would apply a sobriquet. "Stonewall" Jackson never called his favorite horse anything other than Fancy, but his staff and others referred to it as Little Sorrel, and others, as it aged, as Old Sorrel. "My Billy horse" is pretty clear, but when others make a reference the name can be altered in popular memory. Sheridan's Rienzi, due to a poem, was often referred to after 1864 as "Sheridan's Winchester horse" and eventually as Winchester.

Then too, there was much inconsistency among the veterans of the war in how they recorded the stories of their horses. Some, like Lee, were very good about naming and describing their animals. Others were poor. Confederate Brig. Gen. Moxley Sorrel described several horses in his memoir but named only the two which had proven unserviceable to him. Joseph Johnston, Longstreet and Sherman mentioned their horses only very briefly. A times, they leave the reader frustrated. John Cheves Haskell, a Confederate staff officer, described some of his horses — including one that he wrote had been used by Robert E. Lee, recommended to him by President Jefferson Davis, and which Ulysses S. Grant offered to purchase after the war. Truly, this must have been an outstanding animal of exceptional virtues, but Haskell left us but to wonder what its name was.[5]

12

Roster of Civil War Equine Veterans

The following roster contains the names of 706 different equine veterans of the Civil War. Of these, 369 of them were used by Union forces, 295 by Confederate, and 43 were provably used by both sides. One or more horses are identified as having been used by 79 Union and 71 Confederate generals. Two (Grace Darling and Whitey) had also been used during the Mexican War of 13 years before. Both were the property of Confederate generals which had been left behind on their plantations, captured, and subsequently used by Union forces. The overwhelming majority of equines listed are horses, with only 6 mules, 1 Shetland pony and 1 donkey listed.

Equines are listed in alphabetical sequence under all names or sobriquets by which they were called during the war. In the case of animals called or known by more than one name, information about that horse is included with the more correct or frequent name, and cross-references are provided from other names to that one. Sobriquets are given within quotation marks to distinguish them from actual names. Some animals are known to us today solely by such a nickname. In almost all cases where an equine's ownership changed, the name used by either a prior or a subsequent owner is unknown.

Information provided about listed horses varies greatly in both detail and length. To some extent this is because the author wished to include only what information about them was definite. Since practically all Civil War riders used more than one horse during the war and even during the same period, many of their references to a characteristic or event relating to "my horse" cannot be specifically related to a named horse. Even if a reference was only the next chapter or even a few pages after the naming of a horse, it is not presumed that the reference was to that horse. The author felt it better to be sure rather than to assume. In a few instances there will be found, in brackets, comments from the author. Most of these are to add explanation of an unusual name that refers to some classical or historical figure. A very few of them provide commentary.

The sequence of information given in the roster is:

1. **Name** or "**Sobriquet**" of the equine — italicized and in bold print.
   Names which have appeared in some listings of Civil War horses that are definitely false are included here but followed with the word, "ERROR" and some explanation of the error.
2. Army in which the animal served — CS for Confederate, U.S. for Union.

3. Highest rank held by the master. Standard military abbreviations are used for ranks.
4. Unit, in parentheses, of the master. This does not apply for generals, but when an equine was used by the general prior to achieving that rank, his prior rank and unit are identified in the text. The postal service's 2-character state abbreviations are used.
5. Additional names or sobriquets by which the equine was or is known.
6. Descriptive information about the equine to the extent known.
   a. Breed.
   b. Sex. "Mare" is of course a female. Both "gelding" and "stallion" identify a male. "Male" is used when the source refers to the animal as "he" but does not specify whether it was a stallion or a gelding. Where the source did not specify, sex is omitted.
   Probably in many cases the name will imply the sex of the equine. "Charley" or "Simon" could be taken to indicate a male animal and "Princess" a female. This is, however, not always the case. The name "Ruby" would imply female, but there is one horse in the roster so named that was identified by the source (its owner) as a male. Use of names to guess the sex of an animal is therefore left to the discretion of the reader.
   c. Color and marks. Readers are invited to utilize Appendix A for clarification of the colors and marks used in relation to horses and mules.
   d. Other characteristics or abilities.
7. Other information as available includes how named, age, where and how obtained, wounds, death, and postwar life. If nothing else, an attempt is made to advise of the period(s) during which an animal was in use, but this information does not preclude use in other periods — it is just limited to those periods about which the author is certain.

At the end of the roster are appended two brief additional lists. One presents some civilian horses of the Civil War years that are of some interest. The second evaluates the horses identified in Richard Adams's novel *Traveller*. The names of some of these animals have begun to appear in lists available on the World Wide Web and are erroneous. The appended list endeavors to identify those which are of doubtful accuracy.

"Abe"—U.S.—OH Union Light Guard
Long-legged and high-headed. Called *"Abe"* by the young sons of President Lincoln who used this horse (belonging to an OH mounted company formed by the OH Gov. to serve as bodyguards to the president) for rides about Washington, D.C.[1]

Abe—see *General Shaler*.

Ajax—CS Gen. Robert E. Lee.
Sorrel mare. Obtained by Lee after Second Manassas.[2] Died 1868 and buried at Washington and Lee University, Lexington, VA.[3]

Albion—CS citizen ("Carter's Farm," SC) Thomas Puryear
    U.S. (2nd Brig., 4th Div., XV Corps)
One of two racehorses taken when Col. Robert N. Adams's brigade approached the town of Camden, SC, from the north on Feb. 1, 1865, and encountered Puryear fleeing north with his animals.[4]

Aldebaran—U.S. Maj. Gen. Philip H. Sheridan

Sheridan used this horse early in the war while still a colonel.[5] (Aldebaran is a star in the constellation Taurus and one of the four "royal stars" in Persian mythology that marked positions of equinoxes and solstices.)

Alice— CS citizen (near Vicksburg, MS) Emilie Riley McKinley

U.S. (Osterhaus's Division)

Mare. Taken May 1863 by Union troops, June 16, 1863. Miss McKinley visited Union Provost officer in unsuccessful effort to recover the horse, which she knew to be with the division of U.S. Gen. Osterhaus.[6]

Almond Eye— U.S. Maj. Gen. Benjamin F. Butler

Named for the peculiar formation of its eyes.[7] An enduring anecdote about this horse is related in Moore's *Anecdotes, Poetry and Incidents of the War: North and South* (1867). While at the Petersburg front in 1864, Butler received word that the horse had been accidentally killed. He instructed an Irish hostler to skin the horse. After quite some time, the Irishman returned with the skin. Gen. Butler asked why it had taken so long. The response was that it hadn't take so long to skin the horse but that it took some doing to kill it first.[8]

Andy— CS Surgeon (56th GA Inf.) George W. Peddy

Peddy used this horse which was owned by his father-in-law . The horse was wounded once. It was frequently sick.[9]

Arab— CS Pvt. (1st NC Cav.) George J. Handley[10]

May be erroneous. See Henderson's *Arab* below. Handley served in Gen. Wade Hampton's scouts with Henderson. In his book, Henderson mentions Handley's borrowing his horse.

Arab— CS Sgt. (2nd SC Cav.) Edward Prioleau Henderson

Male. Foaled March 11, 1857, out of Pocahontas in Colleton District, SC. Wounded thrice during the war. Returned to SC with its master after the war and 1867–68 was used to pull a plow. For 1 year beginning May 1870 was in Savannah, GA, with Henderson. Then put in the care of Pinckney Henderson (brother of its master) at Hendersonville, SC, where it died aged 27 years (about 1884). Buried at the Henderson family plantation. Purported author of Henderson's memoir, *Autobiography of Arab*.[11] Gen. M.C. Butler recalled this horse when visiting Hendersonville during a political campaign in 1876 and took a ride on *Arab*.[12]

Arab— CS Lt. Col. (1st MS Cav.) John Henry Miller

Raised on Miller's plantation and his favorite horse. Killed during the 1861 Battle of Belmont.[13]

Archy— U.S. Col. (63rd PA Inf.) William Kirkwood

According to Davis, *Life of David Bell Birney*:

Ridden by a Col. Watkins, this horse of Kirkwood's won over 11 other horses entered in the 2nd race (steeplecourse) of 3 races held in celebration of St. Patrick's Day on March 17, 1863, at Falmouth, VA, near the HQ of Gen. David B. Birney.[14]

Ashby— U.S. Brig. Gen. George Henry Gordon

Male, dark bay with black streak down his back from mane to tail, "enormous nostrils."

While colonel of the 2nd MA Inf., his men found the horse riderless after a skirmish near Woodstock, VA, during the 1861 Shenandoah Campaign. Upon seeing the horse, Gordon tested it and then claimed it for his own use. He used this horse throughout the balance of the war.[15]

Attakapas— CS Brig. Gen. Jean Jacques Alfred Alexandre Mouton
Mouton used this horse as colonel of the 18th LA Inf.[16] (The Attakapa were an American Indian group formerly resident in the Acadiana area of Louisiana.)

Auster— see *Black Auster*

Babe— U.S. Musician (40th NY Inf.) Gustav A. Schurmann
An excellent jumper, this horse was used by 13-year-old Schurmann while bugler for Gen. Phil Kearny and was stabled with Kearny's own horse.[17]

Baldy— U.S. Maj. Gen. David Hunter
    U.S. Maj. Gen. George Gordon Meade
Also referred to as "*Old Baldy.*" Brown with a white face. Raised on the Western frontier. Gen. Hunter used this horse (his name for it is not known) at First Manassas, where it was wounded twice. He turned it over to the Quartermaster Department Meade purchased it in September 1861 and renamed it *Baldy* because of its white face (a dark horse with a white face was referred to as being "bald"). It had a racking gait and was used as Meade's parade horse. It was wounded at Antietam and left for dead but found grazing on the battlefield with a deep neck wound. The horse was again wounded by a bullet in the ribs on the 2nd day of Gettysburg, and yet again at the 1864 Battle of Weldon Railroad, when it was retired and sent under care of a member of the 1st Pennsylvania Cav. to Meade's country home. (Another account says that the horse was retired to the farm of a Capt. Sam Ringwalt shortly after Grant made his headquarters with the Army of the Potomac.[18]) It remained there 7 years, at which time it was given to John J. Davis, a blacksmith of Jenkington, Morgan Co., PA. *Baldy* was in Meade's Nov. funeral procession. Davis kept the horse until it was unable to rise after lying down. On December 16, 1882, it was put down by administration of poison. A week

Head of Gen. Meade's Baldy. Veterans unearthed Baldy's remains and cut off his head and hooves for preservation in memory of the general (photograph by Don Wiles, courtesy Don Wiles and the Old Baldy Civil War Round Table of Philadelphia).

later, 2 veterans — H.W.B. Hervey and Albert C. Johnston — exhumed it and cut off the head and forehooves, which they had preserved. The head was given to the George G. Meade Post No. 1 of the Grand Army of the Republic's Department of Pennsylvania. It was displayed at the post and then at the Grand Army of the Republic Museum, which succeeded on the post's site on Griscom Avenue. It was restored in 1979 by the Old Baldy Civil War Round Table and the Civil War Museum on Pine St. in Philadelphia, which thereafter displayed it. When that museum closed in 2008 it ultimately went back to the Grand Army of the Republic Library and Museum on Griscom St. in Philadelphia, where it is now on display. One of the forehooves is in possession of the Old York Road Historical Society of Jenkintown, PA.[19] The "Old Baldy Civil War Round Table" in Philadelphia is named after this horse.[20]

Ball — CS Brig. Gen. Robert Hopkins Hatton
This horse was shot from beneath the general on May 31, 1862, during the Battle of Seven Pines. Soon after the dismounted general was slain as well.[21]

Ball — CS Chaplain (35th AL Inf.) Robert A. Wilson
In use April 1862 in the vicinity of Corinth, MS.[22]

Baltimore — CS Col. (Jeff Davis Legion MS Cav.) J. Fred Waring[23]

Banjo — CS Pvt. (16th MS Inf.) David Holt
In April 1865, Holt was a paroled prisoner returning through MS on this horse to his unit in VA.[24]

Barney — U.S. Col. (1st ME Cav.) E.J. Conger
Used during the 1864 Battle of Bermuda Hundred.[25]

Barney — U.S. Brig. Gen. Emerson Opdycke
Male. Taken with Opdycke from Cleveland, OH, at beginning of the war. "I have changed the name, because I did not like to call him Major." Invalided near Jasper, TN, on September 2, 1863.[26] Killed beneath the general on July 13, 1864, during the Atlanta campaign.[27]

Battery Horse U.S. artillery unknown
In October 1863 raced against Gen. Kilpatrick's ***Lively*** at James City, VA, racecourse.[28]

Bay Bob — CS Col. (15th TX Cav. Dismounted) George Sweet
When the 15th and 18th TX Cav. regiments were dismounted, Sweet became unpopular because of his training and drilling the units as infantry. One night, members of the 18th shaved the mane and tail of the horse.[29]

Bayard — U.S. Maj. Gen. Philip Kearny
Light brown. Kearney was riding this horse when he was killed during the Battle of Chantilly.[30] Gen. Robert E. Lee had it sent through the lines to Kearny's widow.[31] (The original Bayard was a horse belonging to Charlemagne.)

Beauregard — CS Capt. (staff of Cleburne) Irving Ashby Buck
In use 1863 about Tullahoma, TN.[32]

Beauregard — CS Maj. (staff of Gen. Longstreet) Thomas Jewett Goree
Very lame and foundered in early 1865.[33]

Beauregard — CS Maj. Gen. Wade Hampton

Male, 16.5 hands high. Mortally wounded at Gettysburg (the general received a wound at the same time). Though wounded, it followed Hampton to the hospital, where it lay down outside and died.[34]

Beauregard— CS Pvt. (Forrest's Scouts) Robert M. Martin
Gray, high head and slimber limbs. In use at the 1861 Battle of Sacramento, KY.[35]

Beauregard— U.S. Maj. Gen. George Stoneman
During "Stoneman's Raid" in July 1864 near Atlanta, a cannon shot struck just behind Stoneman's leg, mortally wounding the horse. Stoneman cried.[36]

Beauregard— CS Pvt. (1st MD Cav.) James Russell Wheeler.
          CS Capt. (1st MD Cav.) William Independence Rasin.
Wheeler rode this horse until, wounded, he was captured a second time. Rasin, his company commander, then rode the horse for the remainder of the war.[37] The horse was with him at Appomattox. The animal lived until 1883.[38]

Bell— see ***Bellfounder*** following.

Bella— CS Col. (staff of Gen. R.E. Lee) Walter Herron Taylor
Female, black, "little nag." Had been the horse ridden by his wife and daughter. Absent in October 1863, Gen. J.E.B. Stuart loaned Taylor Lilly Dandridge. Bella arrived at the camp near Brandy Station on the 31st of that month. Wounded at Spotsylvania, she recovered by August 1864.[39]

Belle— CS Pvt. (?? VA Cav.) Walter Buck
When Buck was killed at Upperville, VA, in June 1863, a cousin returned the horse to his family.[40]

Belle— CS Maj. Gen. Stephen Dodson Ramseur
Mare, dappled gray. Purchased April 1863.[41]

Belle Mosby— CS unknown unit or rider
          U.S. Farrier (18th PA Cav.) Joseph R. Phillips
Mare. Captured near Staunton, VA, in the spring of 1865 when about 4.5 years old. After the war, Phillips took her home with him and cared for it until it died at a little over 34 years.[42]

Bellfounder— U.S. Brig. Gen. Thomas Kilby Smith
Also referred to as "Belle." Called "my favorite" by Smith. Unscathed at Shiloh. In use about Corinth May 31, 1862. Stolen October 16, 1862, near Memphis.[43]

Bemis Horse— U.S. master unknown.
Morgan, black, 15 hands high. American Morgan Horse Register No. 685. Foaled during the 1840s, son of Billy Root. Owned by a Mr. Bryan of Georgia, VT, and later sold to the army.[44] Had won 3rd place at 1853 Vermont State Fair. Killed in battle.[45]

Bench-leg(s)— CS Gen. Matthew Calbraith Butler
Chestnut. The name was occasioned by its crooked hind legs. On June 9, 1863, a bursting shell crushed Butler's leg (he was at that time Col. of the 2nd SC Cav.) and disemboweled the horse.[46]

Beppo— U.S. Brig. Gen. Hugh Judson Kilpatrick
Dark sorrel. A good jumper. Shot through the heart during the Battle of Aldie.[47]

Berold— U.S. Col. (54th MA Inf.) Charles Russell Lowell Jr.
  Since its wounding at Battle of Antietam, this horse was no longer fit for military service and was given over to the use of Lowell's wife.[48]

Bess— U.S. Brig. Gen. George A. Custer
  Coal black. In use August 1863.[49]

Bess— CS Pvt. (43rd VA Cav. Bn.) Hugh T. Walters
  Mare. Walters was using this horse during the summer of 1864 raid on Georgetown and described her as "a superb animal, handsome as a picture and distinguished among the boys for her speed and endurance."[50]

Bess—see *Black Bess*

Bessie— ERROR
  Found on some lists of Civil War horses as belonging to CS Col. (2nd MD Cav. Bn.) Harry A. Gilmor. Apparently a misreading of a reference in Gilmor's *Four Years in the Saddle* to Miss Bessie Shackleford.

Bessie— U.S. Brig. Gen. Horatio Phillips Van Cleve
  Mare. During the Battle of Murfreesboro, the general and this horse were wounded by the same bullet. After healing, Bessie carried Van Cleve for the remainder of the war. Van Cleve was seen on the evening of the 1st day of the Battle of Chickamauga with his arms around the neck of Bessie mourning the heavy casualties of his division.[51] After the war, she became the Van Cleve's carriage horse. When she died at age 20, Bessie was buried near the Van Cleve barn.[52]

Betty— U.S. Lt. Col. (staff of XX Corps) Horace Newton Fisher
  KY thoroughbred. Taken at Lexington, KY.[53]

Betty— U.S. Surgeon (1st PA Cav.) D. B. Hotchkin
  Small, dark bay mare described as "beautiful and swift." During the Battle of Gettysburg, she saved her owner by outracing a cannonball down a Gettysburg street.[54]

Betty Root— U.S. Lt. (1st VT Cav.) Jacob Trussel
  Morgan. Wounded 1863. In 1872 owned by Asa Livingston of St. Johnsbury, VT.[55]

Bevis— CS Col. (19th SC Inf.) Cornelius Irving Walker
  So-named by a "Miss Sinclair." In use about Corinth, MS, in May 1862.[56]

Big Indian— CS Lt. (staff of Gen. J.E.B. Stuart) Richard Byrd Kennon
  Thoroughbred. Said to be a magnificent swimmer but ruined at the beginning of the Gettysburg campaign by an effort at swimming the Potomac River in the vicinity of Rowan's Ford.[57]

Big Sorrel— CS Lt. Gen. Thomas Jonathan "Stonewall" Jackson
  Gelding, sorrel. Obtained at Harpers Ferry in 1861 at the same time as Fancy. Was unreliable in battle, causing Jackson to begin use of Fancy.[58]

Bill— see *Billy* (Bartlett's) following.

Bill— U.S. Lt. (121st PA Inf.) Joshua Garsed
  Light-colored.[59]

Bill— CS Col. (2nd MD Cav. Bn.) Harry W. Gilmor.

Sorrel. Became lame and left behind at Swartz's Mill, VA, in June 1863 during the Gettysburg Campaign. Later recovered and in use October 1864.[60]

Bill— U.S. Brig. Gen. Henry J. Hunt

Pale colored. In use during the Battle of Gettysburg.[61]

Bill— U.S. Col. (2nd MA Cav.) Charles Russell Lowell

While charging a Conf. battery of Breckinridge's Corps in 1864, the horse was shot in 3 places. It was so wounded that it had to be destroyed.[62]

Bill— CS Maj. (7th VA Cav.) John E. Myers

White. One of several killed underneath Myers during the war.[63] After he had ridden the horse for 2 years, it was killed beneath him at the Battle of Trevillian Station in 1864.[64]

Bill— U.S. Maj. Gen. Alfred Pleasanton

White. Used in Philadelphia to pull a cart at the Schuylkill Arsenal until Pleasanton obtained it sometime in 1862.[65] When Gen. George G. Meade's Baldy was seriously wounded on the 2nd day of the Battle of Gettysburg, Pleasanton loaned Bill to Meade who, unused to the horse, had difficulty controlling it.[66]

Bill— U.S. Lt. Col. (19th Ohio Inf.) Henry Granville Stratton

Male, chestnut sorrel, "little," and described as "an unfavorable looking animal but a jewel to ride." Stratton obtained the horse in December 1862 near Gallatin, TN. While in Ohio the first months of 1863 recovering from a Murfreesboro wound, the horse was used by regiment's commanding officer, Col. Charles F. Manderson, whose own horse had died of a stomach wound.[67]

Bill— U.S. Col. (4th IA Cav.) Edward F. Winslow

Bay. Wounded in a leg during the Battle of Westport in 1864. Led to the Arkansas River and taken by steamboat to St. Louis by the regiment. Burned to death with other animals on the steamboat *Maria* on the way from St. Louis to Louisville.[68]

Bill—U.S. Pvt. (2nd MA Lt. Arty Battery) unknown Vermont soldier

After having borne its master almost 3 years, Bill's jaw was shot off by a musket ball during the 1864 Battle of Mansfield, but Bill still carried the soldier to safety at Pleasant Hill, LA.[69]

Billie— CS Lt. Col. (22nd VA Inf.) Andrew W. Barbee

    CS Capt. (unit not known) Bob Moorman

    CS Pvt. (19th VA Cav.) John A. McNeil

Blood bay, 15.5 hands high, aged 5 years in 1863. Barbee had ridden the horse for a year, but due to his heavy weight, Billie's back was damaged and it became unfit for service. Barbee sold it to Moorman, who sold it to McNeil's father. When McNeil took the horse and accompanied (at age 17, he had not yet enlisted but accompanied the raid since his father had recently lost 200 head of cattle to Federal raiders) the 19th VA Cav. on the April 1863 raid, the unit passed the 22nd VA Inf. Some of the soldiers recognized the horse and called to the Col. that his horse was there. Barbee told McNeil its history.[70]

Billy— CS unknown unit and rider — Morgan's cavalry

    U.S. Chaplain (70th IN Inf.) Archibald C. Allen and others

Captured October 1862 in KY from Morgan's CS cavalry by the 70th. The chaplain bought it from the QM but soon sold it to another. The only horse in its brigade not to die during the campaign to Atlanta, it died a natural death postwar at the age of 32.[71]

Billy— U.S. Brig. Gen. William Francis Bartlett
Black, "little." Because of a briar caught in its skin, Billy twice threw the one-legged Bartlett (then Col. of the 57th MA Infantry) the day before the Battle of the Wilderness. When Bartlett was wounded during that battle, he was carried from the field by Billy.[72] Bartlett had possessed this horse as early as November 1862 in VA and took it with him to the Siege of Port Hudson.[73] During one assault on Port Hudson defenses, the horse jumped numerous obstructions, causing a wounded Bartlett to exclaim, "Did you see Billy? Why, he jumped like a rabbit."[74]

Billy— U.S. Brig. Gen. Francis Channing Barlow
"Old bay." Barlow (then Col. of the 61st New York Inf.) was in a bad mood the morning of the Battle of Malvern Hill because this horse had been shot dead beneath him the night before (June 30, 1862).[75]

Billy— U.S. Capt. (57th NY Inf.) Josiah Marshall Favill
Used during the 1862 Peninsula Campaign.[76]

Billy— U.S. Maj. (2nd MA Cav.) William H. Forbes
In September 1864 the horse was killed and Forbes wounded and captured in the Shenandoah Valley.[77]

Billy— U.S. Brig. Gen. James Abram Garfield
Male. Slightly wounded during Battle of Chickamauga.[78]

Billy— U.S. Lt. (staff of Gibbon) Frank Aretas Haskell
Male. Used during the Battles of Second Manassas and Fredericksburg, this animal was wounded during the 2nd day at Gettysburg when a bullet entered its chest just in front of his rider's leg and air escaped from the wound.[79]

Billy— U.S. Surgeon (1st IA Cav.) Charles H. Lothrop
Cross between Texas horses and mustangs. Aged about 5 years in early 1865 when purchased in gold for equivalent of $5,000 Confederate bills. Died about 30 years in 1890. Originally a racer. Lothrop shod the horse only once and had to remove the shoes as the horse was not accustomed to them.[80]

Billy— U.S. Col. (105th PA Inf.) Amor A. McKnight
Gelding, bay. Ridden by a Lt. McHenry, was one of 7 horses in the 1st (steeplechase) of 3 races held in celebration of St. Patrick's Day on March 17, 1863, at Falmouth, VA, near the HQ of Gen. David B. Birney.[81]

Billy— U.S. Col. (9th IL Mtd. Inf.) August Mersey
While leading the 2nd Brig., 2nd Div., XV Corps, in an attack on Bald Hill during the Battle of Atlanta, this horse was killed and Mersey wounded. The colonel exclaimed, "Oh, my poor Billy! My poor Billy!"[82]

Billy— CS Sgt. (2nd SC Cav.) William A. "Bill" Mickler
Fast horse.[83]

Billy—U.S. Chaplain (37th MA Inf.) Frank C. Morse
  In use November 1862 in VA.[84]

Billy—U.S. Chaplain (72nd NY Inf.) Levi Warren Norton
  Male. His favorite.[85]

Billy—U.S. Col. (5th NY Cav.) James Penfield
  A Morgan.[86]

Billy—U.S. Maj. (87th PA Inf.) Noah G. Ruhl
  In use from May 1863, when Ruhl was promoted to major.[87]

Billy—CS Brig. Gen. Claudius Wistar Sears
  During the December 1864 Battle of Nashville, Gen. Sears was wounded in the left
  leg when a shot passed through Billy whom he had ridden throughout the entire war.
  Standing on one foot, Sears was heard exclaiming, "Poor Billy! Poor Billy!"[88]

Billy—U.S. Col. (57th PA Inf.) Peter Sides
  According to Davis, *Life of David Bell Birney*:
  Ridden by Col. C.H.T. Collis, one of 12 horses in the 2nd (steeplechase) race held in
  celebration of St. Patrick's Day on March 17, 1863, at Falmouth, VA, near the HQ of
  Gen. David B. Birney. Billy slipped in the mud on the last turn but got up and finished
  the course without the rider.[89]

Billy—U.S. Saddler Sgt. (1st OH Cav.) George W. Spielman
  Having loaned this horse to a Sgt. Chapin to go out on picket, Spielman was captured
  on July 25, 1862, near Courtland, AL, when the camp was attacked.[90]

Billy—U.S. Maj. Gen. George H. Thomas
  Bay, large. Described as calm, unhurried and deliberate. Named after Thomas's friend,
  Maj. Gen. William T. Sherman.[91]

Billy—U.S. Col. (1st NY Art.) Charles Shiels Wainwright
  While on the way to Gettysburg, this horse threw two shoes, forcing Wainwright to
  stop at a farmhouse and have his battery's forge shoe it.[92]

Billy—U.S. Capt. (125th OH Inf.) E.G. Whitesides
  Bay. Killed beneath Whitesides during the September 1863 Battle of Chickamauga.[93]

Billy—U.S. Surgeon (55th MA Inf.) Burt Green Wilder
  Male. In use 1863 through 1865 occupation duty in South Carolina.[94]

Billy—U.S. Brig. Gen. Alpheus S. Williams
  Used by Williams during the 1865 campaign in the Carolinas. On one occasion, after
  36 hours without being fed, the horse had to forage on stunted bushes and rice straw
  and became indifferent to spur or whip.[95]

Billy Bowlegs—CS 2nd Lt. (staff of Stuart) Francis Smith Robertson
  Lt. Robertson requested that his father send him this horse in a letter of July 20, 1862.
  Apparently a different horse was sent.[96]

Black—CS Brig. Gen. Rufus Clay Barringer
      CS Sgt. (5th NC Cav.) _____ Ratcliff
  Black. During the Battle of Buckland Mills, VA, on October 19, 1863, the horse tired
  and became unmanageable and threw itself and its rider against the wall of a building,

temporarily disabling then–Maj. Barringer of the 1st NC Cav.[97] Barringer was still using this horse during the 1864 Bristoe Campaign.[98] A Sgt. Ratcliff of the 5th NC Cav. captured a horse which by now Gen. Barringer persuaded the sergeant to swap to him for Black.[99]

Black Auster— CS Lt. Gen. William J. Hardee
Also referred to as "Auster" and as "Shiloh." Black. Referred to by the general as "my beautiful black," this horse was shot in one of its shoulders during the Battle of Shiloh and was featured prominently by name in the poem, "General Hardee at the Battle of Shiloh." In Hardee's 1873 funeral procession at Selma, AL.[100] (The original Black Auster was a horse in the poem "The Battle of Lake Regillus" in Thomas Babbington Macauley's *Lays of Ancient Rome*. Many black horses have been called after it.)

Black Bess— CS Brig. Gen. John Hunt Morgan
Also referred to as "Bess." Mare, deep glossy black with thoroughbred points, 15 hands high. Perhaps a blend of Canadian and thoroughbred. Sire was the KY saddle-horse stallion Drennan. Given to Morgan in September 1861 when he left KY by a Mr. Vila. It was captured May 6, 1862, at Lebanon, TN.[101] Subsequently "a Yankee traveled her about the country showing her at 25 cents a sight."[102] Said to have been the general's "favorite." Though the horse was not with him at the time of his death at Greenville, TN, in 1864, a picture of Morgan with this horse is included on a historic marker there.[103] A statue, *General John H. Morgan and his Bess*, is located at Lexington, KY. Believing that a hero should not be shown on a mare, the sculptor added testicles to the horse. Students at the nearby University of Kentucky sometimes paint the testicles in the school colors of blue and white. This statue and the painting of its testicles have been lampooned in an anonymous 18-stanza poem, "The Ballad of Black Bess."[104]

Black Bess— CS guerrilla (MO) James Clark Quantrill
Mare, black, a Morgan or thoroughbred. Quantrill was given this horse in March 1861, probably by a Mr. Morgan Walker. The horse had lost an eye by some accident but had a fine form, splendid qualities and was a swift runner.[105]

Black Bill— CS Col. (2nd MD Cav. Bn.) Harry A. Gilmor
A spare mount which Gilmor used near Bunker Hill, VA, in September 1864.[106]

Black Burns— see ***Burns***

Black Charley— U.S. Lt. (5th MA Battery) John B. Hyde
Coal black. Friends in New Bedford, MA, donated $200 in gold which Hyde used for the purchase of this horse in Washington, D.C., in December 1861.[107]

Black Cloud— CS Col. (GA Agent for Cotton Export) Charles A.L. Lamar
Lamar was riding this horse when he was killed during the April 1865 Battle of Columbus, GA.[108]

Black Diamond— U.S. Capt. (64th NY Inf.) Lewis H. Fassitt
Ridden by Col. Thomas Welsh on of 4 horses in the 3rd (flat course) race held March 17, 1863, in celebration of St. Patrick's Day at Falmouth, VA, near the HQ of Gen. David B. Birney.[109]

Black Dick— U.S. Pvt. (5th NY Cav.) George Black
Male, Morgan, black. Purchased at beginning of the war at Westport, NY. Captured

March 8, 1863, by Mosby's men (same time as they captured Gen. E.H. Stoughton) but escaped and returned to the regiment. Later was disabled and condemned.[110]

Black Dick—U.S. Pvt. (5th NY Cav.) Alphares H. Moore
    U.S. Pvt. (5th NY Cav.) Joseph Osier
Male, Morgan, black. Purchased at beginning of the war from Madison Clark of Westport, NY. Moore loaned it to Osier the winter of 1862–63 for picket duty. The entire picket, including Osier and Black Dick, were captured by Mosby's men.[111]

Black Hawk—CS Maj. Gen. William Brimage Bate
Morgan. Related to Sheridan's Rienzi.[112] Formerly called Canada Chief due to its Canadian pacer bloodline. When Bate was Col. of the 2nd TN Inf., at the Battle of Shiloh in early 1862, both Bate and the horse were wounded. The horse followed Bate to the hospital tent, stuck its head in the door, then walked a few paces away and fell dead.[113]

Black Jack—U.S. Maj. Gen. John A. Logan
Was in use by the general in April 1865 in NC.[114]

Black Jim—U.S. Capt. (QM Dept.) William Gates Le Duc
CS unknown unit and rider Thoroughbred, male, raven black. This horse refused to work in harness. Le Duc used it from 1862 with the Army of the Potomac and with the Army of the Cumberland until after the fall of Atlanta. He left this horse with his orderly at Atlanta when he took leave. He didn't return before Sherman left Atlanta on his march. The orderly was killed and the horse captured by Confederates in SC in early 1865.[115]

Blackhawk—U.S. Capt. (4th TN Mounted) William Hathaway
Fast—had once paced a mile in 2:30. In use in 1865.[116]

Blackie—U.S. Maj. Gen. George G. Meade
Black. Obtained December 1861 for $125 and trade of another horse. A wound during the Battle of Glendale took 18 months to heal. Meade called this his "show horse."[117]

Blackjack—CS President Jefferson Finis Davis
Said to be the president's "favorite" horse and the one depicted with Davis on the Stone Mountain Confederate Memorial near Atlanta, GA.[118]

Blake—CS Chaplain (Palmetto Sharpshooters, SC) James McDowell
Male. The chaplain rode this horse throughout the war including the Richmond battles, Second Manassas, Antietam campaign, to Tennessee and back, the Wilderness, and the retreat to Appomattox. Ridden home to South Carolina after the war. Died near Manning, SC, in 1885 and buried there. Little girls decorated the grave with flowers and ten shots were fired over the grave during services.[119]

Blenheim—U.S. Col. Richard Shackelford
    CS soldier (Morgan's cavalry) _____ Conway
Captured by CS Capt. James Matthews and awarded to Conway.[120]

Blucher—CS Maj. Gen. William Dorsey Pender
In December 1862, the general received $600 from the government for this horse, which had been killed.[121]

Bludgeon—U.S. Sgt. (1st ME Cav.) Winsor B. Smith
 After losing a horse at Gettysburg, Smith was given this one by an infantry QM. Every time he got near the horse, it would step on his feet.[122]

Blue Bird—CS Capt. (various KY commands) Edward O. Guerrant
 "Pony." In use April 1863 when Guerrant had it shod.[123]

Blue Devil—CS Brig. Gen. Richard Lee Turberville Beale
 While Beale was still Col. of the 9th VA Cav., during the Battle of Reams Station, this horse was shot in the head.[124]

Bob—U.S. Brig. Gen. Charles Russell Lowell[125]

Bob—U.S. Col. (24th KY Inf.) Charles D. Pennebaker
 Bay. Upon Pennebaker's death, this horse was remembered in a memorial poem, "My War-Horse Bob."[126]

Bob—U.S. Maj. Gen. John Sedgewick
 On July 12, 1862, the general wrote his sister that he had lost this horse, which had been with him a long time, in one of the actions of the Peninsula Campaign.[127]

Bob—see *Old Joe* (of Toland Jones and Walter G. Knight) following.

Bob—see *Old Bob* (of A. Lincoln) following.

Bob-tail—CS Pvt. (8th KY Cav.) Vincent Eastham
 This East Tennessee mountaineer was riding this "spavined nag" when he joined the unit.[128]

"Bob-Tail Bremer"—see *Bremer* following.

Bobby—U.S. Lt. Col. (51st PA Inf.) Edwin Schall
 In use 1863 in MS campaigning before Jackson and Vicksburg and May 1864 on march through VA. Also spelled Bobbie by the same source.[129]

Bonaparte—CS Capt. (12th VA Cav.) Robert W. Baylor Sr.
 CS Pvt. (12th VA Cav.) Robert W. Baylor Jr.
 CS Capt. (12th VA Cav.) George Baylor
 Also referred to as "Bony." Male. Owned and ridden by Capt. Robt. Baylor until he was wounded and captured on April 27, 1862, at McGaheysville (the horse escaped with the unit). It then went to Pvt. Robt. Baylor Jr. When he was killed in action at Parker's near Fredericksburg, Bonaparte was inherited by Capt. George Baylor, a brother. "Bony" (as George Baylor sometimes referred to it) was wounded during a skirmish May 29, 1864, at Sappony Church, Dinwiddie Co., VA, near Reams Station and died the next day.[130]

Boney—U.S. Maj. Gen. William Starke Rosecrans
 Gray. Said to be his favorite. Ridden alternately with Tobey during the Murfreesboro and Chickamauga battles.[131]

Bony—see *Bonaparte* (Baylor's) preceding.

Bony—U.S. Col. (24th WI Inf.) Charles H. Larrabee
 The Col. was using this horse in 1861.[132]

Boomerang—U.S. Brig. Gen. John McArthur
 This horse used when McArthur was Col. of the 12th IL Infantry. It was named due to its tendency to move backward.[133]

Boston— U.S. Maj. (68th PA Inf.) John A. Danks
According to Davis, *Life of David Bell Birney*:
Ridden by a Col. Crawford, one of 12 horses in the 2nd (steeplechase) race held near
the HQ of Gen. David B. Birney at Falmouth, VA, in celebration of St. Patrick's Day
on March 17, 1863.[134]

Bostona— CS 2nd Lt. (staff of Stuart) Francis Smith Robertson
Mare, thoroughbred, "long and tall." Raised by Robertson's father and sent to him in
the spring of 1863.[135] This horse almost ran away with Robertson while he was riding
her during the Battle of Brandy Station.[136] Robertson wrote in his memoirs that Bostona
was "a good-meaning, poor raw-boned creature" and he later swapped her for a large
mare which he found tied in the woods during the Gettysburg campaign.[137]

Brandy— CS Maj. (1st CS Eng.) William Willis Blackford
     CS Lt. (staff of Stuart) Theodore S. Garnett
Garnett received this horse as a swap from Blackford for Lily of the Valley.[138]

Brandy— CS Lt. (28th TX Cav. Dismtd.) Theophilus Perry
Wrote his wife March 8, 1863, from White Sulphur Springs, AR, that, since the horse
was doing poorly due to lack of fodder, he was sending it home to recuperate with
Pvt. Billy Hargrove, who had a 60-day furlough. The horse arrived home in Texas on
March 23, 1863. A month later, Perry was writing his wife to send him the horse as
he needed it.[139]

Breckinridge— CS officer (staff of Gen. Breckinridge) name unknown.[140]
     U.S. Maj. Gen. Philip Sheridan
Gray, this horse had been captured from a CS officer (whose name of the horse is
unknown) on the staff of Gen. John C. Breckinridge during the Battle of Missionary
Ridge.[141] A spare horse, it was used at Cedar Creek in addition to Rienzi.[142]

Bremer— CS Pvt. (1st MS Cav.) J.G. Deupree
During the Battle of Shiloh, while its tail was raised, a cannonball cut away half of its
tail including bone. Known in the unit as "Bob-Tail Bremer" afterwards.[143]

Brenda— CS 2nd Lt. (staff of Gen. J.E.B. Stuart) Francis Smith Robertson
Robertson requested this horse be sent to him by his father in a March 3, 1863, letter.
Instead, Bostona was sent.[144]

Brother to Brother— U.S. Lt. Col. (1st MA Cav.) H. B. Sargent
Obtained from Canada at the beginning of the war, it was an accomplished jumper
but its temper made it incompatible with cavalry service.[145]

Brown Bess— U.S. Lt. Col. (7th ME Inf.) Edwin C. Mason
Mare, brown. In May 1864, the horse's good jumping ability saved Mason from capture
by Mosby's command. Died during the 1864 Battle of the Wilderness when struck by
7 bullets.[146]

Brown Roan— CS Gen. Robert E. Lee
Also called Brownie and The Roan. Brown roan. Purchased in western Virginia in
1861, used in the Carolinas in early 1862, began to go blind during the Seven Days
Battle.[147]

Brownie— see ***Brown Roan***

Brown's Horse— U.S. Officer (1st RI Cav.) _____ Brown
CS unknown unit and rider
Fast racer. Captured Nov. 1862 near Aldie, VA. So-named by Confederates when they heard Union prisoners calling it "Brown's horse."[148]

Brydon's Nellie— U.S. Sgt. (5th NY Cav.) James Brydon
Mare, Morgan, chestnut. Prewar was used to tow canal boats on the Champlain Canal. In 1863 a hoof was hit by a shell burst. Lamed, it had to be condemned.[149]

Bucephalus— CS Capt. (4th AL Inf.) Reuben Vaughan Kidd
Gray. His favorite.[150]
(The original horse of this name was the horse of Alexander the Great of Macedon.)

Bucephalus— CS Maj. Gen. Sterling Price
Gray. Price used this horse during his fall 1864 raid into Missouri.[151]

Buckner— CS Capt. (3rd TN Inf.) Flavel Clingan Barber
In use March 1863 at Vicksburg.[152]

Bug— U.S. Lt. Col. (1st ME Cav.) Jonathan P. Cilley
Brown with an easy lope but "terrible" trot. Then-Major Cilley was riding this horse during the Bristow Station campaign.[153]

Bullet— CS Col. (15th MS Inf.) Michael Farrell
In use February 1863 in vicinity Canton, MS.[154]

Bullet— CS Maj. Gen. James Ewell Brown "Jeb" Stuart
CS Maj. (staff of Stuart) Henry Brainerd McClellan
Bay. Given to Stuart by a man from Louisa Co., VA. Used at Yellow Tavern, after which the mortally wounded Stuart gave it to McClellan.[155] Stuart never called it anything other than "Pony."[156]

Bully— U.S. Brig. Gen. George Crook
Said to be his favorite horse.[157]

Bully— U.S. Sgt. (Ringgold Cav. Bn. PA) Adam Wickerham
The horse was shot on 3 different occasions, including a cavalry skirmish near Burlington, WV, but survived 3 years of war and was taken home by Wickerham. When it died, he buried it with honors of war.[158]

Burnie— CS unknown unit and rider
U.S. Capt. (23rd MA Inf.) George M. Whipple
Captured April 1862 at New Berne, NC, and named after Gen. Ambrose E. Burnside. It was ordered turned in to the QM shortly later.[159]

Burns— U.S. Maj. Gen. George Brinton McClellan
Also known as Black Burns. Black. Named after an army friend who gave him the horse. The general rode this horse only in the mornings as it had a habit of bolting for the stable at mealtimes.[160] (Brig. Gen. William Wallace Burns had been McClellan's Chief Commissary during the 1861 West Virginia campaign.)

Burnside— U.S. 1st Lt. (2nd MA Inf.) Daniel A. Oakey
10 hands high. Raced vs. Little Mac November 22, 1862, near Sharpsburg, MD.[161]

Burnside—U.S. Brig. Gen. Orlando Bolivar Willcox
 Horse temporarily disabled during the Battle of Antietam.[162]

"Bushwack"—CS Capt. (4th KY Cav.) Barney Giltner
 Chestnut sorrel. When Giltner obtained the horse it was "fat, sleek and handsome," but neglect by its owner soon had it emaciated and unkempt. Some vandal cut off its foretop locks and cut its tail hairs short and square (this sort of prank was often played upon unpopular officers), after which it was known as "Bushwack" in the regiment.[163]

Butler—CS Maj. Gen. Matthew Galbraith Butler
      CS Maj. Gen. Wade Hampton
 Bay. A good jumper, it had been presented to Hampton by Gen. Butler, who had served as a colonel under Hampton early in the war. At Appomattox, Hampton won a jumping contest over U.S. Maj. Gen. Hugh Judson Kilpatrick's Old Spot.[164]

Butler—CS Pvt. (1st NC Cav.) George J. Handley[165]

Caesar—CS Brig. Gen. Henry Gray
 Big. Asked after the Battle of Mansfield if he had not thought that the Yankees would get him, Gray responded that he had been afraid that "they might get Caesar."[174]

Caesar—U.S. Capt. (staff of Gen. von Gilsa) Frederick Otto von Fritsch
 Bay. Purchased for $400, this horse was an excellent jumper. Used at Chancellorsville; when its nose was torn off by a piece of shell, von Fritsch had to shoot it thrice in order to put it down.[175]

Calamity—CS Pvt. (4th LA Cav.) James A. Stone
 Replaced May 1864 by Prosperity following.[166]

Calico—U.S. Chaplain (1st DE Inf.) Thomas G. Murphy
 Piebald. Wounded while being ridden during the Battle of Antietam by Lt. J.P. Postles, the regimental acting adjutant.[167]

Cam—U.S. Surgeon (5th MI Inf.) Moses Gunn
 Gunn was using the horse during 1861 in the vicinity of Alexandria, VA.[168]

Camelback—U.S. Pvt. (15th PA Cav.) Howard E. Buzby
 In use in March and April 1865 during Stoneman's Raid in western North Carolina.[169]

Captain—CS Maj. Gen. Wade Hampton
 Hampton was riding this horse during the Battle of Brandy Station.[170]

Captain—U.S. Brig. Gen. Thomas Kilby Smith
 Male, bay. In use April 17, 1862, near Shiloh.[171]

Captive—CS unknown unit and rider
      U.S. Chaplain (5th NY Inf.) Gordon Wilson
 Male. Captured by Zouaves near Hampton, VA, in August 1861.[172]

Castle Thunder—CS Pvt. (16th MS Inf.) David Holt
 Paroled prisoner Holt was using this horse to return to his unit in VA when he lost it near Brookhaven, MS.[173]

Censor—CS civilian (SC) Thomas Puryear of "Carter's Farm"
      U.S. (2nd Brig., 4th Div., XV Corps)
 One of two racehorses captured near Camden, SC, on February 21, 1865, when Col.

Robert N. Thomas's brigade approached the town from the north and encountered Puryear fleeing north with his animals.[176] Later, Confederate cavalry encountered the Union troops racing the two horses.[177]

Champ — CS Lt. Gen. Ambrose Powell Hill

    CS Sgt. (staff of Hill) George W. Tucker

Stallion, gray. Hill acquired this horse at the Cedar Mountain battlefield and rode it exclusively thereafter. When Hill was killed in action at Petersburg in March 1865, Sgt. Tucker, his courier, changed to this horse and reported Hill's death to Lee. Tucker rode the animal for the remaining weeks of the war.[178]

Champ — CS Capt. (43rd VA Cav. Bn.) William Rowley Smith

    CS Pvt. (43rd VA Cav. Bn.) John William Munson

After Smith's death in battle in January 1864, Munson purchased the horse.[179]

Chancellor — CS Maj. Gen. James Ewell Brown "Jeb" Stuart

Bay. Shot jumping over the Hazel Grove breastworks at Chancellorsville. Died soon thereafter at the home of Stuart's cousin, Alexander H.H. Stuart.[180]

Chancellor — CS Sgt. (3rd Richmond Howitzers) George D. Thaxton

Colt. So named after following its dam through battles including Chancellorsville.[181]

Charlemagne — U.S. Brig. Gen. Joshua Lawrence Chamberlain

This horse was wounded three times while Chamberlain was astride it. The 2nd wound was in the foreleg on November 17, 1863, near Warrenton, VA. The 3rd wound was on March 29, 1864, near Petersburg when a bullet passed through the horse's neck muscle and then also wounded the general. Chamberlain rode this horse during the Grand Review of the Army of the Potomac in Washington at the war's end.[182]

Charley — CS Capt. (staff of J.H. Morgan) Edward O. Guerrant

Gray. Used during the October 11, 1863, East TN Battle of Rheatown. Had distemper in May 1864 when Guerrant called it "now my favorite."[183]

Charley — U.S. Brig. Gen. Rufus King

Male, thoroughbred.[184]

Charley — U.S. Col. (11th NJ Inf.) Robert McAllister

In use from 1861 (when McAllister was Lt. Col. of the 1st NJ Inf) through at least 1863, the horse was sick with lung fever for a period during April 1863. McAllister directed his wife that if he should die, this horse should be taken home for the children to ride.[185]

Charley — U.S. Maj. (55th MA Inf.) Charles W. Phifer

Died 1865 while on occupation duty in South Carolina.[186]

Charley — CS guerrilla (MO) William Clark Quantrill

Brown. Acquired at the Battle of Independence, MO, it was ridden by Quantrill from Lawrence, KS, through the end of the war. It became a vicious animal, controllable only by Quantrill — it would strike, bite, kick and squeal when approached by others. A few days before Quantrill's death in 1865 in Kentucky, the horse was accidentally hamstrung while its shoes were being pared,[187] with the main tendon of its right hind-leg cut.[188]

Charley — U.S. Lt. Col. (2nd RI Inf.) Elisha Hunt Rhodes

A Canadian. Purchased November 19, 1863, at Camp Sedgwick, VA. Described by Rhodes as "tough and just the kind of beast I need for rough work."[189]

Charley—U.S. Pvt. (5th NY Cav.) Hiram Underhill
  CS unit and rider unknown
Male, Morgan, bay, 16 hands high. Raised prewar by Frank Dudley of Crown Point, NY. Developed a sore back and was thereafter used to pull an ambulance. Captured June 30, 1863, near Hanover, PA.[190]

Charlie—U.S. Maj. Gen. Nathaniel Prentis Banks
Wounded at Battle of Cedar Mountain, 1862. Loaned by Banks to Gen. U.S. Grant during his summer 1863 visit to New Orleans. Grant described it as "viscious and little-used." It threw Grant over its head when startled, causing serious injury to the general.[191]

Charlie—U.S. Sgt. (Signal Corps) Allen D. "Frank" Frankenberry
In use during Stoneman's March 1865 raid in western NC.[192]

Charlie—U.S. Maj. Gen. Oliver Otis Howard
In early April 1862 during the Peninsula campaign. Howard unsuccessfully tried to jump a creek on this horse and they became mired. The horse was able to free itself.[193]

Charlie—U.S. Col. (18th NH Inf.) Thomas Leonard Livermore
Could race the quarter-mile with a rider on its back in 25 seconds. Livermore was often challenged to race his horse against others.[194]

Charlie—CS Chaplain (2nd VA Cav.) Randolph Harrison McKim
Bay, little, "blooded," of Messenger stock, formerly the horse of McKim's wife. McKim encountered it by accident in the possession of a soldier in the late spring of 1863 near Staunton, VA. He swapped his own horse (a bay Morgan named Roy) for it, promising the other soldier it would not be used in battle but sent to his wife. After Gettysburg, he did send it via a furloughed soldier, but it arrived weeks later in "deplorable" condition and almost totally blind. It was therefore useless to his wife, so McKim decided to use it himself with the army. Though blind, the horse was used throughout Early's 1864 campaigns.[195]

Charlie—U.S. Brig. Gen. James Dada Morgan
Bay. In use during the Atlanta Campaign.[196]

Charlie—U.S. Col. (67th OH Inf.) Marcus M. Spiegel
Presented to Spiegel in October 1862 by Chicago friends while visiting there.[197]

Charly—U.S. Brig. Gen. John White Geary
Black. Died late 1864 near Milledgeville, GA.[198]

Chester—CS Col. (25th SC Inf.) John G. Pressley
  CS Maj. (25th SC Inf.) Thomas J. Glover
When Pressley was seriously wounded at Walthall Junction about the Petersburg lines in May 1864, he instructed that this horse be turned over to Maj. Glover.[199]

Chickamauga—CS Gen. Braxton Bragg
After his September 1863 victory in the Battle of Chickamauga, Walthall's Brigade presented Bragg with a horse which they had given this name.[200]

Chickamauga—CS Maj., name and unit unknown
  U.S. Brig. Gen. Daniel McCook
After the September 1863 Battle of Chickamauga, the horse of a captured Confederate major was given to McCook and afterwards known as McCook's "Chickamauga pacer."[201]

Chickamauga— CS Brig. Gen. Alfred Jefferson Vaughan Jr.

While Vaughan was at winter quarters, Dalton, GA, upon his promotion to Brig. Gen. in late 1863, his old regiment (13th TN Inf.) purchased this horse of Gray Eagle stock for $3,000 and presented it to him.[202]

China— U.S. Capt. (1st ME Cav.) John A. Heald

His "favorite." Heald was using the horse during the 1865 Battle of Sailor's Creek.[203]

Cincinnati— U.S. Lt. Gen. Ulysses Simpson Grant

Bay, large (17.5 hands high per some sources). Son of Lexington (Sherman's horse), which was said to be fastest thoroughbred in the United States. Called by Grant a "fine trotter" and "the finest horse that I have ever seen." A Mr. S.S. Grant of St. Louis gave the horse to Grant (the general was visiting his son Frederick there) with the stipulation that it never be mistreated. Grant rarely let others ride the animal with exceptions being President Lincoln and Admiral Jacob Ammen. In 1865, Grant refused an offer of $10,000 for the horse. It accompanied Grant to the White House when Grant became president. The horse died at the Maryland home of Admiral Ammen in 1878.[204]

Cincinnatus— CS Maj. Gen. John Bankhead Magruder

On September 26, 1864, District of Texas commander Magruder rode this horse while inspecting Walker's Texas Division at Monticello, AR.[205]

Clay—CS Lt. Col. (41st AL Inf.) Theodore Gilliard Trimmier

Male, claybank with black mane and long tail. Trimmier obtained the horse at Murfreesboro, TN, and used it in the campaigns of Murfreesboro, Chickamauga, Knoxville, and Petersburg until his own death on March 31, 1865, at White Oak Road, VA. For the final two weeks of war, the horse was used by a "Mr. Waiters" (not on unit rolls), who was cook and hostler for Trimmier. Waiters rode the horse back to Pickens Co., AL, and turned it over to the Lt. Col.'s widow and 5 young children. When Mrs. Trimmier removed to MS, she gave the horse to "a good colored man" who promised to care for it and to never sell the horse to another.[206]

Claybank— U.S. Lt. Gen. Ulysses Simpson Grant

Also called "Old Yellow"— so dubbed by men of the 31st IL Inf. because of its claybank color.Purchased by Grant just before leaving IL (while Col. of the 31st IL Inf.) on an expedition into MO. It proved unserviceable and Jack was purchased.[207]

Clifton— CS Asst. Surgeon Gen. William Rhodes Capehart

Male, Morgan, bright chestnut, 15.25 hands high, 960 lbs. American Morgan Horse Registry #457. Foaled 1852. Bred by William Bellows of Walpole, NH. Sired by Hale's Green Mountain Morgan out of chestnut mare Gifford Morgan. At 3 months sold to Silas Hale of South Royalston, MA; at 18 months to S.H. Edgerly of Manchester, NH; and soon thereafter to F.H. Lyford, who owned it until at least 1857. Won a 5-mile walk race at Manchester, NH, in September 1857. Prior to the Civil War, sold to North Carolinian Capehart, who was attending a medical school in VA when the war began. This horse was killed in a cavalry engagement near Cheraw, SC, in 1864.[208]

Clodhopper— U.S. Col. (1st MA Cav.) Robert Williams

This horse, a fine steeplechaser, was obtained in Canada by officers of the regiment and presented to Williams at the beginning of the regiment. The Col. used it seldom since it turned out to be almost useless as a cavalry charger.[209]

Cockeye— U.S. Lt. Col. (5th NY Cav.) James A. Penfield
Morgan. Penfield was captured and the horse killed July 6, 1863, at Hagerstown, MD.[210]

Coldwater— U.S. Brig. Gen. Orlando Bolivar Willcox
In use May 1861 about Washington, D.C.[211]

Colonel— U.S. Maj. Gen. Joseph Hooker
A "big, white horse." The animal was wounded at the Williamsburg and Antietam battles.[212]

Comet— CS Maj. (staff of Gen. J.E.B. Stuart) William Willis Blackford
(Blackford was, late in the war, promoted to Lt. Col., 1st CS Engineers.)
Male, dark mahogany bay (almost brown) with black mane, tail and legs and a white star on his forehead, compact but powerful build. His sire was Hamlet out of a daughter of Prima Donna. A 1st cousin of Magic. Used from the beginning of the war until the Battle of Chantilly in 1862, when it was wounded by a piece of an exploding shell that struck it in the neck. Though Comet recovered, this grievous wound prevented its further use during the war.[213]

Coquette— CS Lt. Col. (43rd VA Cav. Bn.) John Singleton Mosby
Thoroughbred. Purchased October 1864 by Mosby's men from proceeds of the "Greenback Raid" and presented to Mosby.[214]

Cornwall— U.S. Maj. Gen. John Sedgewick
Named for the general's hometown of Cornwall, CT. In use at Gettysburg.[215]

Crampton— U.S. Brig. Gen. William Francis Bartlett
After the 1862 Battle of Crampton's Gap, MD, Bartlett renamed one of his horses this.[216]

Croppie— U.S. (Army of the James) unknown
Had had some success on race tracks at Washington, D.C., so soldiers used this horse in races.[217]

Cuffy— CS Lt. Gen. Richard Heron Anderson[218]

Custis Lee— U.S. Brig. Gen. George Armstrong Custer
Pacer. After it was captured at the 1865 Battle of Five Forks, Custer acquired this smooth-gaited animal for his wife.[219] Custer went on a solo buffalo hunt near the Smokey Hill River of Kansas in 1867. During the chase, a buffalo turned on him and Custer accidentally discharged his pistol, killing this horse, which was his wife's favorite.[220]

Cyclops— U.S. 1st Lt. (54th MA Inf.) John Ritchie
Capt. Charles E. Tucker used this horse of Quartermaster Ritchie during a skirmish at Mill Branch, SC, during Potter's Raid in April 1865.[221]

Dahlgren— U.S. Col. (Army of the Potomac Cavalry Corps) Ulric Dahlgren
　　　CS unknown unit and rider
Supposed to have been the horse ridden by Dahlgren at Hagerstown, MD, and when he was wounded at Gettysburg. He used it during the Kilpatrick-Dahlgren

Raid of February 1864. It was later observed on a VA farm, where Union soldiers heard it being called by this name. It was taken to Washington but became sick and died.[222]

Dan— CS Brig. Gen. Richard Lee Turberville Beale

Bay. While Col. of the 9th VA Cav., Beale used this horse during Stuart's ride around McClellan's Army of the Potomac in 1862.[223]

Dan— U.S. Col. (116th NY Inf.) Edwin P. Chapin

Stallion, KY thoroughbred, black. This horse was a gift to Chapin from E.P. Dorr of Buffalo, NY, and officers of the regiment upon at the time of organization.[224]

Dan— U.S. Brig. Gen. Alexander Hays

Killed during the Battle of Gettysburg.[225]

Dandy— U.S. Maj. (36th WI Inf.) Harvey M. Brown

Cream-colored, KY bred.[226]

Dandy— U.S. Brig. Gen. George Armstrong Custer[227]

Dandy— U.S. Bugler (1st NJ Art. Bty. B) Toddy Williams

During the Chancellorsville Campaign, this horse reared up, striking Williams on the head with his forefeet and knocking him out of the saddle.[228]

Daniel Webster— U.S. Maj. Gen. George Brinton McClellan

Sometimes referred to as "Devil Dan."[229] Dark bay, large. A favorite, the horse had been presented to McClellan by Joseph Alsop and other "railroad friends" of Cincinnati. Was in use during the Battle of Antietam.[230]

Decatur— U.S. Maj. Gen. Philip Kearny

Light bay. Killed during the Battle of Seven Pines when shot through the neck.[231]

Dendy— U.S. Maj. (118th PA Inf.) Charles P. Herring

The horse was loaned to Capt. Francis Adams Donaldson during the Battle of Bristoe Station.[232]

"Devil Dan"— see *Daniel Webster* preceding.

Dick— U.S. Surgeon (11th U.S. Inf.) John Shaw Billings

Used 1861–62 while Billings was assigned to a general hospital in Washington and after assigned to the 11th. Sold to the QM for $140 on December 4, 1863.[233]

Dick— CS Maj. (Good's/Douglas's TX Arty. Battery) James Postell Douglas

Obtained from a stock farm in KY in fall 1862 as Bragg's army was falling back.[234]

Dick— U.S. Col. (9th MA Inf.) Patrick T. Hanley

Was used fording the North Ana River (at Jericho Ford), VA, in 1864.[235]

Dick— U.S. Lt. (staff of Gibbon) Frank Aretas Haskell

This was the 2nd horse that Haskell rode during the Battle of Gettysburg. On the 3rd day it was struck repeatedly; its right thigh was ripped open by a piece of a shell, and 3 bullets lodged deep in its body.[236]

Dick— U.S. Lt. (24th NY Inf.) Robert Oliver Jr.

Male. Foaled about 1852. Presented to Oliver by friends at the beginning of the war. When the officer died of illness during the war, he asked his father to care for Dick.

The father rode the horse postwar in 4th of July parades in Oswego, NY. The horse died 1885 at age 33. One hoof is preserved by the Oswego County Historical Society.[237]

Dick— U.S. Lt. Col. (57th NY Inf.) Philip J. Parisen

When killed in action at Antietam, Parisen was riding this horse.[238]

Dick— CS Pvt. (TX Cav.) A.E. Rentfrow

In 1862 from Fort Chadbourne, TX, Rentfrow wrote his sister that he had been involved in racing since he'd arrived. He had lost much money racing this horse and had bet it on a future race.[239]

Dick— U.S. Capt. (2nd NY Lt. Arty.) Jacob Roemer

In use 1863 during Siege of Vicksburg.[240]

Dick Ewell— CS Col. (6th LA Inf.) Isaac G. Seymour

This horse was hit in the leg during the Battle of the Wilderness.[241]

Dick Turpin— CS Maj. (staff of Longstreet) Thomas Jewett Goree

"A perfect little mustang of a horse."[242]

Dicks— CS Capt. (various KY commands) Edward O. Guerrant

The horse was sick during April 1863.[243]

Dixie— CS Brig. Gen. Edward Porter Alexander

"A rather large dark bay." Purchased at the beginning of the war. During the 2nd day at Gettysburg, the horse received a severe gash from a shell fragment. During the Battle of Spotsylvania, a piece of shell about 2 inches square struck the horse in the neck. A captain observed that the horse was mortally wounded and inquired if it should be put down. Alexander initially agreed but then changed his mind. An examination found that it was only a flesh wound and the horse recovered in about 6 weeks. Postwar, it accompanied Alexander to Washington, GA.[244]

Dixie— CS Maj. Gen. Patrick Ronayne Cleburne

Killed (struck by a cannonball[245]) at 1862 Battle of Perryville while Cleburne was mounted upon it.[246]

Dixie— CS Maj. (staff of Gen. T.J. Jackson and others) Henry Kyd Douglas.[247]

Dixie— CS Sgt. Manson Sherrill Jolly

Purported alternate name for Ironsides following.

Dixie— CS Maj. Gen. Fitzhugh Lee

Bay. While Lt. Col. of the 1st VA Cav., Lee was using this horse February 1862 in the vicinity of Falls Church, VA.[248]

Dixie— CS Brig. Gen. Lewis Henry Little

The Missourian began the war in April 1861 riding this horse.[249]

Doc— CS Lt. (3rd SC Inf.) Y.J. Pope

Survived the war.[250]

Doll— U.S. Chaplain (148th PA Inf.) William Henry Stephens

Second horse obtained and used as his pack horse.[251]

Dolly— U.S. Chaplain (52nd MA Inf.) John Farwell Moors

Too lame to use. Moors had to borrow another horse on March 5, 1862, to deliver the regiment's mail.[252]

Dolly— CS Sgt. (2nd VA Cav.) Robert W. Parker
    On May 17, 1862, in use at Madison Court House, VA.[253]

Dolly— U.S. Maj. Gen. William Tecumseh Sherman (as Dolly)
        CS Lt. (arty. Section, Gen. J. R. Chalmers' Div.) James Bleecker (as Sherman)
Confederates captured this horse on a train, which Sherman had only recently exited, at Collierville, TN, on October 11, 1863. Sherman obtained another horse from the area, which the owner tried to reclaim from him. Sherman related that he gave the man a note on CS Gen. Chalmers for Dolly. Meeting Sherman after the war, Chalmers told him that the man had hunted him down and tried to present the note.[254] After the capture, Bleecker's servant, Burton, named it Sherman and would boast, "Master captured old Sherman."[255]

Don— CS Pvt. (2nd SC Cav.) J. Stanyard "Jack" Shoolbred
        U.S. Lt. (8th IL Cav.) George A. Gamble
Bay with black legs. Ridden from the beginning of the war by Shoolbred until both were captured by the 8th IL Cav. in Prince William County, VA, in late 1863. It was thereafter ridden by the adjutant of the 8th IL Cavalry.[256]

Don Juan— U.S. Brig. Gen. George Armstrong Custer
Thoroughbred, dark mottled gray, 4-mile racer. Captured by Custer's scouts from a stud farm just prior to the surrender at Appomattox. Custer rode it during the Grand Review at Washington after the war and then sent it to his home at Monroe, MI. It was exhibited at a state fair, where it killed a groom. The horse died a year later of heart disease.[257]

Draco— CS Capt. (4th AL Inf.) Reuben Vaughan Kidd[258]

Duff Green— CS Capt. (escort bn., Gen. Jas. R. Chalmers) Bill Tucker
Male. Actually the horse of his brother, Fenton Tucker, it was recognizable throughout the division because of its gait. In late 1864, while being used by the captain in a charge near the Duck River of Tennessee, it was killed when a cedar tree's sharp limb pierced it.[259]

Duke— CS Maj. Gen. Stephen Dodson Ramseur[260]

Dunlap's Mare— U.S. Pvt. (5th NY Cav.) Robert Dunlap
Mare, Morgan, bay. Raised at Crown Point, NY. Was stunned by a shot in the head at Hagerstown, MD, during a charge July 6, 1863, but arose and ran to Union lines. During Wilson's 1864 raid she became tired out and was ordered to be put down, but the sergeant so instructed instead left her grazing in a pasture.[261]

Ebony— U.S. Maj. Gen. Benjamin Franklin Butler
Stallion. Loaned to Pres. Lincoln during his March 1864 visit to the Army of the James, it bolted while the President was riding it.[262]

Eclipse— U.S. Maj. Gen. Daniel Edgar Sickles
        U.S. Maj. Gen. David Bell Birney
Presented to Birney by Sickels. Led by Birney's servant in Birney's Philadelphia funeral procession in October 1864.[263]

Education—CS Pvt. (1st NC Cav.) Rufus Winfield Colvard
So named since Colvard had been a school teacher in Ashe and Wilkes Counties, NC.[264]

Edward—Black Prince—CS Capt. (various KY commands) Edward O. Guerrant
In April 1862 it had been debilitated but was improved after grazing.[265]

Edward the Black Prince—CS Dr. (9th KY Inf., Mtd.) Walter J. Byrne
In use in GA in January 1865. Sore-backed at that time.[266]

Egypt—U.S. Lt. Gen. Ulysses S. Grant
Called "a good saddle horse" by Grant, it was purchased as a gift for Grant by citizens
of southern Illinois (an area referred to as "Egypt") in January 1864.[267] It was being used
during the 1864 crossing of the Topotomy.[268] Accompanied Grant to the White House.[269]

Elizabeth—U.S. Lt. Col. (14th CT Inf.) Sanford H. Perkins
Mare. This war horse appeared at an 1887 meeting in New Britain, CT, to raise money
for decoration of Southern battlefields.[270]

Ephraim—U.S. Sgt. (1st MA Cav.) _____ Coolidge
A Canadian with long hair on its fetlocks and a thick mane and tail. "Always fat."
During the crossing of the Pamukey River on June 27, 1864, it was stolen.[271]

Excelsior—U.S. Brig. Gen (ex–Col. NY Inf.) Nelson Appleton Miles
"A splendid Kentucky charger." During an artillery duel September 16, 1862, during
the Antietam Campaign, the horse was pierced by a shell and so mutilated that it had
to be shot at once.[272]

Faderland—U.S. Col. (7th NY Inf.) George W. von Schaik
Ridden by himself, this horse won 2 straight heats over 6 others in the 1st (a steeplechase) race near the HQ of Gen. David B. Birney at Falmouth, VA, on March 17, 1863,
in celebration of St. Patrick's Day.[273] ("Faderland" translates from German as "father-
land.")

Fan—CS Maj. Gen. William Dorsey Pender
Mare. So lame he couldn't ride her in September 1861. In April 1863, Pender determined
to sell her since she had gotten into the habit of eating the tails of other horses.[274]

Fancy—CS Lt. Gen. Thomas Jonathan "Stonewall" Jackson
Also referred to as "Little Sorrel" and "Old Sorrel," though Jackson himself never called
it anything other than Fancy.[275] During its time at the Virginia Military Institute,
when referred to in the minutes of the Institute's Board of Visitors by a name, Fancy
was the only name ever used.[276] Descriptions include a Morgan, 15 hands high,[277] gelding, small, well-rounded, chestnut sorrel, "hue of gingerbread," rawboned and gaunt,
"ugly,"[278] round and fat, compactly built, and well-formed. The horse was raised by
Noah Collins of Somers, CT, and sold to the Union army early in the Civil War.[279]
While occupying Harpers Ferry in 1861, Jackson's force seized a train that had one car
loaded with horses. From these, Jackson selected 2—a large sorrel gelding (see Big
Sorrel) and a smaller sorrel gelding for his wife, which he named Fancy. Finding that
the larger horse was skittish and had a hard gait, he kept the smaller one as well. The
horse had great endurance and was never known to fatigue.[280] The horse had been lost
or stolen when the Antietam Campaign began but was recovered soon after the battle.[281]

When mortally wounded by friendly fire at Chancellorsville, Jackson was riding Fancy. Also wounded, the horse galloped off toward the enemy lines. A few days later it was recovered by Pvt. Thomas R. Yeatman of Stuart's horse artillery.[282] After Chancellorsville, the horse accompanied Mrs. Anna Jackson to the Morrison family farm, where she, her children and the horse lived for several years.[283] Later the horse was sent to the Virginia Military Institute, where Jackson had taught before the war.[284] It was exhibited at numerous fairs and veterans' reunions. In 1880, the horse was taken to the state fair at Richmond, VA, by the Corps of Cadets, who posted a special guard to prevent the taking of hair from his mane or tail for souvenirs.[285] In 1883, Fancy may have participated in the June 28, 1883, parade for the unveiling of the Recumbent Lee statue at Washington and Lee University in Lexington.[286] It then resided at the R.E.

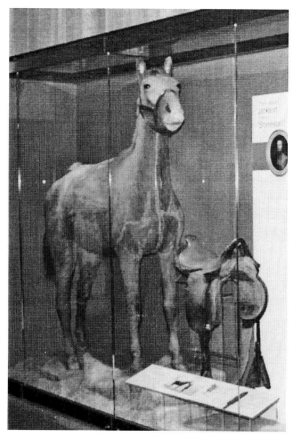

Mounted hide of Jackson's Fancy (courtesy Virginia Military Institute Museum, Lexington, Virginia).

Lee Camp Soldiers' Home for a time. By then he was in poor health and unable to stand, so a sling was made so he could be hoisted to his feet. Fancy broke his back when the sling broke and he fell. He died at age 36 on March 16, 1886. Frederic S. Webster of Washington, D.C., who had participated in the mounting of both Sheridan's Rienzi and Lee's Traveller, began the preservation of the horse's remains. He was allowed to retain the bones in payment for his services. Mounted into an articulated skeleton, they were given to the Carnegie Institute in Pittsburgh, PA. In 1948, that institute permanently loaned the skeleton to VMI and later made it an outright gift.[287] The skeleton was displayed in a biology classroom for almost 40 years until a new biology department building was completed in 1989, at which time they were placed in storage.[288] The United Daughters of the Confederacy campaigned for the bones to be buried.[289] The bones were cremated to simplify burial in a small coffin, and on July 20, 1997, they were buried at the foot of the Stonewall Jackson statue on the VMI parade ground.[290] Fancy's hide had a different journey. Webster used a then-new method of tanning the skin and mounting it on a plaster frame. This work was completed in 1886.[291] The stuffed hide was displayed at the R.E. Lee Camp Soldier's Home, which the U.D.C. inherited in 1935. State funding for the home ceased in 1949 after the death of the last veteran housed there, and the U.D.C. gave the hide to the VMI Museum. It became a popular attraction and students often rubbed its flank "for luck" or pulled a hair from the horse's mane or tail. As the hide became threadbare, a Plexiglas enclosure was built around it.[292] Restoration work on Fancy's hide was completed in 2007. In 1992, "Little Sorrel Lane" was dedicated in a Sommers, CT, subdivision.[293]

Fancy— U.S. Maj. Gen. John Fulton Reynolds
Stallion, black.[294] The general was riding this horse when he was mortally wounded at Gettysburg.[295]

Fannie— U.S. Surgeon (121st NY Inf.) Daniel M. Holt[296]

Fannie— CS Gen. Joseph Eggleston Johnston
Thoroughbred, gray. Never wounded, it survived the war.[297]

Fanny— U.S. Maj. Gen. John Gibbon
Gray. In use at Gettysburg.[298] (Gibbon's wife, Frances, was nicknamed "Fannie.")

Fanny— CS Pvt. (4th AL Cav.) John Allen Wyeth
Thoroughbred. Use began in March 1863.[299]

Fasco— U.S. Col. (8th NY Inf.)
        Felix Constantin Alexander Johann Nepomuk, Prince zu Salm-Salm
Salm-Salm rode his own horse against 6 others in the 1st (steeplechase) race held near the Falmouth, VA, HQ of Gen. David B. Birney on March 17, 1863, celebrating St. Patrick's Day. Fasco stumbled and threw Salm-Salm in the first heat.[300]

Faugh-a-Ballagh— U.S. Col. (88th NY Inf.) Patrick Kelly[301]
The name is from the motto of the 26th MA Inf. of the Irish Brigade of the Army of the Potomac, of which Kelly was sometime commander. It translates "Here We Go!"

Faugh-a-Ballaugh—U.S. Brig. Gen. William Harris Lytle
While he was commanding the 10th OH Inf. at the Battle of Carnifax Ferry in WV on September 10, 1861, a Minié ball passed through Lytle's leg, then entered and killed this horse.[302]

Fink— CS Maj. Gen. Earl Van Dorn
When transferred to Texas late in 1861, Van Dorn took at least two horses with him, but at New Orleans he sold one of them (but not Fink), with the money to be sent to his wife.[303]

Fire-Eater— CS Gen. Albert Sidney Johnston
(Some sources spell the name Fireeater, but the general's son used the hyphen.) Thoroughbred, bay. Johnston was riding this horse when mortally wounded at the Battle of Shiloh. The horse was shot in 4 places during the same battle but survived.[304]

Firefly— CS Maj. Gen. Robert Emmett Rodes[305]

Fleeta— CS spy Belle Boyd
Her favorite mount, it was trained to kneel at command. Prompt obedience to this command enabled Boyd to evade detection on several occasions.[306] (Some sources spell the name Fleeter, but this is in error, as both her biographer Sigaud and Henry Kyd Douglas[307] use Fleeta.)

Fleeter— erroneous spelling; see Fleeta immediately preceding.

Fleetfoot— CS Lt. Col. (staff of Gen. R.E. Lee) Walter H. Taylor
Used at Gettysburg.[308]

Fly— U.S. Pvt. (1st IN Cav.) George M. Barrett
Later referred to as "Old Fly." Mare, darker-colored with dark mane and tail and a white star on its forehead. Purchased with its dam by Posey Co., IN, farmer G.A. Barrett in 1855 when a new colt. Named by Barrett's son, George M., who took the 6-year-old horse with him when he enlisted in the 1st IN Cav. (one of the few Union cavalry units in which the men were allowed to provide their own mounts) on July 21, 1861. Service was in several campaigns for control of the Mississippi River. On one occasion, when surrounded by Confederates, Barrett escaped by jumping the horse off a bluff into a river and swimming across. At the end of his 3-year term of service, the government offered him $150 for the horse. He declined and took Fly back to the family farm. The horse performed farm work from then on and appeared at local parades and veterans' reunions. As it aged, it was sometimes referred to as Old Fly. The horse died at about age 39 in 1893. The tail was kept by the family for over 100 years. The tail and bones are exhibited at the Working Men's Institute at New Harmony, IN. Subject of the book, *Fly Like the Wind*.[309]

Fly by Night— CS Lt. Gen. James Longstreet
While serving in Tennessee, Longstreet was sent this horse from VA by Gen. Lee.[310]

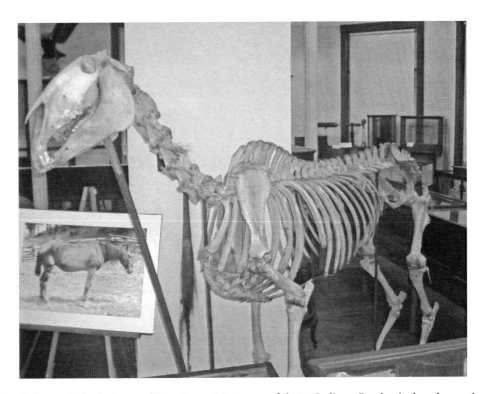

The skeleton of Fly, the horse of Pvt. George M. Barrett of the 1st Indiana Cavalry, is the sole remaining complete skeleton of a Civil War equine (photograph by Stephen Cochran, courtesy New Harmony Working Men's Institute, New Harmony, Indiana).

Flying Ant— CS Lt. (1st GA Regulars) John Porter Fort

Mare. In 1861 or 1862 while a Pvt. in a FL coastal defense cavalry company, Fort traded his original horse Red Robin for this one, which was considered to be a very vicious and dangerous animal, but he was able to break her of bad habits. When he joined the infantry in January 1863, he sold this horse to a resident of Quincy, FL, for $55 in gold, which he never received.[311]

Folko—U.S. Lt. (5th MA Battery) W. S. Appleton

Dark-colored. Used during the Battle of Five Forks in 1865 and during the Grand Review of the Army on May 22, 1865. Sent home by express. Won a prize of $25 and a diploma at the New England Horse Fair held at Saugas, MA.[312]

4th Alabama— CS Brig. Gen. William Henry Chase Whiting

Named in honor of the 4th AL Inf., whose members raised $1,000 to purchase the horse and present it to the general.[313]

Fox— U.S. Lt. Gen. Ulysses Simpson Grant

Roan. Powerful and spirited with great endurance. Used during the Fort Donelson battles and at Shiloh.[314]

Fox— U.S. Pvt. (2nd KS State Militia) Samuel J. Reader

Used during the October 1864 Battle of Westport (MO).[315]

Francis Marion— U.S. Brig. Gen. Galusha Pennypacker

When still colonel of the 97th PA Inf. leading a brigade at Fort Gilmer, Pennypacker had this horse shot from beneath him.[316]

Frank— U.S. Capt. (5th NY Cav.) Elmer J. Barker

Male, Morgan, bay, pacer. Killed in action at Ashland Station, VA, on June 1, 1864.

Frank— CS Brig. Gen. Cullen Andrews Battle

"An ancient race horse" used April 1865 by Battle at Tuskegee, AL, in escaping Wilson's Raid.[317]

Frank— U.S. Col. (148th PA Inf.) James Addams Beaver

Male. Beaver (then Lt. Col., 45th PA Inf.) purchased this horse from J. Harris Linn of the Milesburg (PA) Iron Works at the beginning of the war. When the 45th went by ship to the Carolinas, Frank was lamed seriously when thrown from the ship, but recovered enough to be ridden.[318]

Frank— U.S. Saddler (12th OH Cav.) Abraham Conger

When drawn by Conger at Lexington, KY, it was an unbroken cold, 5 or 6 years old.[319] The horse died in 1886 at age 28 with an obituary by a GAR member appearing in the *Bucyrus* (Ohio) *Journal* and was buried on a nearby farm.[320]

Frank— CS Surgeon (56th GA Inf.) George W. Peddy

Sold in Nov. 1861 to "Gen. Cooper" (unidentified) in Georgia on promise of $300.[321]

Frank Halligas—U.S. Surgeon (121st NY Inf.) Daniel M. Holt

The horse ran off during the Overland Campaign in May 1864.[322]

Frantic— CS Maj. Gen. William Henry Fitzhugh "Rooney" Lee

Brown. Though his favorite horse was an iron gray, Lee kept this horse under saddle and always available. In use 1861.[323]

Gabriel—U.S. 5th MA Battery

Male. Was never hitched on march or in battle but would always stay with the detachment's horses. Had a bad habit of rushing to water. Was eventually condemned and turned over to the QM, but one of its sometime riders (Sgt. Stiles) retrieved him. Never wounded. Among those who rode this horse were Sgt. William H. Peacock, Corp. Chase, Sgt. Stiles and Lt. Scott (at Gettysburg).[324]

Gaines' Denmark—CS (Cavalry of Gen. J.H. Morgan)

Stallion, black with white hind feet. Sired by Denmark out of the Stevenson Mare. Foaled 1851. Used in the command of Gen. John Hunt Morgan.[325] A foundation progenitor of the American Saddle Horse breed.[326] More than 60 percent of all horses in the first three registry volumes of the American Saddlebred Horse Association were traced to this horse.[327]

"Gallant Gray"—see *Tom Telegraph*

Gauley—CS Brig. Gen. Alexander Welch Reynolds

While Col. of the 58th NC Inf., Reynolds was called "Old Gauley" by his men.[328]

Gen. Sheridan—U.S. unit and rider unknown

A Shelburne Morgan.[329]

General—CS Sgt. (courier for Stuart) Benjamin Franklin Weller

    CS Maj. Gen. James Ewell Brown "Jeb" Stuart

    CS Maj. (staff of Stuart then Hampton) Andrew Reid Venable

Iron gray. Stuart purchased the horse in the winter of 1863–64 after three of his mounts had died of glanders. He was riding this "stout gray" when mortally wounded at Yellow Tavern. Before dying, he gave this horse to Major Venable.[330]

The General—see under T

General Blair—U.S. Brig. Gen. John Aaron Rawlings

This staff officer of Grant named the horse after U.S. Maj. Gen. Francis P. Blair Jr., who commanded a corps in the Army of the Tennessee.[331]

General Jackson—U.S. Col. (5th NY Cav.) Othneil DeForrest

Dapple gray. Presented to DeForrest in October 1861 by friends in New York City. The horse was from Cherry Valley and at the time of presentation about 7 years old.[332] Based upon the date and location, it would seem that the General Jackson it was named after was probably Andrew Jackson.

General Jeb—CS Chaplain (3rd VA Cav.) and spy Thomas Nelson Conrad

Stallion, had "red eye." Used only for dress parades and Sunday religious meetings.[333]

General Shaler—U.S. Brig. Gen. Alexander Shaler (as Abe)

    CS Maj. Gen. John Brown Gordon

    U.S. Col. (and Bvt. Brig. Gen.) John Irvin Curtin (as Abe?)

Stallion, thoroughbred, bay. A noted horse in the Union army, it was captured with Shaler by a Georgia infantry brigade during the Battle of the Wilderness in 1864 and presented to Gordon. The first night he had it, the horse saved Gen. Gordon when he rode into the lines of Gen. Sedgewick. After Appomattox, Gordon sold the horse to Curtin for sufficient funds to return home. Afterwards, he learned that Curtin had resold the horse at a profit.[334]

General Thomas— CS Pvt. (1st AR Inf.) William E. Bevens
During 1863, a captured horse was given to the regiment's surgeon, Dr. Arnold, who gave it to Bevens, who was assisting him. When the doctor was unable to draw forage for 2 animals, Bevens had to give the horse up and was again left afoot. Bevens did not say why he named the horse General Thomas.[335] (Gen. Bryan M. Thomas was the only "Gen. Thomas" serving in the Army of Tennessee at the time.)

George— CS Maj. (staff of Gen. M.C. Butler) John R. Blocker
Sorrel. In use during the 1864 Battle of Bethesda Church in VA.[336]

George— CS Lt. (staff of Gen. Featherstone) William P. Drennan
In use during the 1863 Battle of Champion Hill, MS.[337]

George— CS (MO State Guard) Lt. Col. (staff of 3rd Div.) Richard H. Musser
Musser had slept overnight in a cabin between the 2 days of the Battle of Pea Ridge and awoke to discover that his horse outside the cabin had been killed by artillery fire.[338]

George— see Redmond following.

George— CS Maj. Gen. James Ewell Brown "Jeb" Stuart
This horse was brought to Stuart at the beginning of the war by civilian volunteer aide (and cousin and brother-in-law) Peter W. Hairston as a gift. After about 6 months, Stuart sold it, since it could not take the strain of war.[339]

George M. Patchen— U.S. Brig. Gen. La Fayette Curry Baker
Generally referred to as Patchen. Stallion, blood bay with black points and a white star, 16 hands high, of thoroughbred and Canadian ancestry. Foaled 1849 in Monmouth Co., NJ. Its sire was Cassius M. Clay and its dam was the property of George M. Patchen of Brooklyn, NY, after whom it was named. Put to stud in 1853. Exhibited 1st in 1855 at the U.S. Agricultural Fair in Philadelphia and 1856 at the New Jersey Agricultural Fair, at both of which it won races. (It raced mostly in harness but also under saddle in its earlier racing days.) Its first public race was in October 1858 vs. Ethan Allen, which won that race, but never again beat Patchen. This began a career racing in New York and Washington, D.C. Its owner after 1858 was William Waltermire of Kingsbridge, NY. After July 1, 1863, when it beat Gen. Butler 4 of 6 times, it never raced again. It was taken sick in early 1864 and died May 1, 1864.[340] In his book, Gen. Baker referred to using "The celebrated race-horse Patchen" during the 1862 Second Manassas campaign.[341] At that time, Baker was the Col. of the 1st DC Cav. This horse was the subject of Currier & Ives prints. Several of its descendants carried "Patchen" as part of their names, and the California ghost town of Patchen was named after a son of this Civil War horse.

Georgia's Brigade— ERROR
One source identifies a horse of this name as belonging to CS Gen. John Brown Gordon, along with three others (Mayre, General Milroy, and General Shaler), stating that it was a thoroughbred gray gift from the Georgia Brigade from their pay and that it was killed in the Wilderness in 1864.[342] This is an error. It was Mayre that the men of the Georgia Brigade purchased for Gordon, and it was Mayre killed at the Battle of Monocacy.[343]

Gertie—U.S. Maj. Gen. George Gordon Meade[344]

Gim Crack—CS Lt. Col. (staff of Gen. J.A. Wharton) Francis Richard Lubbock
Male. Raised on Lubbock's TX ranch. Left in care of a New Iberia, LA, hotelkeeper while Lubbock visited Richmond after being elected TX governor. Taken to Austin with the governor. On April 10, 1864, led to Shreveport, LA, when Lubbock went to join the army after his term as governor expired.[345]

Gimlet—U.S. Pvt. (Army of the Potomac secret service) John C. Babcock
Dark-colored. Used by Babcock throughout the war. Pictured with Babcock by photographer Alexander Gardner.[346]

Ginnie—CS Lt. (Cobb's GA Legion & Commissary Dept.) Samuel Augustus Burney
Mare. Burney wrote his wife on July 24, 1864, that it was well that he had this horse with him since if Sherman's army got into the home area they'd take it.[347]

Glencoe—CS Capt. (staff of Gen. J.C. Breckinridge) A. Keene Richards
CS Brig. Gen. John Hunt Morgan
U.S. Brig. Gen. James Murrell Shackleford
U.S. Bvt. Lt. Gen. Winfield Scott (?)
Actually Glencoe Jr. Given to Morgan by a Kentucky horse breeder to replace Black Bess, who had been lost at Lebanon, TN. Morgan's subordinate and brother-in-law, Gen. Basil Duke said of this horse: Gelding. High-crested bay with thoroughbred points, 16 hands high. Given to Morgan in summer 1862 by Capt. Keene Richards. Used in the 1863 trans–Ohio raid.[348] Another source said: Mare, thoroughbred, sorrel. Said to be Morgan's favorite. Taken on his trans–Ohio raid in 1863. After his surrender on July 26, 1863, the horse went into possession of Shackleford.[349] Yet another source

John C. Babcock and his horse Gimlet. This is the only known photograph of an enlisted man with his name-identified horse (photograph by Alexander Gardner, Library of Congress).

states that the horse was a gelding and that Shackleford gave the horse to Scott.[350] (Since Scott was 79 years old and had suffered from dropsy and been unable to mount a horse for many years, this seems doubtful.) Gen. Duke's account would seem to be the most authoritative.

Glencoe Jr.— see ***Glencoe*** immediately preceding.
Actual name was Glencoe Jr. since sire was the thoroughbred Glencoe.[351]

Gold Dust— CS Pvt. (4th LA Cav.) Joseph Green Carson
In use May 1864.[352]

Goliath— CS Lt. (3rd VA Cav.) Robert Page
Page left his Cumberland Co., VA, home for the war riding this horse.[353]

Gothic— U.S. Telegrapher (Military Telegraph Corps) D.W. Smith
Male. So called because of its unusual build. Could not be hurried. In use early 1864 on Folly and Morris Islands during siege of Charleston, SC.[354]

Grace— see ***Grace Darling*** immediately following.

Grace Darling— CS Gen. Robert Edward Lee
U.S. unit and rider unknown.
Mare. Lee had used this horse during the Mexican War. Having a young colt, she was left behind on Lee's farm on the Virginia Peninsula in 1862. On August 3, 1862, he wrote to his wife, "I have heard of Grace. She was seen bestrode by some Yankee with her colt by her side."[355]

Grand Old Cannister— ERROR,
see ***Grand Old Cannister & Grape*** immediately following.
This is an erroneous division of the name by some list compilers.

Grand Old Cannister & Grape— U.S. Maj. Gen. Daniel Edgar Sickles
Though the horse was unwounded, Sickles's right leg was mangled by a cannonball while astride it during the 2nd day of the Battle of Gettysburg.[356]

Grape— ERROR see ***Grand Old Cannister & Grape*** immediately preceding.
This is an erroneous division of the name by some list compilers.

Grater— U.S. Maj. (1st MA Cav.) Henry Lee Higginson
The larger of the Major's two horses (the other was Nutmeg).[357]

Gray Alice— CS Brig. Gen. Robert Augustus Toombs
Mare, gray. Used by Toombs while on campaigns July 1861 until his resignation from the army in March 1863 and then thereafter at his GA residence. The horse survived the war and was used by Toombs while trying to evade capture by U.S. troops.[358]

Gray Bill— CS Maj. Gen. Jubal Anderson Early
Gray. The general used this horse in fleeing Virginia postwar.[359]

Gray Eagle— U.S. Lt. Col.. (5th OH Lt. Art.) Andrew Hickenlooper
White neck and breast. During the Battle of Shiloh, this horse was hit, fell, rose up but tumbled, plunging forward. Hickenlooper left it for dead. After his battery retreated, the then–Captain saw a riderless horse approaching the battery. He recognized his own horse, which he had thought dead. The horse's neck and breast were stained red with blood, but it served him the remainder of the day.[360]

Grease— CS Lt. (staff of Gens. Churchill then Price) (John C. or William?) Wright
CS Surgeon (staff of Gens. Churchill then Price) William M. McPheeters
Chestnut sorrel. McPheeters traded Wright his horse, $75 in gold and $10 in greenbacks for this one at the beginning of Price's 1864 raid into Missouri.[361]

Greenbriar— see *Traveller*
This was the 2nd name of Lee's famous horse.

Grey Eagle— U.S. Maj. Gen. John Buford.[362]
In Buford's funeral procession.[363]

Grey Horse— U.S. unit and rider unknown
CS Svt. (of Gen. Robert H. Hatton) Jerry
Taken at Cheat Mtn. from a U.S. soldier. Jerry used it to pull the wagon containing his and Gen. Hatton's equipment and supplies.[364]

Grey John— CS Capt. (Forrest's escort) Nathan Boone
Tennessee Walker.[365]

Guy— U.S. Surgeon (11th U.S. Inf.) John Shaw Billings
Brown. In June 1862, while at full gallop, stepped in a hole and fell with its weight on Billings. Both recovered. Killed by a shell at Beverly Ford in June 1863.[366]

Guy— U.S. Col. (4th MO Cav.) George E. Waring Jr.
Thoroughbred. Waring's 2nd mount, it proved too light to carry Waring's weight and so was turned over to an orderly.[367]

Guy Darnell— CS Maj. (2nd VA Inf.) Frank B. Jones
Jones bartered the horse away on April 4, 1862, to a Tom Marshall of Happy Creek, VA, since the horse was too small for himself.[368]

Gypsy— CS Capt. (13th AR Inf.) Cuthbert H. Slocomb
Mare, coal black. Capt. Slocomb never took her into battle (he thought her too valuable), but used her as his riding horse on all other occasions. In use in the Atlanta campaign.[369]

Handsome Joe— U.S. Maj. Gen. John Sedgwick
Presented to the general as a testimonial by his old division on June 1, 1863. Its cost was $600.[370] In use during the Battle of Gettysburg.[371] This horse was the model for the equestrian statue of Sedgwick at Gettysburg.[372]

Hardtimes— CS Brig. Gen. Ellison Capers
Sorrel, little. Presented to Capers by men of the 24th SC Infantry when he was colonel of the regiment. Both the horse and Capers were wounded in the Battle of Chickamauga. Due to its wound through the windpipe the horse had difficulty breathing thereafter but survived the war.[373]

Harry— U.S. Brig. Gen. George Armstrong Custer
This horse spooked during the Battle of Aldie, VA, and carried Custer into Confederate lines, almost leading to his capture.[374]

Harry— U.S. Col. (9th MA Inf.) Patrick Robert Guiney
From Culpepper, VA, on September 24, 1863, Guiney mailed 2 photographs of the horse home to his family. In one of the photos, the horse had its eyes closed.[375]

Harry Hays— CS Brig. Gen. Leroy Augustus Stafford
Named after Stafford's superior, CS Maj. Gen. Harry Thompson Hays. Stafford had to keep this horse in motion during battle (1864 — Meade's campaign in northern VA) since it became very frightened by gunfire.[376]

Hatch— U.S. unit and rider unknown
    CS Pvt. (Miss Cav., Forrest's command) Thomas D. Duncan
Captured slightly wounded January 1, 1864, at Jack's Creek, TN, and named "in memory" of the Union col. commanding at Bolivar, TN.[377] (This was Col. [later Brig. Gen.] Edward Hatch of the 2nd IA Cav.)

Henry— U.S. Svt. (of Gen. Willcox) Henry
In use June 1861 about Alexandria, VA.[378]

Hero— CS Lt. Gen. James Longstreet
Called "Haro" by Longstreet's Irish hostler. Sired by Red Eye, which had won a 16-mile race several years before the war. Longstreet's favorite; he was mounted on it during Battle of the Wilderness when wounded by friendly fire.[379] It was used at Fredericksburg, Antietam and Gettysburg,[380] as well as during the Wilderness.

Hessian— CS Chaplain (12th MS Inf.) Charles Holt Dobbs
Purchased June 1863 in PA for a watch and chain. The horse became sick but recovered prior to the army's return to VA.[381]

Hiatoga— U.S. Pvt. (16th IL Cav.) John McElroy
    CS Sgt. (1st VA Cav.) name unknown
Captured 1864 in VA, McElroy was among prisoners being escorted to Bristol, VA, when he recognized his horse being ridden by the Conf. Sgt.[382] (Hiatoga was the name of a family line of Ohio trotting horses during the 1830s through 1850s.)

Highfly— CS Maj. Gen. James Ewell Brown "Jeb" Stuart
Bay. Stuart escaped capture at Verdiersville, VA, on August 14, 1862, by jumping a fence on this horse, which he used regularly. Perhaps one of his favorites.[383]

Highlander— CS Lt. Gen. Nathan Bedford Forrest
A gift from friends in Tennessee, this horse was killed in the Battle of Chickamauga.[384]

Homicide— U.S. Lt. (119th PA Inf.) Charles T. Collis
According to Davis, *Life of David Bell Birney*:
Ridden by Col. (later Brig. Gen.) William Gamble, one of 12 horses entered in the 2nd (steeplechase) race held March 17, 1863, in celebration of St. Patrick's Day near the Falmouth, VA, HQ of Gen. David B. Birney.[385]

Hunter— U.S. Col. (1st U.S. Sharpshooters) Hiram Berdan
Ridden by a Lt. S. Shoup, one of 4 horses in the 3rd race (flat course) held March 17, 1863, in celebration of St. Patrick's Day near the Falmouth, VA, HQ of Gen. David B. Birney.[386]

Hunter— U.S. master unknown
Morgan. Full brother of Regulator. Sold to a Mr. Johnson of Ohio in 1857 or 1858. Died in Ohio after the war.[387]

Independence— U.S. Capt. (31st Bty., NY Lt. Arty.) Gustav von Blucher
Von Blucher rode his own horse against 3 others in the 3rd (flatcourse) race held near

the Falmouth, VA, HQ of Gen. David B. Birney on March 17, 1863, celebrating St. Patrick's Day.[388]

Ironsides—CS Sgt. (1st SC Cav.) Manson Sherrill "Manse" Jolly

Male, gray. Became well-known in association with its master, who terrorized Union Reconstruction troops in Anderson Co., SC, from May 1865 to Sept. 1866, at which time Jolly went to Texas with the horse. On the night of July 8, 1869, while trying to cross a rain-swollen Walkers Creek in Milam Co., TX, they were swept away and both drowned. A few sources (the more prone to legend) give this horse's name as Dixie.[389]

Jack—CS Capt. (2nd NC Inf. Bn.) Charles Frederic Bahnson

In use 1864 during Early's raid on Washington and referred to as Bahnson's "Maryland horse" when Bahnson was Chief QM of Artillery."[390]

Jack—U.S. Lt. (11th NY Cav.) Henry Murray Calvert

Used during Grierson's raid. When Calvert was discharged at Memphis in June 1864 the horse went to the wife of Maj. George W. Smith.[391]

Jack—U.S. Lt. Gen. Ulysses Simpson Grant

Stallion. Cream-colored with silvery mane and hair gradually darker toward the feet. Not large but reliable and sure-footed. Purchased from an Illinois farmer when Grant was Col. of the 21st IL Inf. Used regularly until after Chattanooga, when it was used as an extra horse and for ceremonial occasions. In 1864, it was given to the Sanitary Fair at Chicago, which raffled it for $4,000 used for benefit of the U.S. Sanitary Commission.[392] In his letter of donation, Grant stated that he left IL on Jack in July 1861, that he rode it more than all his other horses combined until called east in March 1864, that he then left the horse with J.R. Jones, the U.S. Marshal of the Northern District of IL, and that it was near 11 years old. He reported it as a good saddle horse and gentle in harness but requiring whip and spur.[393]

Jack—U.S. Lt. (5th NY Cav.) James A. Murdock

Male, Morgan, bay. Contracted colic during Bank's 1862 retreat in Shenandoah Valley and died at Harpers Ferry.[394]

Jack—U.S. Lt. (5th NY Cav.) Lucius Renne

Male, Morgan. Son of Fannie and grandson of Black Hawk. Survived the war, brought back to Crown Point, NY.[395]

Jack—U.S. Chaplain (148th PA Inf.) William Henry Stephens

Sorrel. Purchased for $25 during the last months of the war by the chaplain from a poor Virginia family who needed the money to move north, where opportunities were better for their children. This colt was undersized, long-haired and clubfooted, and Stephens wished to experiment if he could improve its condition. He fed it on potato peelings begged from soldiers' rations. In time its appearance improved and the feet became nearly straight. When the regiment broke camp in the spring of 1865, he turned it loose to shift for itself, but it trotted up to him the next morning and couldn't be driven away. It was then used by some of the soldiers to carry their pans and knapsacks during the Appomattox pursuit and then was taken to Washington. It was sold after the war to a "Dutchman" of Meadow Gap, Huntingdon Co., PA.[396]

Jack—CS Maj. Gen. Joseph Wheeler

CS Col. (staff of Wheeler) William E. Wailes

In April 1865, when Wheeler parted from his command, he gave "his old war-horse" to his adjutant general, though Wailes offered to send it to Wheeler once it was sufficiently recovered.[397]

Jack Hinton—U.S. Brig. Gen. Thomas Francis Meagher

According to Conyngham, *Irish Brigade*, and Mulholland, *Story of 116th Pennsylvania*: Gray. Ridden by Capt. John Gosson, won 1st race vs. 5 other horses, held March 17, 1863, at Falmouth, VA, in celebration of St. Patrick's Day.[398]

Jack Rucker—U.S. Brig. Gen. George Armstrong Custer

Bay. Not a thoroughbred. Held a speed record. Custer was riding this horse during his encounter with Longstreet at Appomattox.[399] Custer won many bets racing this horse, but on one occasion crooks betting against Custer drugged Jack Rucker, causing him to lose a race.[400]

Jacques—U.S. Chaplain (2nd MA Cav.) Charles A. Humphries

Dark-colored. Called "the Parson's Old Cob" by a fellow officer. In use during the winter of 1863–64. Horse captured July 7, 1864, by Mosby's command.[401]

Jake—CS soldier (5th SC Cav.) Jim Smith

Purchased from his father for $1500.[402]

Jane—U.S. Pvt. (5th NY Cav.) Hiram Underhill

Mare, Morgan, black. In over 100 engagements. Survived the war and turned over to the government.[403]

Jason—CS Pvt. (3rd LA Inf.) Pierre Challon

Donkey. Challon, a veteran of the French army, traveled overland with his donkey from California to Missouri to join the Confederates. The donkey became a "pet" of his company (Iberville Rifles) and in the regiment. It was left behind in 1862 when the 3rd Louisiana left its winter quarters in Arkansas for the Pea Ridge campaign.[404]

Jasper—U.S. Maj. Gen. Robert Huston Milroy

Milroy was from Jasper County, IN. Perhaps the horse was named for his home area. During the 1862 Battle of Mill Creek in the Shenandoah Valley, VA, this horse received 2 bullets (1st in a hind leg, 2nd through the left breast and lodging in the right shoulder) and was left for dead on the battlefield.[405]

Jeb—CS Capt. (12th VA Cav.) George Baylor

Little. Would rear up whenever it desired. In use February 1865.[406] (Since the 12th VA Cav. was part of Gen. J.E.B. Stuart's cavalry, perhaps named after him.)

Jeb Stuart—Thomas Nelson Conrad. ERROR. See ***General Jeb***.

Jeb Stuart—CS Maj. (staff of Gen. T.J. Jackson) Henry Kyd Douglas[407]

Jeff—CS Pvt. (9th KY Inf., Mtd.) John W. Jackman

Little. When a member of his company was sent to hospital in February 1865, Jackman got this horse, which he called a "firey little horse," but he noted that its wind was not very good.[408]

Jeff—CS Capt. (staff of Gen. A.P. Stewart) Jim Rawlings

The Chattanoogan rode this horse home after Johnston's 1865 surrender in NC.[409]

"Jeff"—see ***Jefferson Davis*** following.

Jeff Davis— see ***Traveller*** following.
Original name of Lee's famous horse.

Jeff Davis— CS Pvt. (5th SC Cav.) James Michael Barr
Male.[410]

Jeff Davis— U.S. Lt. (16th PA Cav.) Samuel E. Cormany
Male. On December 18, 1862, Cormany wrote his wife that he had a new horse and that he called him "Jeff Davis."[411]

Jeff Davis— U.S. Lt. Gen. Ulysses Simpson Grant
Morgan pacer, black. Sired by Canadian pacer Black Oliver, and was the "best horse in the stable" according to Varina (Mrs. Jefferson) Davis.[412] Captured from the plantation of Joseph Davis, brother of the Confederate president. Grant named it after the Confederate president because of its origin. He had it appraised by a board and purchased it for his son Frederick, but due to its easy riding gait it was used by Grant when traveling long distances. A "kicker." This horse was at the White House with Grant through his presidency. It died long after the war.[413]

Jeff Davis— CS Capt. (staff of J.H. Morgan) Edward O. Guerrant
CS officer (Morgan's cavalry command) Jim Overby.
Calico. Lame with scratches in February 1863. Swapped with $30 for a 16-hands-high sorrel in March 1863.[414]

Jeff Davis— CS Gen. John Bell Hood
Male, roan. Hood's favorite, it was named by Hood's old Texas Brigade. He was never wounded while astride this horse — it had been wounded and he was mounted on other horses when he himself was wounded at Gettysburg and Chickamauga. This was apparently the only horse which Hood took with him from Virginia to Georgia in 1863. After the war, "Old Jeff" was cared for by General Jefferson (John Robert Jefferson Jr. had been a Brig. Gen. of MS militia 1842–1846) and family of Seguin, TX.[415]

Jefferson Davis— U.S. Capt. (5th NY Cav.) Elmer J. Barker
Male. Called "Jeff" sometimes. Not an original horse of the regiment. Captured from Mosby's men. Lived many years after the war on Barker's Sugar Hill Farm in NY, where it is buried with a marble monument.

Jehu— U.S. Capt. (7th IA Cav.) _____ Bartlett
Dark bay with bobtail, straight neck and short ears. This horse was balky — Capt. Bartlett was saved from capture just before the 1862 capture of Memphis, TN, when it balked at his commands to halt.[416]

Jennie— U.S. Maj. (2nd RI Inf.) Sullivan Ballou
On July 21, 1861, during Battle of First Manassas, Ballou and this horse were struck by a cannonball. The horse died soon after on the field, and after a leg amputation, the master several months later.[417]

Jerome— U.S. Col. (3rd OH Inf.) Isaac H. Marrow
Known in camp as the "White Bull." Marrow was using this horse during the western Virginia campaign in 1861.[418]

Jerry—CS Teamster (unknown unit) _____ O'Neil
Mule, 20 years old. This Irish teamster rode this mule home after Johnston's surrender in North Carolina in April 1865.[419]

Jerry—CS Lt. Gen. Leonidas Polk
This was the "Bishop-General's" horse at the time he was killed June 14, 1864, at Pine Mountain, GA. The riderless horse followed the ambulance removing his body.[420]

Jersey—U.S. Col. (Army of the Potomac QM Dept.) James Fowler Rusling
Pony. In use August 1862 near Alexandria, VA.[421] Rusling was from New Jersey.

Jess—U.S. Brig. Gen. Cyrus Hamlin
Mare, Morgan, white. Hamlin captured this horse in WV when serving there as an aide to Frémont. It went with him to LA when Hamlin was commissioned Col. of the 80th U.S.C.T. When the general died in New Orleans of yellow fever in 1867, he requested that his father, former U.S. Vice President Hannibal Hamlin, care for the horse. The elder Hamlin became quite fond of the animal. Jess lived to probably more than 25 years. It broke a leg while in pasture and had to be "put down," to the sorrow of the ex–VP.[422]

Jim—CS Pvt. (5th SC Cav.) James Michael Barr[423]

Jim—CS Pvt. (2nd SC Cav.) Moses Boynton
Sorrel.[424]

Jim—CS Pvt. (21st TX Cav.) James Jasper Sample
This horse lived 17 years.[425]

Jim—U.S. Chaplain (148th PA Inf.) William Henry Stephens
Male, bay, 17.5 hands high. After delivering soldier pay to families in April 1863, the chaplain returned and officers presented him with this horse, which had been brought to the army for another officer. Left in the rear of Cemetery Ridge during Gettysburg, Jim was appropriated by a cavalry officer but recovered the next day. Later, it was stolen but found after 6 weeks in a sutler's team. Stephens used the horse throughout the war, including the Wilderness. After the war, it was taken to Orbisonia, Huntingdon Co., PA, and sold to a wool dealer who treated it well. Stephens often visited it.[426]

Jim Banks—CS Pvt. (43rd VA Cav. Bn.) William H. "Slice" Barbour
In January 1865 during Mosby's "Coffee Raid," this horse was picked up on the road. It was recognized by recently captured Pvt. Jeremiah DeBell "Jerry" Wilson, who was unsuccessful in an effort to escape on it near Upperville, VA.[427]

Jim Crow—CS Chaplain (3rd VA Cav.) and spy Thomas Nelson Conrad
Male, jet black, about 900 lbs, 15 hands high. Would neigh at approach of cavalry or when it heard hoofbeats or nearby animals. Conrad's favorite horse when scouting.[428]

Jinny—CS Maj. Gen. Isaac Trimble
Mare. During Pickett's Charge (3rd day at Gettysburg), Trimble was shot through his left leg while mounted on this horse, which carried him off the field before dying from the same shot. The general wrote of this in his diary for that date: "Poor Jinny, noble horse, I grieve to part thus with you."[429]

Jocko— U.S. Col. (12th IA Inf.) Joseph Jackson Woods
U.S. Maj. (52nd OH Inf.) James T. Holmes
Completely white when foaled, with marks of an Arabian and a Mexican bronco. Woods bought the horse from a MS planter, who had bought it from a Comanche. Bore a scar made by a piece of shell at Vicksburg. Holmes bought the horse from Woods at Kingston, GA, just before the "March to the Sea" began, and used it for that campaign. The only horse of the regiment to survive the Carolinas campaign. Jocko died July 6, 1892, on the Alum Creek, Franklin Co., OH, farm of W.T. Rees after he accidentally broke his leg.[430]

Joe— CS Brig. Gen. States Rights Gist
This horse was shot through the neck during the 1864 Battle of Franklin and began to rear and plunge. Gist had to dismount and continue the advance on foot.[431]

Joe— U.S. Lt. (staff of Gibbon) Frank Aretas Haskell
This horse was killed in the 1862 Battle of Antietam.[432]

Joe— U.S. Capt. (2nd NY Lt. Arty.) Jacob Roemer
Male, gray. Presented to Roemer by citizens of Flushing, NY, in 1862. Twice wounded at the August 9, 1863, Battle of Cedar Mtn., it could no longer be ridden and was put down in a cornfield.[433]

Joe Johnston— CS Brig. Gen. States Rights Gist
Possible full name for *Joe* preceding.[434]

Joe Smith— CS Brig. Gen. Adam Rankin "Stovepipe" Johnson
Male. Johnson used this horse prewar in TX vs. Indians. When he joined the Confederate Army, he left it in Shreveport, where he picked it up in 1861 when he (not yet a general) was ordered to carry dispatches to Austin, TX. It pulled his buggy to Austin. He was still using it postwar in 1869.[435]

John— U.S. Maj. Gen. Thomas Leonidas Crittenden
Gray. When relieved of Corps command in the Army of the Cumberland in October 1863, the general rode this horse to say farewell to his brigades. Afterwards, it was usually ridden by his young son.[436]

John— U.S. Col. (staff of Gen. U.S. Grant) F.S. Duff
CS unit and rider unknown Sorrel. This walking horse was prone to run away. Captured by Confederates.[437]

John— CS Capt. (staff of Gen. Brockenbrough) Wayland Fuller Dunaway
Bay, large. About 5 years old when purchased for Confederate money (seller knew it was therefore "more a gift") near Fredericksburg, VA, in May 1863 after Chancellorsville. Dunaway had just been appointed to staff from the 40th VA Inf.[438]

John— U.S. Dr. (109th PA Inf.) James Langstaff Dunn
Traded off for another horse in September 1863.[439]

John— U.S. Pvt. (1st NJ Arty., Bty. B) Emanuel Raake
After 3 miles of the 1863 "Mud March," the wheel horses of the right section gun were thrown on their backs. Driver Raake was heard telling this horse to get up as soon as the pole yoke was loosened.[440]

John— U.S. Maj. Gen. Lewis "Lew" Wallace

Big horse.[441] Much beloved by Wallace, who remarked in a footnote to his memoirs, "I loved this horse passionately. For five years he was my faithful, intelligent servant and friend...."[442]

John Dillard— CS (cavalry of Gen. John Hunt Morgan)

Stallion, bay with star, snip and one white postern. Bred by a Mr. Vallandigham of Owen Co., KY, and foaled in 1853. Subsequently owned by Dr. Adams of Scott Co., KY; Mr. Manluis St. Claire of Georgetown, KY; Mr. W.H. Richardson of Russell Cave, KY; and finally Mr. L.P. Muir of Paris, KY. Taken to Indiana in 1869 where it died. Served with Gen. John Hunt Morgan's cavalry during the Civil War.[443] A foundation progenitor of the American Saddle Horse breed. Almost 1 percent of the dams of Standard (Trotting) horses in the country in 1890 were sired by this horse.[444]

The John Horse— see under T

Joseph— U.S. Surgeon (5th WI Inf.) Alfred L. Castleman

Probably black. "My faithful and affectionate horse." In use on the Fredericksburg front in December 1862.[445]

Josh— CS Lt. Col. (Poague's Bn. Arty.) William Thomas Poague

"Great jumper." Actually the horse of Poague's brother Jim (1st VA Cav.). Poague used this horse to escape capture after the April 1865 Battle of Sailor's Creek.[446]

Jubal Early— CS Brig. Gen. Roger Atkinson Pryor

Gray. In use November 1864 when Pryor was captured.[447]

June— U.S. (5th NY Cav.) master not known

Mare, Morgan, black. Had many different riders. Survived the war.

Kangaroo— U.S. Col. (staff of Grant) Clark B. Lagow
U.S. Lt. Gen. Ulysses Simpson Grant

Thoroughbred? "Raw-boned." Left by Confederates on the Shiloh battlefield, since it looked apparently "good-for-nothing," it was given as a joke to Col. Lagow, a wealthy man and volunteer aide on Grant's staff. Grant believed the animal to be thoroughbred and offered to take the horse. After a short period of rest and feeding, the horse turned out to be "a magnificent animal." It was named for its appearance and a habit of rearing up on its hind feet and plunging forward when mounted. It was in use during the Vicksburg campaign.[448]

Kate— CS civilian (NC) W.S. Chaffin
U.S. unknown soldiers (Kilpatrick's cavalry)

Taken from Chaffin's farm near Lumber River on March 9, 1865.

Kate— U.S. Lt. Col. (2nd RI Inf.) Elisha Hunt Rhodes

Mare, dark-colored. While regimental adjutant (Lt.) at Camp Sedgewick on December 25, 1863, Rhodes noted in his diary that he had traded a previous horse, Old Abe, for this animal, which he called "one of the finest animals in the Army. She is a beauty and very fast, both running and trotting." On September 15, 1864, he noted, "My mare Kate is a beauty, and I enjoy rides both on duty and for pleasure which I take every day." In March 1865 at Petersburg, a Miss Lena Hunt of Chicago visited the camp with others and was allowed to ride the horse. He took the horse home with him after the war and was joyous to find that the car carrying Kate was attached to his train so that it arrived at Providence on July 18, 1865, with him. His wife later painted a picture of this horse. The mare is referred to as Katie in some of his diary entries.[449]

Kathleen Mavorneen — U.S. QM Capt. (unit not known) _____ Martin
According to Davis, *Life of David Bell Birney*:
Surgeon P.L.F. Reynolds (169th NY Inf.) rode Martin's horse against 6 others in the 1st (steeplechase) race held in celebration of St. Patrick's Day on March 17, 1863, near the HQ of Gen. David B. Birney at Falmouth, VA.[450]
According to Conyngham, *Irish Brigade*, and Mulholland, *Story of 116th Pennsylvania*:
Mare, bay. Owned and ridden by Capt. Martin vs. 5 other horses.[451]

Katie — see ***Kate*** immediately preceding.

Kentuck — U.S. Maj. Gen. George Brinton McClellan
A gift early in the war from Union men of Kentucky (whence named) this was considered to be "a very fine horse."[452]

Kentucky — CS President Jefferson Finis Davis
Bay. The president rode this favorite saddle-horse daily.[453] He was using it in April 1865 in GA while trying to escape Union forces.[454]

King Philip — CS Lt. Gen. Nathan Bedford Forrest
Gelding, large, dapple gray. This horse was a gift from ladies of Georgia.[455] This horse was sluggish until it heard firing, when it would become excitable. It was wounded at Okolona (the 3rd horse Forrest used in this battle) and several later times but survived the war and was with Forrest at the surrender in 1865.[456] Postwar it lived on Forrest's plantation at Sunflower Landing, Coahoma Co., MS. During one visit by Reconstruction troops, the horse charged the blue-uniformed soldiers.[457] When it died, it was buried in one of Forrest's army blankets.[458]

Kit — ERROR
Sometimes found on a list of Civil War horses as belonging to U.S. Brig. Gen James A. Garfield. This mare was actually the horse of his wife during the postwar period.

Kitt — CS Lt. Col. (staff of Stuart) Johan August Heinrich Heros von Borcke
Mule, gray. This animal had a prodigious appetite and would eat anything. It was generally used for "night excursions" around the camps. In use winter 1862–63.[459] A foreign observer, Justus Scheibert of Prussia, recorded the name as Katy and called it "a beautiful white mule."[460]

Kitty — U.S. newspaper sketch artist Edwin Forbes
The *Frank Leslie's Illustrated Newspaper* artist was using this horse during the Battle of Cross Keys.[461]

Kitty — CS Col. (2nd MD Cav. Bn.) Harry A. Gilmor[462]

Klitschka — U.S. Pvt. (4th MO Cav.) Peter Wettstein
U.S. Col. (4th MO Cav.) George E. Waring Jr.
Mare, iron-gray. Purchased 1861 as one of the regiment's original mounts. Assigned by

Kitty. Not surprisingly, sketch artist Edwin Forbes sketched the mare which he used from 1862 through 1865 (Library of Congress).

Col. Waring to his trumpeter, who gave orders to the horse in a mixture of French and German. Wettstein often overloaded the horse. Wettstein drowned fording a river in 1863 and asked the Col. to care for the horse, which he did for the remainder of the war.[463]

Lady Gray— CS Pvt. (5th SC Cav.) James Michael Barr
  Mare, gray.[464]

Lady Margrave— CS Maj. Gen. James Ewell Brown "Jeb" Stuart
  Mare. In Stuart's possession as early as November 24, 1861, when mentioned in a letter to his wife. Along with Skylark, was captured from Stuart's sleeping servant during the 1862 Chambersburg raid.[465]

Lady Mosby— CS Lt. Col. (43rd VA Cav. Bn.) John Singleton Mosby
    U.S. Sgt. (1st NY Cav.) Russell P. Forkery
  Mare, sorrel. On June 11, 1863, Mosby and his wife were visiting the night with James Hathaway near Salem, VA. Sgt. Forkery and a patrol arrived and Mosby escaped capture only by hiding on the home's roof. The horse was taken from the barn and named after Mrs. Mosby by Forkery.[466] (Mosby's name for the horse is not known.)

The Lady Polk— see under T

Lamkins Bill— U.S. Corp. (8th IL Cav.) George M. Roe
  Brought into service from Shabbona, IL. Accused of having "incurable viciousness," so was sold to Roe. Was still in use during the 1862 Antietam campaign.[467]

Lancer— U.S. Brig. Gen. George Armstrong Custer[468]

Lancer— U.S. Maj. (6th PA Cav.) Henry C. Phelan

Phelan referred to it as "little." Using it, he escaped Confederate cavalry during the 1863 Battle of Brandy Station by leaping a 5-foot stone wall.[469]

Lazarus— U.S. QM Sgt. (3rd MA Cav.) Samuel Corning
Had a bad habit of standing up on its hind legs. After Port Hudson, the horse fell, almost leading to Corning's capture by "guerrillas."[470]

Lee— CS Capt. (Dearing's VA Art. Bn.) William C. Marshall
This animal was killed July 3, 1863, during the Battle of Gettysburg.[471]

Leet— U.S. Brig. Gen. Alexander Hays
Hays named the horse after the Leet family of Leet Township, PA.[472] A gift from the Shields family, Leet was severely wounded during the Battle of Gettysburg.[473]

Lexington— U.S. Maj. Gen. William Tecumsh Sherman
Stallion, thoroughbred. A noted Kentucky race horse, it was the sire of Grant's horse Cincinnati.[474] Sherman used this horse from Atlanta through the Grand Review after the war in Washington.

Lieut. Joe Massengale— CS Lt. (4th TN Cav.) Joe Massengale
    CS Col. (4th TN Cav.) Baxter Smith
Bay with qualities of a thoroughbred. When Massengale was killed at the Battle of Fayetteville, NC, in April 1865, men of the regiment purchased it for the Col., collecting $2,600 for Massengale's family. Smith rode it until surrender. Postwar the horse became conspicuous at reunions and was named the regimental mascot. It died aged 26 years.[475]

Lightfoot— U.S. Col. (1st NY Cav.) Andrew T. McReynolds
    U.S. Lt. (1st NY Cav.) B.F. McReynolds
Light dappled gray. Presented to Col. McReynolds at New York City in 1861. When he left service in 1864, given to his son. Sold after the war to a Philadelphia merchant for $1,000, to be used as a riding horse for the ladies of the merchant's family.[476]

Lilly Dandridge— CS Maj. Gen. James Ewell Brown "Jeb" Stuart
    CS Col. (staff of Gen. R.E. Lee) Walter Herron Taylor (on loan)
Mare, thoroughbred, brown, small. Too small for himself to use, Stuart provided the horse to Taylor to use as long as needed.[477] Stuart had his headquarters at "The Bower," Jefferson Co., WV, plantation of Adam Stephen Dandridge, July 28–October 10, 1862.

Lily— see ***Lily of the Valley*** following

Lily of the Valley— CS Maj. (staff of Stuart) James Thomas Watt Harrison
    CS Maj. Gen. James Ewell Brown "Jeb" Stuart
    CS Lt. (staff of Stuart) Theodore S. Garnett
    CS Lt. Col. (1st CS Eng.) William Willis Blackford
    CS Lt. Francis S. Robertson
Mare, black. Stuart was given this horse by Harrison, a relative on his staff. A "camp horse," this animal was ridden by Stuart's wife, Flora, when visiting the general. Sometimes referred to as Lily for short. Sold for $1,500 to Garnett during the winter of 1863–64. Garnett later swapped it to Blackford for a horse named Brandy. Near the end of the war, Blackford loaned the horse to his brother-in-law Robertson. After the war, the horse was purchased from Blackford by Alexander Stuart for $500.[478] Blackford,

who called the horse Lilly, wrote that Stuart named this thoroughbred after Miss Lilly Dandridge.[479] (More than likely the same horse as Lilly Dandridge preceding.)

Limber Jim— CS Capt. (12th TX Cav., later guerrilla) Howell A. "Doc" Rayburn
Black. Captured from a Union officer 1862.[480] Or: Chestnut sorrel. Sold after the war at Government auction and died soon after.[481]

Little Billy— U.S. Col. (141st PA Inf.) Henry J. Madill
According to Davis, *Life of David Bell Birney*:
A Lt. Garretson rode Madill's horse against 11 others in the 2nd (a steeplechase) race held to celebrate St. Patrick's Day on March 17, 1863, near the Falmouth, VA, HQ of Gen. David B. Birney.[482]

Little Mac— U.S. Lt. (11th NY Cav.) Henry Murray Calvert
U.S. rank unknown (11th NY Cav.) Orris Martin
Had been used by Calvert in area of Poolesville, NY, in 1861. In June 1865, it was being used by Martin in the vicinity of Memphis.[483]

Little Mac— U.S. 1st Lt. (2nd MA Inf.) Thomas Rodman Robeson
Raced against Burnside (Oakey's) November 22, 1862, near Sharpsburg, MD.[484]

Little Reb— U.S. Lt. Gen. Ulysses Simpson Grant
Shetland pony, black. Used by Grant's youngest son, Jesse, while visiting his father in early 1865. Jesse, mounted on the pony, followed his father and came under fire. A staff officer had to lead the boy off on the pony at a gallop.[485] Also referred to as Rebbie.[486] Also described as a spotted Shetland pony, this animal may have been the property of Charles Buckner Gaines (a gift from his father, William Gaines) of near Vicksburg, MS. It was stolen shortly after the surrender of Vicksburg from the property of the elder Gaines, and young Frederick Dent Grant, son of Gen. Grant, was seen riding it about Vicksburg. The Gaines family protested and the pony was returned, but was soon after again stolen. The Gaines family never saw the pony again nor knew what happened to it.[487]

"Little Sorrel"— see ***Fancy*** preceding.

Lively— U.S. Brig. Gen. Hugh Judson Kilpatrick
Mare. A favorite with Kilpatrick, who raced it in late fall 1862. Raced vs. Battery Horse at James City, VA, racetrack in October 1863.[488]

Liverly— U.S. unit and rider unknown
CS (43rd VA Cav. Bn.) rider unknown
Thoroughbred race horse which fled its rider, a member of Kilpatrick's command, at the time of the Battle of Buckland Mills, VA, on October 19, 1863, and later picked up by some of Mosby's men.[489] (Same as ***Lively*** preceding?)

Long Tom— CS Lt. (6th VA Cav.) Walker Keith Armistead
In use 1863 after the Battle of Gettysburg.[490]

"Lookout"— U.S. Maj. Gen. Joseph Hooker
Male, chestnut-colored, nearly 17 hands high. Original or actual name not known. A ¾ bred out of Mambriono on a half-bred mare. Speedy, it could trot under saddle in 2.45. Bred in Kentucky, it was selected at age 5 (about 1861) for Mr. Ten Broeck as

the finest horse that could be sent to England to exhibit style. Forwarded to New York City, it was there seen by an agent of the French emperor, who offered $1,000 for it. Hooker somehow came into competition and succeeded in purchasing the horse. Ridden during the "Battle Above the Clouds" (Lookout Mountain) in 1863, it was thereafter called "Lookout."[491]

Luck— CS Capt. (various KY commands) Edward O. Guerrant
In use June 1864.[492]

Lucy— U.S. Pvt. (5th NY Cav.) William Barrows
CS unit and rider unknown
Mare, Morgan, black. Daughter of Black Hawk. Raised in Bridport, VT. Captured by Mosby's men.[493]

Lucy— CS Maj. Gen. George Edward Pickett
The general's "courting horse," according to his wife.[494]

Lucy Long— CS Maj. Gen. Janes Ewell Brown "Jeb" Stuart
CS Gen. Robert Edward Lee
Mare, sorrel (not chestnut) with white blaze on forehead and white hind legs, 9 or 10 years old in 1866. She had a fast walk and an easy pace. Bred on Jefferson County, WV, plantation "The Bower" by Stephen Dandridge. Purchased by Stuart — whose headquarters were there September 28–October 10, 1862 — and given to Lee to spell Traveller and was ridden alternately until the spring of 1864 when, due to hard riding and scanty feed, she became broken down and was sent to Henry Co., VA, to recuperate. Lee sent for her before the opening of the Appomattox campaign. She was mixed with public horses under the charge of Maj. J.G. Paxton and reached Danville, VA, and somehow disappeared there. After the war, the horse was noticed in Essex Co., VA; the resemblance to Lee's horse was noted, and he was informed. Wishing to have her in memory of Stuart, Lee purchased her, reimbursing the owner the amount he had paid for the horse (to a person unauthorized to have her). The horse was delivered to his son, Robert E. Lee Jr., in the autumn of 1866 and he took her to Lee at Lexington in December 1865. Part of the journey was by train, and then with Lucy Long pulling a buggy — which surprised Lee, who had been unaware she had ever been broken to harness. Thereafter, Lucy Long served mainly as a mount for Lee's daughters.[495] Her stall was next to that of Traveller.[496] She was boarded out in the countryside for the last ten years of her life and was in good health until about a year before her death — chloroformed at age 33.[497]

Madge— U.S. Col. (24th MA Inf.) Francis A. Osborn
Mare. While in the Bermuda Hundred vicinity, the horse strayed on June 21, 1864, but was found a few days later by the regimental QM and recovered from an artilleryman who had been riding her. She had already been branded with the crossed cannons of artillery.[498]

Maggie— CS Lt. Gen. Richard Stoddart Ewell
Mare, chestnut sorrel. Called a "splendid" animal, it was killed while Ewell was astride it during the 1862 Battle of Mechanicsville.[499]

Maggie— CS Lt. (a reserve VA bn. of arty.) John Sergeant Wise
Lent the horse to a wounded Frank Johnson during the 1865 Appomattox campaign.[500]

Maggie Mitchell— CS Maj. (staff of Gen. J.E.B. Stuart) Benjamin Stephen White
  Mare, black. White's favorite horse. Described as "beautiful" and said to have been able to outrun more rested horses. Though in numerous battles, it survived the war unscathed. Duringthe Gettysburg campaign it carried White 186 miles.[501]

Magic— CS Lt. Col. (1st CS Eng.) William Willis Blackford
  Mare, dark chestnut, 16 hands high, 4 years old in 1863 with a nervous temperament. A 1st cousin of Comet. Used first after Malvern Hill.[502] This horse had strength and endurance and was a good jumper (a July 1863 jump at Hanover, PA, saved Blackford from capture). Blackford's favorite, she survived the war.[503]

Major— U.S. Maj. Gen. Ambrose Everrett Burnside
  After his first horse was killed at First Manassas, Burnside used this one, which he afterwards considered his lucky horse since he and it made it through the rest of the battle unscathed. He was riding this horse upon his 1863 entry into Knoxville. The horse lived 30 years and when it became aged, Burnside could not bring himself to put it down. He asked a friend to do it while he was away in Congress.[504]

Major— U.S. Col. (116th PA Inf.) St. Clair Augustine Mulholland
  According to Conyngham, *Irish Brigade*, and Mulholland, *116th Pennsylvania*: Chestnut. Ridden by QM Wade vs. 5 other horses in 1st race held March 17, 1863, at Falmouth, VA, in celebration of St. Patrick's Day.[505]

Major— see *Barney* (Opdyke's) preceding.

Malty— U.S. Maj. (10th MA Inf.) Dexter F. Parker
  In use January 1863 on the Fredericksburg front.[506]

Manassas— U.S. unit and rider unknown
  CS Lt. Col. (1st CS Eng.) William Willis Blackford
  Male, dappled yellow dun with white mane and tail. Captured on the Second Manassas battlefield. Used for relief of Comet or otherwise Blackford's servant Gilbert would ride it.[507] On one occasion this horse was shot beneath Blackford but survived.[508]

Manassas— CS Col. (VA) John "John Tuck" Sanders
  To avoid its capture by Union forces raiding in the Cripple Creek Valley of southwestern Virginia, Sanders put this horse in the care of Chaplain (19th TN Inf.) David Sullins who was able to secure the horse for Sanders even though cannonading could be heard in nearby Wytheville, VA.[509]

Manassas— U.S. Brig. Gen. Orlando Bolivar Willcox
  Horse killed during the Battle of Antietam.[510]

Mary— CS Lt. (Adjutant, 14th KY Cav.) Leland Hathaway
  U.S. Maj. (MI unit) name unknown
  Mare, 15 hands and 1 inch high. Bred and reared at her owner's home near Deer Park, KY. Hathaway later wrote that during Morgan's Trans-Ohio Raid, the horse "never faltered, never seemed to tire." When Hathaway was captured at the Battle of Buffington's Island, OH, in July 1863, an unknown U.S. major from Michigan noticed Mary and asked about her. Hathaway praised her highly. The officer promised to care for her and send her to his home in Michigan. Hathaway's closing comments about the horse were, "This was the best I could do for my mare.... I never heard of Mary again."[511]

Mary— CS Brig. Gen. Robert Hopkins Hatton

Canadian, mare, black. Had long fetlock hair. Name given by the general's servant, Jerry. After Hatton's death the horse was returned to his TN home. When Hatton was reburied (from VA) at Lebanon, TN, in March 1866, Jerry led the horse in the funeral procession.[512]

Mary Minnehaha— CS Capt. (staff of J.H. Morgan) Edward O. Guerrant

Was shot August 29, 1862, at Lebanon, TN.[513]

Maryland— CS Maj. Gen. Robert Emett Rodes

Black. In use August 1864.[514]

Maryland— see *My Maryland* following.

Max— U.S. Lt. (16th PA Cav.) Samuel E. Cormany

On February 3, 1863, this "little" horse trampled on Cormany's leg.[515]

Max— CS unknown unit and rider

U.S. Col. (4th MO Cav.) George W. Waring Jr.

Dark bay, 16 hands high. Captured from the Confederates. Waring paid $140 for it even though at the time it was in poor condition. The horse recovered with care. Used in campaigns against CS Lt. Gen. N.B. Forrest and grazed by a bullet on one occasion.[516]

Mayre— U.S. officer, name and unit unknown

CS Maj. Gen. John Brown Gordon

This horse was captured by Georgia Brigade troops at Mayre's Heights in December 1862 when, after a U.S. officer had been shot off of its back, it galloped into Confederate lines during the Battle of Fredericksburg. The Georgia brigade troops purchased it from the quartermaster and presented it to Gordon, who afterwards treasured it as being from his soldiers. Gordon described it as "beautiful" and stated that it was ordinarily rather sluggish and required free use of the spur, but was a superb battle horse which would, with its head up and its nostrils distended, bound across ditches and over fences. It was afraid of nothing and was never wounded until it was killed at the 1864 Battle of Monocacy. When visiting the camp, Mrs. Gordon often rode Mayre.[517]

Mazeppa— CS Maj. Gen. James Ewell Brown "Jeb" Stuart

CS Maj. (staff of Stuart) Norman R. Fitzhugh

Mentioned in an October 26, 1862, letter to Mrs. Stuart. She didn't like this horse so it was given to Maj. Fitzhugh.[518]

Medor— U.S. Maj. (6th PA Cav.) J. Henry Hazeltine

"Harry's magnificent horse 'Medor' fell, shot through the flank," on June 8, 1863, during the Battle of Brandy Station.[519]

Meg— see *Meg Merrilies* immediately following.

Meg Merrilies— CS Brig. Gen. Edward Porter Alexander

Mare, bay with a roan spot on one hip. Purchased at the beginning of the war. Alexander described this, his spare horse, as "very pretty." Often ridden by Alexander's servant, Charley. After the war, she was taken to Washington, GA, and left there when Alexander moved to Columbia, SC. Sometimes referred to as Meg, the mare died in 1866.[520]

Methuselah— U.S. Lt. Gen. Ulysses S. Grant

White. Purchased in Galena, IL, when Grant reentered the army as Col. of the 21st Illinois Infantry. It was strong but unfitted for service and replaced by Jack.[521]

Michigander— U.S. Major (1st MA Cav.) Benjamin William Crowninshield
Stallion, sorrel. Purchased from an officer of the 8th Michigan Infantry. Killed at Waynesboro, VA, in October 1864.[522]

Mickey Free— CS Major (1st Richmond Howitzers) Robert Augustus Stiles
In use after the Gettysburg campaign. Killed during the Battle of Spotsylvania when a piece of shell struck it in the head.[523]

Mike— CS 1st Lt. (35th AL Inf.) Albert Theodore Goodloe
In use April 1862 while Goodloe was on scouting duty, later sent home.[524]

Milroy— U.S. Maj. Gen. Robert Huston Milroy?
          CS Maj. Gen. John Brown Gordon
Black, immense sized. Captured by Confederates during the 1862 Shenandoah Valley campaign and given to Gordon by his men. Named after its believed previous owner (what he called it is unknown). Its appearance was described by Gordon as "magnificent." He said that the horse behaved well under cannonading, but, a very fearful horse, it would flee upon approach to the lines of the enemy who were firing. Gordon rode it only once — it ran off 100 yards behind Confederate lines carrying him. He doubted that Milroy would have owned and used such a horse.[525]

Mink— U.S. Pvt. (5th NY Cav.) Robert Dunlap
          U.S. Maj. (5th NY Cav.) Eugene B. Hayward
Mare, Morgan, black. Second rider, Maj. Hayward, used her in over 70 engagements — riding over 70 miles in one day during the Wilderness. Survived the war and returned to Crown Point with the major, who later took it to Wisconsin and then Iowa. It died of a digestive disease in Iowa.[526]

Miranda— CS 2nd Lt. (staff of Gen. J.E.B. Stuart) Francis Smith Robertson
Though his favorite and fastest horse, it had, according to its owner, a talent of avoiding enemy fire by hiding behind the nearest large tree. Robertson was enabled through its speed to escape the enemy while scouting Germania Ford. Near Williamsport, during the retreat from Gettysburg, when startled by a flaring fire, it leaped a canal.[527]

Mr. Yorkshire— U.S. Brig. Gen. Alpheus Starkey Williams
Stallion, thick skin and soft hair. Williams took this horse to war with him from Detroit. In October 1861 he wrote his wife, saying, "It proves a splendid animal, afraid of nothing and full of life and spirit." During a 2-week railroad journey to the west in 1863, it was badly rubbed on both hips.[528]

Mollie— U.S. Pvt. (5th NY Cav.) Charles Holcomb
Mare, Morgan, bay. Holcomb used the horse while a regimental mail carrier. Holcomb purchased the horse from the government after the war and settled in Virginia.[529]

Mollie Glass— CS Jeff Davis (AL) Artillery
Mare. When young Mollie Glass's favorite riding mare Di Vernon stood on its hind legs, she fell off backward, breaking one of her arms. Her father then forbade her to ride it, so she determined to give it to the Confederate army. She donated it to the Jeff Davis Artillery, which had just formed at Selma, AL, and was heading off to Virginia. The bat-

tery changed its name to Mollie Glass in honor of her. It was killed by a wound to the breast during the Battle of Fredericksburg and reported as a casualty by a battery lieutenant in the *Montgomery Weekly Advertiser* of January 7, 1863. Each claiming to have been riding the horse at the time it was shot, four sick and wounded of the battery afterwards visited the young donor to tell of its death. (Mollie subsequently married a Mr. Brown.[530])

Money— CS Lt. (2nd TX Inf.) E.J. Chance
After the war, Chance led this horse home carrying a one-legged Confederate soldier.[531]

Monmouth— ERROR
This gray often appears on lists of Civil War horses. It was actually a Mexican War horse of Civil War Gen. Philip Kearny.[532]

Morgan— CS Brig. Gen. Eppa Hunton
The general was offered $500 for this horse after the war.[533]

Morgan Rattler— U.S. unit and rider unknown
      CS unit and rider unknown
Morgan. Captured at Murfreesboro by Confederates.[534]

Moscow— U.S. Sgt. (21st NY Cav.) James E. Clark
Male. Rescued its wartime master from a battlefield. After the war Clark gave the horse to Sand Lake, NY, resident James G. Averill. A participant in Decoration Day parades, when deemed too old to participate, it heard music and jumped its stable fence but had a heart attack before joining the procession. It was buried at the foot of Averill's grave. A tombstone for the horse was placed in 2001.[535]

Moscow— U.S. Maj. Gen. Philip Kearny
White, large. High-spirited and may have been a favorite.[536]

Moses— U.S. Capt. (Signal Corps) Ocran M. Howard
Selected October 1861 at Georgetown, D.C. Howard was always satisfied with the horse.[537]

Mott— CS Col. (19th MS Inf.) Christopher Haynes Mott
      CS Maj. (staff of Gen. Longstreet) Thomas Walton
      CS Brig. Gen. Gilbert Moxley Sorrel
Male, bay. Brought to Virginia by Col. Mott. After his death at the Battle of Williamsburg, Maj. Walton had possession of the horse. In September 1862, he traded the horse to Sorrel for a small mare and $275. Either Walton or Sorrel named it after the late Colonel Mott (what he called it is unknown). Longstreet advised Sorrel that the horse ate too much but the trade was made anyway. The animal ran away but was later found and returned to Sorrel. The animal was powerful and well-paced but did indeed require too much food. It soon showed ribs and bones, so Sorrel turned it over to the quartermaster.[538]

Mountain Bill— CS Pvt. (9th TX Cav.) Allison Wudville Sparks
While this cavalryman was in a MS hospital in 1862, his horse was used to pull an ambulance.[539]

Mustang— U.S. Brig. Gen. Charles Adam Heckman
On May 6–7, 1864, during the Battle of Port Walthall, the horse was shot and Heckman wounded.[540]

My Maryland— CS Maj. Gen. James Ewell Brown "Jeb" Stuart
Called Maryland for short. Bay. Given to Stuart by troops from Maryland. A gentle

horse, it was used by Mrs. Stuart when she was visiting in camp. It was the last of 3 of Stuart's horses to die of glanders during the winter of 1863–64.[541]

Napoleon—U.S. Bvt. Lt. Gen. Winfield Scott
Bay, 18 hands high. Scott had obtained the horse during the late 1840s. (This was probably the largest war-horse ever—given Scott's huge size, it had to be big.) When Scott became too aged and overweight to ride, the horse pulled his carriage. The horse led Scott's 1867 funeral procession at West Point. The horse died 1870 at age 30.[542]

Napper Tandy—U.S. Brig. Gen. Francis Thomas Meagher
According to Davis, *Life of David Bell Birney*:
A Capt. Whitefield rode the general's horse against 6 others in the 1st (steeplechase) race held March 17, 1863, in celebration of St. Patrick's Day near the Falmouth, VA, HQ of Gen. David B. Birney.[543] An Irish rebel himself, Meagher named the horse after an Irish rebel leader of the 1790s.
According to Conyngham, *Irish Brigade*, and Mulholland, *116th Pennsylvania*:
U.S. Capt. (unit not known) _____ Hogan
Mare, bay. Ridden by Lt. Ryder vs. 5 other horses in 1st race held March 17, 1863, at Falmouth, VA, in celebration of St. Patrick's Day.[544]

Ned—U.S. citizen (Gettysburg) Toby Boyer
        U.S. soldier (name and unit unknown)
This pet pony of a lame, 17-year-old master was appropriated and used by a U.S. soldier during the Battle of Gettysburg. It was recovered after the battle but with a lame ankle and loss of playfulness.[545]

Ned—U.S. Maj. (50th NY Inf.) Ira Spalding
According to Davis, *Life of David Bell Birney*:
A Lt. Kimple rode Ned against 11 others in the 2nd (a steeplechase) race held March 17, 1863, in celebration of St. Patrick's Day near the Falmouth, VA, HQ of Gen. David B. Birney.[546]

Ned Buntline—CS guerrilla (MO) Bill Myers
Bay. With his gray warhorse completely worn down, the Missouri guerrilla rode it to the farm of a friend named McFadden and during the night, unknown to McFadden, "swapped" it for this horse.[547] "Buntline" is a nautical term for the rope at the bottom of a square sail. "Ned Buntline" was the postwar pseudonym of dime novel author Edward Zane Carroll.

Nell—CS Capt. (2nd NC Inf. Bn.) Charles Frederic Bahnson
In January 1863, this horse was sold, as it had the habit of stopping when meeting anything.[548]

Nellie—U.S. citizen (Gettysburg) Joseph Bayly
        CS soldier (name and unit unknown)
This horse, which had belonged to Bayly's deceased daughter, was taken along with 2 others and some unbroken colts by Confederates during the 3rd day of the Battle of Gettysburg.[549]

Nellie—U.S. Brig. Gen. Kenner Garrard
Mare.[550]

Nellie— U.S. Pvt. (5th NY Cav.) Monroe L. Hayward
     U.S. Lt. (5th NY Cav.) James A. Murdock
    Mare, Morgan. Wounded May 4, 1862, near Rockingham Furnace, VA. Killed August 25, 1864, at Kearneysville, VA.[551]

Nellie— CS Sgt. (2nd VA Cav.) Robert W. Parker
    Lame in July 1862. Parker referred to it as "my secession horse."[552]

Nellie— U.S. Cavalry Officer (name unknown)
    Born and raised in Athens Co., OH. When 6 years old it was sold because it disregarded fences and raided the fields of neighbors. The purchaser, a U.S. officer, rode it daily after Morgan's 1863 Trans-Ohio Raid. Nellie was known as a "hard rider" because it was trotting, prancing and going sideways all of the time. In 1864, it was noted as having followed its master's unit for a great distance though not mounted.[553]

Nellie Gray— CS Maj. Gen. Fitzhugh Lee
    Mare, dapple gray with white mane and tail. At one time was selected by Gen. Robert E. Lee to be ridden by President Davis during a planned review of the Army of Northern Virginia. This horse was killed during the Battle of Opequon, VA.[554]

Nelly— U.S. unknown unit and rider
    Taken by Union forces on February 10, 1863, at Paris, VA, from Amanda Virginia "Tee" Edmonds despite her protests.[555]

Nettie— U.S. Chaplain (2nd MA Cav.) Charles A. Humphries
    The horse was put in the charge of a transportation company on October 14, 1864.[556]

"Nig"—see *Nigger* following.

Nigger— U.S. Surgeon (staff of Gen. U.S. Grant) John Hill Brinton
    Male, jet-black. Horse did not have a pleasant temper. Purchased at Cairo, IL, soon after Fort Donelson. "...so named by my Servant. I called him 'Nig' for short."[557] (Brinton, like many other Union officers, had a black servant.)

Nigger Bill— U.S. Capt. (unit not known) _____ Langdon
    According to Conyngham, *Irish Brigade*, and Mulholland, *116th Pennsylvania*: Black. Ridden by Lt. Byron in 1st race vs. 6 other horses on March 17, 1863, at Falmouth, VA, in celebration of St. Patrick's Day.[558]

Nutmeg— U.S. Maj. (1st MA Cav.) Henry Lee Higginson
    Strawberry roan. Purchased from a member of the 3rd Indiana Cav.[559]

Oceola— CS Asst. Surgeon (2nd SC Cav.) W.L. Henderson[560]

Old Abe— U.S. Lt. Col. (2nd RI Inf.) Elisha Hunt Rhodes
    Male, bay with a white mark on his face. Purchased November 15, 1863, near Hazel Run, VA. Rhodes wrote in his diary that it could "run like a deer." Nevertheless, he traded it on December 25, 1863, for another horse (Kate). Rhodes was regimental adjutant at the time.[561]

"Old Baldy"—see *Baldy* preceding.

Old Barber— U.S. Brig. Gen. Benjamin Henry Grierson
    Black. Ridden in numerous engagements in West Tennessee and Memphis vicinity.[562]

Old Battalion—CS Col. (4th AL Inf.) Egbert Jones
In use early 1861 in northern VA.[563]

"Old Bench-leg"—see *Bench-leg* preceding.

Old Bill—CS (GA Militia) Brig. Gen. Charles David Anderson
Sorrell, foaled about 1854. Purchased as a replacement for Selim (following) in 1864 from a soldier who had previously used this horse throughout the war. In 1887, this horse was 33 years old and owned by W.J. Anderson of Houston County, GA.[564]

Old Bill—U.S. Col. (21st NY Cav.) W.B. Tibbit
Survived the war, dying afterwards at Tibbit's family farm near Troy, NY.[565]

Old Billy—U.S. Lt. Col. (5th NY Cav.) James A. Penfield
Male, Morgan. Grandson of Black Hawk. Survived the war and returned to Crown Point, NY, with Penfield. Lived on Penfield's farm for 22 years, dying in 1885 aged about 32. A monument marks its grave.[566]

Old Billy—U.S. Maj. Gen. Andrew Jackson Smith
Male, Ky thoroughbred. Racer. In use July 1863 about Jackson, MS.[567]

Old Black—CS Lt. Col. (staff of Gen. J.E.B. Stuart) Johan August Henrich Heros von Borcke
Kingdom of Prussia Capt. (observer with CS ANV) Justus Scheibert
Scheibert received this horse for his use from Heros von Borcke. Though he described it as in jaded condition, aged, and with a "wretched appearance" (its ribs could be seen), Scheibert still thought it was a "good campaign horse."[568]

Old Blue—U.S. Brig. Gen. Alfred Gibbs
Used during the 1864 Trevillian Raid in VA. Gibbs was at the time colonel of the 130th NY Inf.[569]

Old Bob—U.S. soldier (4th IA Cav.) name unknown
This horse had erratic behavior and was prone to try to bush off its rider under trees and to lie down in water.[570]

Old Bob—U.S. Maj. Gen. Ambrose Everrett Burnside[571]

Old Bob—U.S. President Abraham Lincoln
Also called Bob, Old Robin and Robin (Old Bob seems to be the most common name). Male, reddish-brown bay. The Lincoln family's carriage horse in Springfield, IL, and also used by Lincoln on his legal circuit to areas not reached by railroad. Left behind in Springfield when the Lincolns went to Washington. Followed the hearse in Lincoln's April 1865 funeral procession at Springfield.[572]

"Old Bobtail"—U.S. Maj. Gen. Ambrose Everrett Burnside
One unit history states this was "his trusty old war-horse, long and well known to all soldiers of the Ninth Corps as 'old bob-tail,'" and that this was the horse Burnside always rode when danger was ahead.[573] (This is almost certainly the same as Old Bob preceding and the description meets that of Burnside's "lucky" horse Major. It seems likely that the soldiers called the horse something different from what Burnside had named it.)

Old Brown—CS Brig. Gen. William Nelson Pendleton
This horse was with him at the end of the war.[574]

Old Buck—CS Maj. Gen. George E. Pickett
Staid and indifferent to bursting shells, it was Pickett's "war-horse" per his wife.[575]

Old Bull—U.S. Col. (11th OH Inf.) A.H. Coleman
He rode this favorite horse at Antietam.[576]

Old Charley—U.S. Col. (85th PA Inf.) Joshua B. Howell
With the regiment since November 1861 when presented by Jasper Thompson of Union-town, PA, to Howell. On September 17, 1864, on the Petersburg front, a horse (not this one) accidently fell and killed Howell. Old Charley, then about 10 years old, followed the ambulance used as a hearse.[577]

Old Charlie—CS Brig. Gen. John Adams
The general and the horse were killed at the same time during the Battle of Franklin. Adams fell within the Union lines and Old Charlie atop the Union breastworks.[578]

Old Charlie—U.S. Col. (15th VT Inf.) Redfield Proctor.
In use during the Gettysburg campaign.[579]

Old Chas—U.S. Maj. Gen. Edward Richard Sprigg Canby
Canby, while colonel commanding Union forces in the New Mexico Territory from Fort Craig during early 1861, was using this horse, which was killed beneath him during the Battle of Valverde.[580]

Old Clem—U.S. Col. (1st VT Cav.) Lemuel B. Platt
Morgan. Lost hooves to foot rot in winter 1862–63. Wrenched a shoulder in 1864 while being used by Phillip Ide, was sent to Giesboro Horse Depot (Washington, D.C.) to heal, and was seen July 1864 in army use.[581]

Old Dan—U.S. Pvt. (1st RI Lt. Arty.) Thomas M. Aldrich
When discharged in 1864 after Spotsylvania, Aldrich had to reluctantly leave the horse behind. He kissed it goodbye.[582]

Old Fly—see **Fly** preceding.

Old Fox—CS Col. (1st VA Inf.) F.G. Skinner[583]
Sorrel. Noted as a hunter.[584]

Old Gabe—U.S. Pvt. (36th IL Inf.) Frank W. Raymond
This brigade mail carrier was using this horse during the 1863 Tullahoma Campaign.[585]

Old Glencoe—U.S. Brig. Gen. Thomas Leiper Kane
When the 13th PA Reserves were organized in 1861, they floated on rafts to Harrisburg to be mustered in. A special raft was constructed to transport Old Glencoe, who was the horse of then-Colonel Kane.[586]

Old Gray—U.S. Lt. Col. (7th NH Inf.) Augustus W. Rollins
On October 7, 1864, during the Battle of Laurel Hill, VA, this horse was shot from under the colonel, who was severely injured.[587]

Old Gray—U.S. (Army of the Ohio/Cumberland) artillery
Mare, gray except for a dark black left shoulder, 16 hands high. Of Gray Eagle stock. Purchased after the war by George Drinnon of Hancock Co., TN, then sold to Pleasant Seal of Swan Island on the Clinch River, TN, who sold colts from her. After 8 years, sold to Jackson Seals of Luther, TN, who kept her until death (1893) aged about 35

years. Mistaking lightning and thunder for artillery, the horse would become unmanageable and charge. After death, her hide was tanned.[588]

Old Hatchie— CS unit and rider unknown
> U.S. Brig. Gen. Robert Kingston Scott
> Claybank, big, fast runner. Captured at the 1862 Battle of Hatchie Bridge, TN. Used during the 1864 Atlanta campaign while Scott was colonel of the 68th OH Inf.[589]

Old Jeff— see *Jeff Davis* (Hood's) preceding.

Old Jim— U.S. Pvt. (11th NY Cav.) James D. Hamlin
> In use 1864.[590]

Old Jim— U.S. Col. (83rd PA Inf.) John W. McLane
> The colonel was riding this horse when he was wounded at the Battle of Gaines Mill.[591]

Old Jim— CS Lt. (Army of Tennessee?) _____ McMahon
> Weighed 900 lbs. in 1865. Raised in Sevierville, TN, and went to war with Lt. McMahon. Wounded in the neck somewhere in Tennessee but later used by its master at Atlanta, Savannah, and then South Carolina, where McMahon was killed in battle. The horse wandered onto the plantation of W.T. Williams, where it was long afterwards identified by brands and marks. It entertained crowds at veterans' parades. According to an 1894 report in an Aiken, SC, newspaper it was the oldest surviving Civil War equine.[592]

Old Jim— U.S. Brig. Gen. Strong Vincent[593]

"Old Joe"— CS Maj. Gen. Robert Frederick Hoke
> Male. Formally named San Jose, but Hoke fondly referred to him as "Old Joe." Recovering from a wound, Hoke loaned the horse to Col. Isaac Erwin Avery (6th NC Inf.) who, leading Hoke's brigade during the Battle of Gettysburg, was wounded riding the horse. The horse was returned to Hoke after the campaign. When the war was over, he rode "Old Joe" home and hitched him to a plow.[594]

Old Joe— CS Orderly Sgt. (12th GA Inf. Bn.) Walter G. Knight (as Bob)
> U.S. Col. (113th OH Inf.) Toland Jones
> Gelding, white. Knight had just returned from prisoner of war camp when the owner, Joe Vinson, offered a horse named Bob to him to scout out whereabouts of Union troops supposed to be near Oconee, GA. Knight and the horse were both captured in battle at Sandersville, GA. Knight heard soldiers saying to take the "good horse" to Col. Jones. Jones renamed the horse Old Joe and had it taken to his home at London, OH. Years later, when the horse died, there was an article about it in the *London Democrat*, which was 2 months later copied in the *Sandersville Herald & Georgian*. Knight recognized the horse from the article and contacted the London paper.[595]

Old Joe Hooker— U.S. (1st MA Lt. Arty.)
> With the battery spring of 1864. Sensitive and would tremble with rage at any attention.[596]

Old John— CS Brig. Gen. Junius Daniel
> After his mortal wounding on May 13, 1864, during the Battle of Spotsylvania, among the general's last words were instructions to his servant, Bill, to take care of this horse.[597]

Old John— U.S. Col. (9th VT Inf.) Edward Hastings Ripley
Chestnut.[598]

Old Man— U.S. Maj. (1st MA Cav.) Benjamin William Crowninshield
Liked to kick.[599]

Old Napoleon— CS Pvt. (9th TX Cav.) Allison Wudville Sparks
Gelding, black, large. Valued at $100, this was Sparks's horse at the beginning of the war.[600]

Old Pete— CS Pvt. (5th SC Cav.) James Michael Barr
Barr sent home for this horse, thinking that since it was older it would be more reliable.[601]

Old Pomp— CS Col. (9th/5th KY Inf.) Thomas H. Hunt
In use December 1861.[602]

Old Prince— U.S. Brig. Gen. Lysander Cutler
Dark bay, large. Wounded at Second Manassas but carried Cutler (then Col. of the 6th WI Inf.) off the field.[603]

Old Rebel— CS Brig. Gen. Mark Perrin Lowrey
Lowrey rode this horse off to war in 1861. During the December 1864 Battle of Nashville, the horse was shot out from beneath him. Lowrey mounted another horse and continued to lead his men in battle. He looked back and saw Old Rebel feebly trying to follow until it could not jump over a log, at which time it lay down to die. The general later recalled that he was unable to hold back his tears as he continued to lead the charge.[604]

Old Roan— CS Maj. (20th TN Inf.) Patrick Duffy
During the Battle of Fishing Creek, KY, in January 1862, a bullet passed through Duffy's saddlebags and into the horse, which fell dead.[605]

Old Roan— U.S. Brig. Gen. Solomon Meredith
Shot in the neck during Second Manassas.[606]

Old Robin— see *Old Bob* (of A. Lincoln) preceding.

Old Selim— CS Col. (2nd TN Cav.) Clark Russell Barteau
Used until Barteau's active service ended January 1865.[607]

Old Sled— U.S. Pvt. (4th IL Cav.) Joe Carter
During a July 22, 1863, pursuit of Confederates north of Natchez, the horse got excited and ran into the rear of the Confederate column. It finally fell in a muddy place with Carter falling off (and escaping), arose and headed into Confederate lines.[608]

Old Snip— CS Pvt. (7th TN Inf.) John Milton Hubbard
Had this horse December 2, 1862, near Oxford, MS.[609]

Old Sorrel— CS Pvt. (?? AL Cav) John _____
The master preferred being with the trains, so he was ever ready to loan this horse, which had a mean temper and was very rough-riding, to anyone whose horse was lame or broken down.[610]

Old Sorrel— CS Maj. Gen. John Cabell Breckinridge
Male, bay. Used throughout the war until Cold Harbor in 1864, when a solid shot

struck it in the chest, killing it instantly. A remorseful Breckinridge had fancied that the horse led a charmed life.[611]

Old Sorrel— see **Fancy** (Jackson's)

Old Spot— U.S. Maj. Gen. Hugh Judson Kilpatrick

Arabian, white with spots ("calico"). At Appomattox, lost a jumping contest to CS Gen. Wade Hampton's Butler. Postwar was kept at Kilpatrick's farm at Deckertown, NJ, where it died in 1887 at the age of 40 or more.[612]

Old Spunk— CS civilian (Washington Co., AL) Wilson Hunter

      U.S. soldiers (unknown unit)

Taken late in the war by Union soldiers. A few days later returned to Hunter's plantation at night.[613]

Old Thunder— U.S. Maj. (1st IA Cav.) William M.G. Torrance

In use the winter of 1861–62 near Sedalia, MO.[614]

Old Tom— U.S. Lt. (1st MA Cav.) _____ Merrill

Stallion, mahogany bay. Once had its skull kicked by Old Man but survived.[615]

Old Tom— U.S. Lt. Col. (12th NH Inf.) George D. Savage

Used throughout the war. Survived the war 20 years, dying 2 years after Savage.[616]

Old Wellington— see **Wellington**

Old Whitey— CS unit and rider unknown

      U.S. Sanitary Commission nurse Mrs. Mary A. "Mother" Bickerdyke

White. This malnourished stray horse with sores on its legs was captured at the 1862 Battle of Iuka, MS, and nursed back to health by Mrs. Bickerdyke, who used it for the rest of the war. By invitation of Maj. Gen. John A. Logan, she rode Old Whitey at the general's side during the Grand Review in Washington, D.C., at the end of the war. She always rode the horse sidesaddle though she had only a regulation army saddle.[617]

Old Whitey— CS Brig. Gen. Philip Cook

Male. During the Battle of Winchester, the horse was shot and so stunned that it seemed likely to die, so the general asked a staff officer to shoot him to prevent its capture. Shot in the head, it seemed to revive and wandered off to the rear. The next day a member of Cook's brigade recognized the horse and recovered it from a soldier riding it to the rear and brought it back. Cook used the horse until captured at the Battle of Sailor's Creek. Since he was imprisoned when the war ended, George Wallace, a black servant-soldier of the 12th GA Inf., rode Old Whitey back to GA and delivered him to the general's brother-in-law. The horse lived for 10 or 12 years after the war, and when it died was buried in a coffin made especially for it by Gen. Cook.[618]

Old Whitey— U.S. Maj. (staff of R.B. Hayes) Russell Hastings

      U.S. Brig. Gen. Rutherford Birchard Hayes

Male, white, large, foaled about 1850. Possessed speed, stamina and jumping ability. When Hastings was mortally wounded at the Battle of Opequan, the horse carried him off the field. For the remainder of the war, the horse was kept at Hayes's headquarters. After the war, Hayes sent the horse to the Spiegel Grove, OH, farm of his uncle Sardis Birchard. When Birchard died, the horse was cared for at the neighboring farm of Sarah Jane Grant. She notified Hayes, who was then president, by telegraph on March 20, 1879, of its death. It was buried at Spiegel Grove near where President Hayes was later buried.[619]

Old Whitey— see ***Whitey***

Old Whitie–Thomas Nelson Conrad.[620]— ERROR — see ***Whitie***

Old Woolly— U.S. Pvt. (1st RI Lt. Arty, Bty A) Fred Phillips
While encamped near Falmouth, VA, in 1862, driver Phillips, in response to others who were jumping their mounts, to everyone's surprise jumped Old Woolly over a 4-foot-high bar, clearing it by 2 feet.[621]

"Old Yellow"— see ***Claybank*** preceding.

Osborne— CS Lt. (3rd VA Cav.) Robert T. Hubard Jr.
Hubard sent for this horse when his other was lamed by a nail in a foot. In August 1863, the horse had been sick, infirm or wounded.[622]

Ossawatomie— CS Col. (Rgt. in Pickett's Brigade) _____ M_____
Was the favorite buggy-horse of the colonel's wife. He was unpopular, and the night prior to his regiment's marching through Richmond (Peninsula Campaign) someone shaved the horse's tail.[623] (The soldier telling of this in a letter did not identify the colonel or the unit. No Col. "M" could be identified for any of the regiments that served in Pickett's brigade.)

Patchen— see ***George M. Patchen*** preceding.

Peacock— U.S. Lt. Col. (16th VT Inf.) Charles Cummings
Left in the rear during the Battle of Gettysburg, it was killed by a shell.[624]

Pet— CS Pvt. (unit unknown) Frank "Frenchy" Carpenter
When his wife wrote in 1916 seeking testimony help for his pension application, all that was known of his service was his nickname and the name of his horse.[625]

Pet— CS Sgt. (2nd TX Cav.) William Williston Heartsill
His horse when he joined the "J.P. Lane Rangers" in April 1861.[626]

Pete— U.S. Col. (105th PA Inf.) Amor A. McKnight
According to Davis, *Life of David Bell Birney*:
Col. Henry J. Madill rode McKnight's horse vs. 11 others (including one of his own) in the 2nd (a steeplechase) race held on March 17, 1863, near the Falmouth, VA, HQ of Gen. David B. Birney to celebrate St. Patrick's Day.[627]

Pete— U.S. Col. (8th VT Inf.) Stephen Thomas
Wounded at the Battle of Cedar Creek, the horse was left behind to die, but recovered enough to follow the unit and find Thomas's headquarters that night. Its wounds were dressed and it was sent to Vermont where it "lived to a good old age."[628]

Peytonia— CS Maj. (2nd VA Inf.) Frank B. Jones
In use on March 23, 1862, in the Shenandoah Valley.[629]

Philippi— U.S. Brig. Gen. Benjamin Kelley
   CS Sgt. (4th VA Cav.) John S. Arnold
Given by the citizens of the town to Gen. Kelley, who had been wounded in battle

there. In February 1865, McNeil's (VA) Rangers captured Kelley and Gen. Crook during a raid near Cumberland, MD. The horse became Arnold's share for participation in the raid.[630]

Pink— U.S. Col. (5th NY Cav.) John Hammond
   Male, Morgan. Grandson of Black Hawk. Hammond rode this horse in over 34 battles, including Winchester, Orange Court House, Second Manassas, Hanover, Gettysburg, Hagerstown, and the Wilderness. Survived the war and taken back to Crown Point, NY, by Hammond. When it died in 1886 aged about 30, Hammon erected a granite monument on its grave. The marker credits the horse as having carried its master for 25 years.[631]

Plug— U.S. civilian (NY)
      CS Pvts. Wash. Traweek (Jeff Davis AL Arty.) and J.W. Crawford (6th VA Cav.)
   The 2 privates had escaped from Elmira Prison in NY, and encountering a horse, had both mounted it to facilitate their escape. A farmer called to them, "What are you boys doing with old Plug?" They showed a gun they'd previously found and continued their flight, but soon were pursued by cavalry and the farmer. The cavalry fired and the horse fell. The 2 Confederates continued their flight dismounted.[632]

Plug Ugly— U.S. Brig. Gen. Alpheus Starkey Williams
   "Long." Williams's preferred ride over rough and muddy roads. It was lightly wounded at Chancellorsville when an artillery shell exploded in mud beneath it while Williams was riding it. During the pursuit of Confederates after Gettysburg, Williams tried to leap it over a partially fallen rail fence at the end of a wall. The pair fell 8 to 10 feet without either being hurt. During the 2-week railroad transport to the western theater in October 1862, rubbed on both sides of the car and bared bones on both its head and tail, losing "pretty much all" of its tail. It was also bitten by another horse during the journey.[633]

Pocohontas— CS Brig. Gen. George Hume "Maryland" Steuart[634]

Pocohontas— CS Lt. (a reserve VA bn. of arty.) John Sergeant Wise
   In 1861, Wise was practicing cavalry maneuvers on this horse.[635]

Pomp— U.S. Corp. (5th NY Cav.) Orlando Drake
      U.S. Pvt. (5th NY Cav.) F.H. Barker
      CS unit and rider unknown
   Male, Morgan, black, bobtailed. At the beginning of the war was purchased from Clark Butterfield of Port Henry, NY. Barker and the horse were captured February 8, 1863, near New Baltimore by White's guerrillas.[636]

Pompey— CS Lt. Col. (43rd VA Cav. Bn.) John Singleton Mosby
      U.S. Musician (40th NY Inf.) Gustav A. Schurmann
   Roan mustang. Formerly ridden by Mosby, this horse was presented by the men of the 40th NY Infantry to Schurmann, its 13-year-old bugler. While serving as bugler to Gen. Daniel Sickles, Schurmann met President Lincoln and his son Tad and allowed Tad to ride the horse.[637]

"Pony"—see *Bullet* preceding.

Potomac— U.S. Brig. Gen. William Harrow

An unpopular general, after serving in western Virginia and then with the Army of the Potomac, he was transferred to the west. After Atlanta, his division was broken up and his superior (Maj. Gen. O.O. Howard) refused to give him another command—he finally resigned in April 1865. While still having a command, near Dallas, GA, in 1864, he was the recipient of a box by express (at his expense) which when opened was full of stones and a horse's tail. An enclosed block of wood with a horse's face painted on it had the label, "Head and tail of your Potomac horse." (The shaving of the tail was a common signal to an unpopular officer—this one went a little beyond.[638])

Powell—CS Servant (2nd SC Cav.) Ben
    U.S. unit and rider unknown
Pony. Captured 1862 by Union forces. (Ben was servant and hostler for Sgt. Edward Prioleau Henderson of the regiment.[639])

Pretty—U.S. Brig. Gen. David McMurtie Gregg[640]

Prince—U.S. Capt.. (5th NY Cav.) Elmer J. Barker
Male, Morgan, brown, 15.5 hands high. Could trot a mile in less than 3 minutes. Was wounded May 30, 1863, in a fight with Mosby's men and died 4 weeks later while in the care of a Washington, D.C., veterinarian.[641]

Prince—CS Brig. Gen. Cullen Andrews Battle
Black. Survived the war.[642]

Prince—U.S. Brig. Gen. Joshua Lawrence Chamberlain
Stallion, white. Chamberlain had this horse while still Lt. Col. of the 20th ME Inf. At Shepherdstown, MD, on September 20, 1862, he borrowed another horse (which was shot beneath him) to avoid exposing Prince. During the Battle of Chancellorsville, Prince was wounded in the head.[643]

Prince—CS Lt. Gen. Ambrose Powell Hill
Used by Hill during the Peninsula Campaign and through the Battle of Cedar Mtn.[644]

Prince—U.S. Surgeon (144th NY Inf.) John R. Leal
Used for 3 years of the war, including when Leal was chief medical officer on the staff of Brig. Gen. Robert Brown Potter.[645]

Prince—U.S. Asst. Surgeon (36th IL Inf.) William P. Pierce
Purchased in KY. Taken by a colonel a few days later.[646]

Prince—U.S. Maj. Gen. John Fulton Reynolds
Secondary horse.[647]

Prince—U.S. Capt. (KY) Frederick Shackelford
    CS Capt.(Morgan's cavalry) James Matthews
Very fast horse.[648]

Prince—U.S. Brig. Gen. William Harvey Lamb Wallace
Male, darker in color. Used by the general during the Battle of Shiloh. Was in Wallace's 1862 funeral procession. When it died after the war, Mrs. Wallace had it buried a few feet from the general's grave.[649]

Prince Hal—CS Maj. (8th NC Cav.) John W. Woodfin
Dark-colored.[650]

Princess—CS Lt. Col. Walter Scott
  Mare, sorrel. Scott was riding this horse when serving in Gen. Hindman's command near Little Rock, AR, during the summer of 1862.[651]

Promptly—U.S. Col. (MA 2nd Inf.) George L. Andrews
  This horse was shot in the shoulder and downed during the August 9, 1862, Battle of Cedar Mountain, VA.[652]

Prosperity—CS Pvt. (4th LA Cav.) James A. Stone
  Purchased May 1864 by Stone's mother to replace Calamity preceding. This name was selected as being more auspicious.[653]

Pulaski—CS Capt. (46th VA Inf.) Obadiah Jennings Wise
  When Wise was killed at Roanoke Island, NC, the horse was sent to the family farm about 30 miles west of Richmond, VA. Blind, it was used by CS Brig. Gen. Henry Alexander Wise to escape the Dahlgren raiders in 1864.[654]

Punch—U.S. 2nd Lt. (6th NY Cav.) Isaac A. Collier
  During the summer of 1863, the horse ran away toward enemy lines when the unit was attacked by Mosby's Confederate cavalry. Collier had to run the horse into a rail fence to stop it.[655]

Quaker—U.S. Capt. (12th CT Inf.) John William DeForest
  Male. Described by DeForest as an "old nag." He was riding this horse during Sheridan's 1864 campaign in the Shenandoah Valley. When DeForest lost a spur, the horse began to pivot around and around while in a gully which was under fire. DeForest dug the rowel of the remaining spur in one side of the horse and hit the other side with the flat of his sword, which got thehorse out of the gully.[656]

Queen—U.S. Capt. (unit not known) _____ Kershaw
  Ridden by Capt. Gustav von Blucher against 6 others in the 1st (steeplechase) race held March 17, 1863, in the celebration of St. Patrick's Day near the Falmouth, VA, HQ of Gen. David B. Birney.[657]

Rambler—U.S. Maj. Gen. John Sedgewick[658]

"Rebbie"—see *Little Rebel* preceding.

Rebel—CS Lt. (Fenner's LA Arty) W.T. Cluverius
  The horse was shot in the head and died at New Hope, GA, on May 26, 1864.[659]

Rebel—CS 1st Lt. (VA 1st Richmond Howitzers) William Price Palmer
  Loaned to then–Pvt. Richard A. Stiles in December 1862 to visit his brother.[660]

Red Eye—CS Brig. Gen. Richard Brooke Garnett
  Gelding, thoroughbred, gray. Called "magnificent" and valued at $1,400, it was said to be the 2nd highest valued horse in the 1st Corps of the Army of Northern Virginia. Garnett and the horse were both killed in Pickett's Charge at Gettysburg on July 3, 1863.[661]

Red Oak—U.S. Maj. Gen. Don Carlos Buell
  During the movement to Perryville in 1862, a soldier tried to grab this horse's reins while the general was astride it. Frightened, the horse reared up and fell backward over Buell, who was severely cut and bruised.[662]

Red Oak—U.S. Lt. Col. (12th IL Inf.) Charles Ducat Sr.
Thoroughbred. In use 1862 crossing the Hatchie River, TN.[663]

Red Pepper—CS Maj. Gen. Patrick Ronayne Cleburne
Chestnut bay, large.[664] The horse was wounded in the hip during the 1864 Battle of Spring Hill, TN, when a shell burst overhead.[665]

Red Robin—CS Lt. (1st GA Regulars) John Porter Fort
His original horse while serving as a private in a FL coastal defense cavalry company in northwest Florida. Exchanged it for Flying Ant.[666]

Redmond—U.S. Sgt. (unit unknown) _____ Redmond
    CS Sgt. (2nd SC Cav.) William A. "Bill" Mickler
Bay. Named George by its original master. Captured in 1862 near Brentsville, VA, by Mickler from its mortally wounded master, who requested Mickler to care for it. Sgt. Mickler renamed the animal for this previous owner.[667]

Regulator—CS unknown unit and rider
Morgan. Full brother of Hunter. In Richmond, VA, prior to the war. Sired a number of cavalry horses.[668]

Reindeer—CS Maj. Gen. Simon Bolivar Buckner
Sorrel. While visiting in Greenville, KY, in late 1861, Buckner saw George W. Haden riding this horse, admired it, and offered to buy it. Haden refused the offer but hearing of it, Mrs. Haden had it sent to Buckner. It was stolen at Fort Donelson but later returned to Buckner.[669]

Reno—U.S. Brig. Gen. Orlando Bolivar Willcox
Also called his Washington horse. Killed during the Battle of Antietam.[670]

Richmond—CS Gen. Robert Edward Lee
Stallion, bay, big. This horse was given to Lee by admirers of Richmond (hence the name)[671] and used by him during the 1861 campaign in western Virginia.[672] It lacked stamina and tired easily. It also squealed and bucked around other horses.[673] When later stationed in South Carolina, Lee left it behind in Richmond under the supervision of his son, G.W.C. ("Custis") Lee. He wrote his son from South Carolina in January regarding the need to exercise the horse and about forage returns for it. He also wrote, "I am sorry to hear about his leg [the ailment is not known]. Do not let him have too much grain. I fear he will be great trouble to you, & if you cannot exercise him I do not know what will become of him."[674] On August 3, 1862, Lee wrote his wife that Richmond had died a few days prior. He said that he had ridden it the day before and that it seemed well but was not so in the evening. He thought the horse was only distressed by heat. Since it did not recuperate and was breathing heavily, he had it bled. This seemed to revive the horse and the next morning he administered a purgative to it. At noon, Richmond was reported dead. About Richmond, Lee concluded, "He carried me very faithfully & I shall never have so beautiful animal again."[675]

Rienzi—U.S. Capt. (2nd MI Cav.) Archibald P. Campbell
    U.S. Maj. Gen. Philip Sheridan
Gelding, jet black except for 3 white feet, 16 hands high. Of Morgan stock[676] and descended from Blackhawk.[677] Another source states that its dam was brought from

Sheridan's "Winchester Horse." Rienzi's taxidermed remains are displayed at the Smithsonian Institution's National Museum of American History, Division of Armed Forces History (courtesy Smithsonian Institution).

Canada, and that the sire was a full-blooded fox-hunter and the dam ¾ fox-hunter.[678] Foaled in 1858 near Grand Rapids, MI.[679] Was strongly built and had endurance — could run 5 mph at its natural walking gait. Capt. Campbell distrusted the horse's temperament and seldom rode it. He gave it to Sheridan in 1862 at Rienzi, MS — after which Sheridan renamed the horse (previous name not known). Rienzi was ridden by Sheridan almost exclusively thereafter throughout numerous battles and campaigns during which it was wounded several times. Sheridan retrieved a Union victory on October 19, 1864, after a long ride from Winchester to Cedar Creek.[680] This ride was popularized by two poems — most notably, "Sheridan's Ride" by Thomas Buchanan Read. Neither poem mentioned the horse's name or even particularly concentrated on the horse.[681] Nevertheless, in popular imagination, Rienzi became known as "Winchester." Though some sources say that Gen. Sheridan renamed him,[682] the general never referred to it in his memoirs as other than by Rienzi.[683] Memory became a legend. Humorist Bill Nye in his *Remarks* included an essay, "General Sheridan's Horse" (see Appendix C), which poked fun at this (and by extension) the many conflicting legends that had arisen about the Civil War.[684] When his horse died in 1878,[685] Gen. Sheridan had it stuffed and presented it to the Military Service Institution Museum on Governor's Island at New York City, where it was displayed.[686] Its body was often draped with flowers by veterans on Memorial Day.[687] This museum was destroyed by fire but Rienzi's remains were saved, and in June 1922, the horse was transferred to the Smithsonian Institution in Washington,[688] where it is now displayed in the Hall of Armed Forces History.

Rifle — CS Lt. Gen. Richard Stoddart Ewell
Mare, gray.[689] Described as an "old gray,"[690] "lean,"[691] and a "flea-bitten, bag-o-bones nag."[692] ("Flea-bitten" has nothing to do with fleas or bites but is a color pattern — see Appendix A.) This horse was new to Ewell as of January 1864.[693] He cherished it[694] and was riding it when he surrendered at the Battle of Sailor's Creek in April 1865.[695]

Rinaldo — CS cavalry officer (unit and name not known)
U.S. Col. (1st SC Inf./33rd U.S. Col'd Inf.) Thomas Wentworth Higginson
Sorrel with a white line down its face and 2 white feet. In use in the vicinity of Jacksonville, FL. Ate salt like it was sugar.[696]

Roanoke — CS Capt. (3rd LA Cav.) Beverly Buckner
A "powerful hunter," it was used briefly in May 1861 when Buckner originally joined the army. It was then returned to Buckner's "Winn Forest" plantation in Madison Parish, LA.[697]

Roanoke — CS officer, name and unit unknown
U.S. Brig. Gen. George Armstrong Custer
Thoroughbred gray. Captured from a Confederate officer at the Battle of White Oak Swamp in 1862.[698] During the July 3, 1863, cavalry battle at Gettysburg, this horse stumbled and Custer had to mount another, riderless, horse to continue in the battle.[699]

Robin — see *Old Bob* (of A. Lincoln) preceding.

Robin Hood — U.S. Lt.(unit not known) _____ Dennison
According to Davis, *Life of David Bell Birney*:
A Lt. Searle rode this horse (Dennison was riding Zoozoo) in the 2nd (a steeplechase) race held March 17, 1863, celebrating St. Patrick's Day near the Falmouth, VA, HQ of Gen. David B. Birney.[700]

Rock — CS Maj. (staff of Ewell) George Campbell Brown
Thoroughbred. Used by Brown throughout the war until his capture at the April 1865 Battle of Sailor's Creek. After the war, a North Carolina man named Robards took the horse to his home, but when it would not work, starved it to death.[701]

Roderick— CS Lt. Gen. Nathan Bedford Forrest

Gelding. A gift from a Mr. Cocke of Tennessee, killed during battle at Thompson's Station, TN.[702] The planned community of Roderick Place, TN, is named after this horse, and a statue to Roderick has been erected at its entrance.[703]

Rodney— U.S. Col. (124th IL Inf.) John H. Howe

During the late spring of 1863 near Richmond, LA, during operations to Vicksburg, Howe (then Lt. Col.) received this "valuable horse" from home. He turned out the horse to "play and graze." Somehow, the horse stumbled, breaking its left fore shoulder, and had to be shot.[704]

Rodney— U.S. Col. _____ Vincent

Ridden by a Lt. Chambers, won over 3 other horses in the 3rd (flatcourse) race held on March 17, 1863, in celebration of St. Patrick's Day near the Falmouth, VA, HQ of Gen. David B. Birney.[705]

Roebuck— U.S. Brig. Gen. Orlando Bolivar Willcox

Third horse Willcox used during Battle of Antietam. Used in camp and on the march but not in battle because it was frisky but not vicious.[706]

Romney— U.S. Lt. (11th NY Cav.) Henry Murray Calvert

Male, blood bay with black points. Near Edwards Ferry, VA, it dislocated the whirl bone of its stifle joint and had to walk on 3 legs. Was turned over to the QM when it didn't improve.[707]

Rondy— U.S. Lt. Gen. Ulysses S. Grant

Purchased in Galena, IL. Writing July 1861 to his wife from Naples, IL, Grant advised that he was letting his son, Fred, ride the horse.[708]

Rover— CS Lt. (2nd Creek Mtd.) George Washington Grayson

Credited with saving Grayson's life on several occasions.[709]

Rover— CS Pvt. (6th VA Cav.) Luther W. Hopkins

Mare. "Colts on the farm together" with Hopkins and the first horse he used during the war. In the spring of 1863, he had to desert the horse on the banks of the Shenandoah River in order to avoid capture.[710]

Roy— CS Maj. Gen. Dabney Herndon Maury

In use about Corinth, MS, in 1862. Maury called it "my finest horse."[711]

Roy— CS Chaplain (2nd VA Cav.) Randolph Harrison McKim

Ruby— U.S. Col. (4th MO Cav.) George E. Waring, Jr.

Male. Excellent jumper. The first mount of the colonel, it broke a thigh in a blacksmith shop accident and had to be put down.[712]

Ruksh— U.S. Col. (54th MA Inf.) Charles Russell Lowell Jr.

Stallion, black, large. In use in 1863 at the time the 54th MA Inf. was organized.[713] (In literature, this name is attributed to one of the horses of Achilles and to the horse of Rustum in a poem by Matthew Arnold.)

Saltron— CS Maj. (staff of Longstreet) John W. Fairfax

Stallion, gray. Had been raised at Fairfax's Loudon, VA, estate. While being ridden by Fairfax during the 1862 Battle of Antietam, it was struck in the fundament right under the tail by a cannon shot and killed. Greatly distressed, Fairfax exclaimed to Longstreet about Saltron's death and circumstances. Longstreet replied that Fairfax should be glad that it was not he who had been struck.[714]

Sam—U.S. Capt. (2nd CO Cav.) E. W. Kingsbury
Kingsbury and the horse were both wounded during the 1864 Battle of Newtonia, MO. In some manner at an unknown time they became separated, but in 1881 were somehow reunited. Then about 30 years old, the horse was referred to as Veteran Sam.[715]

Sam—U.S. Maj. Gen. William Tecumseh Sherman
Half-thoroughbred, dark chestnut bay, 5'4" at the withers, weighed about 1,000 lbs. Acquired by Sherman after the Battle of Shiloh to replace a horse that was killed. Named after his friend, U.S. Grant. Used thereafter including, it is believed, during the "March to the Sea." It was wounded several times, including once shot through the neck. After the war, about 1870, Sam was retired to the Frankfort, IL, farm of William Sanger, a Sherman friend. Here it was frequently ridden by Sanger's grandchildren. It died in 1874 and was buried on Sanger's farm near a grove of trees. The farm has since been developed and the precise location is now not known. A metal statue of the horse, with Sherman and Sanger's grandchildren, was placed in downtown Frankfort in 2004.[716] Sherman rode this horse in the Grand Review at Washington after the war.[717]

Sam Patch—CS Gen. Joseph Eggleston Johnston
Described as "a little bay mare."[718] He was using this horse during the 1862 Peninsula Campaign in Virginia.[719]

San Antonio—CS Maj. Gen. Earl Van Dorn
While he was in Texas during 1861, the citizens of San Antonio presented Van Dorn with this horse, which he named after the city.[720]

San Jose—see "*Old Joe*" preceding.

Sardanapalus—CS Brig. Gen. (MO St. Guard) Meriwether "Jeff" Thompson
Stallion, spotted.[721] White. Purchased July 25, 1861, in Missouri.[722] (Sardanapalus was the last king of Assyria, according to ancientGreek writers. Alexander the Great visited his tomb. He was the subject of an 1821 play by Lord Byron.)

Scott—CS Lt. (28th TX Cav. Dismtd.) Theophilus Perry
It had been returned home by August 4, 1862, since it had been doing poorly.[723]

Secesh—CS unknown rider and unit
U.S. Brig. Gen. Thomas Edwin Greenfield Ransom
Cream-colored. A Confederate soldier was killed at Charleston, MO, and this horse was taken in 1861 while Ransom was serving as colonel of the 11th IL Inf.[724]

Secessia—U.S. Brig. Gen. Alexander Hays
"Contraband horse" acquired 1864.[725]

Seliem—CS Pvt. (Balletine's MS Partisan Rangers) Atless Jones Dickson[726]

Selim—CS (GA Militia) Brig. Gen. Charles David Anderson
Black. Wounded during 1864 Battle of Griswoldville, GA. ("Selim" was a common name used in a noted thoroughbred family of the early 1800s.)

Selim— CS Sgt. (cav./ordnance/courier/hospital) William G. Stevenson
U.S. cavalry (unit unknown — command of Ebenezer Dumont)
Stallion with a "finely arched neck." Initially a bit wild when obtained by Stevenson near Bowling Green, KY, in 1861. It threw its master over his head and then broke his kneepan by striking him with his rear legs. Used by Stevenson through the retreat from Nashville, left behind at Corinth during Shiloh, taken to Mobile and Selma, and finally was used during Stevenson's desertion and flight north via Chattanooga. Stevenson and Selim arrived at McMinnville, TN, within Union lines about June 20, 1862. While it was hitched in front of a hotel there, Union cavalry of Gen. Dumont entered the town and appropriated the horse without Stevenson's knowledge.[727]

Sharpsburg— U.S. QM (unit not known) _____McCormick
According to Conyngham, *Irish Brigade*, and Mulholland, *116th Pennsylvania*:
Bay. Ridden by Lt. O'Connor vs. 5 other horses in 1st race held in celebration of St. Patrick's Day on March 17, 1863, at Falmouth, VA.[728]

Shellbark— U.S. Pvt. (70th IN Inf.) "Bird" (actual name unknown)
A POW, "Bird" met and rejoined the regiment in SC in 1865 riding this "long-necked, long-bodied, long-legged, bony horse."[729]

Shenandoah— U.S. Maj. Gen. Nathaniel Prentiss Banks
Purchased in VA. Banks's favorite.[730]

Sheridan— U.S. Maj. Gen. James Harrison Wilson
One source says: Gray. Wounded during the Battle of Selma in April 1865 but rose and so was ridden by Wilson through the remainder of the battle and accompanied him to Macon, GA, where it died in May 1865.[731] Wilson himself wrote that the horse was a gray gelding. During the Battle of Selma, he heard Confederate foes shout, "Shoot the man on the white horse," after which the horse was wounded by a bullet in the breast. There was no trickle of blood, and Sheridan showed neither pain nor fatigue, so it was ridden for the remainder of the battle until 11:00 that night. Two weeks later it was wounded through the neck by a stray shot while crossing the Chattahoochee River bridge at Columbus, GA. It died 2 weeks later at Macon.[732] Named after Gen. Phil Sheridan, under whom Wilson had served in Virginia.

Sherman— see *Dolly* (Sherman's) preceding.

Shiloh— U.S. courier (Army of the Cumberland), name and unit unknown
Male. Used by an anonymous courier in 1863 near Trenton, GA, prior to Chickamauga, to carry a message to Gen. George Thomas. During the journey, while fording a stream, the courier was fired upon and sped away on the horse but noticed its strength was failing. Dismounting, he found that the horse was wounded, with blood flowing down its flanks. It soon died.[733]

Shiloh— CS Lt. Col. (staff of Gen. J. A. Wharton) Richard Francis Lubbock
Lubbock left Austin riding this horse on April 10, 1864, for Shreveport, LA, to join the army.[734]

Shiloh— see *Black Auster*.

Siegel— U.S. Maj. (103rd IL Inf.) Charles W. Wills
Bay, large. Wills used this horse in 1862–63 while adjutant of the 7th Illinois Cav-

alry serving in Missouri (under Gen. Franz Siegel) and then in Tennessee and Mississippi.[735]

Silver Tail— U.S. Surgeon (121st NY Infantry) Daniel M. Holt

Cream-colored with white mane and tail. Used May 15, 1863, at the Battle of Salem Church. Leading about 20 men instructed to follow his horse after the Battle of Chancellorsville, Holt and the horse were halted and captured by Confederate Gen. Kershaw.[736]

Simon— CS enlisted soldier (E.P. Alexander's artillery battery) Jim _____

Mule, white. Balky on an occasion during the march to Gettysburg.[737]

Simon Bolivar— U.S. teamster (Army of the Potomac), name unknown.

Mule. During the 1st day of the Battle of the Wilderness (May 7, 1864), teamsters were ordered into the ranks and sent to the front. As they were marching past the teams, one was recognized by his lead mule, which commenced to bray loudly. Addressing the mule by name, the driver told it to quiet down or it too would be put in the ranks.[738]

Sir Oliver— CS Brig. Gen. John Hunt Morgan

When slain in September 1864 at Greeneville, TN, Morgan was trying to reach the stable where this horse was located.[739]

Skedaddle— U.S. Brig. Gen. Jefferson Columbus Davis

Postwar he kept the horse on his Clark Co., IN, farm.[740]

Skedaddle— CS cavalry command of Brig. Gen. John Hunt Morgan

A "celebrated race horse" which Morgan's command appropriated from a Mr. Clay of Kentucky during one of its raids. Clay pursued with two other horses, which he offered to swap for Skedaddle back. He lost those two horses as well.[741]

Skylark— CS Maj. Gen. James Ewell Brown "Jeb" Stuart

Stallion, "fleet." A gift to Stuart while at Harpers Ferry in mid–1861 from Charles Alexander Ware. Stuart escaped capture at Verdiersville on this horse. One of two horses (the other was Lady Margrave) captured from Stuart's sleeping servant during the Chambersburg Raid in 1862.[742]

Slasher— U.S. Maj. Gen. John Alexander Logan

Black. Apparently a very fast horse.[743] Period of this horse's use is not known other than that it was ridden by Logan at Atlanta.[744] There is an "urban legend" that this horse is stuffed and stored at the Smithsonian Institution; this story was briefly featured in the intrigue book *The Lost Symbol* by Dan Brown (author of *The Da Vinci Code*). The only stuffed horse in the collection of the Smithsonian is that of Gen. Sheridan's Rienzi.[745]

Sleepy Jeff— U.S. (Army of the James) unknown rider

A good racer which had once belonged to an ambulance train. Soldiers often raced this horse for entertainment.[746]

Slicky— U.S. Maj. Gen. Alfred Pleasanton[747]

Loaned to Gen. Meade on July 2, 1863, during Battle of Gettysburg.[748]

Snip and ***Snap***— CS civilian (Chaplain to Provisional Congress) Basil Manly
      CS army (unknown unit)

"Old." In March 1863 at Montgomery, AL, Confederate impressment agents took these two horses for the military.[749]

Snodder—CS Pvt. (9th KY Inf., Mtd.) John W. Jackman
In use January 1865 in GA. En route to Macon, GA, an inebriated Lt. Henry Buchanan ran his horse into this one, then the mount of an unknown soldier, with both horses and their riders going down. Neither horses nor riders were badly hurt. In February 1865, Pvt. John W. Jackman was using it for foraging.[750]

Soloman—U.S. Brig. Gen. Alexander Hays
This horse was struck by bullets in 8 places when Hays was killed during the Battle of the Wilderness.[751]

Sorghum—CS Pvt. (9th KY Inf., Mtd.) George Pash
Described as "a little scrub of a thing"—so little that when borrowed briefly by Pvt. John W. Jackman, Jackman's feet nearly dragged the ground. In use January 1865 in GA.[752]

Spike—U.S. Maj. (2nd OH Cav.) Luman Harris Tenney
In use, November 1863, January 1864, and June 1864 in East Tennessee.[753]

Spot—U.S. Col. (1st DE Inf.) John W. Andrews
Horse killed during the Battle of Antietam.[754]

Spot—CS Col. name and unit unknown
         U.S. Brig. Gen. Hugh Judson Kilpatrick
Arab. Captured during 1862 from a Confederate colonel.[755]

Star—see **Star of the East** immediately following.

Star of the East—CS Maj. Gen. James Ewell Brown "Jeb" Stuart
Sorrel with light mane and tail. It came from Fauquier Co., VA, and was used from the beginning of the war until the winter of 1863–64, when it died of glanders at camp near Orange Court House, VA.[756]

The Star of the West—see under T

Stonewall—CS Maj. Gen. Patrick Roynane Cleburne
Bay. Went missing near Dalton, GA, in May 1864.[757]

Stonewall—CS (Morton's GA Battery)
This was the horse of the color bearer during the May 1863 Battle of Raymond, MS.[758]

Stony—U.S. Brig. Gen. William Grose
Gray. Wounded at Murfreesboro while in use by then–Col. (36th IN Inf.) Grose. Later died and was buried in the Sequatchee Valley, TN.[759]

Stumbler—U.S. Lt. (unit not known) _____ Searle
According to Davis, *Life of David Bell Birney*:
A Lt. Moorhead rode Searle's horse (Searle was riding Robin Hood) in the 2nd race (a steeplechase) held March 17, 1863, celebrating St. Patrick's Day near the Falmouth, VA, HQ of Gen. David B. Birney.[760]

Sukey—U.S. Lt. (5th NY Cav.) Lucius Renne
         U.S. Pvt. (5th NY Cav.) Charles Holcomb
         U.S. Pvt. (5th NY Cav.) Dave Robbins

Mare, Morgan, sorrel. In 1863 won a race organized by Gen. Kilpatrick. While a regimental mail carrier, Robbins and the horse were captured by Mosby's men.[761]

Sultan— U.S. Lt. (11th NY Cav.) John Orphin Massey

Male. Massey initially named this horse Sultana until persuaded that was a feminine name. Both Massey and the horse were captured while serving in the Dept. of the Gulf in 1864.[762]

Superior— CS Lt. Gen. Thomas Jonathan "Stonewall" Jackson[763]

Sweet Will— CS Lt. Gen. Alexander Peter Stewart

The general had had 3 horses killed beneath him at the Battle of Resaca[764] and was using this one during the 1864 battles about Atlanta.[765]

Tammany— U.S. Maj. Gen. Daniel Edgar Sickles[766]

The general was riding this horse July 2, 1863, at Gettysburg when struck in the leg by a cannonball — the horse was remarkably untouched and remained calm.[767] (Sickles was a member of New York City's Tammany Hall political machine.)

Tangent— ERROR

Found on some lists of Civil War horses as the property of CS Lt. Gen. Richard Stoddert Ewell. This was a prewar horse which Ewell raced. Curiously, another of Ewell's prewar horses, Tar River, coupled with this horse in accounts, is omitted from lists.

Tarheel— CS Servant (of Gen. Ramseur) Caleb

Caleb swapped this horse away in August 1864 near Bunker Hill, VA.[768]

Tarter— U.S. Capt. (Battery B, U.S. 4th Art.) James Sewart

Taken into U.S. service 1857 at Ft. Leavenworth, KS. Abandoned on the plains due to distemper, it was later turned in in good condition by Indians for a reward. Assigned to then–Sgt. Stewart in 1860. Transferred with the battery by rail to Washington at the war's beginning. During the Battle of Second Manassas, a shell wounded Tarter in both rear legs and cut off its tail at the base. Stewart mounted another horse but found the wounded horse was following after him. Stewart continued to use Tarter after its recovery. President Lincoln commented upon Tarter during a review of the Army of the Potomac. Wounded again at Fredericksburg, it became difficult to steady. Just prior to Gettysburg, it was lamed by a nail and had to be left in the horse lines and afterwards left with a farmer. In August 1863, a tailless horse was observed in a cavalry unit, and Stewart reclaimed Tarter and used it for the remainder of the war. The horse was still with the battery when Stewart transferred to the 18th Inf. in 1866.[769]

Teasle— U.S. unknown

  CS unknown

The property of Dr. Dwight Hitchcock in the Cherokee Nation. Union and Confederate forces both took this horse several times but it would run away and return home.[770] (The name appears to be from a herb with a flower head surrounded by spines.)

Tennessee— U.S. Brig. Gen. William Grose

In use during the 1863 Tullahoma campaign by then–Col. (36th IN Inf.) Grose.[771]

The General— ERROR

A favorite of President John Tyler, this horse is buried on his Sherwood Forest Plantation with an epitaph extolling 21 years' faithful service.[772] It was not, however, "used as a warhorse during the Civil War." It died many years prior to the war.

The John Horse—CS (MO Militia) Pvt. (bodyguard of Gen. D.M. Frost) Jack Murphy
This small horse with long, badly kept hair and an unsteady gait was used by its owner to entice others into racing against it—and won easily. This racing occurred near Camp Jackson, MO (outside of St. Louis), before U.S. forces captured the MO militia encamped there.[773]

The Lady Polk—CS Brig. Gen. Otho French Strahl
        CS Chaplain (1st TN Inf.) Charles Todd Quintard
A few days before the 1864 Battle of Franklin, Gen. Strahl gave this horse to Quintard, who used it through the remainder of the war and until 1869, when he sold it. He donated the proceeds for a memorial stained glass window at St. James Church, Bolivar, TN, in memory of Gen. Strahl and his adjutant, Lt. John Marsh, who were both killed during the Battle of Franklin.[774]

The Star of the West—CS Pvt. (Mitchell Rangers, NC) Romulus M. Brown
Purchased by Brown's father in TX at the start of the war and used in western NC.[775] (This company became part of the 58th NC Inf.)

Thomas—U.S. Asst. Surgeon (19th MI Inf.) John Bennitt
Left Ann Arbor with this horse in November 1861. In December 1862, the horse was lame but being "well taken care of" by the regiment while Bennitt was working at the Division Hospital at Nicholsville, KY.[776]

Thunderbolt—CS Lt. (1st KY Cav. Bn.) Louis Roberts
Described as "crow-bait" and barefooted. Roberts unsuccessfully tried to swap off this horse in February 1862.[777]

Tobey—U.S. Maj. Gen. William Starke Rosecrans
Dappled gray, "nettlesome." Ridden alternately with Boney at Stones River and through Chickamauga.[778]

Tom—U.S. Surgeon (23rd MA Inf.) George Derby
Sorrel, "big." In use at Newport News, VA, in 1862.[779]

Tom—U.S. QM Sgt. (5th OH Cav.) William H. Harding
Dark-colored.[780]

Tom—U.S. Col. (20th CT Inf.) Samuel Ross
Black.[781]

Tom—U.S. Maj. Gen. John Sedgwick
The general wrote to his sister on July 6, 1862, from camp on the James River, VA, saying "My old favorite horse, which I have had ten years, received a ball in the leg, soon after a piece of shell struck him, and within a minute a ball grazed my leg going through and through poor old Tom; he lived a few minutes, groaning most piteously, following me about until he fell."[782]

Tom Taylor—U.S. soldier (1st MA Cav., Co. C) _____ _____
Fast, the horse won several bets match racing for men of the company until, just before the Battle of the Wilderness, it lost to another regiment's horse, which turned out to be a thoroughbred quarterhorse.[783]

Tom Telegraph—CS Brig. Gen. Turner Ashby

Occasionally referred to as "Gallant Gray." Arabian, white. Shot through the lungs on April 17, 1862, north of New Market in Virginia and died the same day one-half mile south of there near the Valley Pike. Henry Kyd Douglas called it "the most beautiful war-horse I ever saw."[784] A bit of its hair was snipped off by a member of the Stonewall Brigade. This sample was later attached to some hair from Stonewall Jackson's Fancy, tied with ribbon and mounted on pasteboard. This artifact is in the collection of the Museum of the Confederacy, as is a flower spray woven from Tom Telegraph's hair, tied by a black ribbon, which was presented to Ashby's mother. The museum also possesses an oval lady's brooch with a gold rim and smooth bone surface in the center. The bone was picked after the war by Sallie E. (Casler) Alexander on the spot where the horse lay after dying and had decayed. Mrs. Alexander's father had lived near there. She made the brooch. Dr. S.C. Henkel had preserved one of the horse's hooves and its thigh bone. Crochet needles were later made of the thigh bone and sold at a Baltimore church fair for $50. The hoof is in the collection of the Museum of the Confederacy.[785]

Tom Tug— U.S. Col. (state rank, staff of MA Gov. John Andrew) Henry Lee
Lee was extremely fond of the horse, which lived to be 25 to 30 years of age.[786]

Tommy— U.S. Col. (unit not known) _____ McGenahan
According to Davis, *Life of David Bell Birney*:
Ridden by Maj. Ira Spalding vs. 11 other horses in the 2nd (a steeplechase) race held on March 17, 1863, in celebration of St. Patrick's Day near the Falmouth, VA, HQ of Gen. David B. Birney.[787]

Tommy— U.S. Maj. (10th MA Inf.) Dexter F. Parker
Parker's favorite, in use October 1862 and killed May 1864 at Spotsylvania.[788]

Topsy—U.S. Lt. (5th NY Cav.) Clark M. Pease
Mare, Morgan, coal black with white stripe on its face, weighed less than 900 lbs. Was an excellent jumper. Killed September 19, 1864, during Battle of Winchester.[789]

Tramp— CS enlisted soldier (John C. Haskell's artillery bn.) Lewis Haskell
A sore-back horse that could be ridden only with a McClellan saddle, it was brought to Virginia from South Carolina by this youngest brother of the battalion commander. While untied, it wandered off during the retreat from Petersburg, but was found soon after.[790]

Traveler— erroneous; see *Traveller*.
The spelling of the name of Gen. Lee's famous horse is frequently encountered with only a single "L." Robert E. Lee himself spelled the name with a double "L,"[791] as did his son, Robert E. Lee Jr.[792]; his early biographer, Armistead L. Long[793]; and his premier biographer, Douglas Southall Freeman.[794] "LL" is therefore considered to be the proper spelling in this work. The "LL" may indicate a very slight difference in pronunciation.

Traveller— CS Capt. James W. Johnston
    CS Maj. Thomas L. Broun
    CS Capt. Joseph M. Broun
    CS Gen. Robert Edward Lee
The most famous horse of the Civil War, its name is very frequently misspelled with a single "L" (see *Traveler* immediately preceding for discussion of the spelling). Previous names of this horse were Jeff Davis and Greenbriar.

Description: Gen. Lee himself described the horse while president of Washington College in a letter (dictated to his daughter, Agnes) to Martha "Markie" Custis Williams:

> If I were an artist like you, I would draw a true picture of Traveller —
> representing his fine proportions, muscular figure, deep chest and short
> back, strong haunches, flat legs, small head, broad forehead, delicate ears,
> quick eye, small feet, and black mane and tail. Such a picture would inspire
> a poet, whose genius could then depict his worth and describe his endurance
> of toil, hunger, thirst, heat, cold, and the dangers and sufferings through
> which he passed. He would dilate upon his sagacity and affection, and his
> invariable response to every wish of his rider. He might even imagine his
> thoughts through the long night marches and the days of battle through which
> he has passed. But I am no artist; I can only say he is a Confederate gray....[795]

A more physical description is that he weighed 1100 lbs, was 16 hands high,[796] was iron-gray with black points, a long mane and flowing tail.[797] Union correspondent Sylvanus Cadwallader, who saw the horse at Appomattox, six years after the war, described it as a "dapple gray."[798] His color had become "almost milk white."[799] Sheridan's adjutant, Col. James W. Forsyth, described the horse at Appomattox as "a fairly well-bred-looking gray in good heart though thin in flesh."[800] Lee's nephew, Maj. Gen. Fitzhugh Lee, wrote after the war that Traveller was "greatly admired for his rapid, springy walk, high spirit, bold carriage and muscular strength."[801] During the early summer of 1863, Lee was accompanied by other officers in a review of Hill's Corps. He rode off on Traveller, and the horse set off with a long lope and never slowed down on the 9-mile circuit. The pace resulted in others' falling out as they and their horses tired out.[802] Jefferson Davis noticed the "rough gait" of the horse and offered to lend Lee one of his own fine horses — Lee declined.[803]

Lineage: Col. Forsyth had reason to comment that Traveller was "well-bred-looking." Some accounts stated that his bloodline was traceable to notable English horses Diomede and Sir Archy.[804] Others claim he was of "premium Greenbriar stock"[805] or of Gray Eagle stock.[806] Many, however, averred that his lineage was not traceable.[807] Though disputed, some sources state that his dam was a half-thoroughbred named Flora.[808] All descriptions and pictures attest that this was indeed a fine horse and must have had superior ancestry.

Early Life: Traveller was born in 1857 at the farm of Andrew Davis Johnston[809] near Blue Sulphur Springs, Greenbriar Co., WV (then VA).[810] Johnston named the horse Jeff Davis (at that time, Davis was a U.S. Senator from Mississippi and former U.S. Secretary of War). He was trained by a young slave named Frank Pace and twice won prizes at local fairs in the county.[811] The horse was carried off to war by the son of Mr. Johnston, Capt. James W. Johnston, who was with Confederate forces in western Virginia (now WV). Lee saw this horse there for the first time and admired it. Supposedly, Johnston told Lee that he was contemplating changing the name of the horse to Greenbriar.[812] Later it was sold by Capt. Johnston for $175 in gold to Major Thomas L. Broun.[813] Broun either bought the horse for,[814] or loaned it to, his brother, Capt. Joseph M. Broun.[815] The Brouns called it Greenbriar.[816] When in the Carolinas in early 1862, Lee again saw the horse, then being used by Capt. Broun at Pocotaligo, SC, and was again attracted to it. Broun offered to give the horse to Lee, but Lee declined. After a trial period of riding the animal, Lee insisted on paying Broun $200 for the horse — Broun's cost plus $25 to cover currency depreciation. (In August 1864, it was appraised at $4,600 in Confederate money.)[817]

With Lee at War: As late as December 29, 1861, Lee had not changed the horse's name. On this date he wrote his son G.W.C. Lee that he had ridden 35 miles on horseback, adding, "I took Greenbriar the whole distance."[818] The story goes that Lee enjoyed riding the horse on his journeys, and finding it a fine traveler, renamed it Traveller.[819] Numerous accounts note Gen. Lee riding Traveller throughout the war including at Second Manassas, Antietam, Chancellorsville, Get-

General Robert E. Lee Mounted on Traveller, Petersburg, 1864. This is the only known wartime photograph of the general on his famous horse (courtesy DeMenti Studio, Richmond, Virginia).

tysburg, the Wilderness, Petersburg, and during the retreat to Appomattox. It has already been explained in Chapter 13 that Traveller is invariably called culpable for the injuries to Lee's hands just prior to Antietam — except for one doctor's account that the guilty animal was a "gift horse." As previously noted, the horse attracted favorable attention from Union officers at Appomattox. Surrendered soldiers passed their hands in farewell over the sides of the horse — attention which he seemed to enjoy, as he would toss his head.[820]

After the War: After Appomattox, Traveller accompanied Lee to Richmond and then to Oakland, and finally carried the general to Lexington, VA, when he became president of Washington College (now Washington and Lee University). When a brick house was built by the college for Lee, a brick stable — with a covered passageway to the house — was also built. Traveller occupied one stall and Lucy Long the other.[821] Lee enjoyed riding his gray about town and the surrounding countryside nearly every afternoon until November 1869, when rides became limited to only when the weather was good.[822] Lee spoiled the horse and many later commented on his very visible affection for it.[823] After Lee died in 1870, Traveller followed his master's hearse in the funeral procession in Lexington.[824]

Death: Traveller survived Lee by only about 2 years. He had gone to the porch for a treat of sugar from Lee's daughters. One noticed that he was limping and advised their brother Custis. He examined the horse and found a nail in one hoof, which he removed. The horse wandered off and seemed to be all right, but the hoof became infected. There was, at that time, no "vet" in the town so local doctors attempted to do what they could.[825] One remedy tried was small doses of chloroform.[826] When Traveller became too weak to stand, a feather bed was placed on the stable floor for him. The condition only worsened and Lee's famous Traveller died of lockjaw at the age of 13 years.[827] His death was reported in the *Lexington Gazette* on June 30, 1871.[828] He was wrapped in his blankets and buried, under the supervision of Custis Lee on the campus of the college.[829]

After Death: After his death, Traveller was buried behind the main buildings of the Washington and Lee campus. About 1875 or 1876, someone unearthed the bones, and then bleached them for display at Rochester, NY. In 1907, Richmond journalist Joseph Bryan purchased the bones and had them mounted and returned to the college.[830] The skeleton was displayed in the Lee Museum at the college until 1929, when they were transferred to a basement to prevent vandalism. In 1971, the horse's bones were reinterred near the Lee Chapel at the college. A plaque was placed on the wall of his old stable.[831]

Traveller is also commemorated by several equestrian statues of Lee, which are discussed in Chapter 19. In 1988, Richard Adams's novel *Traveller* exposed the horse and its life to new generations of Americans. Some parts of Traveller remain today. Three bits of his mane are located in the collection of the Museum of the Confederacy in Richmond. Two of these were donated by Mildred Lee, a granddaughter, and the other is folded in a piece of paper stating that it was pulled from the horse's mane at Bremo, VA, on August 14, 1865. There is also a watch chain made from hair taken from Traveller's tail, which had been presented to Jefferson Davis Jr. and donated to the museum by his sister, Marjorie Hayes Davis.[832]

Trojan — CS? (9th Ky Inf., Mtd.) "Judge"? (possibly James W. Moore?)
Old with only one eye. In use January 1865 in GA. Too sore-backed for "Judge" to ride during a march to Macon, GA. Had served with artillery prior to the mounted infantry. At end of the war, was left in Georgia to pull a plow.[833]

"Trojan Horse" — CS Lt. Gen. Thomas Jonathan "Stonewall" Jackson
After Jackson was injured by a gift horse en route to Antietam, he never rode it again. Some members of his staff afterwards referred to this animal as "the Trojan Horse."[834]

Tulkahoma — see *Tullahoma* following.

Tullahoma — CS Maj. Gen. Alexander Peter Stewart
Stewart's "favorite," he originally named the horse Tulkahoma, after an Indian chief his grandfather had captured, but due to pronunciation problems, the name gradually changed to Tullahoma.[835]

Twist Tail — U.S. unknown cav. unit and rider
CS Pvt. (4th SC Cav.) Alex R. Taylor
CS Pvt. (4th SC Cav.) Barry Bostick
Taylor was captured at Trevilian Station in 1864 when his horse was killed, but he escaped the next day and returned to his unit riding a horse with its tail twisted to one side. He was complaining to the horse, calling it Twist Tail, that he didn't like it.

Riding the horse on December 12, 1864, Taylor captured a bay mare and turned this one loose. Days later, Twist Tail found its way back to the unit — Taylor had to turn in the mare and resume its use. He bought a horse and gave this one to Bostick, who was killed riding Twist Tail in the next action.[836]

Uncle Abe— U.S. Col. (Army of the Potomac QM Dept.) James Fowler Rusling
Gray. In use August 1862 near Alexandria, VA.[837]

Uncle Sam— U.S. Lt. Col. (22nd PA Cav.) Andrew J. Greenfield
Bay. Greenfield had ridden the horse throughout his service. Still in use in July 1864 when Sigel's forces were driven from the Shenandoah Valley.[838]

Van Dorn— U.S. Maj. Gen. Francis Preston Blair Jr.
Brown. In use near Savannah, GA, December 1864. Captured from CS Maj. Gen. Earl Van Dorn and named after him. (The source, a veteran of the 15th IA Inf. of Blair's command, believed the horse recently captured, but since Van Dorn had been murdered May 1863, this would be erroneous. The source wrote that Blair sent Van Dorn a check for $300 in payment after the war — perhaps Blair sent such a check to Van Dorn's widow.)[839]

Veteran Sam— see ***Sam*** (Kingsbury's).

Victory or "***Vic***"—ERROR
This horse sometimes appears on lists of Civil War horses. It was actually a postwar horse of Brig. Gen. George Armstrong Custer (he was riding it at the Battle of the Little Big Horn when killed).[840]

Virginia— CS Maj. Gen. James Ewell Brown "Jeb" Stuart
Mare, thoroughbred, bay. Originally from Maryland. Ridden throughout the Gettysburg campaign up to 50 hours at one stretch. Stuart escaped capture at Hanover, PA, by jumping a ditch on this horse. One of three horses of Stuart's which died of glanders at Orange Court House, VA, during the winter of 1863–64.[841]

Voltaire— CS Brig. Gen. Gilbert Moxley Sorrel
Stallion, little. Sorrel wrote that he "fell in love with" this horse in April 1862 (when on the staff of Longstreet). It proved to be too delicate for army work, so Sorrel gave it to his brother in Richmond, but it "soon went to pieces" anyway.[842]

Waif— U.S. Maj. Gen. James Harrison Wilson
One source says: Black. His favorite and apparently a good jumper, the horse developed boils in January 1865 and had to be sent back to Nashville for treatment. Evidently it did not accompany its master on his Alabama-Georgia raid in March and April of 1865.[843] But Wilson himself wrote: Male, gray bay with black points, 15 hands high and about 850 lbs. Wilson's groom had picked the horse up as a stray during the Siege of Vicksburg and therefore Gen. U.S. Grant (on whose staff Wilson was then serving) named it Waif. Wilson rode the horse for the remainder of the Vicksburg siege and during the Chattanooga campaign (except for loaning it to Grant for the Battle of Missionary Ridge and a few days thereafter). En route to Knoxville, the horse, startled by a steam cock on a steamboat, leaped overboard but was recovered on the bank of the Tennessee River. It was ridden from Knoxville to Lexington, VA. When Wilson became cavalry commander in the West, he took the horse with him to Nashville and

used it during Hood's campaign to that city. During the pursuit of Hood, mud froze on Waif's legs, and he was disabled after breaking through the ice on the road to the Tennessee River. The horse was sent back to the hospital in Nashville, and it was 6 weeks before it was returned fit for service. The horse was used during Wilson's March–April 1865 raid through Alabama into Georgia. After the war, he was given to Wilson's wife to use as saddle horse and to pull her phaeton. He died 15 years after the war (about 1880) in Delaware.[844]

War Eagle— CS Capt. (unknown unit) _____ Gillispie
Male. Said to be his "pet horse" with "free and easy" demeanor. In September 1864, while in Arkansas, Gillispie left the horse with the Stone family near Oak Ridge, LA.[845]

Warren— U.S. Maj. Gen. Benjamin Franklin Butler
Sorrel.[846]

Warren— CS Maj. Gen. Bryan Grimes[847]

Washington— see *Reno* preceding.

Webby— U.S. Brig. Gen. Rutherford Birchard Hayes
New to Col. Hayes of the 23rd OH Inf. during the New River campaign in NC. Hayes rode it daily. It was nearly knocked to the ground on one occasion when lightning struck close by.[848]

Wellington— U.S. Artillery (Griffin's Battery)
U.S. Brig. Gen. George Armstrong Custer
A high jumper,[849] this horse had been used at West Point when Custer was a cadet there. In July 1861, Custer encountered an enlisted man of Griffin's Battery in Washington who had been sent there for this spare battery horse, which had been left behind there. Custer had known this man at West Point. The man allowed Custer to use the horse to carry dispatches from Gen. Scott to McDowell. Custer used the horse at least during the Battle of First Manassas.[850]

"White Bull"—see *Jerome* preceding.

White Eye— U.S. soldier (1st MA Cav.) Richard A. Massey
Male, thoroughbred, sired by Boston. Had been a race horse in Virginia. Due to its poor temper it had several owners in Boston prior to the war. During the Maryland Campaign of 1862, it was being led with a pack on its back along a tow path when it unexpectedly leaped onto a boat, then the other side of the canal, and then into the Potomac, which it swam across.[851]

White Surrey— U.S. Maj. Gen. Joseph Hooker
Ridden by the general in a number of battles, it was with Hooker in early 1864 being transported by barge on the Tennessee River.[852]

Whitey— CS Lt. Gen. Richard Taylor
U.S. Col. (14th IA Inf.) William T. Shaw
U.S. Capt. (14th IA Inf.) Warren C. Jones
White. This horse had been captured from a Mexican officer early during the Mexican war and presented to Gen. Zachary Taylor by his men. He used it for the remainder of the war and took it home with him afterwards. He never referred to the horse as anything other than Whitey — his subordinates called it Old Whitey. When Taylor

was elected president, it went to Washington with him and grazed on the White House lawn. When President Taylor died, the horse was inherited by his son Richard, who kept it on his Louisiana plantation. Richard Taylor joined the Confederate army and rose to the rank of lieutenant general, but did not take this horse with him. During the Red River Campaign of 1864, the Union 14th Iowa Infantry "visited" the Taylor plantation, and despite the protests of Mrs. Taylor that the horse was old and had been the property of President Taylor, took the horse for the use of their colonel. When Col. Shaw died, Capt. Jones became the unit's acting commanding officer and used the horse until the end of the war. Afterwards, the horse was sent to Col. Shaw's Iowa farm where it was used to pull a plow. After two years, Jones bought the horse and retired it.[853]

Whitie — CS Chaplain (3rd VA Cav.) and spy Thomas Nelson Conrad
Male, sorrel with 4 white feet and white forefront. Was undisturbed by gunfire. In April was being used by one of Conrad's couriers, Mortimer B. Ruggles, who, encountering John Wilkes Booth fleeing southward in Virginia after assassinating Lincoln, allowed Booth to ride this horse to the Garrett house on the Rappahannock River, where he was captured.[854]

Whitie — U.S. Col. (9th MA Inf.) Patrick Robert Guiney
Little. Guiney wrote his wife that he had purchased a horse for $300 and would therefore, if she so desired, send this horse to her.[855]

Wild Bill — CS Pvt (16th AR Inf.) Joseph Bailey
Dark bay, medium size. Captured from a Union soldier in the winter of 1861 while Bailey was detached as "captain" of a "guerrilla" group. He sold the horse in late 1864 when again serving with the infantry. He saw it later with field artillery in southern Arkansas.[856]

Wild Bill of the Woods — CS Pvt. (9th KY Inf., Mtd.) James W. Yountz
In use January 1865. Due to "scratches," had bags tied around its feet during movement to Macon, GA.[857]

Willie — U.S. Brig. Gen. Joseph Bradford Carr
Presented to Carr by friends in Troy, NY, the horse was shot five times during the Battle of Gettysburg. Two of the bullets passed through its body, but it continued until hit by the fifth shot.[858]

"Winchester" — see ***Rienzi***.

Wonka — CS civilian (Madison Parish, LA) Sarah Katherine "Kate" Stone
    U.S. soldiers (unknown unit)
Male, blood bay. A gift from Stone's uncle, Bohanan Ragan, when he went into the army in 1861. Unwell but recovered by November 1861. During Union operations about Vicksburg it was hidden in a canebrake. On March 22, 1863, it was brought back to the plantation by a slave and almost immediately taken by U.S. soldiers.[859]

Wyman Horse, The — U.S. 1st Sgt. (5th NY Cav.) Henry Wyman
    Morgan. Killed October 18, 1862, at Thoroughfare Gap.[860]

Yancy — CS Lt. (staff of Anderson) Richard Trumball
    CS Brig. Gen. James Patton Anderson

Male, gray, Kentucky-foaled. Presented to Anderson by Trumball in February 1862. After Anderson's death (1872), his wife left the horse in the care of a former soldier of his command in Memphis, TN. The soldier took the horse to a military funeral, where it became restive, broke its bridle and followed the hearse to the cemetery. Mrs. Anderson and the horse later moved to KY, where a Mr. Adair kept it on his farm. It died there about 1881 at age 25.[861]

Yankee— U.S. (unit not known) Col. _____ Watkins
According to Davis, *Life of David Bell Birney*:
Lt. Boyle rode this horse against 11 others in the 2nd (steeplechase) race held March 17, 1863, celebrating St. Patrick's Day near the Falmouth, VA, HQ of Gen. David B. Birney.[862]

Yellow Horse— U.S. Capt. (1st U.S. Sharpshooters) Henry C. Garrison
Light buckskin in color and therefore given its name. Raced vs. a horse of Col. Biles of the 99th PA Inf. in 1864.[863]

Yorktown— U.S. Artificer (1st RI Lt. Arty.) Dexter P. Pearce
Male. A brown mare, collected in a field early during the Peninsula Campaign, later foaled this colt, which remained with the battery until the end of the war. Afterward, it was taken home by Pearce and kept 25 or 26 years.[864]

Young Giffords— U.S. master unknown.
Morgan. Survived the war.[865]

Young Salem— U.S. Brig. Gen. Erastus Barnard Tyler
Pure white, young, of Grey Eagle stock. Had been purchased in Ohio. The men and officers of his brigade presented this horse to Gen. Tyler in March 1863.[866]

Zella— U.S. Lt. (unit not known) _____ Seibre
Ridden by its owner vs. 6 others in the 1st (steeplechase) race held March 17, 1863, celebrating St. Patrick's Day near the Falmouth, VA, HQ of Gen. David B. Birney.[867]

Zollicoffer— U.S. Col. (15th PA Cav.) William J. Palmer
Black, blooded. At the Battle of Murfreesboro, was being ridden by Maj. Adolph Rosengarten. Together, they were pierced by 14 bullets and died.[868]

Zoozoo— U.S. Col. (114th PA Inf.) Charles H.T. Collis
According to Davis, *Life of David Bell Birney*:
Ridden by a Lt. Dennison against 11 other horses in the 2nd (steeplechase) race held on March 17, 1863, in celebration of St. Patrick's Day near the Falmouth, VA, HQ of Gen. David B. Birney.[869] (Collis commanded the "Collis Zouaves," so the use of the Zouave cheer as a name for his horse was appropriate.)

Some Interesting Civilian Horses of the Civil War Period

Bill— U.S. Stillwell family of Illinois
Mule, black, little. Leander Stillwell rode this mule to enlist in the 61st Illinois Infantry and returned it to his parents' farm the next day (February 1862).[870]

Dick— U.S. civilian Jonathan B. Upson

The owner's nephew, Theodore F. Upson, who had joined the 100th Indiana Infantry, used the animal in a 4th of July parade in 1862 as an aide to the parade marshal after his enlistment but before being mustered in.[871]

Flora Temple— U.S. citizen (Baltimore) William McDonald

Mare. This then-famous trotting horse had been sold in 1858 by Hiram Woodruff for $8,000 to McDonald. In 1861, Mcdonald voiced sympathies for the South. In August of that year the horse was confiscated (or in steps taken toward confiscation) and held at Fort McHenry. It was claimed that McDonald was also imprisoned there with the horse—in the same cell. A. Welsh of Philadelphia owned the horse postwar. Flora Temple died December 21, 1877, aged more than 32 years.[872]

General Butler, ***Hartford Belle*** and ***Prince***— U.S. racehorses

Thousands of soldiers witnessed sulky racing between these 3 horses at Washington's new National Race-Course held in October 1863. General Butler—more often referred to as simply Butler—was a black gelding and the favorite. Hartford Belle was a gray mare. Prince was a bay gelding. General Butler was the winner, taking the 1st, 2nd, and 4th heats. Hartford Belle withdrew after the 2nd heat. Prince won the 3rd heat.[873]

Grant and ***Sherman***— CS civilians Mr. _____ Sargent and Judge (actually J.P.) _____ Hyde

British observer Arthur J.L. Fremantle had traveled across south Texas in a "2-horse hack," the drivers of which were Sargent and Hyde. James A. Longstreet had known them when he had served prewar in Texas. He said their team was named Grant and Sherman.[874] Fremantle described this journey from Brownsville to San Antonio in April 1863 in his own book, *Three Months in the Southern States* (1863). He named both men but wrote that it was a 4-mule, 2-horse team, of which one horse had run away, and did not provide names of any of the animals.[875] Since Longstreet was writing in 1896, and at the time of Fremantle's trip Grant and Sherman were not as prominent as they later became, perhaps these two names are a result of faulty memory.

Harry Bluff— U.S.

Stallion. Sire during Civil War of June Bug.

Ida Mae— U.S.

Quarterhorse foundation dam involved 1864 in a walking race in Ohio.[876]

June Bug— U.S.

Quarterhorse foundation dam sired during Civil War in Greene Co., IL, by Harry Bluff out of Munch Meg.[877]

Lexington— U.S.

Thoroughbred, dark bay with white stockings, 15 hands and 3 inches high. By Boston out of Alice Carneal, foaled 1850. Probably the most famous racehorse and breed sire of the 19th century. At times, was raced under the name Darley. Retired from racing 1855 due to failing eyesight. Though blind by the time of the Civil War, had to be hidden to prevent his taking for military purposes. Died 1875. In 1878, his bones were donated to the Smithsonian Institution, where they were displayed until 2010. Since that time they have been displayed at the International Museum of the Horse in Lexington, KY. Sire of Gen. U.S. Grant's Cincinnati.[878]

Old Billy— CS civilian

   Male. This foundation sire of American quarter horses was born about the beginning of the war. His original owner is said to have kept him chained to a tree (to prevent its being taken) while he was away fighting in the Confederate Army.[879]

Steel Dust— Half sister of June Bug.[880]

"The Woolly-Horse"—U.S. civilian Phineas Taylor Barnum

   A letter of staff officer Theodore Garnett mentions "Sergt. Ben[jamin Franklin] Weller [a courier for Gen. J.E.B. Stuart], as the antebellum owner of the Woolly-Horse."[881] This was a curly-haired horse exhibited by Barnum as the horse with its head where its tail should be (he had it reversed in its stall) and falsely advertised as from Frémont's expedition through the Rocky Mountains.[882]

Horses Named in Richard Adams's Novel Traveller

   Thirty-seven horses are named in this entertaining novel. Horses named in the novel as belonging to Gen. Robert E. Lee, one belonging to Lt. Gen. T.J. "Stonewall" Jackson, one horse of Lt. Gen. A.P. Hill, two belonging to Maj. Gen. J.E.B. Stuart, and one of Lt. Gen. U.S. Grant, are real and are included in the roster and index. These are:

   Ajax, Brown Roan, Champ, Cincinnati, Little Sorrel, Lucy Long, Richmond, Skylark, Star of the East, and Traveller.

One horse named in the novel—Flora (Traveller's dam) is disputable but is mentioned in the roster and is indexed.

   The following horses appearing in the novel are either obvious contrivances or, at the best, not confirmable, and are neither mentioned in the roster nor indexed. These are:

   Bandit, Bluebird, Buckthorn, Crockett, Daffodil, Emerald, Frigate, Frisky, Ivy, Misty, Monarch, Moonlight, Rollo, Ruby, and Ruffian.

   Despite great effort, the names (and masters) of the following horses of the novel have been unverifiable and are neither mentioned in the roster nor indexed:

   Brigand (Gen. William Mahone), Chieftain (Gen. D.H. Hill), Dancer (Capt. Richard E. Wilbourn), Ginger (Gen. Armistead I. Long), Leopard (Maj. Charles S. Venable), Mercury (Col. Charles Marshall), Merlin (Sgt. Tucker), Romeo (Gen. Geo. E. Pickett), Sovereign (Gen. Eppa Hunton), and Thunderer (President Jefferson Davis).

Appendix A: Equine Colors and Marks

Colors of horses are encountered in Civil War stories and accounts more frequently than names. If one is unfamiliar with equines, colors mentioned — and especially marks — can be confusing. In one case, "flea-bitten," the connotation can be completely misleading. To assist the reader in better understanding colors and marks of equines mentioned herein and in other works about the Civil War, this appendix is provided. The definitions provided are summarized, with permission, from Vivienne M. Eby's *The Horse Dictionary: English-Language Terms Used in Equine Care, Feeding, Training, Racing and Show* (Jefferson, NC: McFarland, 1995).

Bald	White facial hair marking that includes both eyes. Entire face might be white.
Bay	Medium brown with black mane and tail. Shade can vary from light to dark. Sometimes a bay can have black lower legs.
Black	Applies to horses with black coat, mane and tail. Can have white face or leg markings.
Blaze	Wide white mark from between the eyes down to the muzzle.
Boot	White hair on leg from hoof up about halfway to the knee.
Brown	Sometimes mistaken for black. Flanks and muzzle are brown.
Buckskin	Yellow with black points. Variations are dark (black hairs with yellow hairs), dusty (yellow with a brownish cast) and silver (cream-colored).
Chestnut	Medium red.
Dapple	Color variation patterns of about 1-inch diameter.

Dun	Generally yellow with brown points. Can have stripes. Several variations:
	Claybank — Red and yellow shades. Coyote — Yellow and black hairs mixed. Red — Variations are: Muddy — Brownish red or yellow. Orange — Apricot-colored. Silver — Cream-colored. Yellow — Yellow.
Flea-Bitten	Gray horse speckled with small black or brown spots.
Gray or Grey	Dark-skinned horse with coat of mixed black and white hairs. Shade can vary from very dark to almost white, except the legs may have gray areas.
Iron Gray	an abundant number of dark hairs mixed with white hairs.
Mottled	Small white spots on the muzzle, around the eyes, on the genitals, or sometimes on the body.
Piebald	Black and white.
Points	Different color on the lips, mane, tail, and sometimes tips of the ears.
Roan	Dark hairs thickly sprinkled with white hairs.
Skewbald	White and some color other than black.
Sorrel	Light red.
Spot	White facial hair marking.
Star	White facial hair marking resembling the shape of a star.
Stocking	White surrounding the leg from hoof to knee.
White	Snow-colored. Gray horses can turn white with age.

Appendix B:
"Charge of the Mule Brigade"

Half a mile, half a mile,
   Half a mile onward,
Right through the Georgia troops
   Broke the two hundred,
"Forward the Mule Brigade!
Charge for the Rebs!"They neighed.
Straight for the Georgia troops
   Broke the two hundred.

"Forward the Mule Brigade!"
Was there a mule dismayed?
Not when the long ears felt
   All their ropes sundered.
Theirs not to make reply,
Theirs not to reason why,
Theirs but to make Rebs fly.
On! to the Georgia troops
   Broke the two hundred.

Mules to the right of them,
Mules to the left of them,
Mules behind them
   Pawed, neighed, and thundered,
Breaking their own confines,
Breaking through Longstreet's lines
Into the Georgia troops,
   Stormed the two hundred.

Wild all their eyes did glare,
Whisked all their tails in air
   Scattering the chivalry there,
While all the world wondered.
Not a mule back bestraddle,
Yet how they all skedaddled–
Fled every Georgian,
Unsabred, unsaddled,
   Scattered and sundered!
How they were routed there
   By the two hundred!

Mules to the right of them,
Mules to the left of them,
Mules behind them
   Pawed, neighed, and thundered;
Followed by hoof and head
Full many a hero fled,
Fain in the last ditch dead,
Back from an ass's jaw
All that was left of them,
   Left by the two hundred.

When can their glory fade?
Oh,the wild charge they made!
   All the world wondered.
Honor the charge they made!
Honor the Mule Brigade,
           Long-eared two hundred!

Appendix C: "General Sheridan's Horse" by Bill Nye

This humorous story was in the book *Remarks*, by Edgar Wilson "Bill" Nye, published in 1887 by M.W. Hazen, New York.

I have always taken a great interest in war incidents, and more so, perhaps, because I wasn't old enough to put down the rebellion myself. I have been very eager to get hold of and hoard up in my memory all its gallant deeds of both sides, and to know the history of those who figured prominently in that great conflict has been one of my ambitions.

I have also watched with interest the steady advancement of Phil Sheridan, the black-eyed warrior with the florid face and the Winchester record. I have also taken some pains to investigate the later history of the old Winchester war horse.

"Old Rienzi died in our stable a few years after the war," said a Chicago livery man to me, a short time ago. "General Sheridan left him with us and instructed us to take good care of him, which we did, but he got old at last, and his teeth failed upon him, and that busted his digestion, and he kind of died of old age, I reckon."

"How did General Sheridan take it?"

"Oh, well, Phil Sheridan is no school girl. He didn't turn away when old Rienzi died and weep the manger full of scalding regret. If you know Sheridan, you know that he don't rip the blue dome of heaven wide open with unavailing wails. He just told us to take care of its remains, patted the old cuss on the head a little and walked off. Phil Sheridan don't go around weeping softly into a pink bordered wipe when a horse dies. He likes a good horse, but Rienzi was no Jay-Eye-See for swiftness, and he wasn't the purtiest horse you ever see, by no means."

"Did you read lately how General Sheridan don't ride on horseback since his old war horse died, and seems to have lost all interest in horses?"

"No, I never did. He no doubt would rather ride in a cable car or a carriage than to jar himself up on a horse. That's all likely enough, but, as I say, he's a matter of fact little fighter from Fighttown. He never stopped to snoot and paw up the ground and sob himself into bronchitis over old Rienzi. He went right on about his business, and, like old King What's-His-name he hollered for another hoss, and the War Department never slipped a cog."

Later on I read that the old war horse was called Winchester and that he was still alive in a blue grass pasture in Kentucky. The report said that old Winchester wasn't very coltish, and that he was evidently failing. I gathered the idea that he was wearing store teeth, and that his memory was a little deficient, but that he might live yet for years. After that I met a New York livery stable prince, at whose place General Sheridan's well-known Winchester war horse died of botts in '71. He told me all about it and how General Sheridan came on from Chicago at the time, and held the horse's head in his lap while the fleet limbs that flew from Winchester down and saved the day, stiffened in the great, mysterious repose of death. He said Sheridan wept like a child, and as he told the touching tale to me I wept also. I say I wept. I wept about a quart, I would say. He said also that the horse's name wasn't Winchester nor Rienzi; it was Jim.

I was sorry to know it. Jim is no name for a war horse who won a victory and a marble bust and a poem. You can't respect a horse much if his name was Jim.

After that I found out that General Sheridan's celebrated Winchester horse was raised in Kentucky, also in Pennsylvania and Michigan; that he went out as a volunteer private; that he was in the regular service prior to the war, and that he was drafted, and that he died on the field of battle, in a sorrel pasture, in '73, in great pain on Governor's Island; that he was buried with Masonic honors by the Good Templars and the Grand Army of the Republic; that he was resurrected by a medical college and dissected; that he was cremated in New Orleans and taxidermized for the Military Museum of New York. Every little while I run up against a new fact relative to this noted beast. He had died in nine different States, and been buried in thirteen different styles, while his soul goes marching on. Evidently we live in an age of information. You can get more information nowadays, such as it is, than you know what to do with.

Appendix D: "Here's Your Mule"

A Farmer came to camp one day,
With milk and eggs to sell,
Upon a mule who oft would stray,
To where no one could tell.
The Farmer, tired of this tramp,
For Hours was made the fool,
By everyone he met in camp,
With "Mister, here's your mule."
Come on, come on,
Come on, old man.
And don't be made a fool,
By everyone you meet in camp,
With "Mister, here's your mule."
His eggs and chickens all were gone
Before the break of day,
The "Mule" was heard of all along,
That's what the soldiers say.
And still he hunted all day long,
Alas! the witless fool,
Whil'st every man would sing the song
Of "Mister, here's your mule."
Come on, come on,
Come on, old man.
And don't be made a fool,
By everyone you meet in camp,
With "Mister, here's your mule."
The soldiers ran in laughing mood,
On mischief were intent;
They lifted "Muley" on their back,
Around from tent to tent.
Thro' this hole, and that, they push'd
His head, — And made a rule,

To shout with humorous voices all,
I say "Mister, here's your mule!"
Come on, come on,
Come on, old man.
And don't be made a fool,
By everyone you meet in camp,
With "Mister, here's your mule."
Alas! one day the mule was miss'd,
Ah! Who could tell his fate?
Search'd early and search'd late,
And as he pass'd from camp to camp
With stricken face — the fool
Cried out to everyone he met,
Oh, "Mister, where's my Mule?"

Sheet music for "Here's Your Mule."

Appendix E: Locations of Civil War Equine Artifacts

Readers desiring to "visit" Civil War equines should phone or email in advance to ascertain the current hours and admission costs of the following museums.

Museum	Artifact(s)
Grand Army of the Republic Museum & Library 4278 Griscom Street Philadelphia, PA 215–289–6484 *http://www.garmuslib@verizon.net*	Gen. George G. Meade's Baldy Mounted head
Museum of the Confederacy 1201 East Clay Street Richmond, VA 804-649-1861 *http://www.moc.org*	Gen. Turner Ashby's Tom Telegraph Desiccated hoof, hair, piece of bone Gen. Robert E. Lee's Traveller Hair from mane and tail Gen. "Stonewall" Jackson's Fancy Hair
New Harmony Working Men's Institute 407 West Tavern Street (Box 368) New Harmony, IN 47631 812-682-4806 *http://www.workingmeninstitute.org*	Pvt. George M. Barrett's Fly Skeleton, part of tail
Old York Road Historical Society c/o The Jenkintown Library 460 Old York Road Jenkintown, PA 19046–2891 215–886–8590 *http://www.oyrhs.org*	Gen. George G. Meade's Baldy One forehoof
Oswego County Historical Society Richardson Bates House Museum 135 East 3rd Street Oswego, NY 13126 315–343–1342 *http://www.ochs.org*	Lt. Robert Oliver's Dick One hoof

Smithsonian Institution
Hall of Military History
Kenneth E. Behring Center
1400 Constitution Avenue
Washington, D.C.
202–633–1000
http://americanhistory.si.edu

Gen. Phil Sheridan's Rienzi
  Taxidermized body

VMI Museum
Virginia Military Institute
415 Letcher Avenue
Lexington, VA 24450
540–464–7334
www.vmi.edu/museum

Gen. "Stonewall" Jackson's Fancy
  Stuffed hide

Chapter Notes

Introduction

1. William M. Morales, *The 41st Alabama Infantry Regiment, Confederate States of America: A Narrative History of a Civil War Regiment from West Central Alabama* (Wyandotte, OK: Gregath, 2001), 66.

2. Richard M. McMurry, *Atlanta 1864: Last Chance for the Confederacy* (Lincoln: University of Nebraska Press, 2000), 30.

3. Joseph E. Johnston, *Narrative of Military Operations During the Civil War* (New York: Da Capo, 1990), 374.

4. W. David Baird, *A Creek Warrior for the Confederacy: The Autobiography of G.W. Grayson* (Norman: University of Oklahoma Press, 1991), 77.

Chapter 1

1. James Pickett Jones, *Yankee Blitzkrieg: Wilson's Raid Through Alabama and Georgia* (Athens: University of Georgia Press, 1987), 7.

2. Russell F. Weigley, *Quartermaster General of the Union Army: A Biography of M.C. Meigs* (New York: Columbia University Press, 1959), 296.

3. Martha L. Crabb, *All Afire to Fight: The Untold Tale of the Civil War's Ninth Texas Cavalry* (New York: Avon, 2000), 11.

4. Jack Coggins, *Arms and Equipment of the Civil War* (New York: Barnes & Noble, 1990), 48.

5. Crabb, 30, citing *Official Records*, Vol. 8, 728.

6. To arrive at full-time units for calculating requirements of horses and mules for various purposes, Frederick A. Dyer's *A Compendium of the War of the Rebellion* (1908) is used for Union units and *Military Service Records: A Select Catalog of National Archives Microfilm Publications* (1985) for Confederate units. In all cases, militia units, less than regimental size units, and units whose service period was less than two years were excluded.

7. Deborah Grace, "The Horse in the Civil War," http://reillysbattery.org/Newsletter/Jul00/deborah_grace.html.

8. Coggins, 63.

9. Lawrence R. Laboda, *From Selma to Appomattox: The History of the Jeff Davis Artillery* (New York: Oxford University Press, 1994), 4.

10. David Cardwell, "A Horse Battery," *Confederate Veteran* (Nov.–Dec. 1988): 6.

11. Coggins, 61.

12. Coggins, 75.

13. Larry J. Daniel, *Cannoneers in Gray: The Field Artillery of the Army of Tennessee, 1860–1865* (Tuscaloosa: University of Alabama Press, 1984), 126.

14. Frederick C. Cross, ed., *Nobly They Served the Union* (USA: Frederick C. Cross, 1975), 17.

15. John Massey, *Reminiscences Giving Sketches of Scenes Through Which the Author Has Passed and Pen Portraits of People Who Have Modified His Life* (Nashville: Methodist Episcopal Church, South, 1916), 189; Robert Hunt Rhodes, *All For the Union: The Civil War Diary and Letters of Elisha Hunt Rhodes* (New York: Orion, 1985), 131.

16. Jean M. Cate and John Spadea, eds., *"If I Live to Come Home": The Civil War Letters of Sergeant John March Cate* (Pittsburgh, PA: Dorrance, 1995), 26.

17. Robert Knox Sneden, *Eye of the Storm: A Civil War Odyssey* (New York: Touchstone, 2002), 155.

18. William Watson, *Life in the Confederate Army Being the Observations and Experience of an Alien in the South During the American Civil War* (New York: Scribner & Welford, 1888), 182.

19. Kevin E. O'Brien, ed., *My Life in the Irish Brigade: The Civil War Memoirs of Private William McCarter, 116th Pennsylvania Infantry* (Campbell, CA: Savas, 1996), 5.

20. John D. Billings, *Hardtack and Coffee, or the Unwritten Story of Army Life* (Lincoln: University of Nebraska Press, 1993), 290.

21. W.S. Morris, L.D. Hartwell and J.B. Kuykendall, *History 31st Regiment Illinois Veterans Organized by John A. Logan* (Herrin, IL: Crossfire, 1991), 132.

22. Webb Garrison, *More Civil War Curiosities* (Nashville: Rutledge Hill, 1995), 190.

23. Terry L. Jones, ed., *Campbell Brown's Civil War: With Ewell and the Army of Northern Virginia* (Baton Rouge: Louisiana State University Press, 2001), 273–4.

24. As numbered by Ezra J. Warner, *Generals in Gray* (Baton Rouge: Louisiana State University Press, 1959) and *Generals in Blue* (Baton Rouge: Louisiana State University Press, 1964).

25. William Tecumseh Sherman, *Memoirs of General William T. Sherman* (2 vols. in 1) (New York: Da Capo, 1984), 178.

26. William Marvel, *Race of the Soil: The Ninth New Hampshire Regiment in the Civil War* (Wilmington, NC: Broadfoot, 1988), 118.

27. Billings, 354.

28. Billings, 357–8.

29. Billings, 360–1.

30. Sherman, 15.

31. Sherman, 22.

32. Sherman, 174–5.

33. Fletcher Pratt, *Civil War in Pictures* (Garden City, NY: Garden City Books, 1955), 201.

34. Weigley, 269.

35. Grace, 3.

36. Weigley, 269.

37. James I. Robertson, Jr., *Stonewall Jackson: The Man, the Soldier, the Legend* (New York: Macmillan, 1997), 330–1.

38. Robertson, *Stonewall Jackson*, 419.

39. Edward Porter Alexander, *Military Memoirs of a Confederate* (New York: Da Capo, 1993), 232.

40. Jubal Anderson Early, *Lieutenant General Jubal A. Early, C.S.A.: An Autobiographical Sketch and Narrative of the War Between the States* (New York: Smithmark, 1994), 256.

41. James H. Brewer, *The Confed-*

erate Negro: Virginia's Craftsmen and Military Laborers, 1861–1865 (Durham: Duke University Press, 1969), 25.

42. Billings, 304.

43. George Worthington Adams, *Doctors in Blue: The Medical History of the Union Army in the Civil War* (Dayton, OH: Morningside, 1985), 34.

44. Billings, 302–3.

45. Adams, 25.

46. Coggins, 119.

47. Adams, 63.

48. Billings, 315.

49. Adams, 62–63.

50. Billings, 313.

51. Adams, 97.

52. Adams, 102.

53. Adams, 100.

54. Garrison, *More Civil War Curiosities*, 190.

55. Jack McLaughlin, *Gettysburg: The Long Encampment* (New York: Bonanza, 1963), 168.

56. Coggins, 108.

57. Charles M. Evans, *War of the Aeronauts: A History of Ballooning During the Civil War* (Mechanicsburg, PA: Stackpole, 2002), 118.

58. Evans, 120.

59. Evans, 180.

60. Evans, 90.

61. Evans, 267.

62. Rex Miller, *Croxton's Raid* (Fort Collins, CO: Old Army Press, 1979), 23–4.

63. O'Brien, 30.

64. William C. Davis and Bell Irvin Wiley, eds., *The Civil War (Compact Edition)* (New York: Black Dog & Leventhal, 1998), 426.

65. Davis and Wiley, 667.

66. Grace, 1.

67. Richard W. Leopold, Arthur S. Link and Stanley Cohen, *Problems in American History*, vol. 1: *Through Reconstruction*, 3rd ed. (Englewood Cliffs, NJ: Prentice-Hall, 1966), 375.

Chapter 2

1. Weigley, 165.

2. Weigley, 167.

3. Weigley, 253.

4. Allan Nevins, *Fremont: Pathmaker of the West*, vol. 2: *Fremont in the Civil War* (New York: Frederick Ungar, 1961), 491.

5. Nevins, 495.

6. Warner, *Generals in Blue*, 303–4.

7. Burton J. Hendrick, *Lincoln's War Cabinet* (Boston: Little, Brown, 1946), 222.

8. Gerry Van der Hervel, *Crowns of Thorns and Glory: Mary Todd Lincoln and Varina Howell Davis: The Two First Ladies of the Civil War* (New York: E.P. Dutton, 1988), 117.

9. Weigley, 187.

10. Weigley, 186.

11. Henry S. Wolcott, "The War's Carnival of Fraud," in *The Annals of the Civil War* (New York: Da Capo, 1994), 712–3.

12. Weigley, 257–8.

13. Edward G. Longacre, *The Cavalry at Gettysburg: A Tactical Study of Mounted Operations during the Civil War's Pivotal Campaign, 9 June–14 July 1863* (Lincoln: University of Nebraska Press, 1993), 54.

14. Philip H. Sheridan, *Personal Memoirs of P.H. Sheridan, General, United States Army*, vol. 1 (New York: Charles L. Webster, 1888), 135.

15. Weigley, 267–9.

16. Miller, 111.

17. Arnold Gates, "Of Men and Mules: A Modest History of Jackassery," *Civil War Times Illustrated* (Nov. 1984): 44.

18. Brewer, 17–8.

19. Clement Eaton, *A History of the Southern Confederacy* (New York: The Free Press, 1965), 107.

20. Frank E. Vandiver, *Their Tattered Flags: The Epic of the Confederacy* (New York: Harper's Magazine Press, 1970), xxx.

21. Frank Vandiver, 275.

22. Joseph T. Glatthar, *Partners in Command: The Relationship Between Leaders in the Civil War* (New York: The Free Press, 1994), 126.

23. Daniel, 125.

24. Dick Nolan, *Benjamin Franklin Butler: The Damnedest Yankee* (Novato, CA: Presidio, 1991), 103.

25. Jeffrey D. Wert, *Mosby's Rangers: The True Adventures of the Most Famous Command of the Civil War* (New York: Touchstone, 1990), 80.

26. Laboda, 3.

27. Daniel, 12.

28. Henry Brainerd McClellan, *The Life and Campaigns of Major-General J.E.B. Stuart* (Edison, NJ: Blue & Gray Press, 1993), 257–8.

29. Susan Leigh Blackford, *Letters From Lee's Army, or Memoirs of Life In and Out of the Army in Virginia During the War Between the States* (New York: Scribner's, 1947), 137.

30. Crabb, 11.

31. Eaton, 107.

32. McClellan, 259.

33. Lowell H. Harrison, *The Civil War in Kentucky* (Lexington: University Press of Kentucky, 197), 69.

34. Harrison, 71.

35. McClellan, 258.

36. McClellan, 259.

37. William A. Fletcher, *Rebel Private, Front and Rear* (New York: Meridian, 1997), 109–122.

38. William C. Davis, *The Orphan Brigade: The Kentucky Confederates Who Couldn't Go Home* (Garden City, NY: Doubleday, 1980), 213.

39. Davis, *Orphan Brigade*, 238–9.

40. Webb Garrison, *Civil War Curiosities: Strange Stories, Oddities, Events and Coincidences* (Nashville: Rutledge Hill, 1994), 67.

41. Stephen Z. Starr, *Jennison's Jayhawkers: A Civil War Cavalry Regiment and Its Commander* (Baton Rouge: Louisiana State University Press, 1993), 283.

42. Bridgette Z. Savage, *Fly Like the Wind* (Stanford, IN: Buckbeech Studios, 2006), 23.

43. Savage, 77–8.

44. Starr, 283.

45. Jacqueline Dorgan Meketa, ed., *Legacy of Honor: The Life of Rafael Chacon, a Nineteenth-Century New Mexican* (Albuquerque: University of New Mexico Press, 1986), 372.

46. Meketa, 119.

47. Meketa, 142.

48. Meketa, 135–43.

49. Meketa, 169.

50. John D. Imboden, "Jackson at Harpers Ferry in 1861," in *Battles and Leaders of the Civil War*, vol. 1 (New York: Thomas Yoseloff, 1956), 122.

51. Michael B. Dougan, *Confederate Arkansas: The People and Policies of a Frontier State in Wartime* (Tuscaloosa: University of Alabama Press, 1976), 106.

52. Daniel, 71.

53. Brewer, 24.

54. Malcolm C. McMillan, *The Alabama Confederate Reader* (Tuscaloosa: University of Alabama Press, 1963), 379.

55. Susan Leigh Blackford, 199.

56. Bruce L. Allardice, *More Generals in Gray* (Baton Rouge: Louisiana State University Press, 1995), 104.

57. Dougan, 106.

58. Eaton, 248.

59. James Pickett Jones, 132.

60. Benjamin P. Thomas, ed., *Three Years With Grant as Recalled by War Correspondent Sylvanus Cadwallader* (Lincoln: University of Nebraska Press, 1996), 239.

61. Henry Steele Commager, ed., *The Blue and the Gray: The Story of the Civil War as Told by Participants*, vol. 2 (New York: Fairfax, 1991), 675–76.

62. W.H.H. Terrell, *Indiana in the War of the Rebellion: Report of the Adjutant General*, vol. 1 (Indianapolis: Indiana Historical Society, 1960), 249–50.

63. Weigley, 276.

64. John Singleton Mosby, *Memoirs* (Nashville: J.S. Sanders, 1995), 259–91.

65. Mildred Lewis Rutherford, *Truths of History: A Historical Perspective of the Civil War from the Southern Viewpoint* (Atlanta, GA: Southern Lion, 1998), 79.

66. Allan Keller, *Morgan's Raid* (Indianapolis: Bobbs-Merrill, 1961), 72.

67. Gene C. Armistead, "Dixie's Civil War Unionists: 1871–1880 Interviews," *Heritage Quest Magazine* 16,

No. 4 (Issue 88, July–August 2000): 37.

68. Gilbert Moxley Sorrel, *Recollections of a Confederate Staff Officer* (New York, NY: Bantam, 1992), 145.

69. Longacre, *Cavalry at Gettysburg*, 97, 99.

70. Jacob Hoke, *The Great Invasion* (New York: Thomas Yoseloff, 1959), 107.

71. Susan Leigh Blackford, 182.

72. Sorrel, 144.

73. Susan Leigh Blackford, 182.

74. Sorrel, 145.

75. Hoke, 144.

76. Keller, 22 and 29.

77. Terrell, 204.

78. Harrison, 58.

79. Keller, 109.

80. Keller, 78.

81. Keller, 128.

82. Terrell, 248–54.

83. B.A. Botkin, *A Civil War Treasury of Tales, Legend and Folklore* (New York: Promontory, 1960), 424–5, citing E.E.E. Rouse, *The Bugle Blast: or, Spirit of the Conflict* (Philadelphia: James Challen & Sons, 1864), 299–301.

84. Mark Mayo Boatner III, *The Civil War Dictionary* (New York: David McKay, 1959), 360.

85. Ulysses S. Grant, *Personal Memoirs of U.S. Grant*, vol. 1 (New York: Charles L. Webster, 1885), 486–7.

86. Sherman, 175.

87. Sherman, 208.

88. Sherman, 206.

89. James Harrison Wilson, "The Union Cavalry in the Hood Campaign," in *Battles and Leaders of the Civil War*, vol. 4 (New York: Thomas Yoseloff, 1956), 471.

90. James Pickett Jones, 18.

91. James Pickett Jones, 96.

92. James Pickett Jones, 101.

93. James Pickett Jones, 96.

94. Walter L. Fleming, *Civil War and Reconstruction in Alabama* (Spartanburg, SC: Reprint Company, 1978), 73.

95. Fleming, 257.

96. Fleming, 74.

97. Starr, 111.

98. Florence Marie Ankeny Cox, *Kiss Josey for Me* (Santa Ana, CA: Friis-Pioneer Press, 1974), 144.

99. Mary E. Kellogg, ed., *Army Life of an Illinois Soldier Including a Day-by-Day Record of Sherman's March to the Sea: Letters and Diary of Charles W. Wills* (Carbondale: Southern Illinois University Press, 1996), 201.

100. Kellogg, 206.

101. Kellogg, 207.

102. Hoke, 179.

103. Hoke, 152.

104. William G. Williams, *Days of Darkness: The Gettysburg Civilians* (New York: Berkley, 1990), 13.

105. William R. Houghton and Mitchell B. Houghton, *Two Boys in the Civil War and After* (Montgomery, AL: Paragon, 1912), 34–36.

106. Keller, 15.

107. William Stanley Hoole and Elizabeth Hoole McArthur, *The Yankee Invasion of West Alabama, March–April 1865* (Tuscaloosa: Confederate Publishing, 1985), 9.

108. Blake A. Magner, *Traveller & Company: The Horses of Gettysburg* (Gettysburg, PA: Farnsworth House Military Impressions, 1995), 17, citing W.P. Conrad and Ted Alexander, *When War Passed This Way* (Shippensburg, PA: 1982).

Chapter 3

1. Weigley, 189.

2. Weigley, 194.

3. Weigley, 256–7.

4. Stephen W. Sears, *Chancellorsville* (Boston: Houghton Mifflin, 1996), 91.

5. Coggins, 52.

6. Freeman Cleaves, *Meade of Gettysburg* (Norman: University of Oklahoma Press, 1991), 55.

7. Starr, 283.

8. Frederick C. Cross, 56.

9. Frederick C. Cross, 121.

10. Frederick C. Cross, 124.

11. Glenda McWhirter Todd, *First Alabama Cavalry, USA* (Bowie, MD: Heritage Books, 1999), 146, 158.

12. Stephen W. Sears, ed., *For Country, Cause & Leader: the Civil War Journal of Charles B. Haydon* (New York: Ticknor & Fields, 1993), 359.

13. Jean Edward Smith, *Grant* (New York: Simon & Schuster, 2001), 302.

14. Crabb, 10.

15. John W. Headley, *Confederate Operations in Canada and New York* (New York: Neale, 1906), 82.

16. Charles M. Cumming, *Yankee Quaker, Confederate General: The Curious Career of Bushrod Rust Johnson* (Rutherford, NJ: Fairleigh Dickinson University Press, 1971), 232.

17. Sorrel, 89–90.

18. Cumming, 233.

19. Herman Hattaway, *General Stephen D. Lee* (Jackson: University Press of Mississippi, 1976), 107.

20. Susan Leigh Blackford, 165.

21. McMillan, 200.

22. Crabb, 163–4.

23. Richard Rollins, ed., *Pickett's Charge: Eyewitness Accounts* (Huntington Beach, CA: Rank & File, 1994), 61. Citing Edmund Berkely, "Rode With Pickett," *Confederate Veteran* 23 (1915): 175.

24. Crabb, 380.

25. Headley, 210.

26. Charles A. Earp, "A Confederate Gray," *Confederate Veteran* 2 (1998): 11.

27. Magner, 48.

28. Randy Steffen, "Fighting Joe Wheeler," *By Valor and Arms: the Journal of American Military History* 1, No. 3 (Spring 1975): 11.

29. Sears, *Chancellorsville*, 360.

30. Leander Stillwell, *The Story of a Common Soldier or Army Life in the Civil War 1861–1865* (USA: Franklin, 1920), 46.

31. Vivienne M. Eby, *The Horse Dictionary: English-Language Terms Used in Equine Care, Feeding, Training, Treatment, Racing and Show* (Jefferson, NC: McFarland, 1995), 149.

32. Elizabeth A. Curler, "Morgan Horses in the Civil War," National Museum of the Morgan Horse, http://www.morganmuseum.org/html/civil-war.html, accessed 04/11/2011, 3.

33. John Cheves Haskell (ed. by Gilbert E. Govan and James W. Livingood), *The Haskell Memoirs* (New York: Putnam's, 1960), 11.

34. John D. Imboden, "Jackson at Harpers Ferry," 124.

35. Kellogg, 11.

36. David Herbert Donald, *Gone for a Soldier: the Civil War Memoirs of Private Alfred Bellard* (Boston: Little, Brown, 1975), 82.

37. Robert Hunt Rhodes, 133.

38. Early, 155–7.

39. J.H. Kidd, *Personal Recollections of a Cavalryman With Custer's Michigan Cavalry Brigade* (New York: Bantam, 1991), 17.

40. Starr, 282.

41. David R. Logsdon, ed., *Eyewitnesses at the Battle of Shiloh* (Nashville: Kettle Mills, 1994), 15.

42. Peter Cozzens, *The Shipwreck of Their Hopes: The Battles for Chattanooga* (Urbana: University of Illinois Press, 1996), 9.

43. Kidd, 17.

44. John L. Collins, "A Prisoner's March from Gettysburg to Staunton," in *Battles and Leaders of the Civil War*, vol. 3 (New York: Thomas Yoseloff, 1956), 430.

45. Clifford Dowdy and Louis H. Manarin, eds., *The Wartime Papers of R.E. Lee* (Boston: Little, Brown, 1961), 243.

46. Magner, 18.

47. Billings, 282.

48. Cate and Spadea, 73.

49. John Wayne Dobson, "Jeremiah Beckworth, Confederate Teamster," *Confederate Veteran* (May–June 1994): 10.

50. Gates, 44.

51. Coggins, 123.

52. Michael Tobias and Jane Gray Morrison, *Donkey: The Mystique of Equus Asinus* (San Francisco: Council Oaks, 2006), 12–13.

53. Coggins, 51.

54. Mosby, 259–91.

55. Todd, 114.

56. Crabb, 84.

57. Crabb, 127.

58. Weigley, 150–1.

59. Pratt, 13.

60. Allen D. Albert, ed., *History of the Forty-Fifth Regiment Pennsylvania Veteran Volunteer Infantry 1861–1865* (Williamsport, PA: Grit, 1912), 226.

61. David L. Day, *My Diary of Rambles With the 25th Mass. Volunteer Infantry with Burnside's Coast Division, 18th Army Corps, and Army of the James* (Milford, MA: King & Billings, 1884), 27–28.

62. Lewis G. Schmidt, *A Civil War History of the 47th Regiment of Pennsylvania Veteran Volunteers: "The Wrong Place at the Wrong Time"* (n.p.: L.G. Schmidt, 1986), 203.

63. Laura Maria Knaggs and Katherine Knaggs Anderson, *Major Robert Clark Knaggs, His Life and Times (1836–1927)* (New York: Carleton, 1992).

64. Weigley, 248.

65. Frank Moore, ed., *The Rebellion Record: A Diary of American Events, With Documents, Narrative, Illustrative Incidents, Poetry, Etc., Supplement*, vol. 1 (New York: Putnam's, Henry Holt, 1864), 606.

66. Grant, vol. 1, 279.

67. Morris, Hartwell and Kuykendall, 25.

68. Todd, 125.

69. Walter Havinghurst, *Voices on the River: The Story of the Mississippi Waterways* (Edison, NJ: Castle, 1964), 187.

70. Garrison, *Civil War Curiosities*, 68.

71. Thomas B. Van Horne, *The Army of the Cumberland* (New York: Smithmark, 1996), 294.

72. Alpheus S. Williams (Milo M. Quaife, ed.), *From the Cannon's Mouth: The Civil War Letters of General Alpheus S. Williams* (Lincoln: University of Nebraska Press, 1995), 267.

73. Joseph E. Johnston, 190.

74. John Bell Hood, *Advance and Retreat* (Edison, NJ: Blue & Gray Press, 1985), 62.

75. Daniel, 106.

76. William W. Averell, "With the Cavalry on the Peninsula," in *Battles and Leaders of the Civil War*, vol. 2 (New York: Thomas Yoseloff, 1956), 429.

77. Edward Longacre, "Boots and Saddles: a Short History of the Cavalry During the Civil War, Part I: The Eastern Theater," *Civil War Times Illustrated* 31, No. 1 (March–April 1992): 36.

78. Margaret Leach, *Reveille in Washington, 1860–1865* (New York: Harper & Brothers, 1941), 112.

79. Edward Longacre, "Boots and Saddles: a Short History of the Cavalry During the Civil War, Part II: The Western Theater," *Civil War Times Illustrated* 31, No. 2 (May–June 1992): 48.

80. Eric J. Wittenberg and Karla Jean Husby, *Under Custer's Command: The Civil War Journal of James Henry Avery* (Washington, D.C.: Brassey's, 2000), 10.

81. William G. Stevenson, *Thirteen Months in the Rebel Army ... by an Impressed New Yorker* (Charleston, SC: Bibliobazaar, 2007), 66.

82. Longacre, "Boots, Part I," 36.

83. Wittenberg and Husby, 107.

84. Botkin, 424–5.

85. Billings, 328–9.

86. Frazar Kirkland, "Horse Incidents at Bull Run," in *The Pictorial Book of Anecdotes of the Rebellion ...* (St. Louis: J.H. Mason, 1889), 499.

87. Crabb, 12.

88. Watson, 170.

89. Longacre, "Boots, Part I," 36.

90. Starr, 115.

91. Crabb, 12.

92. Gates, 41.

93. Donald, 82.

94. John Cheves Haskell, 31.

95. John B. Gordon, *Reminiscences of the Civil War* (New York: Scribner's, 1903), 102.

96. A private of the 6th Virginia Cavalry, "The Death of General J.E.B. Stuart," in *Battles and Leaders of the Civil War*, vol. 4 (New York: Thomas Yoseloff, 1956), 194.

97. Leach, 112.

98. Susan Leigh Blackford, 12.

99. Sears, *Chancellorsville*, 106.

100. Gates, 41.

101. Marvel, 118.

102. Bell Irvin Wiley, *The Life of Billy Yank: The Common Soldier of the Union* (Indianapolis: Charter, 1962), 52.

103. John Cheves Haskell, 14.

104. James Pickett Jones, 17.

105. Coggins, 51.

106. Wittenberg and Husby, 78.

107. James Pickett Jones, 38.

108. Coggins, 53.

109. Mosby, 23.

110. Van der Hervel, 114–15.

111. Van der Hervel, 135–36.

112. Harold A. Cross, *They Sleep Beneath the Mockingbird: Mississippi Burial Sites and Biographies of Confederate Generals* (Murfreesboro, TN: Southern Heritage Press, 1994), 49.

113. Leach, 432.

114. William G. Stevenson, 66.

115. Drew Gilpin Faust, *This Republic of Suffering: Death and the American Civil War* (New York: Vintage, 2008), 261.

116. Steven J. Wright, *The Irish Brigade* (Springfield, PA: Steven Wright, 1992), 52.

117. Sears, *For Country, Cause & Leader*, 345.

118. Mosby, 23.

119. Mosby, 88.

120. Mosby, 332.

121. Wittenberg and Husby, 107.

122. Todd, 149.

123. Grant, vol. 1, 335.

124. Grant, vol. 1, 581–82.

125. Cozzens, *Shipwreck of Their Hopes*, 45.

126. E.P. Alexander, *Military Memoirs*, 232.

127. Fitzhugh Lee, *General Lee: A Biography of Robert E. Lee* (New York: Da Capo, 1994), 210.

128. Douglas Southall Freeman, *R.E. Lee*, an abridgement in one volume by Richard Harwell (New York: Touchstone, 1991), 243.

129. Charles Bracelen Flood, *Lee: The Last Years* (Boston: Houghton Mifflin, 1981), 48.

130. James V. Murfin, *The Gleam of Bayonets: The Battle of Antietam and the Maryland Campaign of 1862* (New York: Curtis, 1965), 90.

131. J.H. Segars, *In Search of Confederate Ancestors: The Guide* (Murfreesboro, TN: Southern Heritage Press, 1993), 51.

132. Robertson, *Stonewall Jackson*, 584.

133. Robertson, *Stonewall Jackson*, 587.

134. Murfin, 90.

135. An English Combatant, *Battle-Fields of the South, from Bull Run to Fredericksburg; With Sketches of the Confederate Commanders, and Gossip of the Camps* (New York: John Bradburn, 1864), 142.

Chapter 4

1. John Taylor, *Bloody Valverde: A Civil War Battle on the Rio Grande, February 21, 1862* (Albuquerque: University of New Mexico Press, 1995), 152.

2. George H. Peters, "The Confederate Invasion of New Mexico and Arizona," in *Battles and Leaders of the Civil War*, vol. 2 (New York: Thomas Yoseloff, 1956), 103–04.

3. Robert Lee Kerby, *The Confederate Invasion of New Mexico and Arizona 1861–1862* (Los Angeles, CA: Westernlore Press, 1958), 67–68.

4. Willard W. Glazier, *Three Years in the Federal Cavalry* (New York: R.H. Ferguson, 1870), 133.

5. Billings, 324.

6. John Beatty, *The Citizen-Soldier, or Memoirs of a Volunteer* (Cincinnati, OH: Wilstach, Baldwin, 1879), 211.

7. Sorrel, 84.

8. Houghton and Houghton, 88–9.

9. Grant, vol. 1, 353–4.

10. Glenn Tucker, *Hancock the Superb* (Indianapolis: Bobbs-Merrill, 1960), 123.

11. Early, 70.

12. John Allen Wyeth, *That Devil Forrest: Life of General Nathan Bedford Forrest* (Baton Rouge: Louisiana State University Press, 1989), 600.

13. Garrison, *Civil War Curiosities*, 74.

14. H.C. Parsons, "Farnsworth's Charge and Death," in *Battles and Leaders of the Civil War*, vol. 3 (New York: Thomas Yoseloff, 1956), 396.

15. Wyeth, *That Devil Forrest*, 601.

16. Kirkland, "Horse Incidents at Bull Run," 499.

17. George Lang, Raymond L. Collins and Gerald F. White, *Medal of Honor Recipients 1863–1994*, vol. 1: *Civil War to 2nd Nicaraguan Campaign* (New York: Facts on File, 1995), 206.

18. Richard Rollins and Dave Shultz, *Guide to Pennsylvania Troops at Gettysburg* (Redondo Beach, CA: Rank & File, 1996), 179.

19. Billings, 327–8.

20. Washington Bryan Crumpton, *A Book of Memories, 1842–1920* (Montgomery, AL: Baptist Mission Board, 1921), 87.

21. Billings, 327.

22. Logsdon, *Eyewitnesses at the Battle of Shiloh*, 90.

23. Daniel, 34–5.

24. Imboden, "Incidents of the First Bull Run," in *Battles and Leaders of the Civil War*, vol. 1 (New York: Thomas Yoseloff, 1956), 234.

25. Cozzens, *Shipwreck of Their Hopes*, 85.

26. Daniel, 21–22

27. Daniel, 22.

28. W. Springer Menge and J. August Shimrak, *The Civil War Notebook of Daniel Chisolm: A Chronicle of Daily Life in the Union Army 1864–1865* (New York: Ballantine, 1989), 15.

29. Daniel, 103.

30. Longacre, *Cavalry at Gettysburg*, 250.

31. Longacre, *Cavalry at Gettysburg*, 254.

32. Cozzens, *Shipwreck of Their Hopes*, 20.

33. Crumpton, 96.

34. Logsdon, *Eyewitnesses at the Battle of Shiloh*, 15.

35. Boatner, "Wheeler's Raid," 911.

36. William M. Lamers, *The Edge of Glory: A Biography of General William S. Rosecrans, U.S.A.* (Baton Rouge: Louisiana State University Press, 1999), 389.

37. Todd, 129.

38. Charles Whalen and Barbara Whalen, *The Fighting McCooks* (Bethesda, MD: Westmoreland, 2006), 307.

39. Peter Cozzens, *The Darkest Days of the War: The Battles of Iuka and Corinth* (Chapel Hill: University of North Carolina Press, 1997), 265.

40. Sorrel, 26.

41. J. Warren Gilbert, *People's Pictorial Edition the Blue and Gray: A History of the Conflicts During Lee's Invasion and Battle of Gettysburg* (Chicago: privately printed, 1922), 69.

42. John G. Walker, "Sharpsburg," in *Battles and Leaders of the Civil War*, vol. 2 (New York: Thomas Yoseloff, 1956), 680.

43. James T. Wilson, *The Black Phalanx: African American Soldiers in the War of Independence, the War of 1812, and the Civil War* (New York: Da Capo, 1994), 297.

44. James T. Wilson, 305.

45. John William DeForest, *A Volunteer's Adventures: A Union Captain's Record of the Civil War* (New Haven: Yale University Press, 1946), 214.

46. Thomas W. Cutrer, *Ben McCulloch and the Frontier Military Tradition* (Chapel Hill: University of North Carolina Press, 1993), 302, 304.

47. Thomas Y. Cartwright, "'Better Confederates Did Not Live': Black Southerners in Nathan Bedford Forrest's Commands," in *Black Southerners in Gray: Essays on Afro-Americans in Confederate Armies* (Murfreesboro, TN: Southern Heritage Press, 1994), 108–9.

48. Richard Rollins, ed., *Pickett's Charge: Eyewitness Accounts* (Redondo Beach, CA: Rank & File, 1994), 60–1.

49. Rollins, *Pickett's Charge*, 130. Citing Robert A. Bright, "Pickett's Charge at Gettysburg," *Confederate Veteran* 31 (1903): 263–66.

50. Horace Porter, *Campaigning With Grant* (New York: Bantam, 1991), 184.

51. Hal Bridges, *Lee's Maverick General: Daniel Harvey Hill* (Lincoln: University of Nebraska Press, 1991), 47

52. John Reuben Thompson, "Lee to the Rear," in *Civil War Poetry: An Anthology* (Mineola, NY: Dover, 1997), 56–8.

53. Samuel R. Watkins, "*Co. Aytch,*" *Maury County Grays, First Tennessee Regiment: or, a Side Show of the Big Show* (New York: Penguin Plume, 1999), 121.

54. Nathaniel Cheairs Hughes Jr., *General William J. Hardee, "Old Reliable"* (Baton Rouge: Louisiana State University Press, 1965), 202–3.

55. James A. Longstreet, "The Invasion of Maryland," in *Battles and Leaders of the Civil War*, vol. 2 (New York: Thomas Yoseloff, 1956), 671. For a slightly variant version, see also James A. Longstreet, *From Manassas to Appomattox: Memoirs of the Civil War* (New York: Mallard, 1991), 254.

56. Sorrel, 84.

57. Grant, 343.

58. Cumming, 233.

59. A.F. Aldridge, "Gen. Joseph Wheeler," *New York Times*, Oct. 9, 1898.

60. Wyeth, *That Devil Forrest*, 536.

61. Wyeth, *That Devil Forrest*, 600–01.

62. William Preston Johnston, *The Life of Gen. Albert Sidney Johnston Embracing His Services in the Armies of The United States, the Republic of Texas, and the Confederate States* (New York: Da Capo, 1997), 612.

63. Elizabeth J. Whaley, *Forgotten Hero: General James B. McPherson* (New York: Exposition, 1955), 159–60.

64. Larry Tagg, *The Generals of Gettysburg: The Leaders of America's Greatest Battle* (Campbell, CA: Savas, 1998), 12, 42, 97, 183, 218–19, 145–46, 249, 327.

65. E.P. Alexander, *Military Memoirs*, 217.

66. Stephen W. Sears, *Landscape Turned Red: The Battle of Antietam* (New York: Book-of-the-Month Club, 1983), 206.

67. Rhodes, 146.

68. Warner, *Generals in Gray*, 350.

69. McClellan, 413–4.

70. Robertson, *Stonewall Jackson*, 730.

71. James I. Robertson Jr., *General A.P. Hill: The Story of a Confederate Warrior* (New York: Vintage, 1992), 317–318.

72. Nathaniel Cheairs Hughes Jr., *Sir Henry Morton Stanley, Confederate* (Baton Rouge: Louisiana State University Press, 2000), 131.

73. Logsdon, *Eyewitnesses at the Battle of Shiloh*, 90.

74. Edward Porter Alexander, *Fighting for the Confederacy; the Personal Recollections of General Edward Porter Alexander* (Chapel Hill: University of North Carolina Press, 1989).

75. Sorrel, 26.

76. Wyeth, *That Devil Forrest*, 600.

77. Mosby, 291.

78. Logsdon, *Eyewitnesses at the Battle of Shiloh*, 50.

79. David Shultz, "*Double Canister at Ten Yards*": *The Federal Artillery and the Repulse of Pickett's Charge* (Redondo Beach, CA: Rank & File, 1995), 27.

80. Cozzens, *Darkest Days of the War*, 123–4

81. Cited in Otto Eisenschiml and Ralph Newman, *The American Iliad: The Epic Story of the Civil War as Narrated by Eyewitnesses and Contemporaries* (Indianapolis: Bobbs-Merrill, 1947), 452.

82. William G. Stevenson, 83.

Chapter 5

1. Magner, 47.

2. Grace, 4.

3. Daniel, 28.

4. George R. Lee, "The Wagonmaster's Letter," *Civil War Times Illustrated* 27, No. 1 (March 1988): 31.

5. Richard H. Orton, *Records of California Men in the War of the Rebel-*

lion *1861 to 1867* (Sacramento, CA: State Office, 1890), 47.

6. Orton, 52.

7. Orton, 58.

8. Orton, 70.

9. John L. Hervey and John Alexander Gorman, "Horse," in *Encyclopaedia Britannica*, vol. 11 (Chicago: Encyclopaedia Britannica, Inc., 1960), 754.

10. Magner, 47.

11. H.V. Redfield, "Characteristics of the Armies," in *Annals of the Civil War* (New York: Da Capo, 1994), 361.

12. Weigley, 270–1.

13. Leach, 186.

14. Brewer, 19.

15. Grace, 4.

16. Benjamin F. Butler, *Autobiography and Personal Reminiscences of Major-General Benj. F. Butler: Butler's Book* (Boston: A.M. Thayer, 1892), 779.

17. Alpheus S. Williams, 33.

18. Grace, 3.

19. Daniel, 124.

20. Sears, *Landscape Turned Red*, 64.

21. Menge and Shimrak, 23.

22. Cozzens, *Shipwreck of Their Hopes*, 9.

23. Alpheus S. Williams, 19.

24. Sears, *Chancellorsville*, 35.

25. McMurry, 31.

26. Houghton and Houghton, 92.

27. B.P. Gallaway, *The Ragged Rebel: A Common Soldier in W.H. Parsons' Texas Cavalry, 1861–1865* (Austin: University of Texas Press, 1988), 81.

28. Billings, 282.

29. Daniel, 95.

30. Cozzens, *Shipwreck of Their Hopes*, 21.

31. Warren Lee Goss, "The Army Mule, Carrier of Victory," *Civil War Times Illustrated* 1, No. 4 (July 1962): 18.

32. Glenda McWhirter Todd, 137.

33. Goss, "The Army Mule," 19.

34. Sneden, 65.

35. George Little and James R. Maxwell, *A History of Lumsden's Battery C.S.A.* (Tuscaloosa: R.E. Rhodes Chapter, United Daughters of the Confederacy, 1905), 15.

36. Daniel, 124.

37. Katherine M. Jones, *Heroines of Dixie: Confederate Women Tell Their Stories of the War* (New York: Konecky & Konecky, 1955), 233.

38. Eby, 13.

39. Sears, *For Country, Cause & Leader*, 355.

40. Cox, 183.

41. Daniel, 107.

42. Cozzens, *Shipwreck of Their Hopes*, 9.

43. Houghton and Houghton, 67–8.

44. Terry L. Jones, *Campbell Brown*, 87.

45. Henry Heth, "Letter from Major-General Henry Heth, of A.P. Hill's Corps, A.N.V.," *Southern Historical Society Papers*, vol. 4, 151–160. http://www/gdg.org/Research/Authored%20Items/shheth2.html, accessed 09/28/2011.

46. Frederick C. Cross, 48.

47. Frederick C. Cross, 55.

48. Cate and Spadea, 180.

49. Rex Miller, 22–23.

50. Cozzens, *Shipwreck of Their Hopes*, 21.

51. Alpheus Williams, 83.

52. Alpheus Williams, 86.

53. James A. Anderson, "The Federal Raid into Central Alabama, April, 1865, Including Wilson's Raid on Selma and Montgomery, and Croxton's Raid on Tuscaloosa," in *The Federal Invasion of Tuscaloosa, 1865* (Tuscaloosa: General Robert E. Rhodes Camp 262 Sons of Confederate Veterans, 1965), 34.

54. Thomas P. Clinton, "The Closing Days of the War of Secession in Tuscaloosa," in *The Federal Invasion of Tuscaloosa* (Tuscaloosa: General Robert E. Rhodes Camp 262 Sons of Confederate Veterans, 1965), 11.

55. Daniel, 47.

56. Daniel, 116.

57. Steven W. Sears, *For County, Cause & Leader*, 345.

58. George R. Lee, 32–33.

59. Morales, 66.

60. Alpheus Williams, 160.

61. Alpheus Williams, 162.

62. Rhodes, 97.

63. Evan Morrison Woodward and Stanley W. Zamonski, eds., *Our Campaigns: The Second Regiment Pennsylvania Reserve Volunteers 1861–1865* (Shippensburg, PA: Burd Street, 1995), 197.

64. Marvel, 123.

65. Donald, 198.

66. Cate and Spadea, 73.

67. Sears, *Chancellorsville*, 20.

68. E.P. Alexander, *Fighting for the Confederacy*, 66.

69. Sneden, 15.

70. Sneden, 40.

71. Sneden, 63.

72. Warren Lee Goss, "Yorktown and Williamsburg — Recollections of a Private," in *Battles and Leaders of the Civil War*, vol. 2 (New York: Thomas Yoseloff, 1956), 192.

73. Cozzens, *Shipwreck of Their Hopes*, 21.

74. E.P. Alexander, *Military Memoirs*, 467.

75. Alpheus Williams, 371–2.

76. Daniel, 179–80.

77. Van Horne, 506.

78. Lamers, 281.

79. Paul Zall, ed., *Blue & Gray Laughing: A Collection of Civil War Soldiers' Humor* (Redondo Beach, CA: Rank & File, 1996), 87, citing Frank Moore, *Anecdotes, Poetry and Incidents of the War* (New York: Scribner's, 1866), 179.

80. Goss, "The Army Mule," 18.

81. Billings, 286.

82. Billings, 284.

83. Gates, 43.

84. Kirkland, 452–53.

85. Zall, 87.

86. Warner, *Generals in Blue*, 155.

87. Richard Shenkman and Kurt Edward Reiger, *One-Night Stands With American History* (New York: Quill, 1982), 112, citing Edward P. Smith, *Incidents of the United States Christian Commission* (Philadelphia: Lippincott, 1869), 88–89.

88. Botkin, 212–13, citing Blackford, *Letters From Lee's Army*, 87–85.

89. Imboden, footnote to "Incidents of the First Bull Run," 238.

90. Noah Brooks, *Washington in Lincoln's Time* (New York: Rinehart, 1958), 55.

91. E.P. Alexander, *Fighting for the Confederacy*, 389–90.

92. Crabb, 84.

93. Coggins, 53.

94. Dowdy and Manarin, 329.

95. Weigley, 266–65, citing Quartermaster General Letter book 68.

96. Lamers, 254.

97. Laboda, 13.

98. Alpheus Williams, 44.

99. Houghton and Houghton, 88.

100. Cutrer, 263.

101. Cutrer, 263.

102. Chip Langston, "Men of Iron," *Civil War Times Illustrated* 43, No. 2 (June 2004): 46.

103. McClellan, 261.

104. Susan Leigh Blackford, 182.

105. Arthur James Lyon Fremantle, *Three Months in the Southern States, April–June 1863* (Lincoln: University of Nebraska Press, 1991), 222–36.

106. Todd, 104.

107. Todd, 147.

108. Fremantle, 251.

109. Coggins, 53.

110. Sneden, 89.

111. Crabb, 163–64.

112. William B. Styple, *With a Flash of His Sword: The Writings of Major Holman S. Melcher, 20th Maine Infantry* (Kearny, NJ: Belle Grove, 1994), 148.

113. Todd, 135.

114. Daniel, 124.

115. Daniel, 125.

116. Peter Svenson, *Battlefield: Farming a Civil War Battleground* (Boston: Faber & Faber, 1992),

117. Grace, 2.

118. J.E.B. Stuart IV, note to author dated Jan. 7, 2011.

119. Billings, 294.

120. Dowdy and Manarin, 328.

121. Eby, 97.

122. Eby, 90–91.

123. Eby, 215.

124. Magner, 47.

125. Eby, 231.

126. Eby, 221.

127. Eby, 150.

128. Carleton Beals, *War Within a War: The Confederacy Against Itself* (Philadelphia: Chilton Books, 1965), 63.

129. Weigley, 269.

130. Robert J. Trout, *They Followed the Plume: The Story of J.E.B. Stuart and His Staff* (Mechanicsburg, PA: Stackpole, 2003), 282.

131. Brewer, 24–25.

132. Keller, 62.

133. Brewer, 24–25.

134. John Cheves Haskell, 70.

135. Knaggs and Anderson, 84.

136. Walter H. Hebert, *Fighting Joe Hooker* (Lincoln: University of Nebraska Press, 1999), 99.

137. Frank Aretes Haskell, *The Battle of Gettysburg* (Cambridge, MA: Riverside, 1958), 91.

138. James Lee McDonough, *Shiloh — in Hell Before Night* (Knoxville: University of Tennessee Press, 1977 6th Printing, 217.

139. Logsdon, *Eyewitnesses at the Battle of Shiloh*, 102.

140. McDonough, 215.

141. Crabb, 239.

142. Todd, 125.

143. James Pickett Jones, 96.

144. Sneden, 64.

145. Victor Hicken, *Illinois in the Civil War* (Urbana: University of Illinois Press, 1991), 42.

146. Sneden, 128.

147. Botkin, 558–60, citing Ida M. Tarbell, "Disbanding the Confederate Army," *McClure's Magazine* 16 (April 1901): 534–535.

148. Todd, 117.

149. Richard Wheeler, *Sherman's March* (New York, NY: Thomas Y. Crowell, 1978), 62, citing Noble C. Williams, *Echoes from the Battlefield or, Southern Life During the War* (Atlanta, GA: Franklin, 1902).

150. Fleming, 73.

151. Massey, 173.

152. Menge and Shimrak, 90.

Chapter 6

1. Mildred Throne, ed., *The Civil War Diary of Cyrus F. Boyd, Fifteenth Iowa Infantry 1861–1863* (Millwood, NY: Kraus Reprints, 1977), 32.

2. Gordon, 102.

3. Sears, *Chancellorsville*, 294.

4. Donald, 96.

5. Woodward, 99.

6. A.B. Weymouth, *A Memorial Sketch of Lieut. Edgar A. Newcomb, of the Nineteenth Mass. Vols.* (Malden, MA: Alvin G. Brown, 1883), 86.

7. John Cannan, *The Spotsylvania Campaign, May 7–21, 1864* (Conshohocken, PA: Combined Books, 1997), 112.

8. Goss, "The Army Mule," 19.

9. E.P. Alexander, *Fighting for the Confederacy*, 542.

10. Porter, 9.

11. Kirkland, 278.

12. Billings, 295.

13. Grant, vol. 2, 41

14. J.L. Coker, footnote about Wauhatchie, in *Battles and Leaders*, vol. 3, 690.

15. Frederick C. Cross, 63.

16. Cozzens, *Shipwreck of Their Hopes*, 88.

17. Underwood, 164.

Chapter 7

1. McMillan, 186, citing John Watson Morton, *The Artillery of Nathan Bedford Forrest's Cavalry* (1909), 91.

2. Richard Nelson Current, *Lincoln's Loyalists: Union Soldiers From the Confederacy* (New York: Oxford University Press, 1992; 1994 paperback printing), 104, 229.

3. For the complete letter from Garfield, see William R. Hartpence, *History of the Fifty-First Indiana Veteran Volunteer Infantry* (Salem, MA: Higginson, 1998), 117–18.

4. Hartpence, 122.

5. Wyeth, *That Devil Forrest*, 170.

6. Hartpence, 123.

7. Hartpence, 133.

8. Brian Steel Wills, *A Battle from the Start: The Life of Nathan Bedford Forrest* (New York: HarperCollins, 1992), 118.

9. Current, 116–18.

10. Wyeth, *That Devil Forrest*, 165.

Chapter 8

1. Eby, 129.

2. Eby, 33–34.

3. Eby, 53.

4. Eby, 172.

5. Eby, 124.

6. Christa Well, "Pagans, Harvard professors = Horse Nibblers," *New York Times*, March 5, 2007.

7. "Hippophagy," *New York Times*, Dec. 12, 1907.

8. World Health Organization, *Joint Meeting of the League of Muslim World and the World Health Organization on Islamic Rules Governing Foods of Animal Origin* (World Health Organization Regional Officer for the Eastern Mediterranean, 1986), 3.

9. Cate and Spadea, 54.

10. Bill Bryson, *Made in America* (London, UK: Black Swan, 1998), 215.

11. Keller, 51.

12. Zall, 7.

13. Hartpence, 22.

14. William C. Davis, *A Taste for War: The Culinary History of the Blue and the Gray* (Mechanicsburg, PA: Stackpole, 2003), 97.

15. Victor Hicken, 351.

16. Cox, 171.

17. Katharine M. Jones, 233, citing Mary Ann Loughborough, *My Cave Life in Vicksburg* (1864).

18. Edward A. Gregory, "Vicksburg During the Siege," in *Annals of*

the Civil War (New York: Da Capo, 1994), 119.

19. Crumpton, 76.

20. Gregory, 120.

21. James R. Arnold, *Grant Wins the War: Decision at Vicksburg*. (New York: John Wiley & Sons, 1997), 275.

22. John C. Pemberton III, *Pemberton: Defender of Vicksburg* (Chapel Hill: University of North Carolina Press, 1970), 219.

23. Ray B. Browne and Lawrence A. Kreiser Jr., *American Popular Culture Through History: The Civil War and Reconstruction* (Westport, CT: Greenwood Press, 2003), 77.

24. Howard C. Wright, *Port Hudson: Its History from and Interior Point of View* (Baton Rouge: Eagle Press, 1978), cited as "Reading 2: the Mule Diet at Port Hudson" by http://www.nps.gov/history/NR/twhp/wwwlps/Lessons/71hudson/ accessed June 2, 2009.

25. Charles McGregor, *History of the Fifteenth Regiment New Hampshire Volunteers 1862–1863* (n.p.: Fifteenth Regiment Association, 1900), 565.

26. Eisenschiml and Newman, 455.

27. Michael B. Ballard, "Disaster & Disgrace: The John C. Pemberton Story," *Alabama Heritage* (University of Alabama, Winter 1993), 18.

28. Browne and Kreiser, 77.

29. DeForest, 146.

30. Katherine M. Jones, 233.

31. Pemberton, 219.

32. Browne and Kreiser, 77.

33. Hicken, 219.

34. Adin B. Underwood, *The Three Years' Service of the Thirty-Third Mass. Infantry Regiment 1861–1865 ...* (Boston: A. Williams, 1881), 153.

35. Beatty, 207.

36. David R. Logsdon, *Eyewitnesses at the Battle of Stones River* (Nashville: Kettle Mills, 1989), 68.

37. Frank J. Jones, "Personal Recollections and Experiences of a Soldier During the War of the Rebellion," in *Sketches of War History: Papers Prepared for the Commandery of the State of Ohio, Military Order of the Loyal Legion of the United States, 1903–1908*, vol. 6 (Cincinnati, OH: Monfort, 1908), 107.

38. S.F. Horrall, *History of the Forty-Second Indiana Volunteer Infantry* (published for the author, 1892), 175.S

39. John Henry Otto, *Memoirs of a Dutch Mudsill: The "War Memories" of John Henry Otto, Captain, Company E, 21st Regiment, Wisconsin Volunteer Infantry* (Kent, OH: Kent State University Press, 2004), xiii, 388.

40. Michael Hendrick Fitch, *Echoes of the Civil War as I Hear Them* (New York: R.F. Fenno, 1905), 108, 111.

41. J. Henry Haynie, *The Nineteenth Illinois: A Memoir of a Regiment of Volunteer Infantry Famous in the Civil War of Fifty Years Ago for its*

Drill, Bravery, and Distinguished Services (Chicago: M.A. Donohue, 1912), 190.

42. Marshall P. Thatcher, *A Hundred Battles in the West, St. Louis to Atlanta, 1861–1865: The Second Michigan Cavalry ...* (Detroit, MI: the author, 1884), 268.

43. Richard Lowe, *A Texas Cavalry Officer: The Diary and Letters of James C. Bates* (Baton Rouge: Louisiana State University Press, 1999), 64.

44. Garrison, *Civil War Curiosities,* 73.

45. Joseph Ripley Chandler Ward, *History of the One Hundred Sixth Regiment Pennsylvania Volunteers, 2d Brigade, 2d Division, 2d Corps, 1861–1865* (Philadelphia: Grant, Faires & Rodgers, 1883), 49.

46. William M. McPheeters, with Cynthia Dehaven Pitcock and Bill J. Gurley, eds., *I Acted From Principle: The Civil War Diary of Dr. William M. McPheeters* (Fayetteville: University of Arkansas Press, 2002), 243.

47. Little and Maxwell, 52–3.

48. Aurora Hunt, *The Army of the Pacific, 1860–1866* (Mechanicsburg, PA: Stackpole, 2004), 218.

49. Steven J. Wright.

50. Mark Miller, *"If I Should Live": A History of the Sixteenth Arkansas Confederate Infantry, 1861–1863* (Conway, AR: Arkansas Research, 2000), 76.

51. Fitch, 107.

52. Browne and Kreiser, 77.

53. Mark Miller, 76.

54. Crumpton, 76.

55. Gregory, 119.

56. Little and Maxwell, 53.

57. W.H. Tunnard, "Reminiscences of the Third Louisiana (Confederate) Infantry in the Trenches in Front of Logan's Division," in *A Soldier's Story of the Siege of Vicksburg, From the Diary of Osborne H. Oldroyd With Confederate Accounts from Authentic Sources* (Springfield, IL: for the author, 1885), 138.

58. John M. Stanyan, *A History of the Eighth Regiment of New Hampshire Volunteers: Including Its Service as Infantry, Second N.H. Cavalry and Veteran Battalion in the Civil War of 1861–1865 Covering a Period of Three Years, Ten Months, and Nineteen Days* (Concord, NH: I.C. Evans, 1892), 300.

59. Howard C. Wright, *Port Hudson: Its History from an Interior Point of View* (Baton Rouge: Eagle, 1978).

60. E.E. Houston, "History of Vaughn's Confederate Brigade," in *A Soldier's Story of the Siege of Vicksburg, From the Diary of Osborn H. Oldroyd With Confederate Accounts from Authentic Sources* (Chicago, IL: for the author, 1885), 155.

Chapter 9

1. Wiley, *Life of Billy Yank*; Bell Irvin Wiley, *The Life of Johnny Reb: The Common Soldier of the Confederacy* (Baton Rouge: Louisiana State University Press, 1992).

2. Harris Andrews, Christopher Nelson, Brian Pohanka and Harry Roach, *Photographs of American Civil War Cavalry* (East Stroudsburg, PA: Guidon, 1988), 29.

3. Kenneth E. Olson, *Music and Musket: Bands and Bandsmen of the American Civil War* (Westport, CT: Greenwood Press, 1981), 166–67.

4. O'Brien, 160.

5. Wheeler, 38.

6. Katherine M. Jones, 340–41.

7. Olson, 207, 215.

8. Olson, 206–07.

9. McClellan, 423.

10. Burke Davis, *Jeb Stuart: The Last Cavalier* (New York, NY: Wings, 1992), 70.

11. Olson, 171.

12. Todd, 149 and 153.

13. Cate and Spadea, 11.

14. Steven J. Wright, 42.

15. Morris, Hartwell and Kuykendall, 51.

16. Winston Groom, *Shrouds of Glory: From Atlanta to Nashville–The Last Great Campaign of the Civil War* (New York: Atlantic Monthly, 1995), 151.

17. Terry L. Jones, 347.

18. Harrison, 70.

19. William M. Polk, "General Polk and the Battle of Belmont," in *Battles and Leaders of the Civil War,* vol. 1 (New York: Thomas Yoseloff, 1956), 357.

20. John Cheves Haskell, 70.

21. David Paul Smith, *Frontier Defense in the Civil War: Texas' Rangers and Rebels* (College Station: Texas A&M Press, 1992), 21.

22. David Paul Smith, 179.

23. Wiley, *Life of Johnny Reb,* 38.

24. Starr, 215.

25. Wills, 303–04.

26. Elias Porter Pellet, *History of the 114th Regiment, New York State Volunteers* (Norwich, NY: Telegraph & Chronicle Power Press Print, 1866), 159.

27. Kidd, 147.

28. John Cheves Haskell, 70.

29. John Cheves Haskell, 14.

30. Craig L. Symonds, *Joseph E. Johnston: A Civil War Biography* (New York: W.W. Norton, 1992), 132.

31. William C. Davis, *Breckinridge: Statesman, Soldier, Symbol* (Baton Rouge: Louisiana State University Press, 1974), 364.

32. William C. Davis, *Diary of a Confederate Soldier: John S. Jackman of the Orphan Brigade* (Columbia: University of South Carolina Press, 1990), 101.

33. Lynda Lasswell Crist, ed., *The Papers of Jefferson Davis: October 1863–August 1864,* vol. 10 (Baton Rouge: Louisiana State University Press, 1999), 70.

34. Beatty, 268, 272, 275, 278, 355.

35. Leach, 259–60.

36. Noah Andre Trudeau, *The Last Citadel: Petersburg, Virginia, June 1864–April 1865* (Baton Rouge: Louisiana State University Press, 1991), 298.

37. William Corby, *Memoirs of Chaplain Life* (Chicago: O'Donnell, 1893), 138–145.

38. St. Clair Augustine Mulholland, *The Story of the 116th Regiment Pennsylvania Volunteers in the War of the Rebellion: The Record of a Gallant Command* (Philadelphia: F. McManus Jr., 1903), 77.

39. Oliver Wilson Davis, *Life of David Bell Birney, Major-General, United States Volunteers* (Philadelphia: King & Baird, 1867), 115–116.

40. David Porter Conyngham, *The Irish Brigade and Its Campaigns* (New York: William McSorey, 1867), 376–377.

41. Michael Cavanagh, *Memoirs of Gen. Thomas Francis Meagher: Comprising the Leading Events of His Career Chronologically Arranged, With Selections From His Speeches, Lectures and Miscellaneous Writings Including Personal Reminiscences* (Worcester, MA: Messenger, 1892), 478.

42. Cavanagh, 479.

43. Davis, 118.

44. Frederick Clark Floyd, *History of the Fortieth (Mozart) Regiment New York Volunteers, Which Was Composed of Four Companies From New York, Four Companies From Massachusetts, and Two Companies From Pennsylvania* (Boston: F.H. Gilson, 1909), 194.

45. Cavanagh, 479.

46. Mulholland, 80.

47. Oliver Wilson Davis, 116–118.

48. Menge and Shimrak, 68.

Chapter 10

1. Harrison, 102.

2. Fleming, 254.

3. Leopold, Link and Cohen, 390, citing Edward Younger, ed., *Inside the Confederate Government: The Diary of Robert Garlick Hill Kean* (New York: Oxford University Press, 1957), 213–15.

4. Dougan, 106.

5. Fremantle, 238.

6. Sally Jenkins and John Stauffer, *The State of Jones: The Small Southern County that Seceded from the Confederacy* (New York: Doubleday, 2009), 121.

7. Massey, 217.

8. Grant, vol. 2, 492–93.

9. Eisenschiml and Newman, 453.

10. E.P. Alexander, *Military Memoirs*, 613.

11. Sherman, 363.

12. Joseph E. Johnston, 413.

13. Hughes, *General William J. Hardee*, 295.

14. Richard Taylor, *Destruction and Reconstruction: Personal Experiences of the Late War* (New York: Longmans, Green, 1955), 276–77.

15. James Pickett Jones, 139.

16. Gordon, 104.

17. Richard Taylor, 279.

18. Gallaway, 130.

19. Savage, 78–86.

20. Robert Hunt Rhodes, 247.

21. Edna H. Evans, *Famous Horses and Their People* (Brattleboro, VT: Stephen Greene, 1975), 76.

22. Starr, 377.

23. Burton Egbert Stevenson, *Poems of American History* (Boston: Houghton Mifflin, 1922), 521.

24. Lois Hill, *Poems and Songs of the Civil War* (New York: Barnes & Noble, 1996), 87–89.

25. Mosby, 127.

26. Jenkins and Stauffer, 149.

27. William Palmer Hopkins, *The Seventh Regiment Rhode Island Volunteers in the Civil War 1862–1865* (Providence, RI: Snow & Farnham, 1903), 283.

28. Commager, 582.

29. Commager, 441.

30. Richard Taylor, 350–352 (footnote by editor Richard B. Harwell).

31. C. Drew. Vicki Betts submitted the entire poem to the Authentic Campaigner website, http://www.authentic-campaigner.com/forum/archive/index.php/t-3223.html, accessed 10/01/2011.

32. Hughes, *General William J. Hardee*, 113.

33. Catherine M. Wright, "Horse-Related Objects in the MOC Collections," letter and notes to author (Dec. 14, 2010), 2.

34. A.R. Small, *The Sixteenth Maine Regiment in the War of the Rebellion 1861–1865* (Portland, ME: B. Thurston for the Regimental Association, 1886), 221–223.

35. Edward Prioleau Henderson, *Autobiography of Arab* (Columbia, SC: R.L. Bryan, 1901).

36. "Famous Horses of the Civil War," http://library.thinkquest.org/06Aug/01591/horse.html, 3.

37. Catherine M. Wright.

38. Sue Wunder, "This Civil War hero … was a horse," *Christian Science Monitor* (April 11, 2006), http://csmonitor.com/2006/0411/p18So2-hfks.html.

39. Keith Gibson, "Civil War Horse Undergoes Make-over," *Virginia Military Institute, http://vmi.edu/NewsCenter.aspx?id=*15775, accessed Mar. 24, 2009.

40. Martha Boltz, "Bones of Warhorse Will be Interred Near Jackson," *Washington Times* (July 19, 1997), http://users.erols.com/va-udc/times.html, accessed March 24, 2009.

41. "Winchester, General Philip H. Sheridan's War Horse," Smithsonian Institution, http://www.si.edu/Encyclopedia_SI/nmah/horse.html, accessed March 24, 2009.

42. Edward Colimore, "Old Baldy to Return to Frankford Civil War Museum," *Philadelphia Inquirer*, March 8, 2010.

43. Magner, 43.

44. Magner, 43.

45. Magner, 8.

46. Magner, 12, 47.

47. Magner, 9.

48. Chester L. Somers, "Lee's Superb Equestrian in Richmond," *Confederate Veteran* (July–August 1994), 21.

49. James Loewen, *Lies Across America: What Our Historic Sites Get Wrong* (New York: The New Press, 1999), 164–65.

50. Stanley Howard and Terrie Howard, "Death of Gen. John Hunt Morgan Marker," Historical Marker Database (Oct. 7, 2009 — accessed Dec. 22, 2010), http://www.hmdb.org/marker.asp?marker=23081, 2.

51. Earp, 14.

52. Karen Buffett-Smith, "Forgotten Soldiers; the Horses of the New York 5th Cavalry Company H and Their Service During the U.S. Civil War," 11–14. www.freewebs.com/.../5th%20new%20cavalry%20horses.doc.

53. Lisa Campbell, "The Origin of the War Horse," *NSL Newsletter* (Summer 2002), National Sporting Library & Museum, Middleburg, VA, via http://www.nsl.org/warhourse.htm, 1 and supplemental information from Maureen Gustafson, Library Director of Communications & Education, dated Dec. 3, 2010, to author.

54. "Roderick Place, Tennessee," http://www.roderickplace.com (updated 2008, accessed 10/18/2011).

Chapter 11

1. Keller, 182.

2. James H. Stevenson, *"Boots and Saddles": A History of the First Volunteer Cavalry of the War, Known as the First New York (Lincoln) Cavalry, and Also as the Sabre Regiment, its Organization, Campaigns and Battles* (Harrisburg: Patriot, 1879), 143.

3. Buffet-Smith, 1.

4. Benjamin William Crowninshield, *A History of the First Regiment of Massachusetts Cavalry Volunteers* (Boston: Houghton Mifflin, 1891), 287–90.

5. John Cheves Haskell, 98.

Chapter 12

1. Smith Stimmel, *Personal Reminiscences of Abraham Lincoln* (Minneapolis: W.H.M. Adams, 1928), 28.

2. Boatner, 479.

3. Elizabeth Whipkey, notes to author on "Who's Who in Horsedom," dated Dec. 15, 2010, 123.

4. John G. Barrett, *Sherman's March Through the Carolinas* (Chapel Hill: University of North Carolina Press, 1956), 101.

5. Garrison, *Civil War Curiosities*, 77.

6. Gordon A. Cotton, ed., *From the Pen of a She-Rebel: The Civil War Diary of Emilie Riley McKinley* (Columbia: University of South Carolina Press, 2001), 22, 32, 53.

7. Theodore F. Rodenbough, "Famous Chargers," in *The Photographic History of the Civil War*, vol. 4: *The Cavalry* (New York: Review of Reviews, 191), 318.

8. Frank Moore, *Anecdotes*, 509.

9. George P. Cuttino, ed. *Saddle Bag & Spinning Wheel: Being the Civil War Letters of George W. Peddy, M.D., Surgeon, 56th Georgia Volunteer Regiment, C.S.A., and his Wife Kate Featherstone Peddy* (Macon: Mercer University Press, 2008), 194, 203, 242, 244, 246–49, 253, 285.

10. "Roster of General Wade Hampton's 'Iron Scouts,'" 2.

11. Henderson, entire book.

12. Ulysses Robert Brooks, *Butler and His Cavalry in the War of Secession 1861–1865* (Columbia, SC: The State Company, 1990), 231.

13. J.G. Deupree, "Reminiscences of Service With the First Mississippi Cavalry," in *Publications of the Mississippi Historical Society*, vol. 7 (Oxford, MS: Mississippi Historical Society, 1903), 98.

14. Oliver Wilson Davis, 117.

15. Frederic A. Wallace, *Framingham's Civil War Hero: The Life of General George H. Gordon* (Charleston, SC: History Press, 2011), 50.

16. William Arceneaux, *Acadian General: Alfred Mouton and the Civil War* (Lafayette: University of Southwestern Louisiana Press, 1981), 48.

17. A Special Correspondent, "Gen. Phil Kearny's Bugler, Story of Gus Schurmann's Evolution from Boot-Black to President's Son's Companion," 3. http://dmna.state.nyu.us/historic/reghist/civil/infantry/40thInf/, accessed 01/31/2011.

18. Cleaves, 234.

19. David Rowland (President, Old York Road Historical Society), email to author, dated 10/07/2011.

20. Compiled from Boatner, 40–41; Cleaves, 55, 79, 168, 234, 351; Magner, 6–7, 9; McLaughlin, 92; 1882 newspaper article and W.C. Storrick, *Gettysburg: The Place, the Battles, the*

Outcome (New York: Barnes & Noble, 1994), 65–66; Colimore. 21. James Vaulx Drake, *Life of General Robert Hatton Including His Most Important Speeches Together, With Much of His Washington & Army Correspondence* (Nashville: Marshall & Bruce, 1867), 424.

22. Albert Theodore Goodloe, *Confederate Echoes: A Voice from the South in the Days of Secession and of the Southern Confederacy* (Nashville: Publishing House of the M[ethodist] E[piscopal] Church, South, 1907), 83.

23. Donald A. Hopkins, *The Little Jeff: The Jeff Davis Legion, Cavalry, Army of Northern Virginia* (Shippensburg, PA: White Mane, 1999), 185.

24. Thomas D. Cockrell and Michael B. Ballard, *A Mississippi Rebel in the Army of Northern Virginia: The Civil War Memoirs of Private David Holt* (Baton Rouge: Louisiana State University Press, 2001), 352.

25. Edward Parsons Tobie, *History of the First Maine Cavalry 1861–1865* (Boston: Emery & Hughes, 1887), 329.

26. Glenn V. Longacre and John E. Haas, eds., *To Battle for God and the Right: The Civil War Letterbooks of Emerson Opdycke* (Champaign: University of Illinois Press, 2003), 75–76, 90.

27. Charles T. Clark, *Opdycke Tigers, 125th O.V.I.: A History of the Regiment and of the Campaigns and Battles of the Army of the Cumberland* (Columbus, OH: Spahr & Glenn, 1895), 180, 288.

28. John Esten Cooke, *Wearing of the Gray: Being Personal Portraits, Scenes and Adventures of the War* (New York: E.B. Treat, 1867), 265.

29. John R. Lundberg, *Granbury's Texas Brigade* (Baton Rouge: Louisiana State University Press, 2012), 47.

30. Boatner, 449.

31. Garrison, *Civil War Curiosities*, 71.

32. Mauriel Joslyn, *A Meteor Shining Brightly: Essays on the Life and Career of Major General Patrick R. Cleburne* (Macon: Mercer University Press, 2000), 65.

33. Thomas W. Cutrer, ed., *Longstreet's Aide, the Civil War Letters of Major Thomas J. Goree* (Charlottesville: University Press of Virginia, 1995), 149.

34. James Grant Wilson, "Famous American War Horses," *The Outlook Illustrated Monthly* (Jan. 2, 1896): 57.

35. Otto Arthur Rothbert, *A History of Muhlenberg County* (Louisville, KY: John P. Morton, 1913), 262.

36. David Evans, *Stoneman's Horsemen: Union Cavalry Operations in the Atlanta Campaign* (Bloomington: Indiana University Press, 1999), 334.

37. Donna J. Williams, "James Russell Wheeler," in *United Daughters of the Confederacy Patriot Ancestor Album* (Paducah, KY: Turner, 1999), 19–20.

38. Garrison, *Civil War Curiosities*, 75.

39. R. Lockwood Tower, ed., *Lee's Adjutant: The Wartime Letters of Colonel Walter Herron Taylor, 1862–1865* (Columbia: University of South Carolina Press, 1995), 18, 81, 115, 288.

40. John Gregory Selby, ed., *Virginians at War: The Civil War Experiences pf Seven Young Confederates* (Wilmington, DE: Scholarly Resources, 2002), 134.

41. Stephen Dodson Ramseur and George D. Kundahl, ed., *The Bravest of the Brave: The Correspondence of Stephen Dodson Ramseur* (Chapel Hill: University of North Carolina Press, 2010), 124.

42. Theodore F. Rodenbough, Henry C. Potter, and William P. Seal, publication committee, *History of the Eighteenth Regiment of Cavalry, Pennsylvania Volunteers, (163rd Regiment of the Line) 1862–1865* (New York: Publication Committee, 1909), 32.

43. Walter George Smith, *Life and Letters of Thomas Kilby Smith, Brevet Major-General United States Volunteers, 1820–1887* (New York: Putnam's, 1898), 193, 211, 245.

44. Curler, 2.

45. Meredith M. Sears, "The Elusive Civil War Morgan," The Ultimate Horse Site, http://www.ultimatehorsesite.com/articles/sears_civilwar... 1.

46. Samuel J. Martin, *Southern Hero: Matthew Calbraith Butler, Confederate General, Hampton Red Shirt, and U.S. Senator* (Mechanicsburg, PA: Stackpole, 2001), 74.

47. James Grant Wilson, "Famous American War-Horses," 56.

48. Carol Bundy, *The Nature of Sacrifice: A Biography of Charles Russell Lowell, Jr., 1835–64* (New York: Macmillan, 2005), 347, 280.

49. Jeffrey D. Wert, *Custer: The Controversial Life of George Armstrong Custer* (New York: Simon & Schuster, 1996), 171.

50. James J. Williamson, *Mosby's Rangers: A Record of Operations of the Forty-Third Battalion Virginia Cavalry From its Organization to the Surrender* (New York: Ralph B. Kenyon, 1896), 486.

51. Robert P. Lott Jr., *Van Cleve at Chickamauga: The Study of a Division's Performance in Battle* (master's thesis, General Stagg College, 1996), 120.

52. "Horatio and Charlotte Van Cleve House, 603 5th Street, South East, Minneapolis, Minnesota," http://www.placeography.org/index.php/Horatio_and_Charlotte_Van_Cleve_House.

53. Horace Cecil Fisher, *The Personal Experience of Colonel Horace Newton Fisher in the Civil War: A Staff Officer's Story* (n.p.: T. Todd, 1960), 45.

54. Magner, 30–31.

55. Curler, 1.

56. William Lee White and Charles Denny Runion, eds., *Great Things are Expected of Us: The Letters of Colonel C. Irvine Walker, 10th South Carolina Infantry, C.S.A.* (Knoxville: University of Tennessee Press, 2009), 9.

57. Trout, *They Followed the Plume*, 190.

58. Robertson, *Stonewall Jackson*, 230.

59. Survivor's Association (121st PA Inf.), *History of the 121st Regiment Pennsylvania Volunteers: "An Account From The Ranks"* (Philadelphia: Catholic Standard & Times, 1906), 40.

60. Harry W. Gilmor, *Four Years in the Saddle* (New York: Harper & Brothers, 1866), 88, 267.

61. Edward G. Longacre, *The Man Behind the Guns: A Military Biography of General Henry Hunt, Commander of Artillery, Army of the Potomac* (New York: Da Capo, 2002), 158.

62. James McLean, *California Sabers: The 2nd Massachusetts Cavalry in the Civil War* (Bloomington: Indiana University Press, 2000), 138.

63. William Naylor McDonald and Bushrod C. Washington, ed., *A History of the Laurel Brigade Originally, the Ashby Cavalry of the Army of Northern Virginia and Chew's Battery* (Baltimore, MD: Sun Job Printing Office, 1907), 118–119.

64. James B. Avirett, *The Memoirs of General Turner Ashby and His Compeers* (Baltimore, MD: Selby & Dulany, 1867).

65. Frank H. Taylor, *Philadelphia in the Civil War 1861–1865* (Glenside, PA: J.M. Santarelli, 1991), 25.

66. Anthony Waskie, "'Old Baldy,' General Meade's Warhorse." http://isc.temple.edu/awakie/Old%20Baldy%Article.htm, accessed 10/05/2011.

67. Frederick C. Cross, 18, 42, 54.

68. William Forse Scott, *The Story of a Cavalry Regiment: The Career of the Fourth Iowa Veteran Volunteers From Kansas to Georgia, 1861–1865* (New York: Putnam's, 1892), 325.

69. Gary D. Joiner, ed., *Little to Eat and Mud to Drink: Letters, Diaries, and Memoirs from the Red River Campaigns, 1863–1864* (Knoxville: University of Tennessee Press, 2007), 56.

70. John A. McNeil, "The Imboden Raid and Its Effects," in *Southern Historical Society Papers*, vol. 34 (Richmond: Southern Historical Society, 1906), 303–304.

71. Samuel Merrill, *The Seventieth Indiana Volunteer Infantry in the War of the Rebellion* (Indianapolis: Bowen-Merrill, 1900), 37.

72. Thomas B. Buell, *The Warrior Generals: Combat Leadership in the Civil War* (New York: Crown, 1997), 85, 87.

73. Warren Wilkinson, *Mother, May You Never See the Sights I Have Seen: The Fifty-Seventh Massachusetts Veteran Volunteer Infantry 1864–1865* (New York: Harper & Row, 1990), 61, 73, 77–78.

74. Francis Winthrop Palfrey, *Memoir of William Francis Bartlett* (Boston: Houghton, Osgood, 1878), 65.

75. Edward Cunningham, *The Port Hudson Campaign, 1862–1863* (Baton Rouge: Louisiana State University Press, 1994), 86.

76. Josiah Marshall Favill, *The Diary of a Young Officer Serving With the Armies of the United States During the War of the Rebellion* (Chicago: R.R. Donnelley & Sons, 1909), 146.

77. Charles A. Humphries, *Field, Camp, Hospital and Prison in the Civil War, 1863–1865* (Boston: George H. Ellis, 1981), 162.

78. James Moorhead Perry, *Touched With Fire: Five Presidents and the Civil War Battles that Made Them* (Cambridge, MA: Public Affairs (Perseus), 2003).

79. Frank Aretes Haskell, 63–64.

80. Charles H. Lothrop, *A History of the First Regiment Iowa Cavalry Veteran Volunteers From Its Organization in 1861 to Its Muster Out of the United States Service in 1865* (Lyons, IA: Beers & Eaton, 1890), 351–52.

81. Oliver Wilson Davis, 115.

82. Robert N. Adams, "The Battle and Capture of Atlanta," read March 18, 1893, in *Glimpses of the Nation's Struggle, Papers Read Before the Minnesota Commandery of the Military Order of the Loyal Legion of the United States, Fourth Series*, vol. 3 (St. Paul, MN: H.L. Collins, 1899), 157.

83. Henderson, 74.

84. James Lorenzo Bowen, *History of the Thirty-seventh Regiment Mass. Volunteers in the Civil War of 1861–1865 with a Comprehensive Sketch of the Doings of Massachusetts as a State, and of the Principal Campaigns of the War* (Holyoke, MA: Clark W. Bryan, 1884), 93.

85. Benedict R. Maryniak, *The Spirit Divided: Memoirs of Civil War Chaplains: The Union* (Macon: Mercer University Press, 2007), 45,

86. M.E. Wolf, untitled list, http://civilwartalk.com/forums/campfire-chat-general-Discussion/2733>, updated March 12, 2008, accessed June 4, 2009.

87. George Reeser Prowell, *History of the Eighty-seventh Regiment, Pennsylvania Volunteers: Prepared From Official Records, Diaries and Other Authentic Sources of Information* (York, PA: York Daily, 1903), 105.

88. Harold A. Cross, 90.

89. Oliver Wilson Davis, 116.

90. William Leontes Curry, *Four Years in the Saddle: History of First Regiment, Ohio Volunteer Cavalry, War of the Rebellion ... 1861–1865* (Columbus, OH: Champlin, 1898), 348.

91. Garrison, *Civil War Curiosities*, 77.

92. Allan Nevins, ed., "A Diary of Battle: The Personal Journals of Colonel Charles S. Wainwright, 1861–1865," from Voices of Battle, Gettysburg National Military Park Virtual Tour, http://www.nps.gov/archive/get/gettour/sidebar/wainwright.html.

93. Charles T. Clark, 126.

94. Burt Green Wilder, *Practicing Medicine in a Black Regiment: The Civil War Diary of Burt G. Wilder, 5th Massachusetts* (Amherst: University of Massachusetts Press, 2010), 56–7, 188, 219–20, 253.

95. Alpheus S. Williams, 371.

96. Robert J. Trout, *In the Saddle With Stuart: The Story of Frank Smith Robertson of Stuart's Staff* (Gettysburg, PA: Thomas, 1998), 19.

97. "General Barringer & the 1st North Carolina Cavalry," http://first-nccav.home.mindspirng.com/nc1hist2.html, 8.

98. Chris J. Hartley, *Stuart's Tarheels: James B. Gordon and His North Carolina Cavalry in the Civil War* (Jefferson, NC: McFarland, 2011), 188.

99. "General Barringer & the 1st North Carolina Cavalry," 11.

100. Hughes, *General William J. Hardee*, 112–13, 313.

101. Basil Wilson Duke, *Reminiscences of General Basil W. Duke, C S.A.* (Garden City, NY: Doubleday, Page, 1911), 290–292.

102. Thomas Franklin Berry, *Four Years With Morgan and Forrest* (Oklahoma City: Harlow-Ratliff, 1914), 69.

103. Howard and Howard, "Death of Gen. John Hunt Morgan Marker."

104. Loewen, 164–65.

105. William Elsey Connelley, *Quantrill and the Border Wars* (New York: Smithmark, 1996), 180.

106. Gilmor, 245.

107. United States Army Fifth Massachusetts Battery, *History of the Fifth Massachusetts Battery, Organized October 3, 1861, Mustered Out June 12, 1865* (Boston: Luther E. Cowles, 1902), 91–92.

108. "Black Cloud, the horse Col. Lamar was riding," *Confederate Veteran* 3, No. 5 (May 1895): 131.

109. Oliver Wilson Davis, 118.

110. Buffett-Smith, 13.

111. Buffett-Smith, 12.

112. Wolf, 1.

113. Lawrence Scanlan, *Wild About Horses: Our Timeless Passion for the Horse* (New York: HarperCollins, 1998), 142–43.

114. Mary S.C. Logan, *Reminiscences of a Soldier's Wife: An Autobiography by Mrs. John A. Logan* (New York: Scribner's, 1916).

115. William Gates Le Duc, *The Business of War: The Recollections of a Civil War Quartermaster* (St. Paul, MN: Minnesota Historical Society Press, 2004), 68–69.

116. James Alex Baggett, *Homegrown Yankees: Tennessee's Union Cavalry* (Baton Rouge: Louisiana State University Press, 2009), 156–57.

117. Waskie, 2, 4.

118. "Stone Mountain Confederate Memorial," Georgia Civil War Commission, http://www.facebook.com/pages/Georgia_Civil_War_Commission/120462404685199, accessed 10/06/2011.

119. "Rev. James McDowell's Civil War Horse's Death," *New Orleans Daily Picayune*, Aug. 16, 1885, 10. http://boards.ancestry.co.uk/localities.northam.usa.states.southcarolina..., accessed 01/24/2011/

120. Byron Archibald Dunn, *Raiding With Morgan* (Chicago: A.C. McClurg, 1903), 113–14.

121. William Woods Hassler, *One of Lee's Best Men: The Civil War Letters of General William Dorsey Pender* (Chapel Hill: University of North Carolina Press, 1999; orig. pub. 1965), 190.

122. Tobie, 190.

123. William C. Davis and Meredith L. Swentor, *Bluegrass Confederate: The Headquarters Diary of Edward O. Guerrant* (Baton Rouge: Louisiana State University Press, 1999), 214.

124. George William Beale, *A Lieutenant in Lee's Army* (Boston: Gorham, 1918), 185.

125. Edward Waldo Emerson, *Life and Letters of Charles Russell Lowell: Captain Sixth Unites States Cavalry, Colonel Second Massachusetts Cavalry, Brigadier-General United States Volunteers* (Boston: Houghton Mifflin, 1907), 27.

126. John Alexander Joyce, *A Checkered Life* (Chicago: S.P. Rounds Jr., 1883), 312.

127. John Sedgwick and George William Curtis, ed., *Correspondence of John Sedgwick, Major-General*, vol. 2 (New York: DeVinne Press, 1903), 74–75.

128. Keller, 43.

129. Thomas H. Parker, *History of the 51st Regiment of P.V. and V.V. from its Organization at Camp Curtin, Harrisburg, Pa., in 1861, to its Being Mustered Out of the United States Service at Alexandria, Va., July 27th, 1865* (Philadelphia: King & David, Printers, 1869), 369, 543.

130. George Baylor, *Bull Run to Bull Run: or, Four Years in the Army of Northern Virginia, Containing a Detailed Account of the Career and Adventures of the Baylor Light Horse, Company B, Twelfth Virginia Cavalry, C.S.A.,*

with *Leaves from My Scrap Book* (Richmond: B.E. Johnson, 1900), 85, 230.

131. Lamers, 217.

132. William J.K. Beaudot, *The 24th Wisconsin Infantry in the Civil War: The Biography of a Regiment* (Mechanicsburg, PA: Stackpole Books, 2003), 60.

133. Garrison, *Civil War Curiosities*, 76.

134. Oliver Wilson Davis, 117.

135. Trout, *In the Saddle With Stuart*, 62.

136. Trout, *They Followed the Plume*, 237.

137. Trout, *In the Saddle With Stuart*, 62.

138. Stuart, notes dated Jan. 7, 2011, to author.

139. Theophilus Perry, Harriet Perry, and M. Jane Johansson, ed., *Widows by the Thousand: The Civil War Letters of Theophilus and Harriet Perry, 1862–1864* (Fayetteville: University of Arkansas Press, 2000), 109, 113, 127.

140. Sheridan, 266.

141. Thomas A. Lewis, *The Guns of Cedar Creek* (New York: Harper & Row, 1988), 252, 275.

142. Thomas A. Lewis, 252, 275; Porter, 285.

143. Deupree, 90.

144. Trout, *In the Saddle With Stuart*, 28.

145. Crowninshield, 289.

146. Edwin C. Mason, "Through the Wilderness to the Bloody Angle at Spottsylvania Court House," in *Glimpses of the Nation's Struggle. Fourth Series. Papers Read Before the Minnesota Commandery of the Military Order of the Loyal Legion of the United States, 1892–1897* (St. Paul, MN: H.L. Collins, 1898), 296.

147. Boatner, 479.

148. Cooke, 287.

149. Buffett-Smith, 12.

150. Alice V.D. Pierrepont, *Reuben Vaughan Kidd: Soldier of the Confederacy* (Petersburg, VA: n.p., 1947), 133.

151. Fred Berry Jr., *Ozark Blood: Kin and Kind in the Civil War* (Bloomington, IN: Anchor House, 2006), 200.

152. Flavel Clingan Barber, *Holding the Line: The Third Tennessee Infantry, 1861–1864* (Kent, OH: Kent State University Press, 1994.

153. Tobie, 203.

154. Daniel W. Barefoot, *Let Us Die Like Men: Behind the Dying Words of Confederate Warriors* (Winston-Salem, NC: John F. Blair, 2005), 230.

155. James Grant Wilson, "Famous American War Horses," 57.

156. Stuart.

157. William Howard Armstrong, *Major McKinley: William McKinley and the Civil War* (Kent, OH: Kent State University Press, 2000), 85.

158. John W. Elwood, *Elwood's Sto-*

ries of the Old Ringgold Cavalry, 1847–1865: The First Three Year Cavalry of the Civil War* (Coal Center, PA: published by the author, 1914), 138, 288–89.

159. Herbert E. Valentine, *Story of Co. F, 23rd Massachusetts Volunteers in the War for the Union 1861–1865* (Boston: W.B. Clarke, 1896), 18.

160. Rodenbough, 304.

161. Robert Gould Shaw and Russell Duncan, ed., *Blue-Eyed Child of Fortune: The Civil War Letters of Robert Gould Shaw* (Athens: University of Georgia Press, 1992), 260.

162. Orlando Bolivar Willcox and Robert Garth Scott, ed., *Forgotten Valor: The Memoirs, Journals & Civil War Letters of Orlando B. Willcox* (Kent, OH: Kent State University Press, 1999), 367.

163. George Dallas Musgrove, *Kentucky Cavaliers in Dixie: Reminiscences of a Confederate Cavalryman* (Lincoln: University of Nevada Press Bison Books, 1999), 96.

164. Fairfax Downey, *Famous Horses of the Civil War* (New York: Thomas Nelson & Sons, 1959), 60–63.

165. "Roster of General Wade Hampton's 'Iron Scouts,'" 2.

166. John Q. Anderson, ed., *Brockenburn: The Journal of Kate Stone 1861–1868* (Baton Rouge: Louisiana State University Press, 1995), 282.

167. William P. Seville, *History of the First Regiment Delaware Volunteers, from the Commencement of the "Three Months' Service" to the Final Muster-Out at the Close of the Rebellion* (Wilmington, DE: Historical Society of Delaware, 1884), 49.

168. Jane Augusta Terry Gunn, *Memorial Sketches of Doctor Moses Gunn, by His Wife, With Extracts From His Letters and Eulogistic Tributes From His Colleagues and* Friends (Chicago: W.T. Keener, 1889), 74.

169. Chris J. Hartley, *Stoneman's Raid, 1865* (Winston-Salem, NC: John F. Blair, 2010), 87, 90, 91, 103.

170. Longacre, *Cavalry at Gettysburg*, 78.

171. Walter George Smith, 194, 353.

172. Alfred Davenport, *Camp and Field Life of the Fifth New York Volunteer Infantry (Duryee Zouaves)* (New York: Dick & Fitzgerald, 1879), 439, 443.

173. Cockrell and Bullard, 346.

174. Arthur W. Bergeron, *The Civil War Reminiscences of Major Silas T. Grisamore, C.S.A.* (Baton Rouge: Louisiana State University Press, 1993), 187.

175. Joseph Tyler Butts, *A Gallant Captain of the Civil War Being the Record of the Extraordinary Adventures of Frederick Otto Baron von Fritsch Compiled From His War Record in

Washington and His Private Papers* (New York: F. Tennyson Neely, 1902), 36, 47, 55, 84.

176. Barrett, 101.

177. Ulysses Robert Brooks, *Butler and His Cavalry*, 470.

178. James I. Robertson Jr., *General A.P. Hill*, 109, 291, 314, 317–18.

179. Zarvona, untitled list, http://cs.bloodhorse.com/blogs/thoroughbred-bloggers-Alliance/archive.

180. Stuart.

181. Magner, 18.

182. Mark Nesbitt, *Through Blood & Fire: Selected Civil War Papers of Major General Joshua Chamberlain* (Mechanicsburg, PA: Stackpole, 1996), 114, 157, 198.

183. Davis and Swentor, 346, 456.

184. David W. Blight, *A Slave No More: Two Men Who Escaped to Freedom Including Their Own Narratives of Emancipation* (Orlando: Harcourt, 2007), 197.

185. Robert McAllister and James I. Robertson Jr., ed., *The Civil War Letters of General Robert McAllister* (Baton Rouge: Louisiana State University Press, 1998), 81, 92, 111, 135, 296, 329, 361.

186. Wilder, 253.

187. Connelley, 466.

188. John Newman Edwards, *Noted Guerillas, or the Warfare of the Border.* (St. Louis: Bryan, Brand, 1877), 390–91.

189. Robert Hunt Rhodes, 133.

190. Buffett-Smith, 12.

191. James Grant Wilson, "Famous American War Horses," 57.

192. Hartley, 88.

193. Oliver Otis Howard, *Autobiography of Oliver Otis Howard, Major General United States Army*, vol. 1 (New York: Baker & Taylor, 1908), 212.

194. Thomas Leonard Livermore, *Days and Events 1860–1866* (Boston: Houghton Mifflin, 1920), 395.

195. Randolph Harrison McKim, *A Soldier's Recollections: Leaves from the Diary of a Young Confederate With an Oration on the Motives and Aims of the Soldier of the South* (New York: Longmans, Green, 1921), 214–15, 233.

196. Ephraim A. Wilson, *Memoirs of the War* (Cleveland: W.M. Baune, 1893), 319.

197. Marcus M. Spiegel, *A Jewish Colonel in the Civil War: Marcus M. Spiegel of the Ohio Volunteers* (Lincoln: Bison, 1995), 175.

198. William Alan Blair, *A Politician Goes to War: The Civil War Letters of John White Geary* (State College: Pennsylvania State University Press, 1991), 218.

199. William Valmore Izlar, *A Sketch of the War Record of the Edisto Rifles, 1861–1865* (Columbia, SC: The State Co., 1914), 48.

200. Judith Lee Hallock, *Braxton*

Bragg and Confederate Defeat, vol. 2 (Tuscaloosa: University of Alabama Press, 1991), 154.

201. Henry J. Aten, *History of the Eighty-fifth Regiment, Illinois Volunteer Infantry* (Hiawatha, KS: The Regimental Association, 1901), 103.

202. Alfred Jefferson Vaughan, *Personal Record of the Thirteenth Regiment, Tennessee Infantry by Its Old Commander* (Memphis, TN: S.C. Toof, 1897), 84–85.

203. Tobie, 527.

204. Compiled from Boatner, 353; Smith, *Grant*, 303; Marie Kelsey, "Ulysses S. Grant and His Horses During and After the Civil War," College of St. Scholastica, http://faculty.css.edu/mkelsey/usgrant/horse2.html.

205. Joseph Palmer Blessington, *The Campaigns of Walker's Texas Division* (New York: Lange, Little, 1875), 278.

206. Morales, 429.

207. Augustus L. Chetlain, "Recollections of General U.S. Grant," in *Military Essays and Recollections: Papers Read Before the Commandery of the State of Illinois, Military Order of the Loyal Legion of the United States* (Chicago: A.C. McClurg, 1891), 20.

208. "Morgan Horse Guide," http://morganhorseguide.com/index.php?page=clifton (2010).

209. Crowninshield, 289.

210. Buffett-Smith, 11.

211. Willcox and Scott, 255.

212. Hebert, 91.

213. William Willis Blackford, *War Years with Jeb Stuart* (Baton Rouge: Louisiana State University Press, 1993), 21–23, 85, 136.

214. Wert, *Mosby's Rangers*, 235.

215. Tagg, 105.

216. Mark A. Snell, *From First to Last: The Life of Major General William B. Franklin* (Bronx, NY: Fordham University Press, 2002), 184.

217. Livermore, 396.

218. Zarvona.

219. Jay Monaghan, *Custer: The Life of General George Armstrong Custer* (Fargo, ND: Bison, 1971), 248.

220. Wert, *Custer*, 255.

221. Luis Fenollosa Emilio, *History of the Fifty-fourth Regiment of Massachusetts Volunteer Infantry 1863–1865*, 2nd ed. (Boston: Boston Book, 1894).

222. John Adolphus Dahlgren, *Memoir of Ulric Dahlgren by His Father Rear-Admiral Dahlgren* (Philadelphia: J.B. Lippincott, 1872), 276–77.

223. Beale, 29.

224. Orton S. Clark, *The One Hundred and Sixteenth Regiment of New York State Volunteers Being a Complete History of its Organization and of Its Nearly Three Years of Active Service in the Great Rebellion* (Buffalo, NY: Matthews & Warren, 1868), 23.

225. Gilbert Adams Hays, *Under the Red Patch: Story of the Sixty-third*

Regiment Pennsylvania Volunteers 1861-1865 (Pittsburgh: Market Review, 1908).

226. James M. Aubery, *The Thirty-Sixth Wisconsin Volunteer Infantry, 1st Brigade, 2d Division, 2d Army Corps, Army of the Potomac. An Authentic Record of the Regiment from Its Organization to Its Muster Out. A Complete Roster of Its Officers and Men With Their Record*, etc. (n.p.: n.p., 1900), 39.

227. Wolf, 2.

228. Michael Hanifen, *History of Battery B First New Jersey Artillery* (Ottawa, IL: Republican-Times, Printers, 1905), 46.

229. Boatner, 524.

230. Stephen W. Sears, *George B. McClellan: The Young Napoleon* (New York: Ticknor & Fields, 1988), 71, 134, 280, 289.

231. Boatner, 449.

232. Gregory Acker, ed., *Inside the Army of the Potomac: The Civil War Experience of Captain Francis Adams Donaldson* (Mechanicsburg, PA: Stackpole, 1998), 363.

233. Fielding H. Garrison, *John Shaw Billings: A Memoir* (New York: Putnam's, 1915), 34, 71.

234. James Postell Douglas and Samuel A. Thompson, ed., *Douglas's Texas Battery* (Tyler, TX: Smith County Historical Society, 1966), viii.

235. Daniel George Macnamara, *The History of the Ninth Regiment Massachusetts Volunteer Infantry, Second Brigade, First Division, Fifth Army Corps, Army of the Potomac, June, 1861–June, 1864* (Boston: E.B. Stillings, 1899), 397.

236. Frank Aretes Haskell, 139–40.

237. Downey, 118–119.

238. Gilbert Frederick, *The Story of a Regiment, Being a Record of the Military Services of the Fifty-Seventh New York State Volunteer Infantry in the War of the Rebellion* (Chicago: Fifty-Seventh Veteran Assoc., 1895), 103.

239. Wiley, *Life of Johnny Reb*, 38.

240. Jacob Roemer, *Reminiscences of the War of the Rebellion* (Flushing, NY: Estate of Jacob Roemer, 1897), 124.

241. Terry L. Jones, *Lee's Tigers: The Louisiana Infantry in the Army of Northern Virginia* (Baton Rouge: Louisiana State University Press, 2002), 183.

242. Cutrer, *Longstreet's Aide*, 226.

243. Davis and Swentor, 214.

244. E.P. Alexander, *Fighting for the Confederacy*, 39, 243, 369–30.

245. Joslyn, 55.

246. Garrison, *Civil War Curiosities*, 75.

247. Longstreet, *From Manassas to Appomattox*, 46.

248. F.A. Bond, "Fitzhugh Lee as a Lieutenant Colonel in a Skirmish," in *The War of the Sixties*, ed. by E.R. Hutchins (New York: Neale, 1912), 213.

249. Albert Castel, "The Diary of General Henry Little, C.S.A.," *Civil War Times Illustrated* 11, No. 6 (Oct. 1972): 4.

250. D. Augustus Dickert, *History of Kershaw's Brigade, With Complete Roll of Companies, Biographical Sketches, Incidents, Anecdotes, Etc.* (Newberry, SC: Elbert H. Aull, 1899), 227–28.

251. Emory H. Stephens, "The Story of the Chaplain," in *The Story of Our Regiment: A History of the 148th Pennsylvania Vols. Written by the Comrades* (Des Moines, IA: Kenyon, 1904), 202–203.

252. John Franklin Moors, *History of the Fifty-second Regiment Massachusetts Volunteers* (Boston: George H. Ellis, 1893), 65.

253. Catherine M. Wright, *Lee's Last Casualty: The Life and Letters of Sgt. Robert W. Parker, Second Virginia Cavalry* (Knoxville: University of Tennessee Press, 2008), 75.

254. E.O. Hurd, "The Battle of Collierville," in *Sketches of War History, 1861–1865: Papers Prepared for the Commandery of the State of Ohio, Military Order of the Loyal Legion of the United States, 1896–1903*, vol. 5 (Cincinnati: R. Clarke, 1903), 248, 250.

255. James Dinkins, *1861 to 1865, by an Old Johnnie: Personal Recollections and Experiences in the Confederate Army* (Cincinnati: R. Clarke, 1897), 115.

256. Henderson, 64; Ulysses Robert Brooks, 19, 232.

257. Frederick Whittaker, *A Life of Major General George A. Custer* (Lincoln: University of Nebraska Press, 2008), 313.

258. Pierrepont, 133.

259. Dinkins, 229.

260. Ramseur and Kundahl, 124.

261. Buffett-Smith, 12.

262. James Grant Wilson, *Biographical Sketches of Illinois Officers Engaged in the War Against the Rebellion of 1861*, 3rd ed. (Chicago: James Rarnet, 1863), 58.

263. Oliver Wilson Davis, 305.

264. Greg Mast, "CS Pvt. Rufus Winfield Colvard," in *State Troops and Volunteers: A Photographic Record of North Carolina Civil War Soldiers*, vol. 1 (Raleigh, NC: Office of Archives & History, North Carolina Dept. of Cultural Resources, 1998). http://statetroopsandvolunteers.com/vollgal.html.

265. Davis and Swentor, 74.

266. William C. Davis — ed., *Diary of a Confederate Soldier*, 156.

267. "Grant the Equestrian," *Ulysses S. Grant Homepage*, http://granthomepage.com.

268. Benjamin P. Thomas, 232.

269. Kelsey.

270. Charles Davis Page, *History of the Fourteenth Regiment, Connecticut Vol. Infantry* (Meriden, CT: Horton, 1906), 352.

271. Crowninshield, 290.

272. Nelson Appleton Miles, *Serving the Republic: Memoirs of the Civil and Military Life of Nelson A. Miles, Lieutenant-General, United States Army* (New York: Harper & Brothers, 1911), 44.

273. Oliver Wilson Davis, 116.

274. Hassler, 53, 300.

275. Robertson, *Stonewall Jackson*, 230.

276. William Couper, *One Hundred Years at V.M.I.*, vol. 3 (Richmond: Garrett & Massie, 1939), 371.

277. Boltz, B-3.

278. Robertson, *Stonewall Jackson*, 230, 291, 471, 480, 486.

279. Dyon Stefano, "Street Named for Little Sorrel," *Civil War Times Illustrated* 31, No. 1 (March–Apr. 1992), 41.

280. Robertson, *Stonewall Jackson*, 230.

281. Robertson, *Stonewall Jackson*, 584, 893.

282. Robertson, *Stonewall Jackson*, 730, 916.

283. Robertson, *Stonewall Jackson*, 922; Stefanon, 41.

284. Robertson, *Stonewall Jackson*, 922.

285. Robertson, *Stonewall Jackson*, 922; Stefanon, 41.

286. Couper, 371.

287. Boltz, 2.

288. Lisa Fine, "Horse's Bones Finally Receive Proper Burial: VMI Ceremony Honors Jackson's Steed," *Richmond Times-Dispatch*, July 21, 1997, B-1 and B-3.

289. Boltz, 3.

290. Fine, B-1 and B-3.

291. Boltz, 2.

292. Boltz, 4.

293. Stefanon, 41.

294. Magner, 46.

295. "Our Fleet—Gettysburg Segway Tours," SegTours, LLC. http://segtours.com/team.html, 2.

296. James M. Greiner, Janet L. Coryell, and James R. Smith, eds. *A Surgeon's Civil War: The Letters and Diary of Daniel M. Holt, M.D.* (Kent, OH: Kent State University Press, 1994), 55, 58, 60.

297. James Grant Wilson, "Famous American War Horses," 56.

298. Jeffrey D. Wert, *Gettysburg, Day Three* (New York: Touchstone, 2001), 196.

299. John Allen Wyeth, *With Sabre and Scalpel: The Autobiography of a Soldier and Surgeon* (New York: Harper & Brothers, 1914), 200.

300. Oliver Wilson Davis, 116.

301. Magner, 46.

302. David S. Heidler and Jeanne T. Heidler, eds. *Encyclopedia of the American Civil War: A Political, Social, and Military History*, 5 vols. in 1 (Santa Barbara, CA: ABC-CLIO, 2000), 1236.

303. Emily Van Dorn Miller, *A Soldier's Honor: With Reminiscences of Major-General Van Dorn* (New York: Abbey Press, 1902), 46.

304. William Preston Johnston, 612.

305. Magner, 46.

306. Louis A. Sigaud, *Belle Boyd: Confederate Spy* (Richmond: Dietz, 1944), 25.

307. Botkin, 139.

308. Scott Bowden and Bill Ward, *Last Chance for Victory: Robert E. Lee and the Gettysburg Campaign* (New York: Da Capo, 2003), 180; Magner, 46.

309. Savage, entire book.

310. William Garrett Piston, *Lee's Tarnished Lieutenant: James Longstreet and His Place in Southern History* (Athens: University of Georgia Press, 1987), 90.

311. John Porter Fort, *John Porter Fort: A Memorial and Personal Reminiscences* (New York: Knickerbocker, 1918), 20.

312. *History of the Fifth Massachusetts Battery*, 389, 706–707.

313. Jeffrey D. Stocker, ed., *From Huntsville to Appomattox: R.T. Coles's History of the 4th Regiment, Alabama Volunteer Infantry, C.S.A., Army of Northern Virginia* (Knoxville: University of Tennessee Press, 2005), 33.

314. "Grant the Equestrian," 1.

315. Howard N. Monnett, *Action Before Westport, 1864* (Boulder: University Press of Colorado, 1995), 70.

316. Heidler and Heidler, 1486.

317. Cullen Andrews Battle, *Third Alabama! The Civil War Memoir of Brigadier General Cullen Andrews Battle, C.S.A.* (Tuscaloosa: University of Alabama Press, 2000), 150.

318. James Addams Beaver, "The Campaigns of 1863 and 1864," in *The Story of Our Regiment: A History of the 148th Pennsylvania Vols. Written by the Comrades* (Des Moines, IA: Kenyon, 1904), 103.

319. Hartley, 29.

320. Caire McCullogh, "Photos from the Past: Frank (Veteran of Company I, 12th Ohio Volunteer Cavalry," http://suvce.org/past/frank12ove.htm, accessed 10/05/2011.

321. Cuttinbig, 13, 16.

322. Greiner, Coryell, and Smith, 183.

323. Mary Daughtry, *Gray Cavalier: The Life and Wars of General W.H.F. "Rooney" Lee* (New York: Da Capo, 2002), 55.

324. *History of the Fifth Massachusetts Battery*, 594.

325. Bonnie L. Hendricks and Anthony A. Dent, *International Encyclopedia of Horse Breeds* (Norman: University of Oklahoma Press, 1995), 26.

326. Association for Entry of Pedigrees of Saddle Horses in America, *The Register of the American Saddle Horse Breeder's Association* (Louisville, KY: *Courier-Journal* Job Printing, 1911), xxiv.

327. "Race Horse Breeds," IGI Boards, http://www.walkerswest.com/History/AmericanSaddlebreds.htm, accessed 10/06/2011.

328. Michael C. Hardy, *The Fifty-Eighth North Carolina Troops: Tar Heels in the Army of Tennessee* (Jefferson, NC: McFarland, 2010), 85.

329. Meredith M. Sears, 1.

330. Stuart.

331. Porter, 39.

332. Louis Napoleon Boudrye, *Historic Records of the Fifth New York Cavalry, First Ira Harris Guard, Its Organization, Marches, Raids, Scouts, Engagements and General Service During the Rebellion of 1861–1865, With Observations of the Author by the Way Giving Sketches of the Armies of the Potomac and of the Shenandoah, Also, Interesting Accounts of Prison Life and of the Secret Service* (Albany, NY: S.R. Gray, 1865), 224.

333. Thomas Nelson Conrad, *The Rebel Scout: A Thrilling History of Scouting Life in the Southern Army* (Westminster, MD: Heritage, 2009), 65.

334. Gordon, 103–04, 265.

335. William E. Bevens, *Reminiscences of a Private: William E. Bevens of the First Arkansas Infantry, C.S.A.* (Fayetteville: University of Arkansas Press, 1992), 137.

336. Ulysses Robert Brooks, 207.

337. Timothy B. Smith, *Champion Hill: Decisive Battle for Vicksburg* (New York, NY: Savas Beatie, 2006), 118.

338. Richard H. Musser, "The Battle of Pea Ridge," 2nd Missouri Cavalry C.S.A., http://2ndmocavcsa.tripod.com, Accessed 10/02/2011., citing *Daily (St. Louis) Missouri Republican*, November 21 and 28, 1886.

339. Trout, *They Followed the Plume*, 90, 170; Stuart.

340. F.V., "History of the Stallion, George M. Patchen," *Wallace's Monthly* 4, No. 1 (Feb. 1878): 512–524.

341. La Fayette Curry Baker, *History of the United States Secret Service* (Philadelphia: L.C. Baker, 1867), 330–334.

342. Wolf, 7.

343. Gordon, 103–04, 265, 313.

344. Magner, 46.

345. Francis Richard Lubbock, *Six Decades in Texas or Memoirs of Francis Richard Lubbock, Governor of Texas in War-Time, 1861–1863, a Personal Experience in Business, War and Politics* (Austin, TX: Ben C. Jones, 1900), 325, 330, 535–36.

346. Francis Trevelyan Miller, ed., *Photographic History of the Civil War*, vol. 8 (New York: Review of Reviews, 1911), frontispiece photograph and caption.

347. Samuel Augustus Burney and Nat S. Turner, ed., *A Southern Soldier's Letters Home: The Civil War Letters of Samuel A. Burney, Cobb's Legion, Army of Northern Virginia* (Macon: Mercer University Press, 2002), 278.

348. Duke, 290–292.

349. Keller, 27, 227.

350. Whipkey.

351. Randolph Hollingsworth, *Lexington, Queen of the Bluegrass.* Charleston, SC: Arcadia, 2004.

352. John Q. Anderson, 282.

353. William Meade Dame, *From the Rapidan to Richmond and the Spotsylvania Campaign: A Sketch in Personal Narrative of the Scenes a Soldier Saw* (Baltimore, MD: Green-Lucas, 1920), 111.

354. William R. Plum, *The Military Telegraph During the Civil War in the United States With an Exposition of Ancient and Modern Means of Communication, and of the Federal and Confederate Cipher Systems, Also a Running Account of the War Between the States,* vol. 2 (Chicago: Jansen, McClurg, 1882), 29.

355. Armistead I. Long, *Memoirs of Robert E. Lee: His Military and Personal History* (Secaucus, NJ: Blue & Gray Press, 1983), 132.

356. Magner, 46.

357. Crowninshield, 290.

358. Pleasant Alexander Stovall, *Robert Toombs, Statesman, Speaker, Soldier, Sage: ...* (New York: Cassell, 1892), 288.

359. Jubal A. Early Preservation Trust, "Early's Homeplace," http://www.jubalearly.org/history.html, accessed 10/01/2011.

360. Andrew Hickenlooper, "The Battle of Shiloh, Part I," in *Sketches of War History, 1861–8165: Papers Prepared for The Commandery of the State of Ohio, Military Order of the Loyal Legion of the United States, 1896–1903,* vol. 5 (Cincinnati, OH: R. Clarke, 1903), 415–417.

361. McPheeters, Pitcock and Gurley, 205.

362. Magner, 46.

363. "Our Fleet — Gettysburg Segway Tours," 3.

364. Drake, 381.

365. Wolf, 2.

366. Fielding H. Garrison, 57.

367. Downey, 114.

368. Margaretta Barton Colt, *Defend the Valley: A Shenandoah Family in the Civil War* (New York: Oxford University Press, 1999), 129.

369. Nathaniel Cheairs Hughes Jr., *The Civil War Memoir of Philip Daingerfield Stephenson, D.D.: Private, Company K, 13th Arkansas Volunteer Infantry, Loader, Piece No. 4, 5th Company, Washington Artillery, Army of Tennessee, C.S.A.* (Baton Rouge: Louisiana State University Press, 1998), 170.

370. Sedgwick, 130–31, 146.

371. Magner, 46.

372. Hubert M. Sedgwick, excerpt from *A Sedgwick Genealogy: Descendants of Deacon Benjamin Sedgwick* (New Haven: New Haven Colony Historical Society, 1961), http://www.sedgwick.org/na/families/robert1613/B./2/9/2/B292-sedgewick-gen-john-article, accessed 10/06/2011.

373. Walter Branham Capers, *The Soldier-Bishop, Ellison Capers* (New York: Neale, 1912), 76.

374. Longacre, *The Cavalry at Gettysburg,* 108.

375. Christian G. Samito, *Commanding Boston's Irish Ninth: The Civil War Letters of Colonel Patrick R. Guiney, Ninth Massachusetts Volunteer Infantry* (Bronx, NY: Fordham University Press, 1998), 220.

376. Terry L. Jones, *Lee's Tigers,* 188.

377. Thomas D. Duncan, *Recollections of Thomas D. Duncan, a Confederate Soldier* (Nashville: McQuiddy Publishing, 1922.

378. Willcox and Scott, 275.

379. James Grant Wilson, "Famous American War Horses," 56–57.

380. Jeffrey D. Wert, *General James Longstreet: The Confederacy's Most Controversial Soldier — A Biography* (New York, NY: Simon & Schuster, 1993), 218, 256, 259.

381. John Wesley Brinsfield Jr., ed., *The Spirit Divided: Memoirs of Civil War Chaplains: The Confederacy* (Macon: Mercer University Press, 2006), 78, citing Charles Holt Dobbs, "Reminiscences of an Army Chaplain" (1874)

382. John McElroy, *Andersonville: A Story of Rebel Military Prisons. Fifteen Months a Guest of the So-Called Southern Confederacy, a Private Soldier's Experience in Richmond, Andersonville, Savannah, Millen, Blackshear, and Florence* (Toledo, OH: D.R. Locke, 1879), 65, 70.

383. Stuart and Boatner, 816.

384. Wyeth, *That Devil Forrest,* 600–601.

385. Oliver Wilson Davis, 117.

386. Oliver Wilson Davis, 118.

387. Meredith M. Sears, 1.

388. Oliver Wilson Davis, 118.

389. Louise Ayer Vandiver, *Traditions and History of Anderson County* (Atlanta, GA: Ruralist Press, 1928), 228–29, 249; Sanders Homepage (Sanders Family Web Page), http://SandersWeb.net, accessed 07/16/2012; "Manse Jolly Took Last Ride Here 102 Years Ago," *Anderson (SC) Daily Mail,* January 29, 1969; Thomas E. Turner, "Legendary Rebel Lies in Remote Grave," *Dallas Morning News,* March 27, 1965.

390. Charles Frederic Bahnson and Sarah Bahnson Chapman, eds., *Bright and Gloomy Days: The Civil War Correspondence of Captain Charles Bahnson, a Moravian Confederate* (Knoxville: University of Tennessee Press, 2003), 131.

391. Henry Murray Calvert, *Reminiscences of a Boy in Blue 1862–1865* (New York: Putnam's, 1920), 230.

392. "Grant the Equestrian"; Boatner, 353.

393. Stella A. Coatsworth, *The Loyal People of the North-West: A Record of Prominent Persons, Places and Events, During Eight Years of Unparalleled American History* (Chicago: Goodman & Donnelley, 1869), 258–259.

394. Buffett-Smith, 12.

395. Buffett-Smith, 11.

396. Stephens, 205.

397. W.C. Dodson, *Campaigns of Wheeler and His Cavalry 1861–1865 From Material Furnished by Gen. Joseph Wheeler to Which is Added His Concise and Graphic Account of the Santiago Campaign of 1898* (Atlanta, GA: Hudgins, 1899), 360–61.

398. Conyngham, 376–377; Mulholland, 80–81.

399. James Grant Wilson, "Famous American Horses," 58.

400. Downey, 57.

401. Humphries, 6, 25.

402. James Michael Barr and Thomas D. Mays, ed., *Let Us Meet in Heaven: The Civil War Letters of James Michael Barr, 5th South Carolina Cavalry* (Abilene, TX: McWhinney Foundation Press, 2000), 202.

403. Buffett-Smith, 12.

404. Watson, 264–67, 336.

405. Jonathan A. Noyalas, *"My Will is Absolute Law": A Biography of Union General Robert H. Milroy* (Jefferson, NC: McFarland, 2006), 49.

406. Baylor, 308–09.

407. Henry Kyd Douglas, *I Rode with Stonewall: The War Experiences of the Youngest Member of Jackson's Staff* (Chapel Hill: University of North Carolina Press, 1968), 387.

408. William C. Davis, *Diary of a Confederate Soldier,* 160.

409. B.L. Riddle, "Coming Home From Greensboro, N.C.," *Confederate Veteran* 3, No. 10 (Oct. 1895): 308; Bromfield Lewis Ridley, *Battles and Sketches of the Army of Tennessee* (Mexico, MO: Missouri, 1906), 476.

410. Barr, 201.

411. James C. Mohr, ed. *The Cormany Diaries: A Northern Family in the Civil War* (Pittsburgh: University of Pittsburgh Press, 1982), 268.

412. Van der Hervel, 51.

413. Boatner, 353; "Grant the Equestrian," 2; Porter, 79, 152; Jean Edward Smith, 303, 376; Kelsey, 2–3.

414. Davis and Swentor, 215, 240.

415. Hood, 61, 64.

416. Washington Davis, *Camp-Fire Chats of the Civil War; Being the Incident, Adventure and Wayside Exploit of the Bivouac and Battle Field as Related

by *Veteran Soldiers Themselves* (Chicago: Lewis, 1882), 25–26.

417. Robin Young, *For Love & Liberty: The Untold Civil War Story of Major Sullivan Ballou & His Famous Love Letter* (New York: Thunder's Mouth, 2006), 266, 488.

418. Beatty, 29.

419. Riddle, 308, Ridley, 476.

420. Catherine Barrett Robertson Burnam, "Death and Funeral of Bishop-General Leonidas Polk," Saint Paul's Church, Augusta, GA, http://www.saintpauls.org/cbf/burnamPolk.php, accessed 09/28/2011.

421. James Fowler Rusling, *Men and Things I Saw in Civil War Days* (New York: Eaton & Mains, 1899), 272.

422. Charles Eugene Hamlin, *The Life and Times of Hannibal Hamlin* (Cambridge, MA: Riverside, 1899), 575–76.

423. Barr, 237.

424. Henderson, 47–48.

425. Mary Frances Robert, "James Jasper Sample," *United Daughters of the Confederacy Patriot Ancestor Album* (Paducah, KY: Turner, 1999), 167.

426. Stephens, 202.

427. John Scott, *Partisan Life with Col. John S. Mosby* (New York: Harper & Brothers, 1867), 448.

428. Conrad, 65, 91.

429. Svenson, 208; Helen P. Trimpi, *Crimson Confederates: Harvard Men Who Fought for the South* (Knoxville: University of Tennessee Press, 2010), 97 (for horse surname).

430. Nixon B. Stewart, *Dan McCook's Regiment, 52nd O.V.I.: A History of the Regiment, its Campaigns and Battles from 1862 to 1865* (n.p.: the author, 1900), 148.

431. David R. Logsdon, *Eyewitnesses at the Battle of Franklin* (Nashville: Kettle Mills, 1991), 17.

432. Frank Aretes Haskell, 64.

433. Roemer, 49, 62–63.

434. Trimpi, 97.

435. Adam Rankin Johnson and William J. Davis, ed., *The Partisan Rangers of the Confederate States Army* (Louisville, KY: Geo. G. Fetter, 1904), 5, 38, 73, 218.

436. William Babcock Hazen, *A Narrative of Military Service by General W.B. Hazen* (Boston: Ticknor, 1885), 152.

437. Wayland Fuller Dunaway, *Reminiscences of a Rebel* (New York: Neale, 1913), 80.

438. Paul B. Kerr. *Civil War Surgeon: Biography of James Langstaff Dunn, M.D.* (Bloomington, IL: Paul B. Kerr, 2005), 120.

439. Walter George Smith, 370.

440. Hanifen, 42.

441. Havinghurst, 173.

442. Lew Wallace, *Smoke, Sound & Fury: The Civil War Memoirs of Major-General Lew Wallace, U.S. Volunteers*

(Philadelphia: Polyglot, 2004), 79, 165.

443. I.B. Nall, *The Register of the American Saddle-Horse Breeders Association (Incorporated)*, vol. 2 (Chicago: Brown-Cooper, 1901— compiled originally 1893), xvi.

444. Association for Entry of Pedigrees of Saddle Horses in America, xxiv.

445. Alfred L. Castleman, *The Army of the Potomac, Behind the Scenes: A Diary of Unwritten History; from the Organization of the Army, by General George McClellan, to the Close of the Campaign in Virginia, About the First Day of January, 1863* (Milwaukee, WI: Strickland, 1863), 259.

446. William Thomas Poague (ed. by Monroe F. Cockrell, Bell Irvin Wiley and Robert K. Krick), *Gunner With Stonewall: Reminiscences of William Thomas Poague* (Lincoln: University of Nebraska Press), 112.

447. Sara Agnes Rice Pryor, *Reminiscences of Peace and War* (New York: Macmillan, 1970; orig. pub. 1904), 306.

448. "Grant the Equestrian."

449. Robert Hunt Rhodes, 136, 151, 156, 182, 219, 247.

450. Oliver Wilson Davis, 116.

451. Conyngham, 376–77; Mulholland, 80.

452. Stephen W. Sears, *George B. McClellan*, 134.

453. Botkin, 536.

454. John Henninger Reagan, *Memoirs, With Special Reference to Secession and the Civil War* (New York: Neale, 1906), 214.

455. Earp, 11.

456. Wyeth, *That Devil Forrest*, 600–01.

457. Cartwright, 99.

458. Earp, 11.

459. Johan August Heinrich Heros von Borcke, *Memoirs of the Confederate War for Independence* (Philadelphia: J.B. Lippincott, 1867), 326, 332.

460. Justus Scheibert (William Stanley Hoole, ed.; Joseph C. Hayes, translator), *Seven Months in the Rebel States During the North American War, 1863* (Tuscaloosa: University of Alabama Press, 2009), 42.

461. Svenson, 43.

462. Zarvona.

463. George E. Waring Jr., *Whip and Spur* (Boston: James R. Osgood, 1875), 70–73, 75, 77–78, 82, 88, 90.

464. Barr, 192.

465. Stuart.

466. Wert, *Mosby's Rangers*, 87.

467. Abner Hard, *History of the Eighth Cavalry Regiment Illinois Volunteers, During the Great Rebellion* (Aurora, IL: n.p., 1868), 172.

468. Magner, 46.

469. Edward G. Longacre, "A Race for Life at Brandy Station," *Civil War Times Illustrated* 17, No. 9 (Jan. 1979): 35.

470. James K. Ewer, *The Third Massachusetts Cavalry in the War for the Union* (Maplewood, MA: Wm. G.J. Perry, 1903), 356.

471. Rollins, *Pickett's Charge*, 130.

472. Fair Oaks Volunteer Fire Dept., "Leet Township and Fair Oaks History," fovfd.org/aboutfovfd.htm, accessed 10/02/2011.

473. Hays, 416, 424.

474. "Grant the Equestrian."

475. George B. Guild, *A Brief Narrative of the Fourth Tennessee Cavalry Regiment, Wheeler's Corps, Army of Tennessee* (Nashville: n.p., 1913), 251.

476. William Harrison Beach, *The First New York (Lincoln) Cavalry From April 19, 1861 to July 7, 1865* (New York: Lincoln Cavalry Association, 1902), 40.

477. Tower, 81.

478. Burke Davis, *Jeb Stuart*, 369–70; Stuart.

479. William Willis Blackford, 304.

480. Pris, "Howel A. 'Doc' Rayburn," Civil War Buff: the Civil War in Arkansas (01/10/2011), http://civilwarbuff.org/wp/2011/01/howel-a-doc-rayburn/, accessed 10/01/2011.

481. Ronald S. Coddington, *Faces of the Confederacy: An Album of Southern Soldiers and Their Stories* (Baltimore: Johns Hopkins University Press, 2008), 15.

482. Oliver Wilson Davis, 117.

483. Calvert, 340.

484. Shaw, 260.

485. Porter, 214.

486. Isabel Ross, *The President's Wife: Mary Todd Lincoln, a Biography* (New York: Putnam's, 1973), 224.

487. Francis McRae Ward, "Chapter Three — Fear and Gloom Covers the Land. Grant's Move From Milliken's Bend to Vicksburg," in "*Vignettes" of the Civil War* (unpublished; written 1961, Tallulah, LA), pages not numbered.

488. Cooke, 265.

489. Ulysses Robert Brooks, *Stories of the Confederacy* (Columbia, SC: The State Company, 1912), 207.

490. Luther W. Hopkins, *From Bull Run to Appomattox: A Boy's View* (Baltimore: Fleet-McGinley, 1908), 120.

491. Kirkland, 465.

492. Davis and Swentor, 457.

493. Buffett-Smith, 13.

494. "General Pickett: Mrs. Pickett Tells the Story of Her Husband's Career," *New York Times*, Sept. 23, 1899.

495. Robert Edward Lee Jr., *Recollections and Letters of General Robert E. Lee by Captain Robert E. Lee, His Son* (New York: Doubleday, Page, 1905), 250–52.

496. Flood, 212.

497. Robert E. Lee Jr., 251.

498. Alfred Seelye Roe, *The Twenty-fourth Regiment Massachusetts Volunteers 1861–1866 "New England Guard*

Regiment" (Worcester, MA: Twenty-fourth Veteran Association, 1907), 321.

499. Donald C. Pfanz, *Richard S. Ewell: A Soldier's Life* (Chapel Hill: University of North Carolina Press, 1998), 363.

500. John Sergeant Wise, *The End of an Era* (Boston, MA: Houghton Mifflin, 1899), 432.

501. Trout, *They Followed the Plume*, 281.

502. W.W. Blackford, 85–87.

503. Trout, *They Followed the Plume*, 66.

504. Gregg A. Mierka, "Rhode Island's Own: U.S. Major General Ambrose Everett Burnside," Major General Ambrose Everett Burnside Civil War Home Page Biography (http://webspace.webring,com/people/ig/gsgreene/burnside/html, accessed 01/24/2011).

505. Conyngham, 376–377; Mulholland, 80–81.

506. Alfred Seelye Roe, *The Tenth Regiment, Massachusetts Volunteer Infantry, 1861–1864: a Western Massachusetts Regiment* (Springfield, MA: Tenth Regiment Veteran Association, 1909), 166.

507. W.W. Blackford, 48, 89.

508. Trout, *They Followed the Plume*, 66.

509. David Sullins, *Recollections of an Old Man: Seventy Years in Dixie, 1827–1897* (Bristol, TN: King, 1910), 289.

510. Willcox and Scott, 366.

511. Keller, 181–82.

512. Drake, 380.

513. Davis and Swentor, 135.

514. G. Ward Hubbs, ed., *Voices From Company D: Diaries by the Greensboro Guards, Fifth Alabama Infantry Regiment, Army of Northern Virginia* (Athens: University of Georgia Press, 2003), 195; Darrell L. Collins, *Major General Robert E. Rodes of the Army of Northern Virginia* (New York: Savas Beatie, 2008), 311.

515. Mohr, 279.

516. Downey, 113–116.

517. Gordon, 103, 313.

518. Stuart.

519. Longacre, "A Race for Life at Brandy Station," 32–33.

520. E.P. Alexander, *Fighting for the Confederacy*, 39, 76.

521. "Grant the Equestrian."

522. Crowninshield, 289.

523. Robert Augustus Stiles, *Four Years Under Marse Robert* (New York: Neale, 1910), 234, 251, 261.

524. Goodloe, 81, 83.

525. Gordon, 102–03.

526. Buffett-Smith, 13.

527. Trout, *They Followed the Plume*, 237, 239.

528. Alpheus S. Williams, 19, 166.

529. Buffett-Smith, 12.

530. Laboda, 318–19.

531. Joseph E. Chance, *The Second Texas Infantry: From Shiloh to Vicksburg* (Austin, TX: Eakin Press, 1984), 144.

532. James Grant Wilson, "Famous American War Horses," 56.

533. Clement A. Evans, ed., *Confederate Military History...*vol. 3 (Atlanta: Confederate Publishing, 1899), 607.

534. Meredith M. Sears, 1.

535. Diane DeBlois, "Monuments to Legendary Horses," The Ephemera Society of America, http://www.ephemerasociety.org/articles/DeBlois_Monuments.html. Dated 2010, accessed 01/24/2011.

536. Garrison, *Civil War Curiosities*, 76.

537. Joseph Willard Brown, *The Signal Corps, U.S.A., in the War of the Rebellion* (Boston: U.S. Veteran Signal Corps Assn., 1896), 246.

538. Sorrel, 89–90.

539. Crabb, 218.

540. Valentine, 137.

541. Stuart.

542. James Grant Wilson, "Famous American War Horses," 58.

543. Oliver Wilson Davis, 116.

544. Conyngham, 376–77; Mulholland, 80–81.

545. Magner, 35.

546. Oliver Wilson Davis, 117.

547. Kirkland, 306–308.

548. Bahnson and Chapman, 49–50.

549. William G. Williams, 165–66.

550. Garrison, *Civil War Curiosities*, 76.

551. Buffett-Smith, 12.

552. Wright, *Lee's Last Casualty*, 79, 82.

553. Kirkland, 500–01.

554. James Grant Wilson, "Famous American War Horses," 57.

555. Selby, 95.

556. Humphries, 408.

557. John Hill Brinton, *Personal Memoirs of John H. Brinton, Major and Surgeon, U.S.V., 1861–1865* (New York: Neale, 1914), 115, 135, 146.

558. Conyngham, 376–377; Mulholland, 80–81.

559. Crowninshield, 290.

560. Henderson, 11.

561. Robert Hunt Rhodes, 132, 136.

562. Bruce J. Dinges and Shirley A. Leckie, eds., *A Just and Righteous Cause: Benjamin H. Grierson's Civil War Memoirs* (Carbondale: Southern Illinois University Press, 2008.

563. Stocker, 20.

564. "Houston County GA Archives News ... Gen. C.D. Anderson & W.J. Anderson, October 14, 1887," from *Marion County Patriot* 41 (October 14, 1887): 10.

565. John C. Bonnell, *Sabres in the Shenandoah: The 21st New York Cavalry, 1863–1866* (Shippensburg, PA: Burd Street, 1996), 98.

566. Buffett-Smith, 11, 14.

567. Terrence J. Winschel, ed., *The Civil War Diary of a Common Soldier:*

Willis Wiley of the 77th Illinois (Baton Rouge: Louisiana State University Press, 2001), 66.

568. Scheibert, 42.

569. J.R. Bowen, *Regimental History of the First New York Dragoons (Originally the 130th N.Y. Vol. Infantry) During Three Years of Active Service in the Great Civil War* (n.p.: the author, 1900), 197.

570. William Forse Scott, 392.

571. "Ambrose Burnside," Interesting History, http://www.interestinghistory.info/Ambrose-Burnside.html.

572. Lloyd Lewis, *Myths After Lincoln* (New York: Reader's Club, 1941), 130; Ruth Painter Randall, *Lincoln's Animal Friends* (New York: Little, Brown, 1958), 99–114; "Abraham Lincoln, Pets and Children," The Lincoln Institute Presents Abraham Lincoln's Classroom, 3, http://abrahamlincolnclassroom.org/Library/newsletter.asp?ID=126&CRLI=174, accessed 10/25/11

573. Leander W. Cogswell, *A History of the Eleventh New Hampshire Regiment Volunteer Infantry in the Rebellion War 1861–1865 Covering its Entire Service, With Interesting Scenes of Army Life and Graphic Details of Battles, Skirmishes, Sieges, Marches, and hardships in Which its Officers and Men Participated* (Concord, NH: Republican Press Association, 1892), 314.

574. Susan Pendleton Lee, *Memoirs of William Nelson Pendleton, D.D.; Rector of Latimer Parrish, Lexington, Virginia; Brigadier-General C.S.A.; Chief of Artillery, Army of Northern Virginia* (Philadelphia: J.B. Lippincott, 1893), 405.

575. "General Pickett: Mrs. Pickett Tells the Story of Her Husband's Career," *New York Times*, Sept. 23, 1899.

576. J.H. Horton and Solomon Teverbaugh, *A History of the Eleventh Regiment (Ohio Volunteer Infantry) Contain-ing the Military Record of Each Officer and Enlisted Man of the Command—a List of Deaths—an Account of the Veterans—Incidents of the Field and Camp—Names of the Three Months Volunteers, Etc., Etc.* (Dayton, OH: W.J. Shuey, 1866), 74.

577. Luther Samuel Dickey, *History of the Eighty-fifth Regiment Pennsylvania Volunteer Infantry 1861–1865: Comprising an Authentic Narrative of Casey's Division at the Battle of Seven Pines* (New York: J.C. & W.E. Powers, 1915), 379.

578. Sam Davis Elliott, *Doctor Quintard, Chaplain C.S.A. and Second Bishop of Tennessee: The Memoir and Civil War Diary of Charles Todd Quintard* (Baton Rouge: Louisiana State University Press, 2003), 100, 191.

579. Howard Coffin, *Nine Months to Gettysburg: Stannard's Vermonters and the Repulse of Pickett's Charge* (Woodstock, VT: Countryman, 1997), pages not numbered.

580. John Taylor, 28, 85, 92, 163.

581. Curler, 2.

582. Thomas M. Aldrich, *The History of Battery A, First Regiment Rhode Island Light Artillery in the War to Preserve the Union 1861–1865* (Providence, RI: Snow & Farnham, 1904), 337.

583. Garrison, *Civil War Curiosities*, 76.

584. "Our Fleet — Gettysburg Segway Tours," 5.

585. Lyman G. Bennett and William M. Haigh, *History of the Thirty-sixth Regiment Illinois Volunteers During the War of the Rebellion* (Aurora, IL: Knickerbocker & Hodder, 1876), 500.

586. Osmund Rhodes Howard Thompson and William H. Rauch, *History of the "Bucktails" Kane Rifle Regiment of the Pennsylvania Reserve Corps (13th Pennsylvania Reserves, 42nd of the Line)* (Philadelphia: Electric, 1906) 13.

587. Henry F.W. Little, *The Seventh Regiment New Hampshire Volunteers in the War of the Rebellion* (Concord, NH: Ira C. Evans, 1896), 470.

588. "Men, Mount Your Horses," 3, citing *Rogersville (TN) Review* (1893).

589. McElroy, 272.

590. Thomas West Smith, *The Story of a Cavalry Regiment "Scott's 900" Eleventh New York Cavalry from the St. Lawrence River to the Gulf of Mexico 1861–1865* (n.p.: Veteran Association of the Regiment, 1897), 302.

591. Oliver Willcox Norton, *Army Letters 1861–1865 Being Extracts from Private Letters to Relatives and Friends from a Soldier in the Field During the Late Civil War with an Appendix Containing Copies of Some Official Documents, Papers and Addresses of Later Date* (n.p.: the author for private circulation, 1903), 167.

592. "Famous Horses of the Civil War," 3.

593. Magner, 46.

594. Daniel W. Barefoot, *General Robert F. Hoke: Lee's Modest Warrior* (Winston-Salem, NC: John F. Blair, 2002), 90–91–323–324, 380.

595. Francis Marion McAdams, *Every-Day Soldier Life, or a History of the One Hundred and Thirteenth Ohio Infantry* (Columbus, OH: Chas. M. Cott, 1884), 369.

596. Andrew J. Bennett, *The Story of the First Massachusetts Light Battery Attached to the Sixth Corps. A Glance Events in the Armies of the Potomac and Shenandoah, From the Summer of 1861 to the Autumn of 1864* (Boston: Deland & Barta, 1886), 140.

597. "Sketch of General Junius Daniel," *The Land We Love: A Monthly Magazine Devoted to Literature, Military, History, and Agriculture* 5, No. 2 (June 1868): 105.

598. Otto Eisenschiml, ed., *Vermont General: The Unusual War Experience of Edward Hastings Ripley, 1862–1865* (Old Greenwich, CT: Devin-Adari, 1960), 249.

599. Crowninshield, 289–90.

600. Crabb, 10.

601. Barr, 222.

602. Edwin Porter Thompson, *History of the First Kentucky Brigade* (n.p.: Caxton, 1868), 420.

603. Lance J. Herdegen, *The Men Stood Like Iron: How the Iron Brigade Won its Name* (Bloomington: Indiana University Press, 1997), 95, 103.

604. Harold A. Cross, 155.

605. William Joseph McMurray, *History of the Twentieth Tennessee Regiment Volunteer Infantry, C.S.A.* (Nashville: Publication Committee 20th Tennessee Infantry, 1904), 123.

606. Herdegen, 111.

607. Richard R. Hancock, *Hancock's Diary or, a History of the Second Tennessee Cavalry, With Sketches of First and Seventh Battalions; Also, Portraits and Biographical Sketches* (Nashville: Brandon, 1887), 525.

608. Phineas Orlando Avery, *History of the Fourth Illinois Cavalry Regiment* (Humboldt, NE: The Enterprise, 1903), 171.

609. John Milton Hubbard, *Notes of a Private* (Memphis, TN: E.H. Clarke & Brother, 1909), 41.

610. Dodson, 311.

611. William C. Davis, *Breckinridge*, 304, 437–38.

612. Downey, 55–56, 61–63.

613. Andrew Ward, *The Slaves' War: The Civil War in the Words of Former Slaves* (New York: Houghton Mifflin, 2008), 49.

614. Lothrop, 370.

615. Crowninshield, 289–290.

616. A.W. Bartlett, *History of the Twelfth Regiment New Hampshire Volunteers in the War of the Rebellion* (Concord, NH: Ira C. Evans, 1897), 369.

617. Barbara Schock, "What Mother Bickerdyke Did During the Civil War," *The Zephyr* (Galesburg, IL), August 5 & 12, 2010. http://www.thezephyr.com/bickerdykewar.htm, accessed 10/02/2011.

618. Hancock, 525.

619. "Old Whitey," *Paper Trail: Selected Manuscripts in the Collection of the Rutherford B. Hayes Presidential Center* 8 (August 2004). http://www.rbhayes.org/hayes/manunews, accessed 01/31/2011.

620. John Bakeless, *Spies of the Confederacy* (Philadelphia: J.B. Lippincott, 1970), 67.

621. Aldrich, 157.

622. Robert Thurston Hubard and Thomas P. Nanzig, ed., *The Civil War Memoirs of a Virginia Cavalryman: Lt. Robert T. Hubard, Jr.* (Tuscaloosa: University of Alabama Press, 2007), 122.

623. J.B. Polley, *A Soldier's Letters to Charming Nellie* (New York: Neale, 1908), 101–02.

624. Jeffrey D. Marshall, ed., *A War of the People: Vermont Civil War Letters* (Hanover, NH: University Press of New England, 1999), 169.

625. Mary Carpenter, untitled notice, *Confederate Veteran* 24, No. 11 (Nov. 1916): 525.

626. Stephen B. Oates, *Confederate Cavalry West of the River* (Austin: University of Texas Press, 1991), 57.

627. Oliver Wilson Davis, 117.

628. George N. Carpenter, *History of the Eighth Regiment Vermont Volunteers 1861–1865* (Boston: Deland & Barta, 1886), 231.

629. Colt, 129.

630. John Overton Casler, *Four Years in the Stonewall Brigade* (Girard, KS: Appeal, 1906), 340.

631. Buffett-Smith, 11, 14.

632. Clay W. Holmes, *The Elmira Prison Camp: A History of the Military Prison at Elmira, N.Y., July 6, 1864 to July 10, 1865* (New York: Putnam's, 1912), 198.

633. Alpheus S. Williams, 166, 197, 236–37, 267.

634. Magner, 46.

635. John Sergeant Wise, 168.

636. Buffett-Smith, 12.

637. A Special Correspondent, 4.

638. Kellogg, 248.

639. Henderson, 11, 39, and 51.

640. Magner, 46.

641. Buffett-Smith, 11.

642. Battle, 150.

643. Nesbitt, 23, 55.

644. James I. Robertson Jr., *General A.P. Hill*, 48, 79.

645. James Harvey McKee, *Back "in War Times": History of the 144th Regiment, New York Volunteer Infantry, with Itinerary, Showing Contemporaneous Date of the Important Battles of the Civil War* (Unadilla, NY: Times Office, 1903), 273.

646. Bennett and Haigh, 352.

647. Magner, 46.

648. Dunn, *Raiding with Morgan*, 113, 190; Byron Archibald Dunn, *On General Thomas's Staff* (Chicago: A.C. McClurg, 1899), 79–81.

649. Jim Huffstodt, *Hard Dying Men: The Story of General W.H.L. Wallace, General T.E.G. Ransom, and Their "Old Eleventh" Illinois Infantry and the American Civil War* (Bowie, MD: Heritage Books, 1991), 101, 267.

650. Walter Clark, *Histories of the Several Regiments and Battalions from North Carolina in the Great War 1861–1865 Written by Members of the Respective Commands*, vol. 4 (Goldsboro, NC: Nash Brothers, 1901), 110.

651. Botkin, 186.

652. Henry Newton Comey and Lyman Richard Comey, eds., *A Legacy of Valor: The Memoirs and Letters of Captain Henry Newton Comey, 2nd*

Massachusetts Infantry (Knoxville: University of Tennessee Press, 2004), 61.

653. John Q. Anderson, 282.

654. Barton H. Wise, *The Life of Henry A. Wise of Virginia, 1806–1876* (New York: Macmillan, 1899), 332.

655. Hillman A. Hall, Chairman, Committee of Regimental History, *History of the Sixth New York Cavalry (Second Ira Harris Guard, Second Brigade — First Division — Cavalry Corps, Army of the Potomac 1861–1865 Compiled From Letters, Diaries, Recollections and Official Records* (Worcester, MA: Blanchard, 1908), 390.

656. Deforest, 225.

657. Oliver Wilson Davis, 116.

658. Magner, 46.

659. Fannie A. Beers, *A Record of Personal Experiences and Adventures During Four Years of War* (Philadelphia: J.B. Lippincott, 1889), 238.

660. Stiles, 152–53.

661. Rollins, *Pickett's Charge*, 61, 155.

662. Stephen D. Engle, *Don Carlos Buell* (Chapel Hill: University of North Carolina Press, 1999).

663. Arthur Charles Ducat Sr., *Memoir of Gen. A.C. Ducat* (Chicago: Rand McNally, 1897), 28.

664. Joslyn, 154.

665. Thomas A. Head, *Campaigns and Battles of the Sixteenth Regiment, Tennessee Volunteers in the War Between the States, With Incidental Sketches of the Part Performed by Other Tennessee Troops in the Same War, 1861–1865* (Nashville: Cumberland Presbyterian, 1885), 374; Craig L. Symonds, *Stonewall of the West: Patrick Cleburne and the Civil War* (Lawrence: University of Kansas Press, 1997), 252.

666. Fort, 20.

667. Henderson, 63.

668. Meredith M. Sears, 1.

669. Lisa D. Piper, "Airdrie and General Buckner," http://lisapiper.com/index, accessed 12/18/2011.

670. Willcox and Scott, 366–67.

671. Boatner, 479.

672. Dowdy and Manarin, 67.

673. Boatner, 479.

674. Dowdy and Manarin, 100.

675. Dowdy and Mararin, 243.

676. Sheridan, vol. 1, 177–178.

677. Porter, 296.

678. Thatcher, 291–292.

679. Edna H. Evans, 89.

680. Sheridan, vol. 1, 177–178.

681. For the poems of both Read and Herman Melville's "Sheridan at Cedar Creek," see Burton Egbert Stevenson, *Poems of American History* (1876; available on the Internet).

682. Roy Morris Jr., *Sheridan: The Life and Wars of General Phil Sheridan* (New York: Crown, 1992), 220.

683. Sheridan, vol. 1, 177–178.

684. Edgar Wilson "Bill" Nye, *Remarks* (New York: M.W. Hazen, 1887).

685. Sheridan, vol. 1, 180.

686. Sydney H. Kasper, "Rienzi's Story," *Civil War Times Illustrated* 27, No. 9 (Jan. 1989): 25.

687. Porter, 296.

688. Kasper, 25.

689. Pfanz, 351.

690. Burke Davis, *To Appomattox: Nine April Days, 1865* (New York: Rinehart, 1959), 40.

691. Burke Davis, *To Appomattox*, 248.

692. D.A. Kinsley, *Custer: A Soldier's Story* (New York: Promontory, 1988), 279.

693. Pfanz, 351.

694. Garrison, *Civil War Curiosities*, 75.

695. Kinsley, 279.

696. Thomas Wentworth Higginson and Christopher Looby, ed., *Letters and Journals of Thomas Wentworth Higginson, 1846–1906* (Boston: Houghton Mifflin, 1921), 189, 194.

697. John Q. Anderson, 19.

698. Kinsley, 81.

699. Longacre, *The Cavalry at Gettysburg*, 238.

700. Oliver Wilson Davis, 117.

701. Terry L. Jones, 22, 197.

702. Wyeth, *That Devil Forrest*, 600–01.

703. "Roderick Place, Tennessee."

704. R.L. Howard, *History of the 124th Regiment Illinois Infantry Volunteers Otherwise Known as the "Hundred and Two Dozen" from August 1862, to August 1865* (Springfield, IL: H.W. Brokker, 1880), 71.

705. Oliver Wilson Davis, 118.

706. Willcox and Scott, 368.

707. Calvert, 33, 94.

708. John Y. Simon, ed., *The Papers of Ulysses S. Grant*, vol. 2: *April–September 1861* (Carbondale: Southern Illinois University Press, 1969), 51–52, 59.

709. Baird, 77, 80.

710. Luther W. Hopkins, 209.

711. Dabney Herndon Maury, *Recollections of a Virginian in the Mexican, Indian and Civil Wars* (New York: Scribner's, 1894), 164.

712. Waring, 53–54, 59, 65–66, 87.

713. Bundy, 280.

714. Sorrel, 65–66.

715. Jennie Edwards, *John N. Edwards: Biography, Memoirs, Reminiscences and Recollections: His Brilliant Career As a Soldier, Author and Journalist: Choice Collection of His Most Notable and Interesting Newspaper Articles, Together With Some Unpublished Poems and Many Private letters, Also a Reprint of Expedition to Mexico, an Unwritten Leaf of the War* (Kansas City: Jennie Edwards, 1889), 165–66.

716. Colleen Mastony, "Sherman's Horse," *Chicago Tribune*, January 31, 2008; Burke Davis, *Sherman's March* (New York: Random House, 1980), 7; Donald Cartwell, *Civil War 101* (New York: Gramercy, 2001), 23; "Sam, the

Horse," Saw the Elephant, http://sawtheelephant.blogspot.com/2011/03, accessed 05/23/2011.

717. Andrew J. Boies, *Record of the Thirty-Third Massachusetts Volunteer Infantry From Aug. 1862 to Aug. 1865* (Fitchbure, MA: Sentinel, 1880), 129.

718. Symonds, *Joseph E. Johnston*, 150.

719. Carol Kettenburg Dubbs, *Defend This Old Town: Williamsburg During the Civil War* (Baton Rouge: Louisiana State University Press, 2002), 156.

720. Arthur B. Carter, *The Tarnished Cavalier: Major General Earl Van Dorn, C.S.A.* (Knoxville: University of Tennessee Press, 1999), 32.

721. Garrison, *Civil War Curiosities*, 76.

722. Doris Land Mueller, *M. Jeff Thompson: Missouri's Swamp Fox for the Confederacy* (Columbia: University of Missouri Press, 2007), 29.

723. Perry, Perry and Johansson, 16.

724. James Grant Wilson, *Biographical Sketches*, 33.

725. Wayne Mahood, *Alexander "Fighting Elleck" Hays: The Life of a Civil War General from West Point to the Wilderness* (Jefferson, NC: McFarland, 2005), 123, 126.

726. Rebecca Maxwell Trafford, "Atless Jones Dickson and Celestine Josephine Chatham," *United Daughters of the Confederacy Patriot Ancestor Album* (Paducah, KY: Turner, 1999), 79.

727. William G. Stevenson, 106, 109.

728. Conyngham, 376–377; Mulholland, 80–81.

729. Merrill, 244.

730. James Grant Wilson, "Famous American War Horses," 57.

731. James Pickett Jones, 89.

732. James Harrison Wilson, *Under the Old Flag: Recollections of Military Operations in the War for the Union, the Spanish War, the Boxer Rebellion, Etc.*, vol. 2 (New York: D. Appleton, 1912), 229–30.

733. A Trooper, "A Courier's Evening," in Albert Bushnell and Elizabeth Stevens, ed., *The Romance of the Civil War* (New York: Macmillan, 1905), 171–74.

734. Lubbock, 535–36.

735. Kellogg, 103.

736. Greiner, Coryell and Smith, 93–94.

737. Magner, 16.

738. Porter, 69.

739. Howard and Howard, 1.

740. Nathaniel Cheairs Hughes, *Jefferson Davis in Blue: The Life of Sherman's Restless Warrior* (Baton Rouge: Louisiana State University Press, 2006), 399.

741. Kirkland, 488–89.

742. Stuart.

743. Garrison, *Civil War Curiosities*, 76.

744. P. Michael Jones (Exec. Dir., Gen. John A. Logan Museum), letter to author dated May 16, 2011.

745. "Great Logan's Ghost," in *The Citizen Soldier: A Publication of the General John A. Logan Museum* (January 2011), 2.

746. Livermore, 396.

747. Magner, 46.

748. "Our Fleet — Gettysburg Segway Tours," 2–3.

749. A. James Fuller, *Chaplain to the Confederacy: Basil Manly and Baptist Life in the Old South* (Baton Rouge: Louisiana State University Press, 2000).

750. William C. Davis, *Diary of a Confederate Soldier*, 153, 159.

751. Mahood, 147.

752. William C. Davis, *Diary of a Confederate Soldier*, 153.

753. Luman Harris Tenney, *War Diary of Luman Harris Tenney* (Cleveland: Evangelical Publishing House, 1914), 97, 104.

754. Seville, 51.

755. James Grant Wilson, "Famous American War Horses," 55.

756. Stuart

757. Whipkey.

758. Isaac Herman, *Memoirs of a Veteran Who Served as a Private in the '60s in the War Between the States: Personal Incidents, Experiences and Observations* (Atlanta, GA: Byrd, 1911), 105.

759. William Grose, *The Story of the Marches, Battles and Incidents of the 36th Regiment Indiana Volunteer Infantry* (New Castle, IN: Courier, 1891), 172.

760. Oliver Wilson Davis, 117.

761. Buffett-Smith, 11.

762. Thomas West Smith, 327.

763. Zarvona.

764. Marshall Wingfield, "Old Straight: A Sketch of the Life and Campaigns of Lieutenant General Alexander P. Stewart, C.S.A.," *Tennessee Historical Society Quarterly* 3, No. 2 (June 1944): 111.

765. "Facing the Enemy at Lovejoy's Station," http://henrycountybattlefield.com.

766. Magner, 46.

767. "Our Fleet — Gettysburg Segway Tours," 3.

768. Ramseur and Kundahl, 257.

769. Augustus C. Buell, *The Cannoneer: Recollections of Service in the Army of the Potomac* (Washington, DC: National Tribune, 1890), 30–31, 197, 389–398.

770. Clarissa W. Confer, *The Cherokee Nation in the Civil War* (Norman: University of Oklahoma Press, 2007), 110.

771. Grose, 129.

772. "The General (horse)," Wikipedia, the free encyclopedia. http://en.wikipedia.org/wiki/the_General_(horse), accessed 10/01/2011.

773. Michael E. Banasik, ed., *Missouri Brothers in Gray: The Reminiscences and Letters of William J. Bull and John P. Bull* (Iowa City, IA: Camp Pope Bookshop, 1998), 20.

774. Elliott, 98.

775. Michael C. Hardy, 9.

776. Robert Beasecker, ed., "*I Hope to Do My Duty*": *The Civil War Letters of John Bennitt, M.D., Surgeon, 19th Michigan Infantry* (Detroit: Wayne State University Press, 2005), 10, 84.

777. Davis and Swentor, 20.

778. Lamers, 217.

779. James A. Emmerton, *A Record of the Twenty-Third Regiment Mass. Vol. Infantry in the War of the Rebellion 1861–1865 With Alphabetical Roster; Company rolls, Portraits, Maps; Etc.* (Boston: William Ware, 1886), 167.

780. Judy Barbour, "William H. Harding," http://judy.kinneys.net/civil.html, updated 1996, accessed June 16, 2009.

781. John W. Storrs, *The "Twentieth Connecticut": A Regimental History* (Ansonia, CT: Naugatuck Valley Sentinel, 1886), 217.

782. John Sedgwick and Curtis, 70.

783. Crowninshield, 290.

784. Virgil Carrington Jones, *Gray Ghosts and Rebel Raiders* (New York: Galahad, 1995), 382.

785. Catherine M. Wright, "Horse-Related Objects in the MOC Collections," Confederate Memorial Literary Society (Dec. 14, 2010); "The Hoof of Turner Ashby's Horse," *Encyclopedia Virginia*, Charlottesville, VA. http://encyclopediavirginia.org/media, accessed 01/31/2011.

786. John Torrey Morse Jr., *Memoir of Colonel Henry Lee With Selections From His Writings and Speeches* (Boston: Little, Brown, 1905), 217.

787. Oliver Wilson Davis, 117.

788. Roe, *The Tenth Regiment, Massachusetts*, 145, 269.

789. Buffett-Smith, 11–12.

790. John Cheves Haskell, 88–90.

791. Flood, 194; Mrs. Lee Duncan Stokes, "Traveller," *United Daughters of the Confederacy Magazine* 51, No. 7 (July 1988): 21; Earp, 14.

792. Flood, 109.

793. Long, consistently.

794. Freeman, consistently.

795. Long, 131.

796. Stokes, 21.

797. Magner, 4.

798. Burke Davis, *To Appomattox*, 379

799. Long, 133.

800. Burke Davis, *To Appomattox*, 387.

801. Fitzhugh Lee, 312.

802. Flood, 109; Earp, 12.

803. Bevin Alexander, *Robert E. Lee's Civil War* (Holbrook, MA: Adams Media, 1998), 6.

804. Stokes, 21.

805. Magner, 4.

806. Earp, 11.

807. Stokes, 21.

808. Downey, 75, for one.

809. Earp, 11.

810. Magner, 4.

811. Earp, 11.

812. Edna H. Evans, 77.

813. Earp, 11; Edna H. Evans, 79.

814. Earp, 11.

815. Magner, 4.

816. Edna H. Evans, 79.

817. Ridley, 560, citing J.N. Broun letter of March 9, 1904.

818. Dowdy and Manarin, 99.

819. Earp, 11.

820. Burke Davis, *To Appomattox*, 394–95.

821. Earp, 12.

822. Freeman, 523.

823. Earp, 12.

824. Magner, 5.

825. Earp, 14.

826. Stokes, 4.

827. Earp, 14.

828. Stokes, 4.

829. Earp, 14.

830. "Traveller's Grave Marker, Lee Chapel, Washington & Lee University, Lexington, Virginia," 2, http://www.flickr.com/photos/10264053@N02/957672032, accessed 05/02/2011.

831. Earp, 14.

832. Catherine M. Wright letter.

833. William C. Davis, *Diary of a Confederate Soldier*, 154, 156, 165.

834. Murfin, 90.

835. Marshall Wingfield, *General A.P. Stewart: His Life and Letters* (West Tennessee Historical Society, 1954), 11.

836. Albert Rhett Elmore, "Incidents of Service With the Charleston Light Dragoons," *Confederate Veteran* 24, No. 11 (Nov. 1916): 538.

837. Rusling, 271.

838. Samuel Clarke Farrar, *The Twenty-second Pennsylvania Cavalry and the Ringgold Battalion, 1861–1865* (Pittsburgh: Twenty-second Pennsylvania Ringgold Cavalry Association, 1911), 257.

839. William Worth Belknap and Loren S. Tyler, *History of the Fifteenth Regiment, Iowa Veteran Volunteer Infantry, From October, 1861, to August, 1865, when Disbanded at the End of the War* (Keokuk, IA: R.B. Ogden & Son, 1887), 424.

840. James Grant Wilson, "Famous American War Horses," 59.

841. Stuart.

842. Sorrel, 65–66.

843. James Pickett Jones, 18.

844. James Harrison Wilson, *Under the Old Flag*, vol. 1, 318–319; vol. 2, 143.

845. John Q. Anderson, 300.

846. James Grant Wilson, 58.

847. Walter Clark, ed., *Histories of the Several Regiments and Battalions from North Carolina in the Great War 1861–1865 Written by members of the Respective Commands*, vol. 1 (Raleigh, NC: E.M. Ussell, 1901), 265.

848. T. Harry Williams, *Hayes of*

the *Twenty-Third: The Civil War Volunteer Officer* (Lincoln: University of Nebraska Bison Books, 1965), 101, 119.

849. Kinsley, 26.

850. Wert, *Custer*, 42.

851. Crowninshield, 287–88.

852. Benjamin Franklin Taylor, *Pictures of Life in Camp and Field*, 3rd ed. (Chicago: S.C. Griggs, 1888), 260–61.

853. Edna H. Evans, 71–76.

854. Conrad, 65.

855. Samito, 190.

856. T. Lindsay Baker, ed., *Confederate Guerilla: The Civil War Memoir of Joseph Bailey* (Fayetteville: University of Arkansas Press, 2007), 44.

857. William C. Davis, *Diary of a Confederate Soldier*, 156.

858. "2nd Regiment Infantry New York Volunteers Civil War Newspaper Clippings," New York State Military Museum and Veterans Research Center, NYS Division of Military and Naval Affairs, http://dmna.state.ny.us/historic/reghist/civil/infantry/2ndInfCWN.htm.

859. John Q. Anderson, 19, 67, 154, 182.

860. Buffett-Smith, 13.

861. James W. Raab. *J. Patton Anderson, Confederate General* (Jefferson, NC: McFarland, 2004).

862. Oliver Wilson Davis, 117.

863. Charles A. Stevens, *Berdan's United States Sharpshooters in the Army of the Potomac 1861–1865* (St. Paul, MN: n.p., 1892), 397.

864. Aldrich, 25.

865. Meredith M. Sears, 1.

866. David W. Rowe, *A Sketch of the 126th Regiment Pennsylvania Volunteers.* (Chambersburg, PA: Cook & Hays, 1869), 27.

867. Oliver Wilson Davis, 116.

868. Charles H. Kirk, *History of the Fifteenth Pennsylvania Volunteer Cavalry: Which Was Recruited and Known As The Anderson Cavalry in the Rebellion of 1861–1865* (Philadelphia: Historical Committee of the Society of the Fifteenth Pennsylvania Cavalry, 1906), 87, 109, 170.

869. Oliver Wilson, Davis, 117.

870. Stillwell, 14.

871. Oscar Osburn Winther, *With Sherman to the Sea: The Civil War Letters, Diaries & Reminiscences of Theodore F. Upson* (Bloomington: Indiana University Press, 1958), 10, 18.

872. Alfred Seelye Roe, *The Fifth Regiment Massachusetts Volunteer Infantry in Its Three Tours of Duty, 1861, 1862-'63, 1864* (Boston: Fifth Regiment Veteran Association, 1911), 286.

873. Leach, 259–60.

874. Longstreet, *From Manassas to Appomattox*, 343–44.

875. Fremantle, 29–52.

876. Robert N. Denhardt, *Foundation Dames of the American Quarter Horse* (Norman: University of Oklahoma Press, 1982), 30–36.

877. Denhardt, *Foundation Dames*, 30–36.

878. "Lexington (horse)," Wikipedia, the free encyclopedia. http://en.wikipedia.org/wiki/Lexington_(horse), accessed 10/07/2011.

879. Robert N. Denhardt, *Foundation Sires of the American Quarter Horse* (Norman: University of Oklahoma Press, 1997), 59.

880. Denhardt, *Foundation Dames*, 30–36.

881. Trout, *They Followed the Plume*, 34.

882. "Biography — Phineas Taylor Barnum," Harpweek Explore History. http://www.abraham lincolncartoons.info/SubPages/Biography.php?UniqueID=1, accessed 01/24/2011.

Bibliography

This bibliography is organized in strict alphabetical sequence, by author or if there is no formal author, by title. Some entries contain such information as the original publication if the entry is a republication or an indication of the information available in the source if it has not been cited in the Chapter Notes. Primary sources (those written contemporary with the event or by a participant in the war) are preceded by an asterisk (*).

The author had an opportunity to review only three unpublished sources. Some 60 case files of the Southern Claims Commission of 1871 were read. These contained what amounts to "almost a census" of horses taken in 1865 by the Union cavalry command of Brig. Gen. John Thomas Croxton in Tuscaloosa County, Alabama. One incident from these files is cited in the book (from a 2000 magazine article by the author). Unpublished letters of two Civil War veterans were read. A series of 24 letters dated May 1863 through April 1864 between Sgt. Burton R. Eppes, Co. B, 2nd Confederate States Engineers, and his wife (ancestors of the author) contained many references to Sgt. Eppes's efforts to obtain a suitable mount and his concern that the Confederate authorities would impress his horse left at home in Marengo County, Alabama. The 13 letters of Pvt. George D. Harmon, Co. A, 30th Iowa Infantry, from April 1864 through April 1865, to his wife, mentions equines only in a December 17, 1864, letter from Savannah, Georgia, in which he estimated that "6000 hoses an muels" were taken during the unit's march from Atlanta to there.

Only works actually used in the writing of this book are listed.

"Abraham Lincoln, Pets and Children." Lincoln Institute Presents Abraham Lincoln's Classroom, 3. http://www.abrahamlincolnclassroom.org/Library/ newsletter.asp?ID=126&CRLI=174, accessed 10/25/2011.

*Acker, Gregory, ed. *Inside the Army of the Potomac: The Civil War Experience of Captain Francis Adams Donaldson.* Mechanicsburg, PA: Stackpole Books, 1998.

Adams, George Worthington. *Doctors in Blue: The Medical History of the Union Army in the Civil War.* Dayton, OH: Press of Morningside, 1985.

Adams, Richard George. *Traveller.* New York: Dell, 1988.

*Adams, Robert N. "The Battle and Capture of Atlanta," read March 18, 1893. In *Glimpses of the Nation's Struggle: Papers Read Before the Minnesota Commandery of the Military Order of the Loyal Legion of the United States, Fourth Series,* vol. 3. St. Paul, MN: H.L. Collins, 1899.

*Albert, Allen D., ed. *History of the Forty-Fifth Regiment Pennsylvania Veteran Volunteer Infantry 1861–1865.* Williamsport, PA: Grit, 1912.

*Aldrich, Thomas M. *The History of Battery A, First Regiment Rhode Island Light Artillery in the War to Preserve the Union 1861–1865.* Providence, RI: Snow & Farnham, 1904.

Aldridge, A.F. "Gen. Joseph Wheeler." *New York Times,* Oct. 9, 1898. Mentions number (29) of horses shot while Wheeler was riding them.

Alexander, Bevin. *Robert E. Lee's Civil War.* Holbrook, MA: Adams Media, 1998.

*Alexander, Edward Porter. *Fighting for the Confederacy: The Personal Recollections of General Edward Porter Alexander.* Chapel Hill: University of North Carolina Press, 1989. Written by author about 1900 and not previously published.

*_____. *Military Memoirs of a Confederate.* New York: Da Capo, 1993. Orig. pub. 1907.

Allardice, Bruce L. *More Generals in Gray.* Baton Rouge: Louisiana State University Press, 1995.

"Ambrose Burnside." *Interesting History.* http://interestinghistory.info/Ambrose- Burnside.html.

Anderson, James A. "The Federal Raid into Central Alabama, April 1865, Including Wilson's Raid on Selma and Montgomery, and Croxton's Raid on Tuscaloosa." In *The Federal Invasion of Tuscaloosa, 1865.* Tuscaloosa: General Robert E. Rodes Camp 262, Sons of Confederate Veterans, 1965. Orig. pub. 1935 as an address.

Anderson, John Q., ed. *Brockenburn: The Journal of*

Kate Stone 1861–1868. Baton Rouge: Louisiana State University Press, 1995. Orig. pub. 1955.

Andrews, Harris, Christopher Nelson, Brian Pohanka and Harry Roach. *Photographs of American Civil War Cavalry*. East Stroudsburg, PA: Guidon, 1988.

Arceneaux, William. *Acadian General: Alfred Mouton and the Civil War*. Lafayette, LA: University of Southwestern Louisiana Press, 1981.

Armistead, Gene C. "Dixie's Civil War Unionists, 1871–1880 Interviews." *Heritage Quest Magazine* 16, No. 4 (Issue 88: July–August 2000): 34–40. Deals with the claims files of the Southern Claims Commission, of which the author reviewed some sixty claims by citizens of Tuscaloosa Co., AL.

Armstrong, William Howard. *Major McKinley: William McKinley and the Civil War*. Kent, OH: Kent State University Press, 2000.

Arnold, James R. *Grant Wins the War: Decision at Vicksburg*. New York: John Wiley & Sons, 1997.

Association for Entry of Pedigrees of Saddle Horses in America. *The Register of American Saddle Horse Breeder's Association*, vol. 4. Louisville, KY: *Courier-Journal* Job Printing, 1911.

*Aten, Henry J. *History of the Eighty-fifth Regiment, Illinois Volunteer Infantry*. Hiawatha, KS: The Regimental Association, 1901.

*Aubery, James M. *The Thirty-Sixth Wisconsin Volunteer Infantry, 1st Brigade, 2d Division, 2d Army Corps, Army of the Potomac. An Authentic Record of the Regiment from its Organization to its Muster Out, a Complete Roster of Its Officers and Men with Their Record*, etc. n.p.: n.p., 1900.

*Averell, William W. "With the Cavalry on the Peninsula." In *Battles and Leaders of the Civil War*, vol. 2. New York: Thomas Yoseloff, 1956. Orig. pub. 1887 by *The Century* magazine.

*Avery, Phineas Orlando. *History of the Fourth Illinois Cavalry Regiment*. Humboldt, NE: The Enterprise, 1903.

*Avirett, James B. *The Memoirs of General Turner Ashby and His Compeers*. Baltimore, MD: Selby & Dulany, 1867.

Baggett, James Alex. *Homegrown Yankees: Tennessee's Union Cavalry*. Baton Rouge: Louisiana State University Press, 2009.

*Bahnson, Charles Frederic, and Sarah Bahnson Chapman, ed. *Bright and Gloomy Days: The Civil War Correspondence of Captain Charles Bahnson, a Moravian Confederate*. Knoxville: University of Tennessee Press, 2003.

*Baird, W. David. *A Creek Warrior for the Confederacy: The Autobiography of G.W. Grayson*. Norman: University of Oklahoma Press, 1991.

Bakeless, John. *Spies of the Confederacy*. Philadelphia: J.B. Lippincott, 1970.

*Baker, La Fayette Curry. *History of the United States Secret Service*. Philadelphia: L.C. Baker, 1867.

*Baker, T. Lindsay, ed. *Confederate Guerrilla: The Civil War Memoir of Joseph Bailey*. Fayetteville: University of Arkansas Press, 2007.

Ballard, Michael B. "Disaster & Disgrace: The John C. Pemberton Story." In *Alabama Heritage* (Winter 1993).

*Banasik, Michael E., ed. *Missouri Brothers in Gray: The Reminiscences and Letters of William and John Bull*. Iowa City, IA: Camp Pope Bookshop, 1998.

*Barber, Flavel Clingan. *Holding the Line: The Third Tennessee Infantry, 1861–1864*. Kent, OH: Kent State University Press, 1994.

Barbour, Judy. "William H. Harding." http://judy.kinneys.net/civil.html. Updated 1996, accessed 06/16/2009.

Barefoot, Daniel W. *General Robert F. Hoke: Lee's Modest Warrior*. Winston-Salem, NC: John F. Blair, 2001.

_____. *Let Us Die Like Men: Behind the Dying Words of Confederate Warriors*. Winston-Salem, NC: John F. Blair, 2005.

*Barr, James Michael, and Thomas D. Mays, ed. *Let Us Meet in Heaven: The Civil War Letters of James Michael Barr, 5th South Carolina Cavalry*. Loveland, CO: McWhinney Foundation Press, 2000.

Barrett, John Gilchrist. *The Civil War in North Carolina*. Chapel Hill: University of North Carolina Press, 1963.

_____. *Sherman's March Through the Carolinas*. Chapel Hill: University of North Carolina Press, 1956.

*Bartlett, A.W. *History of the Twelfth Regiment New Hampshire Volunteers in the War of the Rebellion*. Concord, NH: Ira C. Evans, 1897.

*Battle, Cullen Andrews. *Third Alabama! The Civil War Memoir of Brigadier General Cullen Andrews Battle, C.S.A.* Tuscaloosa: University of Alabama Press, 2000.

*Baylor, George. *Bull Run to Bull Run: or, Four Years in the Army of Northern Virginia, Containing a Detailed Account of the Career and Adventures of the Baylor Light Horse, Company B, Twelfth Virginia Cavalry, C.S.A., with Leaves from My Scrap Book*. Richmond: B.E. Johnson, 1900.

*Beach, William Harrison. *The First New York (Lincoln) Cavalry from April 19, 1861, to July 7, 1865*. New York: Lincoln Cavalry Association, 1902. Beach was adjutant of the regiment.

*Beale, George William. *A Lieutenant of Cavalry in Lee's Army*. Boston: Gorham, 1918. Author a member of the 9th VA Cavalry and son of Brig. Gen. R.L.T. Beale, who was colonel of that regiment.

Beals, Carleton. *War Within a War: The Confederacy Against Itself*. Philadelphia: Chilton, 1965.

*Beasecker, Robert, ed. *"I Hope to Do My Country Service": The Civil War Letters of John Bennitt, M.D., Surgeon, 19th Michigan Infantry*. Detroit: Wayne State University Press, 2005.

*Beatty, John. *The Citizen-Soldier or, Memoirs of a Volunteer*. Cincinnati, OH: Wilstach, Baldwin, 1879.

Beaudot, William J.K. *The 24th Wisconsin Infantry in the Civil War: The Biography of a Regiment*. Mechanicsburg, PA: Stackpole Books, 2003.

*Beaver, James Addams. "The Campaigns of 1863 and 1864." In *The Story of Our Regiment: A History of the 148th Pennsylvania Vols. Written by the Comrades*. Des Moines, IA: Kenyon, 1904.

Beers, Fannie A. *Memories: A Record of Personal Experiences and Adventures During Four Years of War*. Philadelphia: J.B. Lippincott, 1889.

*Belknap, William Worth, and Loren S. Tyler. *History of the Fifteenth Regiment, Iowa Veteran Volunteer Infantry, from October, 1861, to August, 1865, When Disbanded at the End of the War*. Keokuk, IA: R.B. Ogden & Son, 1887.

*Bennett, Andrew J. *The Story of the First Massachusetts Light Battery Attached to the Sixth Corps. A Glance at Events in the Armies of the Potomac and Shenandoah, from the Summer of 1861 to the Autumn of 1864.* Boston: Deland & Barta, 1886. Bennett was a private in the battery.

*Bennett, Lyman G., and William M. Haigh. *History of the Thirty-sixth Regiment Illinois Volunteers.* Aurora: IL: Knickerbocker & Hodder, 1876.

*Bergeron, Arthur W. *The Civil Reminiscences of Major Silas T. Grisamore, C.S.A.* Baton Rouge: Louisiana State University Press, 1993.

Berry, Fred Jr. *Ozark Blood: Kin and Kind in the Civil War.* Bloomington: Anchor House, 2006.

*Berry, Thomas Franklin. *Four Years with Morgan and Forrest.* Oklahoma City: Harlow-Ratliff, 1914.

*Bevens, William E., and Daniel E. Sutherland (introduction). *Reminiscences of a Private: William E. Bevens of the First Arkansas Infantry, C.S.A.* Fayetteville, AR: University of Arkansas Press, 1992.

*Billings, John D. *Hardtack and Coffee, or the Unwritten Story of Army Life.* Lincoln, NE: University of Nebraska Press, 1993. Orig. pub. 1887.

"Biography — Phineas Taylor Barnum." Harpweek Explore History. http://www.abrahamlincolncartoons.info/SubPages/Biography.php?UniqueID=1, accessed 01/24/2011.

"Black Cloud, the horse Col. Lamar was Riding." *Confederate Veteran* 3, No. 5 (May 1895): 131.

*Blackford, Susan Leigh. *Letters From Lee's Army, or Memoirs of Life In and Out of the Army in Virginia During the War Between the States.* New York: Scribner's, 1947. Charles Minor Blackford was a staff officer in the CS Army of Northern Virginia.

*Blackford, William Willis. *War Years with Jeb Stuart.* Baton Rouge: Louisiana State University Press, 1993. Orig. pub. 1945.

*Blair, William Alan. *A Politician Goes to War: The Civil War Letters of John White Geary.* State College: Pennsylvania State University Press, 1991.

*Blessington, Joseph Palmer. *The Campaigns of Walker's Texas Division.* New York: Lange, Little, 1875.

Blight, David W. *A Slave No More: Two Men Who Escaped to Freedom Including Their Own Narratives of Emancipation.* Orlando: Harcourt, 2007.

Boatner, Mark Mayo III. *The Civil War Dictionary.* New York: David McKay, 1959.

*Boies, Andrew J. *Record of the Thirty-Third Massachusetts Volunteer Infantry from Aug. 1862 to Aug. 1865.* Fitchburg, MA: Sentinel, 1880.

*Boltz, Martha. "Bones of Warhorse Will Be Interred Near Jackson." *Washington Times,* July 19, 1997.

*Bond, F.A. "Fitzhugh Lee as a Lieutenant Colonel in a Skirmish." In *The War of the Sixties.* Ed. E.R. Hutchins. New York: Neale, 1912.

Bonnell, John C. *Sabres in the Shenandoah: The 21st New York Cavalry, 1863–1866.* Shippensburg, PA: Burd Street Press, 1996.

Botkin, B.A., ed. *A Civil War Treasury of Tales, Legends and Folklore.* New York: Promontory Press, 1960.

*Boudrye, Louis Napoleon. *Historic Records of the Fifth New York Cavalry, First Ira Harris Guard, Its Organization, Marches, Raids, Scouts, Engagements and Gen-* eral Service During the Rebellion of 1861–1865, With Observations of the Author By the Way Giving Sketches of the Armies of the Potomac and of the Shenandoah, Also, Interesting Accounts of Prison Life and of the Secret Service. 2nd ed. Albany, NY: S.R. Gray, 1865. Boudrye was chaplain of the regiment.

Bowden, Scott, and Bill Ward. *Last Chance for Victory: Robert E. Lee and the Gettysburg Campaign.* New York: Da Capo, 2003.

*Bowen, James Lorenzo. *History of the Thirty-seventh Regiment Mass. Volunteers in the Civil War of 1861–1865, with a Comprehensive Sketch of the Doings of Massachusetts as a State, and of the Principal Campaigns of the War.* Holyoke, MA: Clark W. Bryan, 1884.

*Bowen, J.R. *Regimental History of the First New York Dragoons: (Originally the 130th N.Y. Vol. Infantry) During Three Years of Active Service in the Great Civil War.* n. p.: the author, 1900.

Brewer, James H. *The Confederate Negro: Virginia's Craftsmen and Military Laborers, 1861–1865.* Durham, NC: Duke University Press, 1969. Includes much about the Quartermaster Corps of the Confederacy.

Bridges, Hal. *Lee's Maverick General: Daniel Harvey Hill.* Lincoln: University of Nebraska Press, 1991. Orig. pub. 1961.

*Brinsfield, John Wesley Jr. *The Spirit Divided: Memoirs of Civil War Chaplains: The Confederacy.* Macon: Mercer University Press, 2006.

*Brinton, John Hill. *Personal Memoirs of John H. Brinton, Major and Surgeon, U.S.V., 1861–1865.* New York: Neale, 1914.

*Brooks, Noah (Herbert Mitgang, ed.). *Washington in Lincoln's Time.* New York: Rinehart, 1958. Brooks was a friend and confidant of President Lincoln as well as a wartime correspondent for the *Sacramento Union.*

*Brooks, Ulysses Robert. *Butler and His Cavalry in the War of Secession, 1861–1865.* Columbia: The State Company, 1909.

*_____. *Stories of the Confederacy.* Columbia: The State Company, 1912.

Brown, Dee. "Wilson's Creek." In *Civil War Times Illustrated* 11, No. 1 (April 1972): 8–18.

*Brown, Joseph Willard. *The Signal Corps, U.S.A. in the War of the Rebellion.* Boston: U.S. Veteran Signal Corps Association, 1896.

Browne, Ray B., and Lawrence A. Kreiser Jr. *American Popular Culture Through History: The Civil War and Reconstruction.* Westport, CT: Greenwood Press, 2003.

Bryson, Bill. *Made in America.* London, UK: Black Swan, 1998. Orig. pub. 1994.

*Buell, Augustus C. *The Cannoneer: Recollections of Service in the Army of the Potomac.* Washington, D.C.: National Tribune, 1890. A letter dated October 6, 1889, by Capt. Stewart telling the story of "Tartar" is included, 30–31.

Buell, Thomas B. *The Warrior Generals: Combat Leadership in the Civil War.* New York: Crown, 1997.

Buffett-Smith, Karen. "Forgotten Soldiers: the Horses of the New York 5th Cavalry Company H and Their Service During the U.S. Civil War." http:freewebs.com/.../5th%20new%20cavalry%horses.doc, accessed 01/24/2011.

Bundy, Carol. *The Nature of Sacrifice: A Biography of Charles Russell Lowell, Jr., 1835–64*. New York: Macmillan, 2005.

Burnam, Catherine Barrett Robertson. "Death and Funeral of Bishop-General Leonidas Polk," Saint Paul's Church, Augusta, GA. http://www.saintpauls.org/cbf/burnamPolk.php, accessed 09/28/2011.

*Burney, Samuel Augustus, and Nat S. Turner, ed. *A Southern Soldier's Letters Home: The Civil War Letters of Samuel A. Burney, Cobb's Legion, Army of Northern Virginia*. Macon: Mercer University Press, 2002.

*Butler, Benjamin Franklin. *Autobiography and Personal Reminiscences of Major-General Benj. F. Butler: Butler's Book*. Boston: A.M. Thayer, 1892.

Butts, Joseph Tyler. *A Gallant Captain of the Civil War Being the Record of the Extraordinary Adventures of Frederick Otto Baron von Fritsch Compiled From His War Record in Washington and His Private Papers*. New York: F. Tennyson Neely, 1902.

*Calvert, Henry Murray. *Reminiscences of a Boy in Blue 1862–1865*. New York:Putnam's, 1920.

Campbell, Lisa. "The Origin of the War Horse." *NSL Newsletter* (Summer 2002). National Sporting Library and Museum. http://www.nsl.org/warhorse.html. About the first monument honoring Civil War horses and mules.

Cannan, John. *The Spotsylvania Campaign, May 7–21, 1864*. Conshohocken, PA: Combined Books, 1997.

Capers, Walter Branham. *The Soldier-Bishop, Ellison Capers*. New York: Neale, 1912.

*Cardwell, David. "A Horse Battery." *Confederate Veteran* (Nov.–Dec. 1988): 6–7.

*Carpenter, George N. *History of the Eighth Regiment Vermont Volunteers 1861–1865*. Boston: Deland & Barta, 1886.

Carpenter, Mary. Untitled notice. *Confederate Veteran* 24, No. 11 (Nov. 1916): 525.

Carter, Arthur B. *The Tarnished Cavalier: Major General Earl Van Dorn, C.S.A.* Knoxville: University of Tennessee Press, 1999.

Cartwell, Donald. *Civil War 101*. New York: Gramercy, 2001. 32 horses are listed.

Cartwright, Thomas Y. "'Better Confederates Did Not Live': Black Southerners in Nathan Bedford Forrest's Commands." In *Black Southerners in Gray: Essays on African-Americans in Confederate Armies*. Murfreesboro, TN: Southern Heritage, 1994.

*Casler, John Overton. *Four Years in the Stonewall Brigade*, 2nd ed. Girard, KS: Appeal, 1906. Orig. pub. 1893. Casler was a veteran of the brigade.

*Castel, Albert, ed. "The Diary of General Henry Little, C.S.A." *Civil War Times Illustrated* 11, No. 6 (Oct. 1972): 4–6, 8–11, 41–47.

*Castleman, Alfred L. *The Army of the Potomac Behind the Scenes: A Diary of Unwritten History from the Organization of the Army, by General George McClellan, to the Close of the Campaign in Virginia, About the First Day of January, 1863*. Milwaukee, WI: Strickland, 1863.

*Cate, Jean M., and John Spadea, eds. *If I Live to Come Home: The Civil War Letters of Sergeant John March Cate*. Pittsburgh: Dorrance, 1995.

Cavanagh, Michael. *Memoirs of Gen. Thomas Francis Meagher: Comprising the Leading Events of His Career Chronologically Arranged, With Selections From His Speeches, Lectures and Miscellaneous Writings Including Personal Reminiscences*. Worcester, MA: Messenger Press, 1892.

Chance, Joseph E. *The Second Texas Infantry: From Shiloh to Vicksburg*. Austin: Eakin, 1984.

Chetlain, Augustus L. "Recollections of General U.S. Grant." In *Military Essays and Recollections Papers Read Before the Commandery of the State of Illinois, Military Order of the Loyal Legion of the United States*, vol. I. Chicago: A.C. McClurg, 1891. Chetlain was a staff officer of Grant's.

*Clark, Charles T. *Opdycke Tigers, 125th O.V.I.: A History of the Regiment and of the Campaigns and Battles of the Army of the Cumberland*. Columbus, OH: Spahr & Glenn, 1895.

*Clark, Orton S. *The One Hundred and Sixteenth Regiment of New York State Volunteers Being a Complete History of Its Organization and of Its Nearly Three Years of Active Service in the Great Rebellion*. Buffalo, NY: Matthews & Warren, 1868.

Clark, Walter, ed. *Histories of the Several Regiments and Battalions from North Carolina in the Great War 1861–1865 Written by Members of the Respective Commands*, vol. 1. Raleigh, NC: E.M. Uzzell, 1901.

_____ . *Histories of the Several Regiments and Battalions from North Carolina in the Great War 1861–1865 Written by Members of the Respective Commands*, vol. 4. Goldsboro, NC: Nash Brothers, 1901.

Cleaves, Freeman. *Meade of Gettysburg*. Norman: University of Oklahoma Press, 1991. Orig. pub. 1960.

Clinton, Thomas P. "The Closing Days of the War of Secession in Tuscaloosa." In *The Federal Invasion of Tuscaloosa*. Tuscaloosa: General Robert E. Rhodes Camp 262, Sons of Confederate Veterans, 1965.

Coatsworth, Stella A. *The Loyal People of the North-West: A Record of Prominent Persons, Places and Events, During Eight Years of Unparalleled American History*. Chicago: Goodman & Donnelley, 1869.

*Cockrell, Thomas D., and Michael B. Bullard, eds. *A Mississippi Rebel in the Army of Northern Virginia: The Civil War Memoirs of Private David Holt*. Baton Rouge: Louisiana State University Press, 2001. Orig. pub. 1995.

Coddington, Ronald D. *Faces of the Confederacy: An Album of Southern Soldiers and Their Stories*. Baltimore: Johns Hopkins University Press, 2008.

Coffin, Howard. *Nine Months to Gettysburg: Stannard's Vermonters and the Repulse of Pickett's Charge*. Woodstock, VT: Countryman Press, 1997.

Coggins, Jack. *Arms and Equipment of the Civil War*. New York: Barnes & Noble, 1990. Orig. pub. 1962.

*Cogswell, Leander W. *A History of the Eleventh New Hampshire Regiment Volunteer Infantry in the Rebellion War 1861–1865 Covering its Entire Service, With Interesting Scenes of Army Life, and Graphic Details of Battles, Skirmishes, Sieges, Marches, and Hardships in Which its Officers and Men Participated*. Concord, NH: Republican Press Association, 1891. Cogswell was a member of the regiment.

*Coker, J.L. "Battle of Wauhatchie." In *Battles and Leaders of the Civil War*, vol. 3. New York: Thomas Yoseloff, 1956.

Colimore, Edward. "Old Baldy to Return to Frankford Civil War Museum." *Philadelphia Inquirer*, March 8, 2010.

Collins, Darrell L. *Major General Robert E. Rodes of the Army of Northern Virginia*. New York: Savas Beatie LLC, 2008.

*Collins, John L. "A Prisoner's March from Gettysburg to Staunton." In *Battles and Leaders of the Civil War*, vol. 3. New York: Thomas Yoseloff, 1956.

Colt, Margaretta Barton. *Defend the Valley: A Shenandoah Family in the Civil War*. New York: Oxford University Press, 1999.

*Comey, Henry Newton, and Lyman Richard Comey, eds. *A Legacy of Valor: The Memoirs and Letters of Captain Henry Newton Comey, 2nd Massachusetts Infantry*. Knoxville: University of Tennessee Press, 2004.

*Commager, Henry Steele, ed. *The Blue and the Gray: The Story of the Civil War as Told by Participants* (2 vols. in one). New York: Fairfax, 1991. Orig. pub. 1950.

Confer, Clarissa W. *The Cherokee Nation in the Civil War*. Norman: University of Oklahoma Press, 2007.

Connelley, William Elsey. *Quantrill and the Border Wars*. New York: Smithmark, 1996. Orig. pub. 1909.

*Conrad, Thomas Nelson. *The Rebel Scout: A Thrilling History of Scouting in the Southern Army*. Westminster, MD: Heritage, 2009. Orig. pub. Washington, D.C.: National, 1904.

*Conyngham, David Porter. *The Irish Brigade and Its Campaigns with Some Account of the Corcoran Legion, and Sketches of the Principal Officers*. New York: William McSorley, 1867.

*Cooke, John Esten. *Wearing of the Gray: Being Personal Portraits, Scenes and Adventures of the War*. New York: E.B. Treat, 1867.

*Corby, William. *Memoirs of Chaplain Life*. Chicago: O'Donnell, 1893. Father Corby was chaplain of the Union Irish Brigade.

*Cotton, Gordon A., ed. *From the Pen of a She-Rebel: The Civil War Diary of Emilie Riley McKinley*. Columbia: University of South Carolina Press, 2001.

Couper, William. *One Hundred Years at V.M.I.*, vol. 3. Richmond: Garrett & Massie, 1939.

*Cox, Florence Marie Ankeny. *Kiss Josey for Me*. Santa Ana, CA: Friis-Pioneer Press, 1974. Letters of Capt. Henry G. Ankeny, 4th Iowa Infantry.

Cozzens, Peter. *The Darkest Days of the War: The Battles of Iuka & Corinth*. Chapel Hill, NC: University of North Carolina Press, 1997.

_____. *The Shipwreck of Their Hopes: The Battles for Chattanooga*. Urbana: University of Illinois Press, 1996.

Crabb, Martha L. *All Afire to Fight: The Untold Tale of the Civil War's Ninth Texas Cavalry*. New York: Avon Books, 2000.

*Crist, Lynda Lasswell, ed. *The Papers of Jefferson Davis: October 1863–August 1864*, vol. 10. Baton Rouge: Louisiana State University Press, 1999.

*Croffut, W.A., ed. *Fifty Years in Camp and Field: Diary of Major-General Ethan Allen Hitchcock, U.S.A.* New York: Putnam's, 1909.

*Cross, Frederick C., ed. *Nobly They Served the Union.* N.p.: Frederick C. Cross, 1975. Letters of Henry G. Stratton, officer, 19th Ohio Infantry.

Cross, Harold A. *They Sleep Beneath the Mockingbird: Mississippi Burial Sites and Biographies of Confederate Generals*. Murfreesboro, TN: Southern Heritage Press, 1994.

*Crowninshield, Benjamin William. *A History of the First Regiment of Massachusetts Cavalry Volunteers*. Boston: Houghton Mifflin, 1891.

*Crumpton, Washington Bryan. *A Book of Memories, 1842–1920*. Montgomery, AL: Baptist Mission Board, 1921.

Cumming, Charles M. *Yankee Quaker, Confederate General: The Curious Career of Bushrod Rust Johnson*. Rutherford, NJ: Fairleigh Dickinson University Press, 1971.

Cunningham, Edward. *The Port Hudson Campaign, 1862–1863*. Baton Rouge: Louisiana State University Press, 1994.

Curler, Elizabeth A. "Morgan Horses in the Civil War." National Museum of the Morgan Horse. http://morganmuseum.org/html/civilwar.html, accessed 04/11/2011. 27 horses named.

Current, Richard Nelson. *Lincoln's Loyalists: Union Soldiers From the Confederacy*. New York: Oxford University Press, 1992.

*Curry, William Leontes. *Four Years in the Saddle: History of First Regiment Ohio Volunteer Cavalry, War of the Rebellion ... 1861–1865*. Columbus, OH: Champlin, 1898.

Cutrer, Thomas W. *Ben McCulloch and the Frontier Military Tradition*. Chapel Hill: University of North Carolina Press, 1993.

*_____, ed. *Longstreet's Aide: the Civil War Letters of Major Thomas J. Goree*. Charlottesville: University Press of Virginia, 1995.

*Cuttino, George P., ed. *Saddle Bag & Spinning Wheel: Being the Civil War Letters of George W. Peddy, M.D., Surgeon, 56th Georgia Volunteer Regiment, C.S.A., and his Wife Kate Featherstone Peddy*. Macon: Mercer University Press, 2000. Orig. pub. 1986.

Dahlgren, John Adolphus. *Memoir of Ulric Dahlgren by His Father Rear-Admiral Dahlgren*. Philadelphia: J.B. Lippincott, 1872.

*Dame, William Meade. *From the Rapidan to Richmond and the Spotsylvania Campaign: A Sketch in Personal Narrative of the Scenes a Soldier Saw*. Baltimore: Green-Lucas, 1920.

Daniel, Larry J. *Cannoneers in Gray: The Field Artillery of the Army of Tennessee, 1861–1865*. Tuscaloosa: University of Alabama Press, 1984.

Daughtry, Mary. *Gray Cavalier: The Life and Wars of General W.H.F. "Rooney" Lee*. New York: Da Capo, 2002.

*Davenport, Alfred. *Camp and Field Life of the Fifth New York Volunteer Infantry (Duryee Zouaves)*. New York: Dick & Fitzgerald, 1879.

Davis, Burke. *Jeb Stuart: The Last Cavalier*. New York: Wings, 1992. Orig. pub. 1957.

_____. *Sherman's March*. New York: Random House, 1980.

_____. *To Appomattox: Nine April Days, 1865*. New York: Rinehart, 1959.

Davis, Oliver Wilson. *Life of David Bell Birney, Major-General United States Volunteers*. Philadelphia: King & Baird, 1867. An account of the famous St. Patrick's Day Races held in 1863 involving Gen. Meagher is given on pages 116–118 and includes the names of the horses and riders participating.

*Davis, Washington. *Camp-Fire Chats of the Civil War; Being the Incident, Adventure and Wayside Exploit of the Bivouac and Battle Field as Related by Veteran Soldiers Themselves*. Chicago: Lewis, 1882.

Davis, William C. *Breckinridge: Statesman, Soldier, Symbol*. Baton Rouge: Louisiana State University Press, 1974.

*_____, ed. *Diary of a Confederate Soldier: John S. Jackman of the Orphan Brigade*. Columbia: University of South Carolina Press, 1990.

_____. *The Orphan Brigade: The Kentucky Confederates Who Couldn't Go Home*. Garden City, NY: Doubleday, 1980.

_____. *A Taste for War: The Culinary History of the Blue and the Gray*. Mechanicsburg, PA: Stackpole Books, 2003.

Davis, William C., and Bell Irvin Wiley, eds. *The Civil War (Compact Edition)*. New York: Black Dog & Leventhal, 1998.

*Davis, William C., and Meredith L. Swentor, eds. *Bluegrass Confederate: The Headquarters Diary of Edward O. Guerrant*. Baton Rouge: Louisiana State University Press, 1999. Guerrant used at least 7 horses which he named.

*Day, David L. *My Diary of Rambles With the 25th Mass. Volunteer Infantry with Burnside's Coast Division, 18th Army Corps, and Army of the James*. Milford, MA: King & Billings, 1884.

DeBlois, Diane. "Monuments to Legendary Horses." *The Ephemera Society of America*. http://www.ephemerasociety.org/articles/DeBlois_Monuments.html. Dated 2010, accessed 01/24/2011.

*DeForest, John William. *A Volunteer's Adventures: A Union Captain's Record of the Civil War*. New Haven: Yale University Press, 1946. Written 1890 but not pub. until 1946.

Denhart, Robert M. *Foundation Dames of the American Quarter Horse*. Norman: University of Oklahoma Press and the American Quarter Horse Association, 1982.

_____. *Foundation Sires of the American Quarter Horse*. Norman: University of Oklahoma Press, 1997.

*Deupree, J.G. "Reminiscences of Service with the First Mississippi Cavalry." In*Publications of the Mississippi Historical Society*, vol. 6. Oxford: Mississippi Historical Society, 1903. Deupree was a private in the regiment.

*Dickert, D. Augustus. *History of Kershaw's Brigade, With Complete Roll of Companies, Biographical Sketches, Incidents, Anecdotes, Etc.* Newberry, SC: Elbert H. Aull, 1899.

*Dickey, Luther Samuel. *History of the Eighty-fifth Regiment Pennsylvania Volunteer Infantry, 1861–1865: Comprising an Authentic Narrative of Casey's Division at the Battle of Seven Pines*. New York: J.C. & W.E. Powers, 1915.

*Dinges, Bruce J., and Shirley A. Leckie, eds. *A Just and Righteous Cause: Benjamin H. Grierson's Civil War Memoirs*. Carbondale: Southern Illinois University Press, 2008.

*Dinkins, James. *1861 to 1865, by an Old Johnnie: Personal Recollections and Experiences in the Confederate Army*. Cincinnati: R. Clarke, 1897.

Dobson, John Wayne. "Jeremiah Beckworth, Confederate Teamster." *Confederate Veteran* (May–June 1994): 8–10.

Dodson, W.C., ed. *Campaigns of Wheeler and His Cavalry 1861–1865 from Material Furnished by Gen. Joseph Wheeler to Which is Added His Concise and Graphic Account of the Santiago Campaign of 1898*. Atlanta: Hudgins, 1899.

*Donald, David Herbert. *Gone for a Soldier: The Civil War Memoirs of Private Alfred Bellard*. Boston: Little, Brown, 1975. Bellard was a private in the 5th New Jersey Infantry.

Dougan, Michael B. *Confederate Arkansas: The People and Policies of a Frontier State in Wartime*. Tuscaloosa: University of Alabama Press, 1976.

*Douglas, Henry Kyd. *I Rode with Stonewall: The War Experiences of the Youngest Member of Jackson's Staff*. Chapel Hill: University of North Carolina Press, 1968. Orig. pub. 1946.

*Douglas, James Postell, and Samuel A. Thompson, eds. *Douglas's Texas Battery*. Tyler, TX: Smith County Historical Society, 1966.

*Dowdy, Clifford, and Louis H. Manarin, eds. *The Wartime Papers of R.E. Lee*. Boston: Little, Brown (for Virginia Civil War Commission), 1961.

Downey, Fairfax. *Famous Horses of the Civil War*. New York: Thomas Nelson, 1959.

Drake, James Vaulx. *Life of General Robert Hatton Including His Most Important Speeches Together, With Much of His Washington & Army Correspondence*. Nashville: Marshall & Bruce, 1867.

Drew, C. "The Confederate Soldier's Horse." *Savannah (GA) Republican*, Aug. 21, 1863. Submitted by Vicki Betts to http://www.authentic-campaigner.com/forum/archive/index.php/t-3223.html, accessed 10/01/2011.

Dubbs, Carol Kettenburg. *Defend This Old Town: Williamsburg During the Civil War*. Baton Rouge: Louisiana State University Press, 2002.

*Ducat, Arthur Charles Sr. *Memoir of Gen. A.C. Ducat*. Chicago: Rand McNally, 1897.

*Duke, Basil Wilson. *Reminiscences of General Basil W. Duke, C.S.A.* Garden City, NY: Doubleday, Page, 1911.

*Dunaway, Wayland Fuller. *Reminiscences of a Rebel*. New York: Neale, 1913.

*Duncan, Thomas D. *Recollections of Thomas D. Duncan, a Confederate Soldier*. Nashville: McQuiddy, 1922.

Dunn, Byron Archibald. *On General Thomas's Staff*. Chicago: A.C. McClurg, 1899.

_____. *Raiding With Morgan*. Chicago: A.C. McClurg, 1903.

Dyer, Frederic A. *A Compendium of the War of the Rebellion*, 2 vols. Dayton, OH: Press of Morningside Bookshop, 1979. Orig. pub. 1908.

*Early, Jubal Anderson. *Lieutenant General Jubal Anderson Early, C.S.A.: Autobiographical Sketch and Narrative of the War Between the States. New York: Smithmark, 1994.

Earp, Charles A. "A Confederate Gray." *Confederate Veteran* 2 (1998): 11–15. Very good article about Lee's famous horse, Traveller.

Eaton, Clement. *A History of the Southern Confederacy.* New York: The Free Press, 1965. Orig. pub. 1954.

Eby, Vivienne M. *The Horse Dictionary: English-Language Terms Used in Equine Care, Feeding, Training, Treatment, Racing and Show.* Jefferson, NC: McFarland, 1995.

Edwards, Jennie. *John N. Edwards: Biography, Memoirs, Reminiscences and Recollections: His Brilliant Career as a Soldier, Author and Journalist: Choice Collection of His Most Notable and Interesting Newspaper Articles, Together With Some Unpublished Poems and Many Private Letters, Also a Reprint of Expedition to Mexico, an Unwritten Leaf of the War.* Kansas City: Jennie Edwards, 1889.

Edwards, John Newman. *Noted Guerillas, or the Warfare of the Border.* St. Louis: Bryan, Brand, 1877.

Eisenschiml, Otto, ed. *Vermont General: The Unusual War Experiences of Edward Hastings Ripley, 1862–1865.* Old Greenwich, CT: Devin-Adair, 1960. Ripley was a brevet brigadier general with the actual rank of colonel of the 9th VT Inf.

*Eisenschiml, Otto, and Ralph Newman. *The American Iliad: The Epic Story of the Civil War as Narrated by Eyewitnesses and Contemporaries.* Indianapolis: Bobbs-Merrill, 1947.

*Elliott, Sam Davis, ed. *Doctor Quintard, Chaplain C.S.A. and Second Bishop of Tennessee: The Memoir and Civil War Diary of Charles Todd Quintard.* Baton Rouge: Louisiana State University Press, 2003.

*Elmore, Albert Rhett. "Incidents of Service with the Charleston Light Dragoons." *Confederate Veteran* 24, No. 11 (Nov. 1916): 538–543.

*Elwood, John W. *Elwood's Stories of the Old Ringgold Cavalry, 1861–1865: The First Three Year Cavalry of the Civil War.* Coal Center, PA: the author, 1914.

Emerson, Edward Waldo. *Life and Letters of Charles Russell Lowell, Captain Sixth United States Cavalry, Colonel Second Massachusetts Cavalry, Brigadier-General United States Volunteers.* Boston: Houghton Mifflin, 1907.

*Emilio, Luis Fenollosa. *History of the Fifty-fourth Regiment of Massachusetts Volunteer Infantry 1863–1865.* 2nd ed. Boston: Boston Book, 1894. Orig. pub. 1891. Often reprinted under the title *A Brave Black Regiment.*

*Emmerton, James A. *A Record of the Twenty-Third Regiment Mass. Vol. Infantry in the War of the Rebellion 1861–1865 With Alphabetical Roster; Company Rolls, Portraits; Maps; Etc.* Boston: William Ware, 1886.

Engle, Stephen D. *Don Carlos Buell.* Chapel Hill: University of North Carolina Press, 1999.

"English Combatant, An." *Battle-Fields of the South, from Bull Run to Fredericksburg; With Sketches of Confederate Commanders, and Gossip of the Camps.* New York: John Bradburn, 1864.

"Equine Heroes of Pickett's Charge." *New York Times,* October 12, 1913.

Evans, Charles M. *War of the Aeronauts: A History of Ballooning During the Civil War.* Mechanicsburg, PA: Stackpole Books, 2002.

Evans, Clement Anselm, ed. *Confederate Military History: A Library of Confederate States History in Twelve Volumes, Written by Distinguished Men of the South, and Edited by Gen. Clement A. Evans of Georgia,* vol. 3. Atlanta: Confederate Publishing, 1899.

Evans, David. *Stoneman's Horsemen: Union Cavalry Operations in the Atlanta Campaign.* Bloomington: Indiana University Press, 1999.

Evans, Edna H. *Famous Horses and Their People.* Brattleboro, VT: Stephen Greene, 1975.

*Ewer, James K. *The Third Massachusetts Cavalry in the War for the Union.* Maplewood, MA: Wm. G.J. Perry, 1903.

Fair Oaks (PA) Volunteer Fire Dept. "Leet Township and Fair Oaks History." http://fofd.org/aboutfovFd.htm.

"Famous Horses of the Civil War." http://library.thinkquest.org/o6aug/01591/horses.htm, accessed 06/04/2009. Lists 41 horses by name.

*Farrar, Samuel Clarke. *The Twenty-second Pennsylvania Cavalry and the Ringgold Battalion, 1861–1865.* Pittsburgh: Twenty-second Pennsylvania Ringgold Cavalry Association, 1911.

Faust, Drew Gilpin. *This Republic of Suffering: Death and the American Civil War.* New York: Vintage Books, 2008.

*Favill, Josiah Marshall. *The Diary of a Young Officer Serving with the Armies of the United States During the War of the Rebellion.* Chicago: R.R. Donnelley & Sons, 1909.

*Fine, Lisa. "Horse's Bones Finally Receive Proper Burial: VMI Ceremony Honors Jackson's Steed." *Richmond Times-Dispatch,* July 21, 1997.

*Fisher, Horace Cecil. *The Personal Experience of Colonel Horace Newton Fisher in the Civil War: A Staff Officer's Story.* n.p.: T. Todd, 1960.

*Fitch, Michael Hendrick. *Echoes of the Civil War as I Hear Them.* New York: R.F. Fenno, 1905.

Fleming, Walter L. *Civil War and Reconstruction in Alabama.* Spartanburg, SC: Reprint Co., 1978. Orig. pub. 1905.

*Fletcher, William A. *Rebel Private, Front and Rear.* New York: Meridian, 1997.

Flood, Charles Bracelen. *Lee: The Last Years.* Boston: Houghton Mifflin, 1981.

*Floyd, Frederick Clark. *History of the Fortieth (Mozart) Regiment New York Volunteers, Which Was Composed of Four Companies From New York, Four Companies From Massachusetts, and Two Companies From Pennsylvania.* Boston: F.H. Gilson, 1909.

*Fort, John Porter. *John Porter Fort: A Memorial and Personal Reminiscences.* New York: Knickerbocker, 1918.

*Frederick, Gilbert. *The Story of a Regiment, Being a Record of the Military Services of the Fifty-Seventh New York State Volunteer Infantry in the War of the Rebellion 1861–1865.* Chicago: The Fifty-Seventh Veteran Association, 1895.

Freeman, Douglas Southall. *R.E. Lee* (abridgement in 1 vol. of 4 vols.) New York: Touchstone, 1991.

*Fremantle, Arthur J.L. *Three Months in the Southern*

States, April–June 1863. Lincoln, NE: University of Nebraska Press, 1991. Orig. pub. 1863.

Fuller, A. James. *Chaplain to the Confederacy: Basil Manly and Baptist Life in the Old South.* Baton Rouge: Louisiana State University Press, 2000.

F.V. "History of the Stallion, George M. Patchen." *Wallace's Monthly* 4, No. 1 (Feb. 1878): 512–524.

Gallaway, B.P. *The Ragged Rebel: A Common Soldier in W.H. Parsons' Texas Cavalry, 1861–1865.* Austin: University of Texas Press, 1988.

Garrison, Fielding H. *John Shaw Billings: A Memoir.* New York: Putnam's, 1915.

Garrison, Webb. *Civil War Curiosities: Strange Stories, Oddities, Events and Coincidences.* Nashville: Rutledge Hill, 1994.

_____. *More Civil War Curiosities.* Nashville: Rutledge Hill, 1995.

Gates, Arnold. "Of Men and Mules: A Modest History of Jackassery." *Civil War Times Illustrated* 23, No. 7 (Nov. 1984): 40–46.

"General Barringer & the 1st North Carolina Cavalry." http://firstnccav.home.mindspring.com/nc1hist2.html, accessed 12/21/2011), 8, 9.

"General Pickett: Mrs. Pickett Tells the Story of Her Husband's Career." *New York Times,* Sept. 23, 1899. Names his horses.

*"General Sheridan's Horse, Winchester, Honored." *New York Times,* June 5, 1922.

*Gibson, Keith. "Civil War Horse Undergoes Makeover." Lexington, VA: Virginia Military Institute, 2007. http://vmi.edu/NewsCenter.aspx?id=15775, accessed 03/24/2009.

Gilbert, J. Warren, ed. *People's Pictorial Edition the Blue and Gray: A History of the Conflicts During Lee's Invasion and Battle of Gettysburg.* Chicago: privately printed, 1922.

*Gilmor, Harry W. *Four Years in the Saddle.* New York: Harper & Brothers, 1866.

Glatthar, Joseph T. *Partners in Command: The Relationship Between Leaders in the Civil War.* New York: The Free Press, 1994. Uncorrected 1993 proof.

*Glazier, Willard Worcester. *Three Years in the Federal Cavalry.* New York: R.H. Ferguson, 1870.

*Goodloe, Albert Theodore. *Confederate Echoes: A Voice from the South in the Days of Secession and of the Southern Confederacy.* Nashville: Publishing House of the M[ethodist] E[piscopal] Church, South, 1907.

*Gordon, John B. *Reminiscences of the Civil War.* New York: Scribner's, 1903.

*Goss, Warren Lee. "The Army Mule, Carrier of Victory." *Civil War Times Illustrated* 1, No. 4 (July 1962): 17–19.

*_____. "Yorktown and Williamsburg — Recollections of a Private." In *Battles and Leaders of the Civil War,* vol. 2. New York: Thomas Yoseloff, 1956. Orig. pub. 1887 by *The Century* magazine.

Grace, Deborah. "The Horse in the Civil War." http://www.reillysbattery.org/Newsletter/Jul00, accessed 03/24/2009.

*Grant, Ulysses S. *Personal Memoirs of U.S. Grant,* 2 vols. New York: Charles L. Webster, 1885.

"Grant the Equestrian." *Ulysses S. Grant Homepage,* http://granthomepage.com.

"Great Logan's Ghost." *The Citizen Soldier: A Publication of the General John A Logan Museum* (January 2011).

*Gregory, Edward S. "Vicksburg During the Siege." In *Annals of the Civil War.* New York: Da Capo, 1994, 119–120. Orig. pub. 1878 by *Philadelphia Weekly Times.*

*Grenier, James M., Janet L. Coryell, and James R. Smith, eds. *A Surgeon's Civil War: The Letters and Diary of Daniel M. Holt, M.D.* Kent, OH: Kent State University Press, 1994.

Groom, Winston. *Shrouds of Glory: From Atlanta to Nashville–The Last Great Campaign of the Civil War.* New York: Atlantic Monthly Press, 1995.

*Grose, William (writing as "a member of the regiment"). *The Story of the Marches, Battles and Incidents of the 36th Regiment Indiana Volunteer Infantry.* New Castle, IN: Courier Company Press, 1891.

*Guild, George B. *A Brief Narrative of the Fourth Tennessee Cavalry Regiment, Wheeler's Corps, Army of Tennessee.* Nashville: n.p., 1913.

Gunn, Jane Augusta Terry. *Memorial Sketches of Doctor Moses Gunn, by His Wife, With Extracts from His Letters and Eulogistic Tributes from His Colleagues and Friends.* Chicago: W.T. Keener, 1889.

*Hall, Hillman A., Chairman of Committee on Regimental History. *History of the Sixth New York Cavalry (Second Ira Harris Guard), Second Brigade — First Division — Cavalry Corps, Army of the Potomac 1861–1865 Compiled From Letters, Diaries, Recollections and Official Records.* Worcester, MA: Blanchard Press, 1908.

Hallock, Judith Lee. *Braxton Bragg and Confederate Defeat,* vol. 2. Tuscaloosa: University of Alabama Press, 1991.

Hamlin, Charles Eugene. *The Life and Times of Hannibal Hamlin.* Cambridge, MA: Riverside, 1899.

*Hancock, Richard R. *Hancock's Diary or, a History of the Second Tennessee Cavalry.* Nashville: Brandon, 1887.

*Hanifen, Michael. *History of Battery B First New Jersey Artillery.* Ottawa, IL: Republican-Times, 1905.

*Hard, Abner. *History of the Eighth Cavalry Regiment Illinois Volunteers, During the Great Rebellion.* Aurora, IL: n.p., 1868.

Hardy, Michael C. *The Fifty-Eighth North Carolina Troops: Tar Heels in the Army of Tennessee.* Jefferson, NC: McFarland, 2010.

Harrison, Lowell H. *The Civil War in Kentucky.* Lexington: University Press of Kentucky, 1975. Orig. pub. 1960.

Hartley, Chris J. *Stoneman's Raid, 1865.* Winston-Salem, NC: John F. Blair, 2010.

_____. *Stuart's Tarheels: James B. Gordon and His North Carolina Cavalry in the Civil War.* Jefferson, NC: McFarland, 2011.

*Hartpence, William R. *History of the Fifty-First Indiana Veteran Volunteer Infantry.* Salem, MA: Higginson, 1998. Reprint of orig. pub. 1894. Hartpence was sergeant major of the regiment.

*Haskell, Frank Aretes. *The Battle of Gettysburg.* Cambridge, MA: Riverside Press, 1958. Haskell wrote this account 1863 but it was not published for many years.

*Haskell, John Cheves, with Gilbert E. Govan and James

W. Livingood, eds. *The Haskell Memoirs.* New York: Putnam's, 1960. Haskell was a Confederate staff officer.

*Hassler, William Woods, ed. *One of Lee's Best Men: The Civil War Letters of General William Dorsey Pender.* Chapel Hill: University of North Carolina Press, 1999. Orig. pub. 1965 as *The General and His Lad.*

Hattaway, Herman. *General Stephen D. Lee.* Jackson: University Press of Mississippi, 1976.

Havinghurst, Walter. *Voices on the River: The Story of the Mississippi Waterways.* Edison, NJ: Castle, 1964.

*Haynie, J. Henry. *The Nineteenth Illinois: A Memoir of a Regiment of Volunteer Infantry Famous for its Drill, Bravery, and Distinguished Services.* Chicago: M.A. Donahue, 1912.

*Hays, Gilbert Adams. *Under the Red Patch: Story of the Sixty-third Regiment Pennsylvania Volunteers 1861–1864.* Pittsburgh: Market Review, 1908.

*Hazen, William Babcock. *A Narrative of Military Service by General W.B. Hazen.* Boston: Ticknor, 1985.

*Head, Thomas A. *Campaigns and Battles of the Sixteenth Regiment, Tennessee Volunteers, in the War Between the States, With Incidental Sketches of the Part Performed by Other Tennessee Troops in the Same War, 1861–1865.* Nashville: Cumberland Presbyterian Publishing House, 1885.

*Headley. *Confederate Operations in Canada and New York.* New York: Neale, 1906.

Hebert, Walter H. *Fighting Joe Hooker.* Lincoln: University of Nebraska Press, 1999. Orig. pub. 1944.

Heidler, David S., and Jeanne T. Heidler. *Encyclopedia of the American Civil War: A Political, Social, and Military History,* 5 vols. in 1. Santa Barbara, CA: ABC-CLIO, 2000.

*Henderson, Edward Prioleau. *Autobiography of Arab.* Columbia: R.L. Bryan, 1901.

Hendrick, Burton J. *Lincoln's War Cabinet.* Boston: Little, Brown, 1946.

Hendricks, Bonnie L., and Anthony A. Dent. *International Encyclopedia of Horse Breeds.* Norman: University of Oklahoma Press, 1995.

Henry County Battlefield. "Facing the Enemy at Lovejoy's Station." http://henrycountybattlefield.com.

Herdegen, Lance J. *The Men Stood Like Iron: How the Iron Brigade Won Its Name.* Bloomington: Indiana University Press, 1997.

*Herman, Isaac. *Memoirs of a Veteran Who Served as a Private in the '60s in the War Between the States: Personal Incidents, Experiences and Observations.* Atlanta: Byrd, 1911.

*Heros von Borcke, Johan August Heinrich. *Memoirs of the Confederate War for Independence.* Philadelphia: J.B. Lippincott, 1867.

Hervey, John L., and John Alexander Gorman. "Horse." *Encyclopaedia Britannica,* vol. 11. Chicago: Encyclopaedia Britannica, Inc., 1960.

*Heth, Henry. "Letter from Major-General Henry Heth, of A.P. Hill's Corps, A.N.V." *Southern Historical Society Papers,* vol. 4, 151–160. http://www.gdg.org/Research/Authored%20Items/shheth2.html, accessed 09/28/2011.

Hicken, Victor. *Illinois in the Civil War.* Urbana: University of Illinois Press, 1991. Orig. pub. 1966.

*Hickenlooper, Andrew. "The Battle of Shiloh, Part I."

In *Sketches of War History, 1861–1865: Papers Prepared for the Commandery of the State of Ohio, Military Order of the Loyal Legion of the United States, 1896–1903,* vol. 5. Cincinnati, OH: R. Clarke, 1903.

*Higginson, Thomas Wentworth, and Christopher Looby, ed. *The Complete Civil War Journal and Selected Letters of Thomas Wentworth Higginson.* Chicago: University of Chicago Press, 2000.

Hill, Lois, ed. *Poems and Songs of the Civil War.* New York: Barnes & Noble, 1996.

"Hippophagy." *New York Times,* Dec. 12, 1907, http://query-nytimes.com/mem/archive. Free.

Hoke, Jacob. *The Great Invasion.* New York: Thomas Yoseloff, 1959. Orig. pub. In 1887 as *The Great Invasion of 1863; or General Lee in Pennsylvania.*

Hollingsworth, Randolph. *Lexington, Queen of the Bluegrass.* Charleston, SC: Arcadia, 2004.

Holmes, Clay W. *The Elmira Prison Camp: A History of the Military Prison at Elmira, N.Y., July 6, 1864 to July 19, 1865.* New York: Putnam's, 1912.

*Hood, John Bell. *Advance and Retreat.* Edison, NJ: Blue & Gray Press, 1985. Orig. pub. 1880.

Hoole, William Stanley, and Elizabeth Hoole McArthur. *The Yankee Invasion of West Alabama, March–April 1865, Including the Battle of Trion (Vance), the Battle of Tuscaloosa, the Burning of the University, and the Battle of Romulus.* Tuscaloosa, AL: Confederate Publishing, 1985.

Hopkins, Donald A. *The Little Jeff: The Jeff Davis Legion, Cavalry, Army of Northern Virginia.* Shippensburg, PA: White Mane, 1999.

*Hopkins, Luther W. *From Bull Run to Appomattox: A Boy's View.* Baltimore: Fleet-McGinley, 1908.

*Hopkins, William Palmer. *The Seventh Regiment Rhode Island Volunteers in the Civil War 1861–1865.* Providence, RI: Snow & Farnham, 1903.

"Horatio and Charlotte Van Cleve House, 603 5th Street, South East, Minneapolis, Minnesota." Placeography. http://www.placeography.org/index,php/ Horatio_and_Charlotte_Van_Cleve_House, accessed 10/02/2011.

*Horrall, S.F. *History of the Forty-Second Indiana Volunteer Infantry.* n.p.: published by the author, 1893.

*Horton, J.H., and Solomon Teverbaugh. *A History of the Eleventh Regiment (Ohio Volunteer Infantry) Containing the Military Record of Each Officer and Enlisted Man of the Command — a List of Deaths — an Account of the Veterans — Incidents of the Field and Camp — Names of the Three Month's Volunteers, Etc. Etc.* Dayton, OH: W.J. Shuey, 1866. Both authors were members of the regiment.

*Houghton, William R., and Mitchell B. Houghton. *Two Boys in the Civil War and After.* Montgomery, AL: Paragon, 1912.

*Houston, E.E. "History of Vaughn's Confederate Brigade." In *A Soldier's Story of the Siege of Vicksburg, From the Diary of Osborn H. Oldroyd With Confederate Accounts from Authentic Sources and an Introduction by Brevet Maj.-Gen. M.F. Force.* Springfield, IL: published by the author, 1885.

"Houston County GA Archives News ... Gen. C.D. Anderson and W.J. Anderson, October 14, 1887." *Marion County Patriot* 41 (October 14, 1881): 10.

http://files.usgwarchives.org/ga/houston/newspapers/nw1858gencdad.txt, updated 12/07/2002 by Carla Miles, accessed 10/02/2011.

*Howard, Oliver Otis. *Autobiography of Oliver Otis Howard, Major General United States Army*, vol. 1. New York: Baker & Taylor, 1908.

*Howard, R.L. *History of the 124th Regiment Illinois Volunteer Infantry Volunteers Otherwise Known as the "Hundred and Two Dozen" from August 1862, to August 1865.* Springfield, IL: H.W. Brokker, 1880.

Howard, Stanley, and Terri Howard. "Death of Gen. John Hunt Morgan Marker." *Historical Marker Database*. http://www.hmdb.org/marker.asp?marker=23081.

*Hubard, Robert Thurston Jr., and Thomas P. Nanzig, ed. *The Civil War Memoirs of a Virginia Cavalryman.* Tuscaloosa: University of Alabama Press, 2007.

*Hubbard, John Milton. *Notes of a Private.* Memphis: E.H. Clarke & Brother, 1909.

*Hubbs, G. Ward, ed. *Letters from Company G: Diaries of the Greensboro Guards, Fifth Alabama Infantry Regiment, Army of Northern Virginia.* Athens: University of Georgia Press, 2003.

Huffstodt, Jim. *Hard Dying Men: The Story of General W.H.L. Wallace, General T.E.G. Ransom, and Their "Old Eleventh" Illinois Infantry and the American Civil War.* Bowie, MD: Heritage Books, 1991.

Hughes, Nathaniel Cheairs Jr. *The Civil War Memoir of Philip Daingerfield Stephenson, D.D.: Private, Company K, 13th Arkansas Volunteer Infantry, Loader, Piece No. 4, 5th Company, Washington Artillery, Army of Tennessee C.S.A.* Baton Rouge: Louisiana State University Press, 1998. Orig. pub. 1995 by University of Central Arkansas Press.

_____. *General William J. Hardee, "Old Reliable."* Baton Rouge: Louisiana State University Press, 1912.

_____. *Jefferson Davis in Blue: The Life of Sherman's Restless Warrior.* Baton Rouge: Louisiana State University Press, 2006.

*_____. *Sir Henry Morton Stanley, Confederate.* Baton Rouge: Louisiana State University Press, 2000.

*Humphries, Charles A. *Field, Camp, Hospital and Prison in the Civil War, 1863–1865.* Boston: George H. Ellis, 1918.

Hunt, Aurora. *The Army of the Pacific, 1860–1866.* Mechanicsburg, PA: Stackpole Books, 2004.

*Hurd, E.O. "The Battle of Collierville." In *Sketches of War History, 1861–1865: Papers Prepared for the Commandery of the State of Ohio, Military Order of the Loyal Legion of the United States, 1896–1903,* vol. 5. Cincinnati: R. Clarke, 1903. *Imboden, John D. "Incidents of the First Bull Run." In *Battles and Leaders of the Civil War,* vol. 1. New York: Thomas Yoseloff, 1956. Orig. pub. 1887 by *The Century* magazine.

*_____. "Jackson at Harpers Ferry in 1861." In *Battles and Leaders of the Civil War,* vol. 1. New York: Thomas Yoseloff, 1956. Orig. pub. 1887 by *The Century* magazine.

*Izlar, William Valmore. *A Sketch of the War Record of the Edisto Rifles, 1861–1865.* Columbia: The State Co., 1914.

Jenkins, Sally, and John Stauffer. *The State of Jones: The Small Southern County That Seceded from the Confederacy.* New York: Doubleday, 2009.

*Johnson, Adam Rankin, and William J. Davis, ed. *The Partisan Rangers of the Confederate States Army.* Louisville, KY: George G. Fetter, 1904.

*Johnston, Joseph E. *Narrative of Military Operations During the Civil War.* New York: Da Capo, 1990. Orig. pub. 1874.

Johnston, William Preston. *The Life of Gen. Albert Sidney Johnston Embracing His Services in the Armies of the United States, the Republic of Texas, and the Confederate States.* New York: Da Capo, 1997. Orig. pub. 1879.

*Joiner, Gary D., ed. *Little to Eat and Mud to Drink: Letters, Diaries, and Memoirs from the Red River Campaign, 1863–1864.* Knoxville: University of Tennessee Press, 2007.

*Jones, Frank J. "Personal Recollections and Experiences of a Soldier During the War of the Rebellion." In *Sketches of War History, 1861–1865: Papers Prepared for the Commandery of the State of Ohio, Military Order of the Loyal Legion of the United States, 1903–1908,* vol. 6. Cincinnati: Montfort, 1908.

Jones, James Pickett. *Yankee Blitzkrieg: Wilson's Raid Through Alabama and Georgia.* Athens: University of Georgia Press, 1976. (1987 printing.)

*Jones, Katharine M. *Heroines of Dixie: Confederate Women Tell Their Stories of the War.* New York: Konecky & Konecky, 1955.

Jones, P. Michael. Letter to author dated May 16, 2011.

*Jones, Terry L., ed. *Campbell Brown's Civil War: With Ewell and the Army of Northern Virginia.* Baton Rouge: Louisiana State University Press, 2001.

_____. *Lee's Tigers: The Louisiana Infantry in the Army of Northern Virginia.* Baton Rouge: Louisiana State University Press, 2002.

Joslyn, Mauriel. *A Meteor Shining Brightly: Essays of the Life and Career of Major General Patrick R. Cleburne.* Macon: Mercer University Press, 2000.

*Joyce, John Alexander. *A Checkered Life.* Chicago: S.P. Rounds Jr., 1883.

Jubal A. Early Preservation Trust. "Early's Homeplace." http://www.jubalearly.org/history.html, accessed 10/01/2011.

Kasper, Sydney H. "Rienzi's Story." *Civil War Times Illustrated* 27, No. 9 (Jan. 1989): 20–25.

Keller, Allan. *Morgan's Raid.* Indianapolis, IN: Bobbs-Merrill, 1961.

*Kellogg, Mary E., ed. *Army Life of an Illinois Soldier Including a Day-by-Day Record of Sherman's March to the Sea: Letters and Diary of Charles W. Wills.* Carbondale: Southern Illinois University Press, 1996.

Kelsey, Marie. "Ulysses S. Grant and His Horses During and After the Civil War." Duluth, MN: College of St. Scholastica. http://faculty.css.edu/mkelsey/usgrant/hors2.html, accessed 12/23/2011.

Kerby, Robert Lee. *The Confederate Invasion of New Mexico and Arizona, 1861–1862.* Los Angeles: Westernlore Press, 1958.

Kerr, Paul B. *Civil War Surgeon: Biography of James Langstaff Dunn, M.D.* Bloomington, IL: Paul B. Kerr, 2005.

*Kidd, J.H. *Personal Recollections of a Cavalryman With Custer's Michigan Cavalry Brigade in The Civil War.* New York: Bantam, 1991. Orig. pub. 1908.

Kinsley, D.A. *Custer: A Soldier's Story*. New York: Promontory, 1988.

*Kirk, Charles H. *History of the Fifteenth Pennsylvania Volunteer Cavalry: Which Was Recruited and Known as the Anderson Cavalry in the Rebellion of 1861–1865*. Philadelphia: Historical Committee of the Society of the Fifteenth Pennsylvania Cavalry, 1906.

Kirkland, Frazar. *The Pictorial Book of Anecdotes of the Rebellion or the Funny and Pathetic Side of the War, Embracing the Most Brilliant and Remarkable Anecdotal Events of the Great Conflict in the United States, from the Time of the Memorable Toast of Andrew Jackson, Uttered in 1830, in the Presence of the Original Secession Conspirators, to the Assassination of President Lincoln, and the End of the War. With Famous Words and Deeds of Women*. St. Louis: J.H. Mason, 1889.

Knaggs, Laura Maria, and Katherine Knaggs Anderson. *Major Robert Clark Knaggs: His Life and Times (1836–1927)*. New York: Carleton, 1992.

Laboda, Lawrence R. *From Selma to Appomattox: The History of the Jeff Davis Artillery*. New York: Oxford University Press, 1994.

Lamers, William M. *The Edge of Glory: A Biography of General William S. Rosecrans, U.S.A.* Baton Rouge: Louisiana State University Press, 1999. Orig. pub. 1961.

Lang, George, Raymond L. Collins, and Gerald F. White. *Medal of Honor Recipients 1863–1994*, vol. 1: *Civil War to 2nd Nicaraguan Campaign*. New York: Thomas Yoseloff, 1956.

Langston, Chip. "Men of Iron." *Civil War Times Illustrated* 43, No. 2 (June 2004): 42–47, 59–60, 62.

Leach, Margaret. *Reveille in Washington, 1860–1865*. New York: Harper & Brothers, 1941.

*Le Duc, William Gates. *This Business of War: The Recollections of a Civil War Quartermaster*. St. Paul, MN: Minnesota Historical Society Press, 2004. Orig. pub. as *The Recollections of a Civil War Quartermaster*. St. Paul: North Central Publishing, 1963.

Lee, Fitzhugh. *General Lee: A Biography of Robert E. Lee*. New York: Da Capo, 1994. Orig. pub. 1894.

*Lee, George R., ed. "The Wagonmaster's Letter." *Civil War Times Illustrated* 27, No. 1 (March 1988): 30–33.

*Lee, Robert Edward Jr. *Recollections and Letters of General Robert E. Lee by Captain Robert E. Lee, His Son*. New York: Doubleday, Page, 1905.

Lee, Susan Pendleton. *Memoirs of William Nelson Pendleton, D.D.; Rector of Latimer Parrish, Lexington, Virginia; Brigadier-General C.S.A.; Chief of Artillery, Army of Northern Virginia*. Philadelphia: J.B. Lippincott, 1893. Author was daughter of the general.

Leopold, Richard W., Arthur S. Link, and Stanley Cohen, eds. *Problems in American History*, vol. 1: *Through Reconstruction*. 3rd ed. Englewood Cliffs, NJ: Prentice-Hall, 1966.

Lewis, Lloyd. *Myths After Lincoln*. New York: Readers Club, 1941.

Lewis, Thomas A. *The Guns of Cedar Creek*. New York: Harper & Row, 1988.

"Lexington (horse)." Wikipedia. http://en.wikipedia.org/wiki/Lexington_(horse), accessed 10/07/2011.

"List of horses of the American Civil War." Wikipedia, http://en.wikipedia.org/wiki/List_of_horses_of_the_American_Civil_War. 79 horses are listed.

*Little, George, and James R. Maxwell. *A History of Lumsden's Battery, C.S.A.* Tuscaloosa: R.E. Rhodes Chapter United Daughters of the Confederacy, 1905.

*Little, Henry F.W. *The Seventh Regiment New Hampshire Volunteers in the War of the Rebellion*. Concord, NH: Ira C. Evans, 1896.

*"Little Sorrel Buried at VMI July 20, 1997." http://users.erols.com/va-udc/sorrel.html.

*Livermore, Thomas Leonard. *Days and Events 1860–1866*. Boston: Houghton Mifflin, 1920.

Loewen, James. *Lies Across America: What Our Historic Sites Get Wrong*. New York: The New Press, 1999. Nice section about statue of Gen. John Morgan and his horse Bess.

*Logan, Mary S.C. *Reminiscences of a Soldier's Wife: An Autobiography by Mrs. John A. Logan*. New York: Scribner's, 1916.

*Logsdon, David R., ed. *Eyewitnesses at the Battle of Franklin*. Nashville: Kettle Mills, 1991. Orig. pub. 1988.

*_____, ed. *Eyewitnesses at the Battle of Shiloh*. Nashville: Kettle Mills, 1994.

*_____, ed. *Eyewitnesses at the Battle of Stones River*. Nashville: Kettle Mills, 1989.

*Long, Armistead L. *Memoirs of Robert E. Lee: His Military and Personal History*. Secaucus, NJ: Blue & Gray Press, 1983. Orig. pub. 1886. Author was on Lee's staff.

*Longacre, Edward G., ed. "Boots and Saddles: A Short History of the Cavalry During the Civil War, Part I: The Eastern Theater." *Civil War Times Illustrated* 31, No. 1 (March–April 1992), 34–40.

_____. "Boots and Saddles: A Short History of the Cavalry During the Civil War, Part II: The Western Theater." *Civil War Times Illustrated* 31, No. 2 (May–June 1992): 48–55.

_____. *The Cavalry at Gettysburg: A Technical Study of Mounted Operations During the Civil War's Pivotal Campaign 9 June–14 July 1863*. Lincoln: University of Nebraska Press, 1986. 1993 Bison Books reprint.

_____. *The Man Behind the Guns: A Military Biography of General Henry J. Hunt, Commander of Artillery, Army of the Potomac*. New York: Da Capo, 2002.

_____. "A Race for Life at Brandy Station." *Civil War Times Illustrated* 17, No. 9 (Jan. 1979): 32–38.

*Longacre, Glenn V., and John E. Haas, eds. *To Battle for God and the Right: The Civil War Letterbooks of Emerson Opdycke*. Champaign: University of Illinois Press, 2003.

*Longstreet, James A. *From Manassas to Appomattox: Memoirs of the Civil War*. New York: Mallard, 1991. Orig. pub. 1896.

*_____. "The Invasion of Maryland." In *Battles and Leaders of the Civil War*, vol. 2. New York: Thomas Yoseloff, 1956. Orig. pub. 1887 by *Century Magazine*.

*Lothrop, Charles H. *A History of the First Regiment Iowa Cavalry Veteran Volunteers From Its Organization in 1861 to Its Muster Out of the United States Service in 1865*. Lyons, IA: Beers & Eaton, 1890.

Lott, Robert P. "Van Cleve at Chickamauga: The Study of a Division's Performance in Battle." Master's thesis, General Stagg College, 1996.

*Lowe, Richard. *A Texas Cavalry Officer: The Diary and Letters of James C. Bates*. Baton Rouge: Louisiana State University Press, 1999.

*Lubbock, Francis Richard. *Six Decades in Texas or Memoirs of Francis Richard Lubbock, Governor of Texas in War-Time, 1861–1865, a Personal Experience in Business, War and Politics.* Austin: Ben C. Jones, 1900.

Lundberg, John R. *Granbury's Texas Brigade.* Baton Rouge: Louisiana State University Press, 2012.

*McAdams, Francis Marion. *Every-Day Soldier Life, or a History of the One Hundred and Thirteenth Ohio Volunteer Infantry.* Columbus, OH: Charles M. Cott, 1884.

*McAllister, Robert, and James I. Robertson Jr., eds. *The Civil War Letters of General Robert McAllister.* Baton Rouge: Louisiana State University Press, 1998. Orig. pub. 1965 by Rutgers Univ.

*McClellan, Henry Brainerd. *The Life and Campaigns of Major-General J.E.B. Stuart, Commander of the Cavalry of the Army of Northern Virginia.* Edison, NJ: Blue & Gray Press, 1993. Orig. pub. 1885.

McCullogh, Caire. "Photos from the Past: Frank (Veteran of Company A, 12th Ohio Volunteer Cavalry)." http//suvcw.org/past/frank12ove.htm, accessed 10/05/2011.

*McDonald, William Naylor, and Bushrod C. Washington, ed. *A History of the Laurel Brigade Originally the Ashby Cavalry of the Army of Northern Virginia and Chew's Battery.* Baltimore: Sun Job Printer's Office, 1907. McDonald was a member of the brigade.

McDonough, James Lee. *Shiloh — in Hell Before Night.* Knoxville: University of Tennessee Press, 1977; 6th printing, 1997.

*McElroy, John. *Andersonville: A Story of Rebel Military Prisons. Fifteen Months a Guest of the So-Called Southern Confederacy, a Private Soldier's Experience in Richmond, Andersonville, Savannah, Millen, Blackshear and Florence.* Toledo, OH: D.R. Locke, 1899.

*McGregor, Charles. *History of the Fifteenth Regiment New Hampshire Volunteers 1862–1863.* n.p.: Fifteenth Regiment Association, 1900.

*McKee, James Harvey. *Back "in War Times": History of the 144th Regiment, New York Volunteer Infantry, with Itinerary, Showing Contemporaneous Date of the Important Battle of the Civil War.* Unadilla, NY: Times Office, 1903.

*McKim, Randolph Harrison. *A Soldier's Recollections: Leaves from the Diary of a Young Confederate: With an Oration on the Motives and Aims of the Soldiers of the South.* New York: Longmans, Green, 1921. Orig. pub. 1910.

McLaughlin, Jack. *Gettysburg: The Long Encampment.* New York: Bonanza Books, 1963.

McLean, James. *California Sabers: The 2nd Massachusetts Cavalry in the Civil War.* Bloomington: Indiana University Press, 2000.

McMillan, Malcolm C., ed. *The Alabama Confederate Reader.* Tuscaloosa: University of Alabama Press, 1963.

*McMurray, William Joseph. *History of the Twentieth Tennessee Regiment Volunteer Infantry, C.S.A.* Nashville: Publication Committee (W.J. McMurray, D.J. Roberts, R.J. Neal), 1904.

McMurry, Richard M. *Atlanta 1864: Last Chance for the Confederacy.* Lincoln: University of Nebraska Press, 2000.

*Macnamara, Daniel George. *The History of the Ninth Regiment Massachusetts Volunteer Infantry, Second Brigade, First Division, Fifth Army Corps, Army of the Potomac, June, 1861–June, 1864.* Boston: E.B. Stillings, 1899.

*McNeil, John A. "The Imboden Raid and Its Effects." In *Southern Historical Society Papers,* vol. 34. Richmond: Southern Historical Society, 1906.

*McPheeters, William M., with Cynthia Dehaven Pitcock, and Bill J. Gurley, eds. *I Acted From Principle: The Civil War Diary of Dr. William M. McPheeters.* Fayetteville, AR: University of Arkansas Press, 2002.

Magner, Blake A. *Traveller & Company: The Horses of Gettysburg.* Gettysburg, PA: Farnsworth House Military Impressions, 1995.

Mahood, Wayne. *Alexander "Fighting Elleck" Hays: The Life of a Civil War General from West Point to the Wilderness.* Jefferson, NC: McFarland, 2005.

"Manse Jolly Took Last Ride Here 102 Years Ago." *Anderson (SC) Daily Mail,* January 29, 1969. http://SandersWeb.net, accessed 07/16/2012.

*Marshall, Jeffrey D., ed. *A War of the People: Vermont Civil War Letters.* Hanover, NH: University Press of New England, 1999.

Martin, Samuel J. *Southern Hero: Matthew Calbraith Butler, Confederate General, Hampton Red Shirt, and U.S. Senator.* Mechanicsburg, PA: Stackpole Books, 2001.

Marvel, William. *Race of the Soil: The Ninth New Hampshire Regiment in the Civil War.* Wilmington, NC: Broadfoot, 1988.

*Maryniak, Benedict R., ed. *The Spirit Divided: Memoirs of Civil War Chaplains: The Union.* Macon: Mercer University Press, 2007.

*Mason, Edwin C. "Through the Wilderness to the Bloody Angle at Spotsylvania Court House." In *Glimpses of the Nation's Struggle. Fourth Series. Papers Read Before the Minnesota Commandery of the Military Order of the Loyal Legion of the United States, 1892–1897.* St. Paul, MN: H.L. Collins, 1898.

*Massey, John. *Reminiscences Giving Sketches of Scenes Through Which the Author Has Passed and Pen Portraits of People Who Have Modified His Life.* Nashville: Methodist Episcopal Church, South, 1916.

Mast, Greg. "CS Pvt. Rufus Winfield Colvard." *State Troops and Volunteers: A Photographic Record of North Carolina Civil War Soldiers,* vol. 1. Raleigh, NC: Office of Archives and History, North Carolina Dept. of Cultural Resources, 1998. http://statetroopsandvolunteers.com/vollgal.html, accessed 10/02/2011.

Mastony, Colleen. "Sherman's Horse." *Chicago Tribune,* January 31, 2008.

*Maury, Dabney Herndon. *Recollections of a Virginian in the Mexican, Indian and Civil Wars.* New York: Scribner's, 1894.

Meketa, Jacqueline Dorgan, ed. *Legacy of Honor: The Life of Rafael Chacon, A Nineteenth-Century New Mexican.* Albuquerque, NM: University of New Mexico Press, 1986.

"Men, Mount Your Horses." http://www.angelfire.com/tn/hawkinsscoccivilwar/horses, accessed 10/01/2011.

*Menge, W. Springer, and J. August Shimrak. *The Civil War Notebook of Daniel Chisolm: A Chronicle of Daily*

Life in the Union Army 1864–1865. New York: Ballantine, 1989. A fine description of a horse race is provided by Chisolm.

*Merrill, Samuel. *The Seventieth Indiana Volunteer Infantry in the War of the Rebellion.* Indianapolis: Bowen-Merrill, 1900.

Mierka, Gregg A. "Rhode Island's Own: U.S. Major General Ambrose Everett Burnside," Major General Ambrose Everett Burnside Civil War Home Page Biography, http://webspace.webring.com/people/ig/gsgreene/burnside/html, accessed 01/24/2011.

*Miles, Nelson Appleton. *Serving the Republic: Memoirs of the Civil and Military Life of Nelson A. Miles, Lieutenant–General, United States Army.* New York: Harper & Brothers, 1911.

Miller, Emily Van Dorn. *A Soldier's Honor: With Reminiscences of Major-General Earl Van Dorn.* New York: Abbey Press, 1902.

Miller, Francis Trevelyan, ed. *The Photographic History of the Civil War,* vol. 4. New York: Review of Reviews, 1911. Chapter 11 ("War-Horses"), by Theodore F. Rodenbaugh, pictures and discusses steeds of commanders. Chapter 12 has good information about purchasing horses for the Union cavalry.

_____. *The Photographic History of the Civil War,* vol. 8. New York: Review of Reviews, 1911.

Miller, Mark. *"If I Should Live:" A History of the Sixteenth Arkansas Confederate Infantry, 1861–1865.* Conway, AR: Arkansas Research, Inc., 2000.

Miller, Rex. *Croxton's Raid.* Fort Collins, CO: Old Army Press, 1979.

*Mohr, James C., ed. *The Cormany Diaries: A Northern Family in the Civil War.* Pittsburgh: University of Pittsburgh Press, 1982.

Monaghan, Jay. *Custer: The Life of General George Armstrong Custer.* Fargo, ND: Bison, 1971. Orig. pub. 1959.

Monnett, Howard M. *Action Before Westport, 1864.* Boulder University Press of Colorado, 1995. Orig. pub. 1964.

Moore, Frank. *Anecdotes, Poetry and Incidents of the War: North and South, 1860–1865.* n. p.: Publication Office, Bible House, 1867.

_____, ed. *The Rebellion Record: A Diary of American Events, With Documents, Narrative, Illustrative Incidents, Poetry, Etc., Supplement,* vol. 1. New York: Putnam's, Henry Holt, 1864.

*Moors, John Franklin. *History of the Fifty-second Regiment Massachusetts Volunteers.* Boston: George H. Ellis, 1893.

Morales, William M. *The 41st Alabama Infantry Regiment, Confederate States of America: A Narrative History of a Civil War Regiment from West Central Alabama.* Wyandotte, OK: Gregath, 2001.

"Morgan Horse Guide." http://morganhorseguide.com/index.php?page=clifton, 2010, accessed 04/11/2011.

Morris, Roy Jr. *Sheridan: The Life and Wars of General Phil Sheridan.* New York: Crown, 1992.

*Morris, W.S., L.D. Hartwell, and J.B. Kuykendall. *History 31st Regiment Illinois Volunteers Organized by John A. Logan.* Herrin, IL: Crossfire, 1991. Orig. pub. 1902.

Morse, John Torrey Jr. *Memoir of Colonel Henry Lee*

with Selections from His Writings and Speeches. Boston: Little, Brown, 1905.

*Mosby, John Singleton. *Memoirs.* Nashville: J.S. Sanders, 1995. Orig. pub. 1957.

Mueller, Doris Land. *M. Jeff Thompson: Missouri's Swamp Fox for the Confederacy.* Columbia: University of Missouri Press, 2007.

*Mulholland, St. Clair Augustine. *The Story of the 116th Regiment Pennsylvania Volunteers in the War of the Rebellion: The Record of a Gallant Command.* Philadelphia: F. McManus Jr., 1903.

Murfin, James V. *The Gleam of Bayonets: The Battle of Antietam and the Maryland Campaign of 1862.* New York: Curtis, 1965.

Murray, Pauli. *Proud Shoes: The Story of an American Family.* New York: Harper & Row, 1987. Orig. pub. 1956. Pages 117–123 provide an interesting account of the experiences of a black teamster contracted to the Union Army during 1861 and 1862.

*Musgrove, George Dallas. *Kentucky Cavaliers in Dixie: Reminiscences of a Confederate Cavalryman.* Lincoln: University of Nebraska Press, Bison Books Edition, 1999. Orig. pub. 1957.

Musser, Richard H. "The Battle of Pea Ridge." *2nd Missouri Cavalry C.S.A.* http://2ndmocavcsa.tripod.com/id61.htm, accessed 10/02/2011. Cites the *Daily Missouri Republican,* St. Louis, MO, Nov. 21 and Nov. 26, 1886.

Nall, I.B. *The Register of the American Saddle-Horse Breeders Association (Incorporated),* vol. 2. Chicago: Brown-Cooper, 1901. Orig. compiled 1893.

*Nesbitt, Mark. *Through Blood & Fire: Selected Civil War papers of Colonel Charles S. Wainwright, 1861–1865.* Mechanicsburg, PA: Stackpole, 1996.

Nevins, Allan, ed. "A Diary of Battle: The Personal Journals of Colonel Charles S. Wainwright, 1861–1865." Voices of Battle, Gettysburg National Military Park Virtual Tour.

_____. *Fremont: Pathmaker of the West,* vol. 2: *Fremont in the Civil War.* New York: Frederick Ungar, 1961. Orig. pub. 1939.

Nolan, Dick. *Benjamin Franklin Butler: The Damnedest Yankee.* Novato, CA: Presidio, 1991.

*Norton, Oliver Willcox. *Army Letters 1861–1865 Being Extracts from Private Letters to Relatives and Friends from a Soldier in the Field During the Late Civil War With an Appendix Containing Copies of Some Official Documents, Papers and Addresses of Later Date.* n. p.: the author for private circulation, 1903.

Noyalas, Jonathan A. *"My Will is Absolute Law": A Biography of Union General Robert Milroy.* Jefferson, NC: McFarland, 2006.

Nye, Edgar Wilson "Bill." *Remarks.* New York: M.W. Hazen, 1887.

Oates, Stephen B. *Confederate Cavalry West of the River.* Austin: University of Texas Press, 1991.

*O'Brien, Kevin E., ed. *My Life in the Irish Brigade: The Civil War Memoirs of Private William McCarter, 116th Pennsylvania Infantry.* Campbell, CA: Savas, 1996.

Olcott, Henry S. "The War's Carnival of Fraud." In *The Annals of the Civil War.* New York: Da Capo, 1994. Orig. pub. 1878 by *Philadelphia Weekly Times.*

"Old Whitey." *Paper Trail: Selected Manuscripts in the*

Collection of the Rutherford B. Hayes Presidential Center 8 (August 2004). http://www.rbhayes.org/hayes/manunews/paper_trail_display.asp?nid=72&subj, accessed 01/31/2011.

Olson, Kenneth E. *Music and Musket: Bands and Bandsmen of the American Civil War*. Westport, CT: Greenwood, 1981.

*Orton, Richard H. *Records of California Men in the War of the Rebellion 1861 to 1867*. Sacramento, CA: State Office Supt. of State Printing, 1890.

*Otto, John Henry. *Memoirs of a Dutch Mudsill: The War Memories of John Henry Otto, Captain, Company D, 21st Regiment, Wisconsin Volunteer Infantry*. Kent, OH: Kent State University Press, 2004.

"Our Fleet–Gettysburg Segway Tours." SegTours, LLC. http://segtours.com/team.html, accessed 04/11/2011. 43 horses listed.

*Page, Charles Davis. *History of the Fourteenth Regiment, Connecticut Vol. Infantry*. Meriden, CT: Horton, 1906.

Palfrey, Francis Winthrop. *Memoir of William Francis Bartlett*. Boston: Houghton, Osgood, 1878.

*Parker, Thomas H. *History of the 51st Regiment of P.V. and V.V. from its Organization at Camp Curtin, Harrisburg, Pa., in 1861, to its Being Mustered Out of the United States Service at Alexandria, Va., July 27th, 1865*. Philadelphia: King & Baird, 1882.

*Parsons, H.C. "Farnsworth's Charge and Death." In *Battles and Leaders of the Civil War*, vol. 3. New York: Thomas Yoseloff, 1956. Orig. pub. 1878 by *Century Magazine*.

*Pellet, Elias Porter. *History of the 114th Regiment, New York State Volunteers*. Norwich, NY: Telegraph & Chronicle Power Print, 1866.

Pemberton, John C. III. *Pemberton: Defender of Vicksburg*. Chapel Hill: University of North Carolina Press, 1970. Orig. pub. 1942.

Perry, James Moorhead. *Touched With Fire: Five Presidents and the Civil War Battles That Made Them*. Cambridge, MA: Public Affairs (Perseus), 2003.

*Perry, Theophilus, Harriet Perry, and M. Jane Johansson, ed. *Widows by the Thousands: The Civil War Letters of Theophilus and Harriet Perry, 1862–1864*. Fayetteville, AR: University of Arkansas Press, 2000.

Peters, George H. "The Confederate Invasion of New Mexico and Arizona." In *Battles and Leaders of the Civil War*, vol. 2. New York: Thomas Yoseloff, 1956. Orig. pub. 1878 by *The Century* magazine.

Pfanz, Donald C. *Richard S. Ewell: A Soldier's Life*. Chapel Hill: University of North Carolina Press, 1998.

Pierrepont, Alice V.D. *Reuben Vaughan Kidd: Soldier of the Confederacy*. Petersburg, VA: n.p., 1947.

Piper, Lisa D. "Airdrie and General Buckner." http://lisapiper.com/index, accessed 12/18/2011.

Piston, William Garrett. *Lee's Tarnished Lieutenant: James Longstreet and His Place in Southern History*. Athens: University of Georgia Press, 1987.

*Plum, William R. *The Military Telegraph During the Civil War in the United States With an Exposition of Ancient and Modern Means of Communication, and of the Federal and Confederate Cipher Systems, Also a Running Account of the War Between the States*, vol. 2. Chicago: Jansen, McClurg, 1882.

*Poague, William Thomas (Monroe F. Cockrell, Bell Irvin Wiley and Robert K. Krick, eds.). *Gunner With Stonewall: Reminiscences of William Thomas Poague*. Lincoln: University of Nebraska Press. Orig. pub. 1920 as *Gunner With Stonewall: Reminiscences of William Thomas Poague, a Memoir, Written for His Children in 1903*.

*Polk, William M. "General Polk and the Battle of Belmont." In *Battles and Leaders of the Civil War*, vol. 1. New York: Thomas Yoseloff, 1956. Orig. pub. 1887 by *The Century* magazine.

*Polley, J.B. *A Soldier's Letters to Charming Nellie*. New York: Neale, 1908.

*Porter, Horace. *Campaigning With Grant*. New York: Bantam, 1991. Orig. pub. 1897.

Pratt, Fletcher. *Civil War in Pictures*. Garden City, NY: Garden City Books, 1955.

Pris. "Howel A. 'Doc' Rayburn." Civil War Buff: the Civil War in Arkansas (01/10/2011). http://civilwarbuff.org/wp/2011/01/howel-a-doc-rayburn/, accessed 10/01/2011.

*Prowell, George Reeser. *History of the Eighty-seventh Regiment, Pennsylvania Volunteers: Prepared from Official Records, Diaries, and Other Authentic Sources of Information*. York, PA: York Daily, 1903.

*Pryor, Sara Agnes Rice. *Reminiscences of Peace and War*. New York: Macmillan, 1908; reprinted 1970. Author was wife of CS Brig. Gen. Roger A. Pryor.

Raab, James W. *J. Patton Anderson, Confederate General*. Jefferson, NC: McFarland, 2004.

"Race Horse Breeds." IGN Boards. http://www.walkerswest.com/History/AmericanSaddlebreds.htm, accessed 10/6/2011.

*Ramseur, Stephen Dodson, and George D. Kundahl, ed. *The Bravest of the Brave: The Correspondence of Stephen Dodson Ramseur*. Chapel Hill: University of North Carolina Press, 2010.

Randall, Ruth Painter. *Lincoln's Animal Friends: Incidents About Abraham Lincoln and Animals, Woven into an Intimate Story of His Life*. New York: Little, Brown, 1958.

*Reagan, John Henninger. *Memoirs, With Special Reference to Secession and Civil War*. New York: Neale, 1906.

Redfield, H.V. "Characteristics of the Armies." In *The Annals of the Civil War*. New York: Da Capo, 1994. Orig. pub. 1878 by *Philadelphia Weekly Times*.

"Rev. James McDowell's Civil War Horse's Death." *New Orleans Daily Picayune*, Aug. 16, 1885.

*Rhodes, Osmond, Howard Thompson, and William H. Rauch. *History of the "Bucktails" Kane Rifle Regiment of the Pennsylvania Reserve Corps (13th Pennsylvania of the Line)* Philadelphia: Electric Printing, 1906.

*Rhodes, Robert Hunt, ed. *All for the Union: The Civil War Diary and Letters of Elisha Hunt Rhodes*. New York, NY: Orion, 1985.

*Riddle, B.L. "Coming Home from Greensboro, N.C." *Confederate Veteran* 3, No. 10 (Oct. 1895): 308.

*Ridley, Bromfield Lewis. *Battles and Sketches of the Army of Tennessee*. Mexico, MO: Missouri, 1906. Interesting articles included in the book are "Gen. John H. Morgan's War-Horse, 'Black Bess,' at the Battle of Lebanon" (pp. 97–101) and "General Robert Lee's War Horse 'Traveler'" (pp. 559–563), which includes a letter from Capt. J.N. Broun, owner of the horse before Lee.

Robert, Mary Frances. "James Jasper Sample." *United Daughters of the Confederacy Patriot Ancestor Album.* Paducah, KY: Turner, 1999.

Robertson, James I. Jr., ed. *The Civil War Letters of General Robert McAllister.* Baton Rouge: Louisiana State University Press, 1998.

_____. *General A.P. Hill: The Story of a Confederate Warrior.* New York: Vintage, 1992. Orig. pub. 1987.

_____. *Stonewall Jackson: The Man, the Soldier, the Legend.* New York: Macmillan, 1997.

Rodenbough, Theodore F. "Famous Chargers." In *The Photographic History of the Civil War*, vol. 4: *The Cavalry.* New York: Review of Reviews, 1911.

*Rodenbough, Theodore F., Henry C. Potter, and William P. Seal (publication committee). *History of the Eighteenth Regiment of Cavalry, Pennsylvania Volunteers (163rd Regiment of the Line), 1862–1865.* New York: Publication Committee, 1909.

"Roderick Place, Tennessee." http://www.roderickplace.com. Updated 2008; accessed 10/18/2011.

Roe, Alfred Seelye. *The Fifth Regiment Massachusetts Volunteer Infantry in Its Three Tours of Duty 1861, 1862–63, 1864.* Boston: Fifth Regiment Veteran Association, 1911.

_____. *The Tenth Regiment, Massachusetts Volunteer Infantry, 1861–1864: A Western Massachusetts Regiment.* Springfield, MA: Tenth Regiment Veteran Assn., 1909.

_____. *The Twenty-fourth Regiment Massachusetts Volunteers 1861–1866 "New England Guard Regiment."* Worcester, MA: Twenty-fourth Veterans Association, 1907.

*Roemer, Jacob. *Reminiscences of the War of the Rebellion.* Flushing, NY: Estate of Jacob Roemer, 1897. Roemer was captain of Battery L, 2nd NY Lt. Arty.

*Rollins, Richard, ed. *Pickett's Charge: Eyewitness Accounts.* Redondo Beach, CA: Rank & File, 1994.

Rollins, Richard, and Dave Shultz. *Guide to Pennsylvania Troops at Gettysburg.* Redondo Beach, CA: Rank & File, 1996.

Ross, Isabel. *The President's Wife: Mary Todd Lincoln, a Biography.* New York:Putnam's, 1973.

"Roster of General Wade Hampton's 'Iron Scouts.'" Iron Scouts, Inc. http://www.schistory.net/ironscouts/articles/roster.html. 2003, accessed 04/11/2011. 7 horses are named.

Rothbert, Otto Arthur. *A History of Muhlenberg County.* Louisville, KY: John P. Morton, 1913.

*Rowe, David W. *A Sketch of the 126th Regiment Pennsylvania Volunteers.* Chambersburg, PA: Cook & Hays, 1869.

Rowland, David (President, Old York Road Historical Society, Jenkintown, PA). Email to author dated 10/07/2011.

*Rusling, James Fowler. *Men and Things I Saw in Civil War Days.* New York: Eaton & Mains, 1899.

Rutherford, Mildred Lewis. *Truths of History: A Historical Perspective of the Civil War from the Southern Viewpoint.* Atlanta: Southern Lion Books, 1998. Orig. pub. 1920.

"Sam, the Horse." Saw the Elephant. http://sawtheelephant.blogspot.com/2011/03/, accessed 05/23/2011. Section about Gen. Sherman's horse, Sam.

*Samito, Christian G. *Commanding Boston's Irish Ninth:*

The Civil War Letters of Colonel Patrick R. Guiney, Ninth Massachusetts Infantry. Bronx, NY: Fordham University Press, 1998.

SandersWeb.net Sanders Homepage (Sanders Family Web Page), 2002–2003. http://SandersWeb.net, accessed 07/16/2012.

Savage, Bridgette Z. *Fly Like the Wind.* Stanford, IN: Buckbeech Studios, 2006.

Scanlan, Lawrence. *Wild About Horses: Our Timeless Passion for the Horse.* New York: HarperCollins, 1998.

*Scheibert, Justus (William Stanley Hoole, ed.; Joseph C. Hayes, translator). *Seven Months in the Rebel States During the North American War, 1863.* Tuscaloosa, AL: University of Alabama Press, 2005. 1st translation published 1958. Orig. pub. in German, Stettin, Pomerania, Prussia: von der Nahman, 1868.

Schmidt, Lewis G. *A Civil War History of the 47th Regiment of Pennsylvania Veteran Volunteers "the Wrong Place at the Wrong Time."* n.p.: L.G. Schmidt, 1986.

Schock, Barbara. "What Mother Bickerdyke Did During the Civil War." *The Zephyr* (Galesburg, IL), August 5 & 12, 2010. http://www.thezephyr.com/bickerdyke.htm.

*Scott, John. *Partisan Life with Col. John S. Mosby.* New York: Harper & Brothers, 1867.

*Scott, William Forse. *The Story of a Cavalry Regiment: The Career of the Fourth Iowa Veteran Volunteers from Kansas to Georgia, 1861–1865.* New York:Putnam's, 1892.

Sears, Meredith M. "The Elusive Civil War Morgan," The Ultimate Horse Site,http://ultimatehorsesite.com/articles/sears-civilwar. 2005, accessed 04/11/2011.

Sears, Stephen W. *Chancellorsville.* Boston: Houghton Mifflin, 1986.

*_____, ed. *For Country, Cause & Leader: The Civil War Journal of Charles B. Haydon.* New York: Ticknor & Fields, 1993. Union officer commanded one supply train.

_____. *George B. McClellan: The Young Napoleon.* New York: Ticknor & Fields, 1988.

_____. *Landscape Turned Red: The Battle of Antietam.* New York: Book-of-the-Month Club, 1983.

"2nd Regiment Infantry New York Volunteers Civil War Newspaper Clippings." New York State Military Museum and Veterans Research Center, NYS Division of Military and Naval Affairs. http://dmna.state.ny.us/historic/reghist/civil/infantry/2ndInfCWN, accessed 10/01/2011.

Sedgwick, Hubert M. Excerpt from *A Sedgwick Genealogy: Descendants of Deacon Benjamin Sedgwick.* New Haven: New Haven Colony Historical Society, 1961. http://sedgwick.org/na/families/robert1613/B/2/9/2/B292-sedgwick-gen-john, accessed 10/06/2011.

*Sedgwick, John, and George William Curtis, ed. *Correspondence of John Sedgwick, Major- General*, vol. 2. New York: DeVinne Press, 1903.

Segars, J.H. *In Search of Confederate Ancestors: The Guide.* Murfreesboro, TN: Southern Heritage Press, 1993.

*Selby, John Gregory, ed. *Virginians at War: The Civil War Experience of Seven Young Confederates.* Wilmington, DE: Scholarly Resources, 2002.

*Seville, William P. *History of the First Regiment Delaware Volunteers, From the Commencement of the "Three*

Months' Service" to the Final Muster-Out at the Close of the Rebellion. Wilmington, DE: Historical Society of Delaware, 1884.

*Shaw, Robert Gould, and Russell Duncan, ed. Blue-Eyed Child of Fortune: The Civil War Letters of Robert Gould Shaw. Athens: University of Georgia Press, 1992.

Shenkman, Richard, and Kurt Edward Reiger. One-Night Stands with American History. New York: Quill, 1982.

*Sheridan, Philip Henry. Personal Memoirs of P.H. Sheridan, General, United States Army, 2 vols. New York: Charles L. Webster, 1888.

*Sherman, William Tecumseh. Memoirs of General William T. Sherman, 2 vols. in 1. New York: Da Capo, 1984. Orig. pub. 1875.

Shultz, Dave. "Double Canister at Ten Yards": The Federal Artillery and the Repulse of Pickett's Charge. Redondo Beach, CA: Rank & File, 1995.

Sigaud, Louis A. Belle Boyd: Confederate Spy. Richmond: Dietz, 1944.

*Simon, John Y., ed. The Papers of Ulysses S. Grant, vol. 2: April-September 1861. Carbondale: Southern Illinois University Press, 1969.

"Sketch of General Junius Daniel." The Land We Love: A Monthly Magazine Devoted To Literature, Military, History, and Agriculture 5, No. 2 (June 1868).

*Small, A.R. The Sixteenth Maine Regiment in the War of the Rebellion 1861-1865. Portland, ME: B. Thurston & Co. for the Regimental Association, 1886.

Smith, David Paul. Frontier Defense in the Civil War: Texas' Rangers and Rebels. College Station: Texas A&M University Press, 1992.

Smith, Jean Edward. Grant. New York: Simon & Schuster, 2001.

*Smith, Thomas West. The Story of a Cavalry Regiment "Scott's 900" Eleventh New York Cavalry from the St. Lawrence River to the Gulf of Mexico 1861-1865. n.p.: Veteran Association of the Regiment, 1897.

Smith, Timothy B. Champion Hill: Decisive Battle for Vicksburg. New York: Savas Beatie, 2006.

Smith, Walter George. Life and Letters of Thomas Kilby Smith Brevet Major-General United States Volunteers, 1820-1887. New York: Putnam's, 1898.

*Sneden, Robert Knox, Charles F. Bryan Jr., and Nelson D. Lankford, eds. Eye of the Storm: A Civil War Odyssey. New York: Touchstone, 2002.

Snell, Mark A. From First to Last: The Life of Major General William B. Franklin. Bronx, NY: Fordham University Press, 2002.

Somers, Chester L. "Lee's Superb Equestrian in Richmond." Confederate Veteran (July-August 1994): 20-22.

*Sorrel, Gilbert Moxley. Recollections of a Confederate Staff Officer. New York: Bantam, 1992. Orig. pub. 1905.

Special Correspondent, A. "Gen. Phil Kearny's Bugler: Story of Gus Schurmann's Evolution from Boot-Black to President's Sons' Companion." http://dmna. state.ny.us/historic/reghist/civil/infantry/40thInf/GeneralPhilKearnysbugler, accessed 01/31/2011.

*Spiegel, Marcus M., Jean Powers Soman, and Frank L. Byren, eds. A Jewish Colonel in the Civil War: Mar-

cus M. Spiegel of the Ohio Volunteers. Lincoln: Bison, 1995. Orig. pub. as Your True Marcus: The Civil War Letters of a Jewish Colonel, Kent State University Press, 1985.

*Stanyan, John M. A History of the Eighth Regiment of New Hampshire Volunteers: Including Its Service as Infantry, Second N.H. Cavalry and Veteran Battalion in the Civil War of 1861-1865 Covering a Period of Three Years, Ten Months, and Nineteen Days. Concord, NH: I.C. Evans, 1892.

Starr, Stephen Z. Jennison's Jayhawkers: A Civil War Cavalry Regiment and Its Commander. Baton Rouge: Louisiana State University Press, 1973; 1993 edition.

Stefanon, Dyon. "Street Named for Little Sorrel." Civil War Times Illustrated 31, No. 1. (March-April 1992): 41.

Steffen, Randy. "Fightin' Joe Wheeler." By Valor and Arms: The Journal of American Military History 1, No. 3 (Spring 1975): 6-12.

Stephens, Emory M. "Story of the Chaplain." In The Story of Our Regiment: A History of the 148th Pennsylvania Vols. Written by the Comrades. Joseph Wendel Muffly, ed. Des Moines, IA: Kenyon, 1904.

*Stevens, Charles A. Berdan's United States Sharpshooters in the Army of the Potomac. St. Paul, MN: n.p., 1892.

Stevenson, Burton Egbert. Poems of American History. Boston: Houghton Mifflin, 1922. Orig. pub. 1908.

*Stevenson, James H. "Boots and Saddles": A History of the First Volunteer Cavalry of the War, Known as the First New York (Lincoln) Cavalry, and Also as the Sabre Regiment, Its Organization, Campaigns and Battles. Harrisburg, PA: Patriot, 1879.

*Stevenson, William G. Thirteen Months in the Rebel Army ... by an Impressed New Yorker. Charleston, SC: Bibliobazaar, 2007. Orig. pub. 1863.

*Stewart, Nixon B. Dan McCook's Regiment, 52nd O.V.I.: A History of the Regiment, its Campaigns and Battles from 1862 to 1865. N.p.: the author, 1900.

*Stiles, Robert Augustus. Four Years Under Marse Robert. New York: Neale, 1910. Orig. pub. 1903.

*Stillwell, Leander. The Story of a Common Soldier or Army Life in the Civil War 1861-1865. Atlanta: Franklin, 1920.

*Stimmel, Smith. Personal Reminiscences of Abraham Lincoln. Minneapolis: W.H.M. Adams, 1928. Stimmel was master sergeant of the "Union Light Guard" of Ohio which served as bodyguards at Lincoln's White House.

Stocker, Jeffrey D. From Huntsville to Appomattox: R.T. Coles's History of 4th Regiment, Alabama Volunteer Infantry, C.S.A., Army of Northern Virginia. Knoxville: University of Tennessee Press, 2005.

Stokes, Mrs. Lee Duncan. "Traveller." United Daughters of the Confederacy Magazine 51, No. 7 (July 1988): 21, 4.

"Stone Mountain Confederate Memorial." Georgia Civil War Commission, Atlanta, GA. http://www.facebook.com/pages/Georgia_Civil_War_Commission/120462404685199, accessed 10/06/2011.

Storrick, W.C. Gettysburg: The Place, the Battles, the Outcome. New York: Barnes & Noble, 1994. Orig. pub. 1953.

*Storrs, John W. The "Twentieth Connecticut": A Regi-

mental History. Ansonia, CT: Naugatuck Valley Sentinel, 1886.

Stovall, Pleasant Alexander. *Robert Toombs, Statesman, Speaker, Soldier, Sage: His Career in Congress and on the Hustings — His Work in the Courts — His Record in the Army — His Life at Home.* New York: Cassell, 1892.

Stuart, J.E.B. IV. Notes dated Jan. 7, 2011, to author. Information on Gen. Stuart's horses.

*Styple, William B., ed. *With a Flash of His Sword: The Writings of Major Holman S. Melcher, 20th Maine Infantry.* Kearny: NJ: Belle Grove, 1994.

*Sullins, David. *Recollections of an Old Man: Seventy Years in Dixie 1827–1897.* Bristol, TN: King, 1910.

*Survivors Association (121st PA Inf.). *History of the 121st Regiment Pennsylvania Volunteers: "An Account from the Ranks."* Philadelphia: Catholic Standard & Times, 1906.

Svenson, Peter. *Battlefield: Farming a Civil War Battlefield.* Boston: Faber & Faber, 1992.

Symonds, Craig L. *Joseph E. Johnston: A Civil War Biography.* New York: W.W. Norton, 1992.

_____. *Stonewall of the West: Patrick Cleburne and the Civil War.* Lawrence: University of Kansas Press, 1997.

Tagg, Larry. *The Generals of Gettysburg: The Leaders of America's Greatest Battle.* Campbell, CA: Savas, 1998.

*Taylor, Benjamin Franklin. *Pictures of Life in Camp and Field.* 3rd ed. Chicago: S.C. Griggs, 1888.

Taylor, Frank H. *Philadelphia in the Civil War.* Glenside, PA: J.M. Santarelli, 1991. Orig. pub. 1913. Includes a picture of Meade's Old Bill pulling a cart at an arsenal in 1862.

Taylor, John. *Bloody Valverde: A Civil War Battle on the Rio Grande, February 21, 1862.* Albuquerque, NM: University of New Mexico Press, 1995.

*Taylor, Richard. *Destruction and Reconstruction: Personal Experiences of the Late War.* New York: Longmans, Greene, 1955. Orig. pub. 1877.

*Tenney, Luman Harris. *War Diary of Luman Harris Tenney, 1861–1865.* Cleveland, OH: Evangelical Publishing House, 1914.

*Terrell, W.H.H. *Indiana in the War of the Rebellion: Report of the Adjutant General.* Indianapolis: Indiana Historical Society, 1960. Reprint of vol. 1 of an 8-vol. report by Terrell orig. pub. 1869. Morgan's 1863 Raid and its aftermath covered in detail as it relates to Indiana.

*Thatcher, Marshall P. *A Hundred Battles in the War, St. Louis to Atlanta, 1861–1865, the Second Michigan Cavalry.* Detroit: by the author, 1884.

"The General (horse)." Wikipedia, the free encyclopedia. http://en.wikipedia.org/wiki/The_General_(horse), accessed 10/01/2011.

"The Hoof of Turner Ashby's Horse." *Encyclopedia Virginia.* Charlottesville: Virginia Foundation for the Humanities. http://www.encyclopediavirginai.org/media. Accessed 01/31/2011.

*Thomas, Benjamin P., ed. *Three Years with Grant as Recalled by War Correspondent Sylvanus Cadwallader.* Lincoln: University of Nebraska Press, 1996.

*Thomas, Henry W. *History of the Doles-Cook Brigade, Army of Northern Virginia, C.S.A., Containing Muster Rolls of Each Company of the Fourth, Twelfth, Twenty-First and Forty-Fourth Georgia Regiments, With a Short Sketch of the Services of Each Member, and a Complete History of Each Regiment, by One of Its Members and Other Matters of Interest.* Atlanta: Franklin, 1903.

*Thompson, Edwin Porter. *History of the First Kentucky Brigade.* N.p.: Caxton, 1868.

Thompson, John Reuben. "Lee to the Rear." *Civil War Poetry: An Anthology.* Mineola, NY: Dover, 1997.

*Thompson, Osmond Rhodes Howard, and William H. Rauch. *History of the "Bucktails" Kane Rifle Regiment of the Pennsylvania Reserve Corps (13th Pennsylvania Reserves, 42nd of the Line).* Philadelphia: Electric, 1906.

*Throne, Mildred, ed. *The Civil War Diary of Cyrus F. Boyd, Fifteenth Iowa Infantry 1861–1863.* Millwood, NJ: Kraus Reprint, 1977. Orig. pub. 1953.

Tobias, Michael, and Jane Gray Morrison. *Donkey: The Mystique of Equus Asinus.* San Francisco: Council Oaks, 2006.

*Tobie, Edward Parsons. *History of the First Maine Cavalry 1861–1865.* Boston: Emery & Hughes, 1887.

Todd, Glenda McWhirter. *First Alabama Cavalry, USA.* Bowie, MD: Heritage, 1999.

*Tower, R. Lockwood, ed. *Lee's Adjutant: The Wartime Letters of Colonel Walter Herron Taylor, 1862–1865.* Columbia: University of South Carolina Press, 1995.

Trafford, Rebecca Maxwell. "Atless Jones Dickson and Celestine Josephine Chatham." *United Daughters of the Confederacy Patriot Ancestor Album.* Paducah, KY: Turner, 1999.

"Traveller's Grave Marker, Lee Chapel, Washington & Lee University, Lexington, Virginia." http://www.flickr.com/photos/10264053@N02/957672032, accessed 05/02/2011.

Trimpi, Helen P. *Crimson Confederates: Harvard Men Who Fought for the South.* Knoxville: University of Tennessee Press, 2010.

*"Trooper, A." "A Courier's Evening." In *The Romance of the Civil War: Source Readers in American History,* No. 4. New York: Macmillan, 1905.

Trout, Robert J. *In the Saddle with Stuart: The Story of Frank Smith Robertson of Stuart's Staff.* Gettysburg, PA: Thomas, 1998.

_____. *They Followed the Plume: The Story of J.E.B. Stuart and His Staff.* Mechanicsburg, PA: Stackpole, 2003.

Trudeau, Noah Andre. *The Last Citadel: Petersburg, Virginia, June 1864–April 1865.* Baton Rouge: Louisiana State University Press, 1991.

Tucker, Glenn. *Hancock the Superb.* Indianapolis: Bobbs-Merrill, 1960.

*Tunnard, W.H. "Reminiscences of the Third Louisiana (Confederate) Infantry in the Trenches in Front of Logan's Division." In *A Soldier's Story of the Siege of Vicksburg, From the Diary of Osborn H. Oldroyd With Confederate Accounts from Authentic Sources and an Introduction by Brevet Maj.-Gen. M.F. Force.* Springfield, IL: for the author, 1885.

Turner, Thomas E. "Legendary Rebel Lies in Remote Grave." *Dallas Morning News,* March 27, 1965. http://SandersWeb.net, accessed 07/16/2012.

*Underwood, Adin B. *The Three Years' Service of the*

Thirty-Third Mass. Infantry Regiment 1861–1865, and the Campaigns and Battles of Chancellorsville, Beverly's Ford, Gettysburg, Wauhatchie, Chattanooga, Atlanta, the March to the Sea and Through the Carolinas in Which it Took Part. Boston: A. Williams, 1881.

*United States Army Fifth Massachusetts Battery. *History of the Fifth Massachusetts Battery, Organized October 3, 1861, Mustered Out June 12, 1865.* Boston: Luther E. Cowles, 1902.

*Valentine, Herbert E. *Story of Co. F, 23rd Massachusetts Volunteers in the War for the Union 1861–1865.* Boston: W.B. Clarke, 1896.

Van der Hervel, Gerry. *Crowns of Thorns and Glory: Mary Todd Lincoln and Varina Howell Davis: The Two First Ladies of the Civil War.* New York: E.P. Dutton, 1988.

Van Horne, Thomas B. *The Army of the Cumberland.* New York: Smithmark, 1996. Orig. pub. 1875.

Vandiver, Frank E. *Their Tattered Flags: The Epic of the Confederacy.* New York: Harper's Magazine Press Book, 1970.

Vandiver, Louise Ayer. *Traditions and History of Anderson County.* Atlanta: Ruralist Press, 1928.

*Vaughan, Alfred Jefferson. *Personal Record of the Thirteenth Regiment, Tennessee Infantry by Its Old Commander.* Memphis, TN: S.C. Toof, 1897.

*Walker, John G. "Sharpsburg." In *Battles and Leaders of the Civil War*, vol. 2. New York: Thomas Yoseloff, 1956. Orig. pub. 1887 by *The Century* magazine.

Wallace, Frederic A. *Framingham's Civil War Hero: The Life of General George H. Gordon.* Charleston, SC: History Press, 2011.

*Wallace, Lew. *Smoke, Sound & Fury: The Civil War Memoirs of Major-General Lew Wallace, U.S. Volunteers.* Philadelphia: Polyglot, 2004. Orig. pub. 1901.

Ward, Andrew. *The Slaves' War: The Civil War in the Words of Former Slaves.* New York: Houghton Mifflin, 2008.

Ward, Francis McRae. "*Vignettes" of the Civil War.* Tallulah, LA: unpublished, written 1961. http://www.rootsweb.ancestry.com/~amadisco/articles/ward.

*Ward, Joseph Ripley Chandler. *History of the One Hundred and Sixth Regiment Pennsylvania Volunteers, 2d Brigade, 2d Division, 2d Corps, 1861–1865.* Philadelphia: Grant, Faires & Rodgers, 1883.

*Waring, George E. Jr. *Whip and Spur.* Boston: James R. Osgood, 1875.

Warner, Ezra J. *Generals in Blue: The Lives of the Union Commanders.* Baton Rouge: Louisiana State University Press, 1964.

_____. *Generals in Gray: The Lives of the Confederate Commanders.* Baton Rouge: Louisiana State University Press, 1959.

Waskie, Anthony. "'Old Baldy,' General Meade's Warhorse." http://isc.temple.edu/awaskie/Old%20Baldy%20Article.htm, accessed 10/05/2011.

*Watkins, Samuel R. "*Co. Aytch," Maury County Grays, First Tennessee Regiment: or, a Side Show of the Big Show.* New York: Penguin Plume, 1999. Orig. pub. 1882.

*Watson, William. *Life in the Confederate Army: Being the Observations and Experience of an Alien in the South During the American Civil War.* New York: Scribner & Welford, 1888.

Weigley, Russell F. *Quartermaster General of the Union Army: A Biography of M.C. Meigs.* New York: Columbia University Press, 1959.

Well, Christa. "Pagans, Harvard Professors = Horse Nibblers." *New York Times*, March 5, 2007. http://www.inthemedievalmiddle.com/2007/03/pagans-harvard-professors, accessed 06/02/2009. Information about hippophagy.

Wert, Jeffry D. *Custer: The Controversial Life of George Armstrong Custer.* New York: Simon & Schuster, 1996.

_____. *General James Longstreet: The Confederacy's Most Controversial Soldier—A Biography.* New York: Simon & Schuster, 1993.

_____. *Gettysburg, Day Three.* New York: Touchstone, 2001.

_____. *Mosby's Rangers: The True Adventures of the Most Famous Command of the Civil War.* New York: Touchstone, 1990.

Weymouth, A.B., ed. *A Memorial Sketch of Lieut. Edgar M. Newcomb, of the Nineteenth Mass. Vols.* Malden, MA: Alvin G. Brown (printed for private distribution), 1883.

Whalen, Charles, and Barbara Whalen. *The Fighting McCooks.* Bethesda, MD: Westmoreland, 2006.

Whaley, Elizabeth J. *Forgotten Hero: General James B. McPherson.* New York: Exposition, 1985.

Wheeler, Richard. *Sherman's March.* New York: Thomas Y. Crowell, Publishers, 1978.

Whipkey, Elizabeth. Notes to author on "Who's Who in Horsedom," Dec. 15, 2010.

*White, William Lee, and Charles Denny Runion, eds. *Great Things are Expected of Us: the Letters of Colonel C. Irvine Walker, 10th South Carolina Infantry, C.S.A.* Knoxville: University of Tennessee Press, 2009.

Whittaker, Frederick. *A Life of Major General George A. Custer.* Omaha, NE: University of Nebraska Press, 2008. Orig. pub. 1876 as *A Complete Life of Major General George A. Custer.*

*Wilder, Burt Green, and Richard M. Reid, ed. *Practicing Medicine in a Black Regiment: The Civil War Diary of Burt G. Wilder, 55th Massachusetts.* Amherst: University of Massachusetts Press, 2010.

Wiley, Bell Irvin. *The Life of Billy Yank: The Common Soldier of the Union.* Indianapolis: Charter, 1962. Orig. pub. 1952.

_____. *The Life of Johnny Reb: The Common Soldier of the Confederacy.* Baton Rouge: Louisiana State University Press, 1992. Orig. pub. 1943.

Wilkinson, Warren. *Mother, May You Never See the Sights I Have Seen: The Fifty-Seventh Massachusetts Veteran Volunteer Infantry 1864–1865.* New York: Harper & Row, 1990.

*Willcox, Orlando Bolivar, and Robert Garth Scott, ed. *Forgotten Valor: The Memoirs, Journals & Civil War Letters of Orlando B. Willcox.* Kent, OH: Kent State University Press, 1999.

*Williams, Alpheus S., and Milo M. Quaife, ed. *From the Cannon's Mouth.* Lincoln: University of Nebraska Press, 1995. Orig. pub. 1959.

Williams, Donna J. "James Russell Wheeler." In *United Daughters of the Confederacy Patriot Ancestor Album.* Paducah, KY: Turner, 1999.

Williams, T. Harry. *Hayes of the Twenty-Third: The Civil War Volunteer Officer*. Omaha, NE: University of Nebraska Press Bison Books, 1965. Rutherford B. Hayes is the subject.

Williams, William G. *Days of Darkness: The Gettysburg Civilians*. New York: Berkley, 1990. Orig. pub. 1986.

*Williamson, James J. *Mosby's Rangers: A Record of the Operations of the Forty-Third Battalion Virginia Cavalry From its Organization to the Surrender*. New York: Ralph B. Kenyon, 1896.

Wills, Brian Steel. *A Battle from the Start: The Life of Nathan Bedford Forrest*. New York: HarperCollins, 1992.

*Wilson, Ephraim A. *Memoirs of the War*. Cleveland: W.M. Bayner, 1893.

Wilson, James Grant. *Biographical Sketches of Illinois Officers Engaged in the War Against the Rebellion Of 1861*. 3rd ed. Chicago: James Rarnet, 1863.

_____. "Famous American War Horses." *The Outlook Illustrated Monthly* (Jan. 2, 1896): 51–59.

*Wilson, James Harrison. *Under the Old Flag: Recollections of Military Operations in the War for the Union, the Spanish War, the Boxer Rebellion, Etc.*, 2 vols. New York: D. Appleton, 1912.

*_____. "The Union Cavalry in the Hood Campaign." In *Battles and Leaders of the Civil War*, vol. 4. New York: Thomas Yoseloff, 1956. Orig. pub. 1887 by *Century Magazine*.

Wilson, Joseph T. *The Black Phalanx: African American Soldiers in the War of Independence, the War of 1812, and the Civil War*. New York: Da Capo, 1994. "Winchester, General Phillip Sheridan's War Horse." *Encyclopedia Smithsonian*. http://www.si.edu/Encyclopedia_SI/nmah/horse.html, accessed 03/24/2009. Orig. pub. Hartford, CT: American Publishing, 1890.

Wingfield, Marshall. *General A.P. Stewart: His Life and Letters*. West Tennessee Historical Society, 1954.

_____. "Old Straight: A Sketch of the Life and Campaigns of Lieutenant General Alexander P. Stewart, C.S.A." *Tennessee Historical Society Quarterly* 3, No. 2 (June 1944): 99–130.

*Winschel, Terence J., ed. *The Civil War Diary of a Common Soldier: William Wiley of the 77th Illinois*. Baton Rouge: Louisiana State University Press, 2001.

*Winther, Oscar Osburn. *With Sherman to the Sea: The Civil War Letters, Diaries & Reminiscences of Theodore F. Upson*. Bloomington: Indiana University Press, 1958. Orig. pub. 1943.

Wise, Barton H. *The Life of Henry A. Wise of Virginia*. New York: Macmillan, 1899. Author was grandson of Gov./ Brig. Gen. Henry A. Wise.

*Wise, John Sergeant. *The End of an Era*. Boston: Houghton, Mifflin, 1899.

*Wittenberg, Eric J., and Karla Jean Husby, eds. *Under Custer's Command: The Civil War Journal of James Henry Avery*. Washington, D.C.: Brassey's, 2000.

Wolcott, Henry S. "The War's Carnival of Fraud." In *The Annals of the Civil War*. New York: Da Capo, 1994. Originally published 1878 by *Philadelphia Weekly Times*.

Wolf, M.E. Untitled list. http://civilwartalk.com/forums/campfire-chat-geneal- Discussion/2733. Updated 03/12/2008, accessed 06/04/2009. Lists 64 horses.

*Woodward, Evan Morrison, and Stanley W. Zamonski, ed. *Our Campaigns: The Second Regiment Pennsylvania Reserve Volunteers 1861–1864*. Shippensburg, PA: Burd Street, 1995. Orig. pub. 1865.

World Health Organization. *Joint Meeting of the League of Muslim World and the World Health Organization on Islamic Rules Governing Foods of Animal Origin*. World Health Organization and Regional Office for the Eastern Mediterranean, 1986.

Wright, Catherine M., Collections Manager, Museum of the Confederacy. Letter and notes to Author, dated Dec. 14, 2010.

_____. *Lee's Last Casualty: The Life and Letters of Sgt. Robert W. Parker, Second Virginia Cavalry*. Knoxville: University of Tennessee Press, 2008.

Wright, Howard C. *Port Hudson: Its History from an Interior Point of View*. Baton Rouge: Eagle, 1978. Cited as "Reading 2: The Mule Diet at Port Hudson," by http://www.nps.gov/history/NR/twhp/wwwlps/Lessons/71hudson/, accessed June 2, 2009.

Wright, Steven J. *The Irish Brigade*. Springfield, PA: Steven Wright, 1992.

Wunder, Sue. "This Civil War hero ... was a horse." *Christian Science Monitor* (April 11, 2006). http://csmonitor.com/2006/0411/p18sp2-hfks.html. accessed 06/16/2009. News article about Indiana cavalry horse Fly.

Wyeth, John Allan. *That Devil Forrest: Life of General Nathan Bedford Forrest*. Baton Rouge: Louisiana State University Press, 1989. Orig. pub. 1899.

*_____. *With Sabre and Scalpel: The Autobiography of a Soldier and Surgeon*. New York: Harper & Brothers, 1914.

Young, Robin. *For Love & Liberty: The Untold Civil War Story of Major Sullivan Ballou & His Famous Love Letter*. New York: Thunder's Mouth, 2006.

Zall, Paul, ed. *Blue & Gray Laughing: A Collection of Civil War Soldiers' Humor*. Redondo Beach, CA: Rank & File, 1996.

Zarvona. Untitled list. http://cs.bloodhorse.com/blogs/thoroughbred-bloggers-Alliance/archive. Updated 03/24/2009, accessed 06/04/2009. Lists 47 horses.

Index

Page numbers in **_bold italic_** indicate photographs.

Abe (horses) 105, 108
Abrams, Alexander St.Clair 83, 85
Adair, Mr. 184
Adairsville, GA 44
Adams, Gen. John 159
Adams, Mr. 146
Adams, Richard 99, 180, 186
Adams, Robert N. 108
aeronauts 11–12
Ajax (horse) 104, 108
Alabama Units (CS): Hilliard's Legion 65; Jeff Davis Artillery 154, 164; Lumsden's Battery 85; Semple's Battery 18; 1st Infantry 83; 4th Cavalry 73, 132; 4th Infantry 121, 129, 134, 158; 15th Infantry 25; 35th Infantry 111, 154; 41st Infantry 125
Alabama Units (US): 1st Cavalry 27, 31, 32, 36, 42, 52, 61, 62, 65, 73, 88–89
Albion (horse) 108
Aldebaran (horse) 109
Aldie (VA) Battle 112, 139
Aldrich, Thomas M. 159
Alexander, Gen. Edward Porter 32, 36, 47, 56, 70, 128
Alexander, Sallie E. (Casler) 177
Alice (horse) 109
Alice Carneal (horse) 185
Allen, Archibald C. 114–115
Almond Eye (horse) 109
Alsop, Joseph 127
ambulances 10–11
American Morgan Horse Register 112, 125
American Saddlebred Horse Association 135
Ammen, Admiral Jacob 125
Anderson, Gen. Charles David 158, 171
Anderson, Gen. James Patton 183–184
Anderson, Gen. Richard Heron 126
Anderson, W.J. 158
Andrew, Gov. John 177
Andrews, George L. 106
Andrews, John W. 174
Anecdotes of the Rebellion **68**
Ankenny, Henry 25, 53, 83

Antietam (MD) Battle 10, 27, 37, 43, 44, 46–47, 110, 113, 118, 121–122, 126–128, 130, 140, 145, 148, 152, 159, 167, 170–171, 174, 179–180
Appleton, W.S. 134
Appomattox (VA) Campaign 95–96, 112, 118, 122, 129, 141, 142, 151, 162, 178–179
Arab (horses) 109
Archy (horse) 93, 109
Arkansas Units (CS): 1st Infantry 136; 1st Mounted Rifles 34; 12th Infantry 83; 13th Infantry 139; 16th Infantry 83, 85, 183; 18th Infantry 83
Armies and Departments (CS): of Northern Virginia 10, 17, 32, 51, 52, 61, 63, 88; of Tennessee 3, 17, 24, 32, 52, 56, 62, 91, 136; Trans-Mississippi 52, 96–97
Armies and Departments (US): of the Cumberland 32, 51–52, 53, 69, 72, 74, 84, 91, 118, 145, 159, 172; of the Gulf 175; of the James 51, 126, 129, 173; of the Mississippi 75; of the Mississippi, Military Division 10; of the Ohio 16, 159; of the Potomac 5, 9, 10, 11, 21, 35, 42, **50**, 51, 55, 57, 91–92, 110, 118, 126, 127, 132, 137, 144, 165, 173, 175, 181; of the Tennessee 74, 135; of Virginia 51
Armistead, Gen. Lewis A. 47
Armistead, Walker Keith 150
Arnold, Dr. 136
Arnold, John S. 163–164
Arnold, Matthes 170
artillery 5–6
Asboth, Gen. Alexander S. 28
Ashby (horse) 109–110
Ashby, Gen. Turner 28, 34, 100, 176–177, **194**
Ashland Station, VA 134
Atlanta (GA) Campaign 3, 10, 41, 42–43, 47, 65, 87–88, 111, 112, 114–115, 118, 124, 139, 160, 173, 175
SS _Atlantic_ 31
Attakapas (horse) 110

Auster (horse) 99
Averill, James G. 155
Avery, Isaac Erwin 160
Avery, James Henry 33, 36

Babcock, John C. **137**
Babe (horse) 110
Bahnson, Charles Frederic 141, 156
Bailey, Joseph 183
Bailey, Joseph M. 85
Baker, Gen. La Fayette Curry 136
Baldwin, Gen. William E. 35
Baldy (horse) 26, 101, **110**–111, 194
Ball (horses) 111
Ballou, Sullivan 143
Baltimore (horse) 111
bands 87–88
Banks, Gen. Nathaniel Prentis 36, 124, 172
Barbee, Andrew W. 114
Barber, Flavel Clingan 121
Barbour, William H. "Slice" 144
Baringer, Gen. Rufus Clay 116–117
Barker, Elmer J. 134, 143, 165
Barker, F.H. 164
Barksdale, Gen. William 47
Barlow, Francis Channing 115
Barney (horses) 111
Barnum, Phineas Taylor 186
Barr, James Michael 143–144, 148, 161
Barrett, G.A. 133
Barrett, George M. 100, 133, 194
Barrows, William 151
Barteau, Clark Russell 161
Bartlett, Capt. 143
Bartlett, Gen. William Francis 115, 126
Bate, Gen. William Brimage 118
Battery Horse (horse) 111, 150
Battle, Gen. Cullen Andrews 134, 165
Battles and Leaders **45**, **89**
Bay Bob (horse) 111
Bayard (horse) 111
Baylor, George 119, 142
Baylor, Robert W., Jr. 119
Baylor, Robert W., Sr. 119
Bayly, Joseph 156

Beale, Gen. Richard Lee Turberville 119, 127
Beatty, Gen. John 40, 84, 91
Beauregard (horses) 111–112
Beauregard, Gen. Pierre G.T. 105
Beaver, James Addams 134
Bell (horse) 112
Bella (horse) 112
Bellard, Alfred 28, 56, 67
Belle (horses) 112
Belle Mosby (horse) 112
Bellfounder (horse) 112
Bellows, William 125
Belmont, MO 42, 89, 109
Bemis Horse (horse) 112
Ben (servant) 165
Bench-leg (horse) 112
Bennitt, John 176
Benson, C.D. 98, 193
Beppo (horse) 112
Berdan, Hiram 140
Bermuda Hundred (VA) Battle 111, 151
Berold (horse) 113
Berry, Gen. Hiram 93
Berryville, VA 47
Bess (horses) 101–102, 104, 113
Bessie (horse) 113
Bethseda Church, VA 136
Betty (horses) 113
Betty Root (horse) 113
Bevens, William E. 136
Beverly Ford, VA 139
Bevis (horse) 113
Bickerdyke, Mary A. "Mother" 162
Big Indian (horse) 113
Big Sorrel (horse) 113
Biles, Col. 184
Bill (horses) 113–114, 184
Billie (horse) 114
Billings, John D. **8**, 33, 40, 41, 52, 57, 70, 99
Billings, John Shaw 127, 139
Billy (horses) 94, 114–116
Billy Bowlegs (horse) 116
Billy Root (horse) 112
Birchard, Sardis 162
"Bird," Pvt. 172
Birney, Gen. David Bell 92, 109, 129
Black (horse) 116–117
Black, George 117
Black Auster (horse) 117
Black Bess (horses) 117, 137
Black Bill (horse) 117
Black Burns (horse) *see* Burns (horse)
Black Charley (horse) 117
Black Cloud (horse) 117
Black Diamond (horse) 93, 117
Black Dick (horses) 117–118
Black Hawk (horse) 118, 141, 151, 158, 164, 167
Black Jim (horse) 118
Black Oliver (horse) 143
Blackford, Charles Minor 18, 20, 23, 27, 34, 58, 61

Blackford, William Willis 88, 120, 126, 149–150, 152
Blackhawk (horse) 118
Blackie (horse) 118
Blackjack (horse) 118
Blair, Gen. Francis Preston, Jr. 135, 181
Blair, Montgomery 15
Blake (horse) 118
Bleecker, James 129
Blenheim (horse) 118
Blenker, Gen. Louis 35
Blocker, John R. 136
Blount's Farm (AL) Battle 79
Blucher (horse) 118
Bludgeon (horse) 119
Blue Bird (horse) 119
Blue Devil (horse) 119
Boatner, Mark Mayo 103
Bob (horses) 119
Bob-tail (horse) 119
Bob-Tail Bremer (horse) 119
Bobby (horse) 119
Bonaparte (horse) 119
Boney (horse) 119
Boniface 82
Bony (horses) 119
Boomerang (horse) 119
Boone, Nathan 139
Booth, John Wilkes 183
Bostick, Barry 180
Boston (horses) 120, 185
Bostona (horse) 120
Boyd, Belle 132
Boyd, Cyrus F. 67
Boyer, Toby 156
Boyle, Lt. 184
Boynton, Moses 144
Brady, Matthers 12
Bragg, Gen. Braxton 20, 23, 32, 42, 72, 75, 124
Brandy (horses) 120
Brandy Station (VA) Battle **9**, 112, 120, 122, 148–149, 153
Bratton, Gen. John 69–71
Breckinridge (horse) 120
Breckinridge, Gen. John Cabell 91, 120, 161–162
breeds, horse 18–29, 82
Bremer (horse) 120
Brenda (horse) 120
Bright, Robert A. 44
Brinton, John Hill 157
Bristoe (VA) Campaign 117
Bristow Station (VA) Battle 121
Brooks, Noah 59
Brother to Brother (horse) 120
Broun, Joseph M. 177–179
Broun, Thomas L. 177–178
Brown, Alonzo L. 48
Brown, Dan 173
Brown, George Campbell 8, 169
Brown, Harvey M. 127
Brown, Romulus M. 176
Brown Bess (horse) 120
Brown Roan (horse) 104, 120
Brown's Horse (horse) 121

Bryan, Joseph 180
Bryan, Mr. 112
Brydon, James 121
Brydon's Nellie 121
Bucephalus (horses) 105, 121
Buchanan, Henry 174
Buck, Irving Ashby 111
Buck, Walter 112
Buckland Mills, VA 116–117, 150
Buckner (horse) 121
Buckner, Beverly 169
Buckner, Gen. Simon Bolivar 167
Buell, Gen. Don Calos 166
Buffington's Island (OH) Battle 152
Buford, Gen. Abraham 18, 89
Buford, Gen. John 139
Bug (horse) 121
Bull Run Battles *see* Manassas
Bullet (horses) 104, 121
Bully (horses) 121
"Buntline, Ned" 156
Burlington, WV 121
Burney, Samuel Augustus 137
Burnie (horse) 121
Burns (horse) 121
Burns, Gen. William Wallace 121
Burnside (horses) 121, 122, 150
Burnside, Gen. Ambrose E. 52, 53, 55, 121, 152, 158
Burnside's North Carolina Expedition 31
Burton (servant) 129
Bushwack (horse) 122
Bussler, Mark 100
Butler (horses) 122, 162
Butler, Gen. Benjamin Franklin 17, 51, 109, 129, 182
Butler, Gen. Matthew Calbraith 109, 112, 122
Butler, Nathaniel 99
Butterfield, Clark 164
Buzby, Howard E. 122
Byrne, Walter J. 130
Byron, Lt. 94, 157
Byron, Lord 171

Cache River (AR) Battle 52
cacolet 11
Cadwallader, Sylvanus 178
Caesar (horses) 122
Calamity (horse) 122, 166
Caleb (servant) 175
Calico (horse) 122
California Units (US): California Column 49–50; 1st Infantry 39
Calvert, Henry Murray 141, 150, 170
Cam (horse) 122
Camelback (horse) 122
Cameron, Simon 15
Campbell, Archibald P. 167
Canada Chief (horse) *see* Black Hawk (horse)
Canby, Gen. Edward Richard Sprigg 19, 24, 96, 159
Capehart, William Rhodes 125
Capers, Gen. Ellison 139

Captain (horses) 122
Carlisle, Casper 41
Carnifax Ferry (WV) Battle 132
Carpenter, Frank "Frenchy" 163
Carper, Hercy E. 88
Carr, Gen. Joseph Bradford 183
Carroll, Edward Zane 156
Carson, Joseph Green 138
Carson, "Kit" 19
Carter, Joe 161
Carwell, Donald 103
Cassius M. Clay (horse) 136
Castle Thunder (horse) 122
Castle Thunder Prison (Richmond, VA) 83
Castleman, Alfred L. 146
casualty rates 3
Cate, John March 53, 56, 82, 89
cavalry 5, 18–20
Cavalry Bureau, US 17, 24, 63
Cavalry Museum (Fort Riley, KS) 102
Cedar Creek (VA) Battle 44, 120, 163, 168–169
Cedar Mountain (VA) Battle 123–124, 145, 165–166
Censor (horse) 122–123
Census 12–13, 95
Chacon, Rafael 19–20
Chaffin, W.S. 146
Challon, Pierre 142
Chalmers, Gen. James Ronald 129
Chamberlain, Gen. Joshua Lawrence 123, 165
Chambers, Lt. 170
Chambersburg (PA) Raid 173
Chambliss, John R., Jr. 63
Champ (horses) 123
Champion Hill (MS) Battle 136
Chance, E.J. 155
Chancellor (horses) 104, 123
Chancellorsville, VA 12, 28, 40, 47, 52, 122–123, 126, 130, 145, 164–165, 173, 179
Chantilly (VA) Battle 47, 111, 126
Chapin, Edwin P. 127
Charge of the Mule Brigade (poem) 189; see also Wauhatchee
Charlemagne (horse) 123
Charley (horses) 123–124
Charley (servant) 153
Charlie (horses) 124
Chase, Corp. 135
Chattanooga (TN) Campaign 29, 32, 36, 42, 52, 53, 54, 56, 65, 69, 73, 84, 91, 141, 181
Cheat Mountain (VA) Battle 139
Cheatham, Gen. Benjamin F. 89–90
Cheraw (SC) Battle 125
Chickahominey River (VA) Battle 51, 84
Chickamauga (horses) 105, 124–125
Chickamauga (GA) Battle 18, 41, 42, 52, 113, 115–116, 119, 124–125, 139–140, 143, 172, 176
China (horse) 125

Chisolm, Daniel 42, 51, 65–66, 93
Christian Commission 12
Churchill, Thomas J. 34
Cilley, Jonathan P. 121
Cincinnati (horse) 7, 97, 104, 105, 125, 185
Cincinnatus (horse) 125
Citronelle (AL) Surrender 96
Civil War Curiosities (history) 103
Civil War Dictionary (history) 103
Civil War 101 (website) 103
Clark, James E. 155
Clark, Madison 118
Clay (horse) 125
Clay, Mr. 173
Claybank (horse) 104, 125
Cleburne, Gen. Patrick Ronayne 128, 167, 174
Clifton (horse) 125
Clodhopper (horse) 125–126
Cluverius, W.T. 166
Cochran, Stephen **133**
Cocke, Mr. 170
Cockerill, John A. 42, 47
Cockeye (horse) 126
Coker, J.L. 70
Cold Harbor (VA) Battle 7, 11, 161–162
Coldwater (horse) 126
Coleman, A.H. 159
Collier, Isaac A. 166
Collierville (TN) Battle 129
Collins, John L. 29
Collins, Noah 130
Collis, Charles H.T. 140, 184
Colonel (horse) 126
Colorado Territory Units (US): 2nd Cavalry 171
colors and marks, horse 29, 187–188
Columbia Furnace (VA) Battle 88
Columbus (GA) Battle 117, 172
Colvard, Rufus Winfield 130
Comet (horse) 126
The Confederate Soldier's Horse (poem) 99
Confederate Units (CS): 1st Engineers 126, 149–150, 152
Conger, Abraham 134
Conger, E.J. 111
Connecticut Units (US): 12th Infantry 84, 166; 14th Infantry 130; 20th Infantry 176
Connolly, James A. 65
Conrad, Thomas Nelson 135, 144, 163, 183
Conway, soldier 118
Conyngham, David Peter 92–94, 142, 147, 152, 156–157, 172
Cook, Gen. Philip 162
Coolidge, Sgt. 130
"Copperheads" 22
Coppini, Pompeo 101
Coquette (horse) 126
Corby, Father William 92
Corcoran, Gen. Michael 35
Corinth (MS) Battle 43, 48

Cormany, Samuel E. 143, 153
Corning, Samuel 149
Cornwall (horse) 126
Corps (CS): Breckinridge's 114; Hardee's 91; Hill's 178; Longstreet's (1st) 10, 42, 166
Corps (US): II 92; III 93; V 51; VI 9; IX 158; XI 32, 69, 92; XII 32, 69; XIV 72; XV 55, 108, 115, 122–123; XVI 73, 74; XX 113; XXI 72, 91
Couch, Gen. Darius 92
Cozzens, Peter 71
Cramer, Maj. 65
Crampton (horse) 126
Crampton's Gap (MD) Battle 126
Crawford, Col. 120
Crawford, J.W. 164
Crittenden, Gen. George 28
Crittenden, Gen. Thomas Leonidas 91, 145
Crook, Gen. George 121, 164
Croppie (horse) 126
Cross Keys (VA) Battle 35, 147
Crowninshield, Benjamin William 105, 154, 161
Croxton, Gen. John T. 17, 22, 25, 54
Croxton's Raid 22, 25, 54
Cruft, Gen. Charles 42
Crummer, William F. 64
Crumpton, Washington B. "Wash" 41, 42, 85
Cummings, Charles 163
cursing 57–59
Curtin, John Irvin 135
Curtis, Gen. Samuel 16
Custer, Gen. George Armstrong 5, 88, 90, 104, 113, 126, 127, 129, 139, 142, 148, 169, 181–182
Custis Lee (horse) 104, 126
Cutler, Gen. Lysander 161
Cyclops (horse) 126

Dahlgren (horse) 126–127
Dahlgren, Ulric 126–127
Dan (horses) 127
Dana, Henry 42
Dandridge, Lilly 150
Dandridge, Stephen 151
Dandy (horses) 104, 127
Daniel, Gen. Junius 160
Daniel Webster (horse) 127
Danks, John A. 120
Davis, Gen. Jefferson Columbus 173
Davis, Pres. Jefferson Finis 17, 91, 98, 100, 105, 106, 118, 147, 157, 178
Davis, Jefferson, Jr. 180
Davis, John J. 110
Davis, Marjorie Hayes 180
Davis, Oliver Wilson 92–94
Davis Varina 35, 143
Day, David 31
Death of the Old War Horse (poem) 99
Decatur (horse) 127
DeForest, John William 84, 166

DeForrest, Othneil 135
Delaware Units (US): 1st Infantry 122, 174
DeMenti Studio (Richmond, VA) *179*
Dendy (horse) 127
Denmark (horse) 135
Dennison, Lt. 169, 184
Deupree, J.G. 120
Devil Dan (horse) *see* Daniel Webster (horse)
Dick (horses) 101, 127–128, 185
Dick Ewell (horse) 128
Dick Turpin (horse) 128
Dicks (horse) 128
Dickson, Atless Jones 171
Diomede (horse) 178
diseases, equine 62–63
District of Columbia Units (US): 1st Cavalry 136
Di Vernon (horse) *see* Mollie Glass (horse)
Dixie (horses) 128, 141
Dobbs, Charles Holt 140
Doc (horse) 128
Dodge, Gen. Grenville M. 40, 73–77
Doll (horses) 128
Dolly (horses) 128–129
Don (horse) 129
Don Juan (horse) 104, 129
Donaldson, Francis Adams 127
Donaldson, James L. 17
donkey 30
Dorr, E.P. 127
Douglas, Henry Kyd 128, 132, 142, 177
Douglas, James Postell 127
Downey, Fairfax 99, 103
Draco (horse) 129
Drake, Orlando 164
Drennan (horse) 117
Drennan, William P. 136
Drew, C. 99
Drinnon, George 159
Ducat, Arthur C. 91
Ducat, Charles, Sr. 167
Dudley, Frank 123
Duff, F.S. 145
Duff Green (horse) 129
Duffy, Patrick 161
Dug Gap (AL) Battle 77
Duke (horse) 129
Duke, Gen. Basil 137
Duke, John 54
Dumont, Gen. Ebenezer 172
Dunaway, Wayland Fuller 145
Duncan, Thomas D. 140
Dunlap, Robert 129, 154
Dunlap's Mare (horse) 129
Dunn, Francis W. 27, 31, 36, 52, 61–62, 88–89
Dunn, James Langstaff 145
The Dying War-Horse (poem) 99

Early, Gen. Jubal Anderson 40, 138
Early's Raid on Washington 141

Eastham, Vincent 119
Ebony (horse) 129
Eby, Vivienne M. 187
Eclipse (horse) 129
Edmonds, Amanda Virginia "Tee" 157
Edmonson, Col. 77
Education (horse) 130
Edward — Black Prince (horse) 130
Edward the Black Prince (horse) 130
Edwards, A.R. 88
Edwards, James M. 88
Egypt (horse) *7, 104*, 130
Elisabeth (horse) 130
Ellett, Gen. Alfred W. 75
Elmira Prison (Elmira, NY) 164
Emory, Gen. William H. 44
Engineer Corps 12
Ephraim (horse) 130
Ethan Allen (horse) 136
Ewell, Gen. Richard Stoddart 8, 42, 89, 151, 169, 175
Excelsior (horse) 130

Faderland (horse) 94, 130
Fair Oaks, VA *6*, 64
Fairfax, John W. 170
Famous Horses of the Civil War (history) 99, 103
Fan (horse) 130
Fancy (horses) 28, *29*, 37, 97, 100–101, 103, 106, 130–132, *131*
Fannie (horses) 132, 141
Fanny (horse) 132
Farnsworth, Gen. Elon 41, 47
Farrar, Mr. 15
Farrell, Michael 121
Farrington 41
Fasco (horse) 132
Fassitt, Lewis H. 117
Faugh-a-Ballagh (horse) 132
Faugh-a-Ballaugh (horse) 132
Favill, Josiah Marshall 115
Fink (horse) 132
Fire-Eater (horse) 132
Firefly (horse) 132
Fisher, Horace Newton 113
Fishing Creek (KY) Battle 161
Fisk, Gen. Clinton B. 57–58
Fisk University (Nashville, TN) 58
Fitch, Michael H. 84
Fitzhugh, Norman R. 153
Five Forks (VA) Battle 126, 134
Fleeta (horse) 132
Fleeter (horse) *see* Fleeta (horse)
Fleetfoot (horse) 133
Fletcher, William A. 18–19
Flora Temple (horse) 185
Florida Units (CS): Coast Defense Cavalry 134, 167
Floyd, Frederick C. 92
Fly (horse) 100, *133*, 194
Fly by Night (horse) 133
Fly Like the Wind (history) 100
Flying Ant (horse) 134, 167
Folko (horse) 133
Forbes, Edwin 147–*148*

Forbes, William H. 115
Forkery, Russell P. 148
Forrest, Gen. Nathan Bedford 5, 18, 27, 40–41, 44, 47–*48*, 75–80, 90, 100, 102, 104, 140, 147, 170
Forrest, William 77
Forsyth, James W. 178
Fort, John Porter 134, 167
Fort Donaldson (TN) Battle 40, 47, 134
Fort Gilmer (VA) Battle 134
4th Alabama (horse) 134
Fox (horses) 104, 134
Francis Marion (horse) 134
Frank (horses) 134
Frank Halligas (horse) 134
Frank Leslie's Illustrated Newspaper *50, 64*, 147
Frankenberry, Allen D. "Frank" 124
Franklin, Gen. William B. 98
Franklin (TN) Battle 42, 145, 159, 176
Frantic (horse) 134
Fredericksburg (VA) Battle *43*, 65, 115, 119, 140, 146, 152–155, 175
Freeman, Douglas Southall 37, 177
Fremantle, Arthur J.L. 61, 62, 185
Frémont, Gen. John C. 14–15
Frost, Gen. Daniel Marsh 176

Gabriel (horse) 135
Gaines, Charles Buckner 150
Gaines, William 150
Gaines' Denmark (horse) 135
Gaines Mill (VA) Battle 160
Gallant Gray (horse) *see* Tom Telegraph (horse)
Gamble, George A. 129
Gamble, Gen. William 140
Gardner, Alexander *45, 137*
Garfield, Gen. James A. 72–74, 115, 147
Garner, Chaplain John M. 42
Garnett, Gen. Richard Brooke 28, 47, 166
Garnett, Theodore S. 120, 149–150, 186
Garrard, Gen. Kenner 156
Garrettson, Lt. 150
Garrison, Henry C. 184
Garrison, Webb 103
Garsed, Joshua 113
Gauley (horse) 135
Gaylesville (AL) Battle 79
Geary, Gen. John White 42, 69–71, 88, 124
General (horse) 104, 135; *see also* The General (horse)
The General (horse) 175
General Blair (horse) 135
General Butler (horse) 136, 185
General Hardee at the Battle of Shiloh (poem) 99, 117
General Jackson (horse) 135
General Jeb (horse) 135
General John H. Morgan and his Bess (statue) 117

General Shaler (horse) 105–106, 135
General Thomas (horse) 136
George (horses) 104, 136
George M. Patchen (horse) 136
Georgia Units (CS): Cobb's Legion 137; Morton's Battery 174; 1st Regulars 134, 167; 2nd Infantry 40, 61; 12th Infantry Bn. 160; 44th Infantry 37; 56th Infantry 109, 134
Georgia's Brigade (horse) 136
Germania Ford, VA 47
Germantown (TN) Battle 90
Gertie (horse) 137
Gettysburg (PA) Campaign 10–11, 21–23, 25, 28–29, 31, 40–41, 43–48, *45, 46*, 61, 64, 89, 100–101, 110, 112–116, 119, 124, 126–128, 132–133, 135, 138–140, 143–144, 150, 152, 154, 156, 159–160, 163–164, 166, 169, 173, 175, 179, 181, 183
Gibbon, Frances 132
Gibbon, Gen. John 132
Gibbs, Gen. Alfred 158
Gibson, James F. *6*
Giesboro (MD) Cavalry Depot *16*, 17, 63, 159
Gifford Morgan (horse) 125
Gillispie, Capt. 182
Gilmor, Harry W. 113–114, 117, 147
Giltner, Barney 122
Gim Crack (horse) 137
Gimlet (horse) *137*
Ginnie (horse) 137
Gist, Gen. States Rights 145
Glazier, Willard 40
Glencoe (horse) 137–138
Glencoe Jr. (horse) 138
Glendale (VA) Battle 62, 118
Glover, Thomas J. 124
Gold Dust (horse) 138
Goliath (horse) 138
Goodloe, Albert Theodore 154
Gordon, Gen. George Henry 109–110
Gordon, Gen. John Brown 34, 43, 67, 96, 105, 135, 153–154
Goree, Thomas Jewett 111, 128
Goss, Warren Lee 52, 56, 99
Gothic (horse) 138
Grace Darling (horse) 30, 104, 107, 138
Graham, Capt. 20
Grand Army of the Republic Museum and Library (Philadelphia, PA) 101, 111, 194
Grand Old Cannister (horse) *see* Grand Old Cannister & Grape (horse)
Grand Old Cannister & Grape (horse) 138
Grant (horse) 185
Grant, Frederick Dent 125, 143, 170
Grant, Jesse 150
Grant, Sarah Jane 163

Grant, S.S. 125
Grant, Gen. Ulysses S. *7*, 24, 27, 36, 40, 44, 46, 51, 57, 69, 70, 72, 83, 89–90, 95–96, 104, 106, 124, 125, 130, 134, 141, 143, 146, 150, 153–154, 170–171, 181
Grape (horse) *see* Grand Old Cannister & Grape (horse)
Grater (horse) 138
Gray, Gen. Henry 122
Gray Alice (horse) 138
Gray Bill (horse) 138
Gray Eagle (horse) 125, 138, 159, 178, 184
Graydon, James "Paddy" 39
Grayson, George Washington 4, 170
Grease (horse) 139
Green, Gen. Thomas 98
"Greenback Raid," VA 126
Greenbriar (horse) 106, 139, 178; *see also* Traveller (horse)
Greene, Colton 20
Greenfield , Andrew J. 181
Greenville (LA) Cavalry Depot 17
Greenville (TN) Battle 101–102, 173
Gregg, Gen. David McMurtie 10, 165
Gregory, Edward S. 85
Gregory II, Pope 82
Gregory III, Pope 82
Grey Eagle (horse) 139
Grey John (horse) 139
Grierson, Gen. Benjamin Henry 24, 74, 157
Grierson's Raid 24, 74, 141
Grimes, Gen. Bryan 182
Grisson, John 9
Griswoldville, GA 171
Grose, Gen. William 174–175
Guerrant, Edward G. 119, 123, 128, 130, 143, 151, 153
Guiney, Patrick Robert 139, 183
Gunn, Moses 122
Guy (horses) 139
Guy Darnell (horse) 139
Gypsy (horse) 139

Haden, George W. 167
Hagerstown (MD) 126, 129, 164
Hairston, Peter W. 136
Hale, Silas 125
Hale's Green Mountain Morgan (horse) 125
Halleck, Gen. Henry W. 16, 32
Hamlet (horse) 126
Hamlin, Gen. Cyrus 144
Hamlin, Vice Pres. Hannibal 144
Hamlin, James D. 160
Hammond, John 164
Hampton, Gen. Wade 52, 70, 109, 111–112, 122, 162
Hancock, Gen. Winfield Scott 28, 40, 93
Handly, George J. 109, 122
Handsome Joe (horse) 101, 139
Hanley, Patrick T. 127

Hanover (PA) Battle 124, 152, 164, 181
Hardee, Gen. William J. 17, 44, 99, 117
Harding, William H. 176
Hardtack and Coffee *8*, 57, 70, 99
Hardtimes (horse) 139
Harker, Col. 91
Harman, John A. 20, 58–59
Harper's Weekly *22, 30, 60*
Harris, H.M. 88
Harrisburg (PA) Cavalry Depot 17
Harrison, James Thomas Watt 149
Harrow, Gen. William 164–165
Harry (horses) 104, 139
Harry Bluff (horse) 185
Harry Hays (horse) 140
Hartford Belle (horse) 185
Hartpence, William R. 72, 74, 78, 82
Hasbrouck, Lt. 33
Haskell, Frank Aretas 64, 115, 127, 145
Haskell, John Cheves 63, 106, 177
Haskell, Lewis 177
Hastings, Russell 162
Hatch (horse) 140
Hatch, Gen. Edward 140
Hatchie Bridge (TN) Battle 160, 167
Hathaway, Gilbert 72, 78, 79
Hathaway, Leland 152
Hathaway, William 118
Hatton, Gen. Robert Hopkins 111, 139, 153
Haupt, Gen. Herman J. *43*
Haydon, Charles B. 27, 53
Hayes, Gen. Rutherford Birchard 162–163, 182
Haymarket (VA) Battle 88
Haynie, J. Henry 84
Hays, Gen. Alexander 47, 149, 171, 174
Hays, Gen. Harry Thompson 140
Hayward, Eugene B. 154
Hayward, Monroe L. 157
Hazeltine, J. Henry 153
Headley, John W. 27, 28
Heald, John A. 125
Heartsill, William Williston 163
Heckman, Gen. Charles Adam 155
Henderson, Edward Prioleau 99, 109, 165
Henderson, Pinckney 109
Henderson, W.L. 157
Henkel, S.C. 177
Henry (horse) 140
Henry (servant) 140
Here's Your Mule (song) 98, 192–193
Hero (horse) 140
Herrick, Thomas P. 90
Herring, Charles P. 127
Hervey, H.W.B. 111
Hessian (horse) 140
Heth, Gen. Henry 33, 53
Hiatoga (horse) 140

Hickenlooper, Andrew 138
Higginson, Henry Lee 138, 157
Higginson, Thomas Wentworth 169
Highfly (horse) 140
Highlander (horse) 140
Hill, Gen. Ambrose Powell 47, 67, 123, 165
Hill, Gen. Daniel Harvey 44, 45–46
Hindman, Gen. Thomas C. 48
Hines, Thomas H. 23
Hitchcock, Dwight 175
Hobart, Harrison C. 85
Hog Mountain (AL) Battle 77
Hogan, Capt. 94, 156
Hoke, Gen. Robert Frederick 160
Holcomb, Charles 174
Holmes, James T. 145
Holt, Daniel M. 132, 134, 173
Holt, David 111, 122
Homicide (horse) 140
Hood, Gen. John Bell 32, 143
Hooker, Gen. Joseph 64, 69, 70, 92, 126, 150–151, 182
Hopkins, Luther W. 170
The Horse Dictionary (reference) 187
A Horse for General Lee (history) 99
Horses of Gettysburg—Civil War Minutes (documentary) 100
Hotchkin, D.B. 113
Houghton, Mitchell R. 25
Houghton, William R. 40, 61
Houston, E.E. 86
Houston, Gov. Sam 90
Howard, Ocran M. 155
Howard, Gen. Oliver Otis 44, 47, 70, 85, 92, 124, 165
Howe, John H. 170
Howell, Joshua B. 159
Hubard, Robert T., Jr. 163
Hubbard, John Milton 161
Humphries, Charles A. 142, 157
Hunt, Gen. Henry J. 47, 114
Hunt, Lena 146
Hunt, Thomas H. 161
Hunter (horses) 93, 140
Hunter, Gen. David 110
Hunter, Wilson 162
Hunton, Gen. Eppa 155
Huntsville, AL 27, 80
Hyde, John B. 117
Hyde, J.P. 185

Ida Mae (horse) 185
Illinois Units (US): 2nd Cavalry 19; 4th Cavalry 161; 7th Cavalry 25, 172–173; 8th Cavalry 129, 148; 9th Mounted Infantry 115; 12th Infantry 119, 167; 16th Cavalry 140; 19th Infantry 84; 21st Infantry 141, 154; 24th Infantry 84; 31st Infantry 89, 125; 36th Infantry 159, 165; 45th Infantry 64; 61st Infantry 28, 184; 64th Infantry 27; 80th Infantry 72, 77,

79; 103rd Infantry 172–173; 124th Infantry 170
Imboden, Gen. John D. 42, 58–59
Independence (horse) 93, 140–141
Independence (MO) Battle 123
Indian Territory Units (CS): 2nd Creek Mounted 4, 170
Indiana Units (US): Indiana Legion 21; 1st Cavalry 19, 100, 133; 3rd Cavalry 19, 157; 36th Infantry 174; 42nd Infantry 84; 51st Infantry 72, 74, 77, 79, 80, 82; 70th Infantry 172; 73rd Infantry 72, 77, 78, 79; 100th Infantry 185
International Museum of the Horse (Lexington, KY) 185
Iowa Units (US): 1st Cavalry 19, 115, 162; 4th Cavalry 114, 158; 4th Infantry 25, 53, 83; 7th Cavalry 143; 12th Infantry 145; 14th Infantry 182–183; 15th Infantry 67, 181
Ironsides (horse) 128
Iuka (MS) Battle 162

Jack (horses) 104, 141–142, 154
Jack Hinton (horse) 94, 142
Jack Rucker (horse) 142
Jackman, John W. 105, 142, 174
Jack's Creek (TN) Battle 140
Jackson, Anna 131
Jackson, Gen. Thomas J. "Stonewall" 20, 28, *29*, 37–38, 43, 47, 58–59, 99, 100–101, 113, 130–132, 175, 180, 194–195
Jackson (MS) Battle 119, 158
Jacques (horse) 142
Jake (horse) 142
Jason (donkey) 142
Jasper (horse) 142
Jeb (horse) 142
Jeb Stuart (horses) 142
Jeff (horses) 142
Jeff Davis (horses) *7*, 104, 106, 143
Jefferson, John Robert 143
Jefferson Davis (horse) 143
Jehu (horse) 143
Jenkins, Gen. Albert G. 22
Jennie (horse) 143
Jennifer, Col. 28
Jennison, Charles R. 25
Jerome (horse) 143
Jerry (horses) 144
Jerry (servant) 139, 153
Jersey (horse) 144
Jess (horse) 144
Jim (horses) 144
Jim (soldier) 173
Jim Banks (horse) 144
Jim Crow (horse) 144
Jinny (horse) 144
Jocko (horse) 145
Joe (horses) 145
Joe Johnston (horse) 145
Joe Smith (horse) 145
John (horses) 145–146
John (Private) 161

John Dillard (horse) 146
John Horse (horse) *see* The John Horse (horse)
The John Horse (horse) 176
Johnson, Gen. Adam Rankin "Stovepipe" 145
Johnson, Pres. Andrew 21
Johnson, Gen. Bushrod 27, 46, *47*
Johnson, Frank 151
Johnson, Mr. 140
Johnston, Albert C. 111
Johnston, Gen. Albert Sidney 47, 132
Johnston, Andrew Davis 178
Johnston, James W. 177–178
Johnston, Gen. Joseph Eggleston 3, 32, 35, 52, 91, 96, 100, 106, 132, 171
Jolly, Manson Sherrill "Manse" 128, 141
Jones, Capt. 35
Jones, Egbert 158
Jones, Frank B. 139, 163
Jones, J.R. 141
Jones, Toland 160
Jones, Warren C. 182–183
Joseph (horse) 146
Josh (horse) 146
Jubal Early (horse) 146
June Bug (horse) 185–186

Kane, Gen. Thomas Leiper 159
Kangaroo (horse) 104, 146
Kansas Units (US): 2nd State Militia 134; 7th Cavalry 19, 25, 29, 34, 90
Kate (horses) 146–147, 157
Kathleen Mavorneen (horse) 94, 147
Katie (horse) 97, 147
Kautz, Gen. August *60*
Kean, Robert G.H. 95
Kearney, Gen. Phil 47, 110–111, 127, 155
Kearneysville (VA) Battle 157
Kelley, Gen. Benjamin 163–164
Kelly, Patrick 132
Kelly's Ford (VA) Battle 18
Kemper, Gen. James L. 44
Kennon, Richard Byrd 113
Kentuck (horse) 147
Kentucky (horse) 147
Kentucky Units (CS): "Orphan Brigade" 19; 1st Cavalry 27, 176; 2nd Cavalry 23; 4th Cavalry 122; 5th Infantry 161; 8th Cavalry 119; 9th Infantry 105, 130, 161, 174, 180, 183; 14th Cavalry 152
Kentucky Units (US): 1st Cavalry 19; 4th Infantry 17; 24th Infantry 119
Kershaw, Capt. 166
Kidd, J.H. 29
Kidd, Reuben Vaughan 121, 129
Kilpatrick, Gen. Hugh Judson 16, 42, 90, 111, 112, 122, 150, 162, 175
Kilpatrick-Dahlgren Raid, VA 126–127, 166

Kimple, Lt. 156
King, Gen. Rufus 123
King Philip (horse) 147
Kingsbury, E.E. 171
Kirkland, Frazar *68*, 69
Kirkwood, William 109
Kit (horse) 147
Kitt (mule) 147
Kitty (horses) 147–*148*
Klitschka (horse) 147–148
Knaggs, Robert C. 31, 64
Knight, Walter G. 160
Knoxville (TN) Battle 125
Kurshaw, Capt. 94

Lady Gray (horse) 148
Lady Margrave (horse) 104, 148, 173
Lady Mosby (horse) 148
Lady Polk (horse) *see* The Lady Polk (horse)
The Lady Polk (horse) 176
Lagow, Clark B. 146
Lamar, Charles A.L. 117
Lamkins Bill (horse) 148
Lancer (horses) 104, 148–149
Langdon, Capt. 94, 157
Larrabee, Charles H. 119
Laurel Hill, VA 159
Lawrence (AL) Battle 80
Lawrence (KS) Battle 123
Lawson, Orris A. 73, 74, 75
Lazarus (horse) 149
Leal, John R. 165
Lebanon (TN) Battle 117, 137
Le Duc, William Gates 118
Lee (horse) 149
Lee, Agnes 178
Lee, Gen. Fitzhugh 18, 36–37, 128, 157, 178
Lee, George 55
Lee, George Washington Custis 167, 179–180; *see also* Custis Lee (horse)
Lee, Henry 177
Lee, Mildred 180
Lee, Gen. Robert Edward 28, 30, 33, 36–37, 44, 46, 51, 52, 59, 62, 95, 100–102, 104, 106, 108, 111–112, 120, 123, 133, 138, 151, 157, 167, 177–180, 194
Lee, Robert Edward, Jr. 151, 177
Lee, Gen. Stephen D. 27
Lee, Gen. William Henry Fitzhugh "Rooney" 134
Leet (horse) 149
Leverett, Mrs. 37
Lexington (horse) 125, 149, 185
Libby Prison (Richmond, VA) 80
Library of Congress (Washington, DC) *6–7, 9, 15, 16, 43, 46–48, 57, 73, 92–93, 137, 148*
Lieut. Joe Massengale (horse) 149
Lightfoot (horse) 149
"Lightning Mule Brigade," *see* Streight's Raid
Lilly Dandridge (horse) 104, 112, 149

Lily of the Valley (horse) 104, 106, 120, 149–150
Limber Jim (horse) 150
Lincoln, Pres. Abraham 26, 59, 98, 108, 129, 158, 164, 175
Lincoln, Mary Todd 15, 35
Lincoln, "Tad" 164
Linn, J. Harris 134
Little, Gen. Lewis Henry 128
Little Billy (horse) 150
Little Mac (horse) 121, 150
Little Reb (Shetland pony) 104, 150
Little Sorrel (horse) *see* Fancy (horse)
Little Sorrel Lane, Sommers, CT 132
Lively (horse) 111, 150
Liverly (horse) 150
Livermore, Thomas Leonard 124
Livingston, Asa 113
Logan, Gen. John Alexander 52, 118, 162, 173
London Illustrated News **54**
Long, Armistead L. 177
Long Tom (horse) 150
Longstreet, Gen. James 23, 27, 34, 46, 69–70, 90, 101, 106, 133, 140, 155, 171, 185
Lookout (horse) 150–151
Lookout Mountain (TN) Battle 69, 151
The Lost Symbol (novel) 173
Lothrop, Charles H. 115
Loughborough, Mary Ann 48, 84
Louisiana Units (CS): Fenner's Battery 166; Watson's Battery 42; 3rd Cavalry 169; 3rd Infantry 7, 33–34, 85, 142; 4th Cavalry 122, 138, 166; 6th Infantry 128; 18th Infantry 110; 30th Infantry 86
Lowe, Thaddeus 11
Lowell, Charles Russell, Jr. 113, 114, 119, 170
Lowery, Gen. Mark Perrin 161
Lubbock, Gov. Francis Lubbock 137, 172
Luck (horse) 151
Lucy (horses) 151
Lucy Long (horse) 104, 151, 179
Lyman, George R. 88
Lytle, Gen. William Harris 132

Macauley, Thomas Babington 117
Madge (horse) 151
Madill, Henry J. 150, 163
Maggie (horses) 151
Maggie Mitchell (horse) 152
Magic (horse) 126, 152
Magner, Blake A. 100, 103
Magruder, Gen. John Bankhead 125
Maine Units (US): 1st Cavalry 28, 119, 121, 125; 7th Infantry 120; 19th Infantry 20th Infantry 62
Major (horses) 94, 111, 152, 158
Malty (horse) 152
Malvern Hill (VA) Battle 115, 152

Mambriono (horse) 150
Manassas (horses) 105, 152
Manassas, VA, 1st Battle 12, 26, 29, 33, 41, 42, 65, 110, 143, 152, 182
Manassas, VA, 2nd Battle 51, 108, 115, 118, 152, 161, 164, 175
Manderson, Charles F. 114
Manly, Basil 173–174
Mansfield, Gen. J.K. 47
Mansfield (LA) Battle 114, 122
Marsh, John 176
Marshall, Tom 139
Marshall, William C. 49
Martin, Capt. 94, 147
Martin, Orris 150
Martin, Robert M. 112
Mary (horses) 152–153
Mary Minnehaha (horse) 153
Maryland (horse) 153
Maryland Units (CS): 1st Cavalry 112; 2nd Cavalry Bn. 113–114, 117, 147
Mason, Edwin C. 120
Massachusetts Units (US): 1st Cavalry 105, 120, 125–126, 130, 138, 154, 157, 161–162, 176, 182; 1st Light Artillery 160; 2nd Cavalry 114, 115, 142, 157; 2nd Infantry 109–110, 121, 150, 166; 2nd Light Artillery 114; 3rd Cavalry 149; 5th Battery 117, 134–135; 9th (Bigelow's) Battery 41, *45*; 9th Infantry 127, 139, 183; 10th Battery 62; 10th Infantry 152, 177; 19th Infantry 68; 23rd Infantry 121; 24th Infantry 151; 25th Infantry 31; 33rd Infantry 53, 56, 71, 82, 89; 37th Infantry 116; 52nd Infantry 128–129; 54th Infantry 113, 126, 170; 55th Infantry 116, 123; 57th Infantry 115
Massengale, Joe 149
Massey, John 95
Massey, John Orphin 175
Massey, Richard A. 182
Matthews, James 118, 165
Maury, Gen. Dabney Herndon 170
Max (horse) 153
Maxwell, James R. 85
Maxwell, Ronald F. 100
Mayre (horse) 153
Mazeppa (horse) 104, 153
McAllister, Robert 123
McArthur, Gen. John 119
McClellan, Gen. George Brinton 9, 32, 56, 121, 127, 147
McClellan, H.B. 18, 61
McCook, Gen. Daniel 124
McCook, Gen. Edward 43
McCord, James E. 90
McCormick, Quartermaster 94, 172
McCulloch, Gen. Ben. 44
McCulloch, Henry E. 90
McDonald, William 185
McDowell, Maj. 91
McDowell, James 118

McElroy, John 140
McGaheysville, VA 119
McGenahan, Col. 177
McHenry, Lt. 94
McKim, Randolph Harrison 124, 170
McKinley, Emilie Riley 109
McKinstry, Gen. Justus 14–*15*
McKnight, Armor A. 94, 115, 163
McLane, John W. 160
McMahon, Lt. 160
McNeil, John A. 114
McPheeters, William M. 139
McPherson, Gen. James B. 40, 47
McReynolds, Andrew T. 149
McReynolds, B.F. 149
McWilliams, Charles 79
Meade, Gen. George Gordon 26, 101, 110–111, 114, 118, 137, 194
Meagher, Gen. Thomas 92, 94, 142, 156
Medal of Honor 41
Medical Department. 10–11
Medor (horse) 153
Meg (horse) *see* Meg Merrilies (horse)
Meg Merrilies (horse) 153
Meigs, Gen. Montgomery C. 14, 15, 17, 26, 32, 50, 60
Melcher, Holman S. 62
Melville, Herman 97
Memoirs (John S. Mosby) 21
Meredith, Gen. Solomon 161
Meridian (MS) Campaign 49
Merrill, Lt. 162
Mersey, August 115
Messenger (horse) 124
Methuselah (horse) 104, 153–154
Mexican-American War 30, 138, 155, 182
Michigan Units (US): 2nd Cavalry 28, 84, 167; 2nd Infantry 53; 3rd Cavalry 28; 5th Cavalry 33, 36; 5th Infantry 122; 6th Cavalry 29; 7th Infantry 31, 64; 8th Cavalry 27; 8th Infantry 35; 19th Infantry 176
Michigander (horse) 154
Mickey Free (horse) 154
Mickler, William A. "Bill" 115, 167
Mihalotzy, Goza 84
Mike (horse) 154
Miles, Gen. Nelson Appleton 130
Military Service Institution Museum (New York, NY) 169
Mill Creek (VA) Battle 142
Mill Springs (KY) Battle 42, 47
Miller, John Henry 109
Milroy (horse) 105, 154
Milroy, Gen. Robert Huston 142, 154
Mink (horse) 154
Minnesota Units (US): 1st Infantry 84; 4th Infantry 48
Miranda (horse) 154
Mississippi Units (CS): Ballentine's Patisan Rangers 171; Jeff Davis

Legion 111; 1st Cavalry 109, 120; 12th Infantry 140; 15th Infantry 121; 16th Infantry 111, 122; 19th Infantry 155; 37th Infantry 41, 85
Missouri Units (CS): State Guard 136, 171; 3rd Cavalry 20
Missouri Units (US): 4th Cavalry 139, 147–148, 153, 170; 18th Infantry 42; 25th Infantry 29; 33rd Infantry 58
Mr. Yorkshire (horse) 154
Mollie (horse) 154
Mollie Glass (horse) 154–155
Money (horse) 155
Monmouth (horse) 155
Monocacy (MD) Battle 153
Monterey Springs, PA 42
Moore, Alphares H. 118
Moore, Frank 109
Moore, James W. 180
Moorhead, Lt. 174
Moorman, Bob 114
Moors, John Farwell 128–129
Morgan (horse) 155
Morgan, Gen. James Dada 124
Morgan, Gen. John Hunt 18, 21, 98, 100, 101–102, 104, 117, 137, 173
Morgan, Thomas J. 44
Morgan Rattler (horse) 155
Morgan's Raid North of the Ohio River 21–22, 23–24, 25, 137–138, 152, 157
Morse, Frank C. 116
Morton, Charles 29
Morton, John 52
Morton, Gov. Oliver P. 80
Mosby, John Singleton 17, 21, 26, 35, 47, 126, 148, 164
Mosby's "Coffee Raid" 144
Moscow (horse) 155
Moses (horse) 155
Mott (horse) 105, 155
Mott, Christopher Haynes 155
Mountain Bill (horse) 155
Mouton, Gen. Jean Jacques Alfred Alexander 110
Moyer, H.P. 87
"Mud March" *55*–56, 145
Muhammad, Prophet 82
Muir, L.P. 146
mule characteristics 30
Mulholland, Maj. 94
Mulholland, St.Clair Augustine 93–94, 142, 147, 152, 156–157, 172
Munch Meg (horse) 185
Munson, John William 123
Murdock, James A. 141, 157
Murphy, Jack 176
Murphy, Thomas G. 122
Museum of the Confederacy (Richmond, VA) *100*, 177, 180, 194
Musser, Richard H. 136

Mustang (horse) 155
My Maryland (horse) 104, 155–156
Myering, Frank 88
Myers, Bill 156
Myers, John E. 114

Napoleon (horse) 156
Napoleon Bonaparte, Emperor 10
Napper Tandy (horse) 94, 156
Nashville (TN) Battle 44, 56, 116, 161, 181–182
Nashville (TN) Cavalry Depot 17
National Sporting Library & Museum (Middleburg, VA) *ii*, 102
Ned (horses) 156
Ned Buntline (horse) 156
Nell (horse) 156
Nellie (horses) *68*, 156–157
Nellie Gray (horse) 157
Nelly (horse) 157
Nelson, Gen. William 47
Nettie (horse) 157
New Berne (NC) Battle 121
New Hampshire Units (US): 7th Infantry 159; 8th Infantry 86; 9th Infantry 56; 12th Infantry 162; 18th Infantry 124
New Harmony Working Men's Institute (New Harmony, IN) 100, *133*, 194
New Hope (GA) Battle 166
New Jersey Units (US): 1st Artillery 127, 145; 1st Infantry 123; 5th Infantry 28, 34, 56, 67; 11th Infantry 123
New Market (VA) Battle 177
New Mexico Campaign 49; *see also* Val Verde
New Mexico Territory Units (US): 1st Cavalry 20; 1st Infantry 19
New River (VA) Battle 182
New York Units (US): 1st Artillery 116; 1st Cavalry 19, 103, 148–149; 2nd Light Artillery 128; 5th Cavalry 40, 102, 104, 116–118, 121, 123–124, 126, 129, 134–135, 141–143, 146, 151, 154, 157–158, 164–165, 174, 177, 183; 5th Infantry 122; 6th Cavalry 166; 7th Infantry 130; 8th Infantry 132; 11th Cavalry 141, 150, 160, 170, 175; 21st Cavalry 155, 158; 24th Infantry 101, 127; 31st Battery Light Artillery 140; 40th Infantry 56, 62, 65, 92, 110, 164; 50th Infantry 156; 57th Infantry 115, 128; 61st Infantry 115, 130; 64th Infantry 117; 69th Infantry 89, 93; 70th Infantry 114–115; 72nd Infantry 116; 88th Infantry 132; 116th Infantry 127; 121st Infantry 132, 134, 173; 130th Infantry 158; 137th Infantry 71; 144th Infantry 165; 169th Infantry 147
Newtonia (MO) Battle 171
Nig (horse) *see* Nigger (horse)
Nigger (horse) 157

Nigger Bill (horse) 94, 157
Norris, Sgt. 61
North Carolina Units (CS):
    Mitchell Rangers 176; 1st Cavalry
    109, 116–117, 122, 130; 2nd In-
    fantry Bn. 141, 156; 5th Cavalry
    116–117; 6th Infantry 160; 58th
    Infantry 135, 176
Norton, Levi Warren 116
Nutmeg (horse) 138, 157
Nye, Edgar Wilson "Bill" 98, 169,
    190

Oakey, Daniel A. 121
Oceola (horse) 157
O'Connor, Lt. 94
Oglesby, Gen. Richard J. 75
Ohio Units (US): Union Light
    Guard 108; 1st Cavalry 116; 2nd
    Cavalry 174; 3rd Infantry 73, 74,
    77, 79, 84; 5th Cavalry 176; 5th
    Light Artillery 138; 10th Infantry
    83, 132; 11th Infantry 159; 12th
    Cavalry 134; 19th Infantry 27, 53,
    71, 114; 23rd Infantry 182; 52nd
    Infantry 145; 53rd Infantry 54;
    67th Infantry 124; 68th Infantry
    160; 70th Infantry 42, 47; 113th
    Infantry 160; 125th Infantry 116
Okolona, MS 147
Olcott, Henry S. 16
Old Abe (horse) 157
Old Baldy (horse) see Baldy (horse)
Old Baldy Civil War Round Table
    110–111
Old Barber (horse) 157
Old Battalion (horse) 158
Old Bench-leg (horse) see Bench-
    leg (horse)
Old Bill (horses) 158
Old Billy (horses) 158, 186
Old Black (horse) 158
Old Blue (horse) 158
Old Bob (horses) 158
Old Bobtail (horse) 158
Old Brown (horse) 158
Old Buck (horse) 159
Old Bull (horse) 159
Old Charley (horse) 159
Old Charlie (horses) 159
Old Chas (horse) 159
Old Clem (horse) 159
Old Dan (horse) 159
Old Fly (horse) see Fly (horse)
Old Fox (horse) 159
Old Gabe (horse) 159
Old Glencoe (horse) 159
Old Gray (horses) 159–160
Old Hatchie (horse) 160
Old Jeff (horse) see Jeff Davis
    (horse)
Old Jim (horses) 100, 160
Old Joe (horses) 160
Old Joe Hooker (horse) 160
Old John (horses) 160–161
Old Man (horse) 161
Old Napoleon (horse) 161

Old Pete (horse) 161
Old Pomp (horse) 161
Old Prince (horse) 161
Old Rebel (horse) 161
Old Roan (horse) 161
Old Robin (horse) see Old Bob
    (horse)
Old Selim (horse) 161
Old Sled (horse) 161
Old Snip (horse) 161
Old Sorrel (horses) 161–162
Old Spot (horse) 162
Old Spunk (horse) 162
Old Thunder (horse) 162
Old Tom (horses) 162
Old Wellington (horse) see
    Wellington (horse)
Old White (horse) see White (horse)
Old Whitey (horses) 162–163
Old Whitie (horse) 163
Old Woolly (horse) 163
Old Yellow (horse) 125; see also
    Claybank (horse)
Old York Road Historical Society
    (Jenkintown, PA) 101, 111, 194
Oldroyd, Osborn 83
Oliver, Robert, Jr. 101, 127–128
Oliver, Robert, Sr. 127–128
O'Neil, teamster 144
Opdycke, Gen. Francis Emerson 111
Opequon (VA) Battle 157, 162
Orange Court House (VA) Battle
    164
Osborn, Francis A. 151
Osborne (horse) 163
Osier, Joseph 118
Ossawatomie (horse) 163
O'Sullivan, Timothy 9
Oswego County Historical Society
    (Oswego, NY) 101, 128, 194
Otto, John Henry 84
Overby, Jim 143
Overland Campaign 134

Pace, Frank 178
Page, Robert 138
Palmer, William Price 166
panniers 8
Parisen, Philip J. 128
Parker, Dexter F. 152, 177
Parker, Robert W. 129, 157
Parsons, H.C. 40–41
Parsons, L.E. 20
Parsons, William H. 97
Partridge, Samuel S. 56
Pasco (horse) 94
Pash, George 174
Patchen (horse) see George M.
    Patchen (horse)
Patchen, George M. 136
Patrick, Gen. Marsena 21
Paxton, J.G. 10, 151
Pea Ridge (AR) Battle 44, 136, 142
Peacock, William H. 135
Pearce, Dexter P. 184
Pease, Clark M. 177
Peddy, George W. 109, 134

Pemberton, Gen. John C. 83, 84
Pender, Gen. William Dorsey 47,
    118, 130
Pendleton, Gen. William Nelson
    158
Penfield, James A. 116, 126, 158
Peninsula Campaign (VA) 9, 11, 32,
    34, 56, 67, 84–85, 115, 119, 124,
    138, 163, 165, 171, 184
Pennebaker, Charles D. 119
Pennsylvania 10
Pennsylvania Units (US): Inde-
    pendent Battery 41; Ringgold
    Cavalry Bn. 121; 1st Cavalry 110,
    113; 2nd Reserves Infantry 56;
    3rd Cavalry 19; 4th Reserves In-
    fantry 67; 6th Cavalry 153; 8th
    Cavalry 29; 13th Reserve In-
    fantry; 14th Cavalry 28; 15th
    Cavalry 123; 16th Cavalry 143,
    153; 17th Cavalry 87; 22nd Cav-
    alry 19, 181; 45th Infantry 31, 134;
    47th Infantry 31; 51st Infantry
    119; 63rd Infantry 109; 68th In-
    fantry 119; 83rd Infantry 160;
    85th Infantry 159; 87th Infantry
    116; 99th Infantry 184; 105th In-
    fantry 115, 163; 109th Infantry
    145; 114th Infantry 184; 116th In-
    fantry 42, 51, 65–66, 93, 152;
    118th Infantry 127; 119th Infantry
    140; 121st Infantry 113; 141st In-
    fantry 150; 148th Infantry 128,
    134, 141, 144
Pennypacker, Gen. Galusha 134
Pensacola Expedition (FL) 32
Perkins, Sanford H. 130
Perry, Theophilus 120, 171
Perryville (KY) Battle 27, 46, 65,
    128, 166
Pet (horses) 163
Pete (horses) 163
Peters, George H. 39
Petersburg (VA) Seige 44, 47, 57, 84,
    91, 93, 109, 123, 124, 125, 177, 179
Peytonia (horse) 163
Phelan, Henry C. 148–149
Phifer, Charles W. 123
Philippi (horse) 163–164
Phillips, Fred 163
Phillips, Joseph R. 112
Pickett, Gen. George Edward 44,
    151, 159
Pierce, William P. 165
Pine Mountain (GA) Battle 144
Pink (horse) 164
Platt, Lemuel B. 159
Pleasant Hill (LA) Battle 114
Pleasanton, Gen. Alfred 114, 173
Plug (horse) 164
Plug Ugly (horse) 32, 164
Poague, Jim 146
Poague, William Thomas 146
Pocahontas (horses) 109, 164
Polk, Gen. Leonidas 89, 144
Polk, William M. 89
Pomp (horse) 164

Pompey (horse) 164
Pony (horse) 121; *see also* Bullet (horse)
Pope, Gen. John 32, 36, 51
Pope, Y.J. 128
Port Hudson (LA) Seige 83–86, 115
Port Walthall (VA) Battle 155
Porter, Horace 44, 57, 69
Postles, J.P. 122
Potomac (horse) 164–165
Potter, Gen. Robert Brown 165
Potter's Raid (SC) 126
Powell (horse) 165
pranks 89
Pressley, John G. 124
Pretty (horse) 165
Price, Gen. Sterling 61, 85, 100, 121
Price's 1864 Missouri Raid 139
Prima Donna (horse) 126
Prince (horses) 165, 185
Prince Hal (horse) 165
Princess (horse) 166
Proctor, Redfield 159
Promptly (horse) 166
Prosperity (horse) 122, 166
Pryor, Gen. Roger Atkinson 146
Pulaski (horse) 166
Punch (horse) 166
Puryear, Thomas 108, 122

Quaker (horse) 166
Quantrill, James Clark 117, 123
quartermaster & commissary 8–11, 18
Quartermaster Department 14–17, 23, 26, 50–51, 61, 118, 144
Queen (horse) 94, 166
Quintard, Charles Todd 176

Raake, Emanuel 145
Racine, WI 16
racing 89–94, 109, 115–117, 120, 128, 130, 132, 136, 140–142, 147, 150, 152, 156, 163, 166, 169–170, 172–174, 176, 177, 184–185
Ragan, Bohanan 183
Rambler (horse) 166
Ramseur, Gen. Stephen Dodson 112, 129, 175
Randolph, George W. 62
Ransom, Gen. Thomas Edwin Greenfield 171
Rasin, William Independence 112
Ratcliff, Sgt. 116–117
Rau, Charles H. 88
Rawlings, Gen. John Aaron 135
Rawlins, Jim 142
Rawson, Mary 87–88
Rayburn, Howell A. "Doc" 150
Raymond, Frank W. 159
Raymond (MS) Battle 174
Read, Thomas Buchanan 97, 169
Reader, Samuel J. 134
Ream's Station, VA 41, 119
Rebbie (horse) *see* Little Rebel (horse)
Rebel (horses) 166

Red Eye (horse) 140, 166
Red Oak (horses) 166–167
Red Pepper (horse) 167
Red River Campaign, LA 98, 183
Red Robin (horse) 167
Redfield, H.V. 50
Redmond (horse) 167
Redmond, Sgt. 167
Rees, W.T. 145
Regulator (horse) 140, 167
Renne, Lucius 141, 174
Reno (horse) 167
Rentfrow, A.E. 128
Resaca (GA) Battle 44, 175
Reynolds, Gen. Alexander Welch 135
Reynolds, Dr. 94
Reynolds, Gen. John Fulton 47, 132, 165
Reynolds, P.L.F. 147
Reynolds, Gov. Thomas 61
Rheatown (TN) Battle 123
Rhode Island Units:1st Cavalry 120–121; 1st Light Artillery 159, 163, 184; 2nd Infantry 29, 56, 97, 123, 143, 146–47, 157
Rhodes, Elisha Hunt 29, 56, 97, 123, 146–147, 157
Richards, A. Keene 137
Richardson, W.H. 146
Richmond (horse) 104, 167
Richmond (VA) battles *see* Peninsula Campaign
Rienzi (horse) 97–98, 101, 103, 106, 118, 131, 167–169, *168*, 173, 190–191, 195
Rifle (horse) 169
Rinaldo (horse) 169
Ringwalt, Sam 110
Ripley, Edward Hastings 161
Ripley, Gen. Roswell S. 91
Ritchie, John 126
Roanoke (horses) 104, 169
Roanoke Island, NC 166
Robards, Mr. 169
Robbins, Dave 174
Roberts, Louis 176
Robertson, Francis Smith 116, 120, 149–150, 154
Robertson, James A. 37
Robeson, Thomas Rodman 150
Robin (horse) *see* Old Bob (horse)
Robin Hood (horse) 169
Rock (horse) 169
Rockingham Furnace (VA) Battle 157
Rockville (MD) Invasion 21
Roddy, Gen. Phillip D. 75, 77
Roderick (horse) 102, 170
Rodes, Gen. Robert Emmett 132, 153
Rodney (horses) 93, 170
Roe, George M. 148
Roebuck (horse) 170
Roemer, Jacob 128
Rogers, Andrew F. 72
Rollins, Augustus W. 159

Romney (horse) 170
Rondy (horse) 104, 170
Rosecrans, Gen. William Starke 60, 72, 119, 176
Rosengarten, Adolph 184
Rossville (GA) Battle 41
Rousseau, Gen. Lovell 84, 91
Rover (horse) 170
Rowan, John 53
Roy (horses) 124, 170
Ruby (horse) 170
Rucker, D.H. 15–16
Ruggles, Mortimer B. 183
Ruhl, Noah G. 116
Ruksh (horse) 170
Rusling, James Fowler 144, 181
Russell, Andrew J. *43*
Russell, Milton 79
Ryder, Lt. 94, 156

Sacramento (KY) Battle 112
Sailor's Creek (VA) Battle 125, 162, 169
St. Claire, Manluis 146
St. Louis (MO) Cavalry Depot 17
Salem Church (VA) Battle 173
Salm-Salm, Felix Constantin Alexander Johann Nepomuk, Prince zu 94, 132
Saltron (horse) 170–171
Sam (horses) 105, 171
Sam Patch (horse) 171
Sample, James Jasper 144
Sampson, Emma 78
San Antonio (horse) 171
Sanders, John "John Tuck" Sanders 152
Sandersville (GA) Battle 160
Sanger, William 171
Sanitary Commission, U.S. 12, 27, 141, 162
San Jose (horse) *see* Old Joe (horse)
Sansom, soldier 78
Sappony Church (VA) Battle 119
Sardanapalus (horse) 171
Sargent, H.B. 120
Sargent, Mr. 185
Savage, Bridgette Z. 100
Savage, George D. 162
Sayler's Creek Battle *see* Sailor's Creek (VA) Battle
Schall, Edwin 119
Scheibert, Justus 147, 158
Schurmann, Gustav A. 110, 164
Schurz, Gen. Carl 47
Scott (horse) 171
Scott, Lt. 135
Scott, Gen. Robert Kingdom 160
Scott, Walter 166
Scott, Gen. Winfield 137, 156
Seal, Pleasant 159
Searle, Lt. 174
Sears, Gen. Cladius Wistar 116
Secesh (horse) 171
Secessia (horse) 171
Sedgewick, Gen. John 84, 101, 119, 126, 139, 166, 176

Seibrie, Lt. 94, 184
Seliem (horse) 171
Selim (horses) 158, 171–172
Selma (AL) Battle 24, 65, 117, 172
Seven Days (VA) Battle 10
Seven Pines (VA) Battle 44, 111, 127
Seward, William H. 59
Sewart, James 175
Seymour, Isaac G. 128
Shackelford, Frederick 165
Shackleford, Bessie 113
Shackleford, Gen. James Murrell 137
Shaler, Gen. Alexander 105, 135
Sharpsburg (horse) 94, 172
Sharpsburg Battle see Antietam
Shaw, William T. 182–183
Sheddon, James A. 80
Sheets, James W. 72, 77
Shellbark (horse) 172
Shenandoah (horse) 172
Shenandoah Valley (VA) Campaigns 10, 51- 53, 109–110, 115, 141, 154, 181
Sheridan (horse) 172
Sheridan, Gen. Philip 5, 16, 88, **89**, 97, 101, 104, 109, 120, 167–169, 172, 190–191, 195
Sheridan at Cedar Creek (poem) 97
Sheridan's Ride (poem) 97, 169
Sherman (horses) 129, 185; *see also* Dolly (horse)
Sherman, Gen. William Tecumseh 3, 8–9, 19, 40, 46, 49, 96, 106, 116, 125, 129, 149, 171
Sherman's "March to the Sea" 7, 24, 56, 145, 171
Shields, James 89
Shiloh (horses) 172
Shiloh (TN) Battle 27, 36, 40, 42–48, **64**, 67, 99, 112, 117–118, 120, 122, 132, 134, 138, 146, 165, 171
Shoolbred, J. Stanyard "Jack" 129
Shorter, Gov. John Gill 80
Sibley, Gen. Henry H. 49
Sickles, Gen. Daniel Edgar 92, 129, 138, 164, 175
Siegel (horse) 172–173
Siegel, Gen. Franz 173
Sievers, Frederick William 101
Silver Tail (horse) 173
Simon (mule) 173
Simon Bolivar (mule) 173
Sinclair, Miss 113
Sir Archy (horse) 178
Sir Oliver (horse) 102, 173
Skedaddle (horses) 173
Skinner, F.G. 159
Skylark (horse) 173
Slasher (horse) 173
Sleepy Jeff (horse) 173
Slicky (horse) 173
Slocomb, Cuthbert H. 139
Smith, Gen. Andrew Jackson 158
Smith, Baxter 149
Smith, D.D. 73, 77, 80
Smith, D.W. 138

Smith, George W. 141
Smith, James J. 89
Smith, Jim 142
Smith, John 68
Smith, Gen. Martin L. 83
Smith, Gen. Thomas Kilby 112, 122
Smith, William Rowley 123
Smith, Windsor B. 119
Smithsonian Institution (Washington, DC) 101, **168**–169, 173, 195
Snap (horse) 173–174
Sneden, Robert Knox 56, 62
Snip (horse) 173–174
Snodder (horse) 174
Solomon (horse) 174
Sorghum (horse) 174
Sorrel, Gen. Gilbert Moxley 22, 23, 27, 40, 43, 46, 47, 106, 155, 181
South Carolina Units (CS): Beauregard's Battery 55; Jenkin's Brigade 69–71; Palmetto Sharpshooters 118; 1st Cavalry 141; 2nd Cavalry 99, 105, 112, 115, 129, 144, 165, 167; 3rd Infantry 128; 4th Cavalry 180–181; 5th Cavalry 142, 143–144, 148, 161; 19th Infantry 113; 24th Infantry 139; 25th Infantry 124
South Carolina Units (US), 1st Infantry see United States Units, 33rd Colored Infantry
Southern Claims Commission of 1871 26
Spalding, Ira 156, 177
Sparks, Allison Wudville 155, 161
Speedy (horse) 150
Spencer, William 77
Spiegel, Marcus M. 124
Spielman, George W. 116
Spike (horse) 174
Spot (horses) 174
Spottsylvania (VA) Battle 42, 68, 112, 128, 154, 160, 177
Sprague, John 43
Spring Hill (TN) Battle 167
Springfield (MO) Expedition 15
staff of Gen. J.E.B. Stuart 105, 113, 120, 121, 126, 135, 147, 149–150, 152–154, 158, 186
Stafford, Gen. Leroy Augustus 140
standards for equines 28
Stanley, Henry Morton 47
Stanton, Edwin McM. 42, 80
Stanyan, John M. 86
Star (horse) see Star of the East (horse)
Star of the East (horse) 174
Star of the West (horse) see The Star of the West (horse)
The Star of the West (horse) 176
Starkweather, Lt. 84
Steel Dust (horse) 186
Stephens, William Henry 128, 141, 144
Steuart, Gen. George Hume "Maryland" 164

Stevens, Thaddeus 23
Stevenson, James H. 103
Stevenson, William G. 33, 35, 48, 172
Stevenson Mare (horse) 135
Stewart, Gen. Alexander Peter 175, 180
Stiles, Richard A. 166
Stiles, Robert Augustus 154
Stiles, Sgt. 135
Stillwell, Leander 28, 184
Stone, James A. 166
Stone, Sarah Katharine "Kate" 183
Stone, James A. 122
Stone Mountain Confederate Memorial (Stone Mountain, GA) 118
Stoneman, Gen. George 112
Stoneman's Raid 112, 122, 124
Stone's River Battle see Murfreesboro Battle
Stonewall (horses) 174
Stony (horse) 174
Stoughton, Gen. Edwin H. 26, 118
Strahl, Gen. Otho French 176
Stratton, Henry G. 27, 53, 71, 114
Streight, Abel D. 27, **73**, 72–81
Streight's Raid 27, 72–81
Stuart, Alexander H.H. 123, 149
Stuart, Flora 149
Stuart, Gen. J.E.B. 5, 18, 21, 31, 47, 59, 61, 62, 88, 104, 105, 112, 113, 121, 123, 135, 136, 140, 148–151, 153, 155–156, 173–174, 181
Stuart's Ride Around McClellan, VA 127
Stumbler (horse) 174
Sukey (horse) 174–175
Sultan (horse) 175
Sultana (horse) see Sultan (horse)
Sullins, David 152
Swartz's Mill, VA 113–114
Swaving, Dr. John 36
Sweeney, Sam 88
Sweet, George 111
Sweet Will (horse) 175

Taliaferro brothers 65
Tammany (horse) 175
Tangent (horsse) 175
Tar River (horse) 175
Tarheel (horse) 175
Tarter (horse) 175
Taylor, Alex R. 180
Taylor, Gen. Richard 96, 182–183
Taylor, Walter Herron 112, 133, 149
Taylor, President Zachary 182–183
Teasle (horse) 175
Ten Broeck, Mr. 150–151
Tennessee (horse) 175
Tennessee Units (CS): Marshall's Battery 56; McClung's Battery 42; Morton's Battery 75; Polk's Battery 42; 1st Infantry 176; 2nd Cavalry 161; 2nd Infantry 118; 3rd Infantry 121; 4th Cavalry 75, 77, 149; 7th Infantry 161; 9th Cavalry

75, 77; 10th Cavalry 75; 11th
Cavalry 75, 76; 13th Infantry 125;
18th Cavalry 44; 19th Infantry
152; 20th Infantry 161
Tennessee Units (US): 4th
Mounted 118
Tenney, Luman Harris 174
Tennyson 70
Texas Units (CS): Frontier Regi-
ment 90; Good's/Douglas's Bat-
tery 127; J.P. Lane Rangers 163;
Parson's Cavalry Brigade 52, 97;
Walker's Division 125; Waul's Le-
gion 83; 1st Mounted Rifles 90;
2nd Cavalry 163; 2nd Infantry
155; 8th Cavalry 18; 9th Cavalry
27, 33, 155, 161; 12th Cavalry 150;
15th Cavalry 111; 18th Cavalry 111;
21st Cavalry 144; 28th Cavalry
(Dismounted) 120, 171
That Devil Forrest **76**
Thatcher, Marshall P. 84
Thaxton, George D. 123
Thomas (horse) 176
Thomas, Gen. Bryan M. 136
Thomas, Gen. George H. 17, 21,
56, 116
Thomas, Robert N. 122–123
Thomas, Stephen 163
Thompson, Alan **100**
Thompson, James 41
Thompson, Jasper 159
Thompson, Gen. Meriwether "Jeff"
171
Thompson's Station (TN) Battle 170
Thoroughbred Bloggers Alliance
103
Thoroughfare Gap (VA) Battle 183
Thunderbolt (horse) 176
Thurman, R.W. 88
Tibbit, W.B. 158
Tilden, Gen. Charles W. 99
Tobey (horse) 119, 176
Tom (horses) 176
Tom Taylor (horse) 176
Tom Telegraph (horse) **100**, 176–
177, 194
Tom Tug (horse) 177
Tommy (horses) 177
Toombs, Gen. Robert Augustus 138
Topsy (horse) 177
Torrance, William M.G. 162
Toucey, Isaac 10
training of equines 32–35
Tramp (horse) 177
transportation of equines 30–32
Traveler (horse) *see* Traveller (horse)
Traveller (horse) 28, 37, 97, 101–
104, 106, 131, 151, 177–180, *179*,
194
Traveller (novel) 99–100, 180, 186
*Traveller & Company: the Horses of
Gettysburg* (history) 100, 103
Traveller, horses mentioned in 186
Traweek, Wash. 164
Trevillian Station (VA) Battle 114,
158, 180–181

Trimble, Gen. Isaac 53, 62, 144
Trimmier, Theodore Gilliard 125
Tripler, Dr. Charles S. 11
Trojan (horse) 180
Trojan Horse (horse) 180
Trumball, Richard 183–184
Trussel, Jacob 113
Tucker, Bill 129
Tucker, Charles E. 126
Tucker, George W. 123
Tulkahoma (horse) *see* Tullahoma
(horse)
Tullahoma (horse) 180
Tullahoma (TN) Campaign 72, 91,
111, 159, 175
Tunnard, W.H. 85
Twist Tail (horse) 180–181
Tyler, Gen. Erastus Barnard 184
Tyler, President John 175

Uncle Abe (horse) 181
Uncle Sam (horse) 181
Underhill, Hiram 124, 142
Underwood, Aldin B. 71
United States units (US): "Marine
Brigade" 75; Military Railroads
43; Schuykill Arsenal 114; Sher-
man's Light Artillery Battery 41;
Signal Corps 11, 124, 155; Tele-
graph Corps 138; 1st Sharpshoot-
ers 140, 184; 2nd Artillery **6**; 2nd
Dragoons 28; 4th Artillery 29,
43, 175; 5th Artillery "West Point
Battery" 33, 182; 11th Infantry
127, 139; 14th Colored Infantry
44; 33rd Colored Infantry 169;
80th Colored Infantry 144
University of Kentucky 101, 117
Upperville (VA) Battle 112
Upson, Jonathan B. 185
Upson, Theodore F. 185

Vallandigham, Mr. 146
Valverde (NM) Battle 39–40, 159;
see also New Mexico Campaign
Vananda, Maj. 73, 79
Vance, Gov. Zebulon 63
Van Cleve, Gen. Horatio Phillips
113
Van Dorn (horse) 181
Van Dorn, Gen. Earl 132, 171, 181
Van Horne, Thomas B. 32, 70
Van Wyck, Charles H. 16
Van Wyck Committee 16
Vaughan, Gen. Alfred Jefferson, Jr.
125
Vaughan, Gen. John C. 83, 86
Venable, Andrew Reid 135
Verdiersville (VA) Battle 140, 173
Vermont Units (US): 1st Cavalry
40, 113, 159; 8th Infantry 163; 9th
Infantry 161; 15th Infantry 159;
16th Infantry 163
Veteran Sam (horse) *see* Sam
(horses)
Vic (horse) *see* Victory (horse)
Vicksburg (MS) Campaign 24, 32,

48, 53, 74, 83–86, 96, 98, 119,
121, 128, 145–146, 150, 170, 181,
183
Victory 181
Vila, Mr. 117
Vincent, Col. 170
Vincent, Gen. Strong 160
Vinson, Joe 160
Virginia (horse) 104
Virginia Historical Society (Richmond, VA) 102
Virginia Military Institute (Lexington, VA) *29*, 100–101, 130–132,
195
Virginia Units (CS): "Black Horse
Cavalry" 29; Haskell's Bn. Artillery 177; McNeil's Rangers 164;
Poague's Bn. Artillery 146; 1st
Cavalry 35, 128, 140, 146; 1st Infantry 159; 1st Richmond Howitzers 154, 168; 2nd Cavalry 18,
88, 124, 129, 157, 170; 2nd Infantry 139, 163; 3rd Cavalry 135,
138, 144, 163, 183; 3rd Richmond
Howitzers 30, 123; 4th Cavalry
163; 6th Cavalry 34, 150, 164,
170; 7th Cavalry 114; 9th Cavalry
119, 127; 12th Cavalry 119, 142;
19th Cavalry 114; 22nd Infantry
114; 40th Infantry 145; 43rd Cavalry Bn. 17, 26, 113, 123, 126, 144,
148, 150, 164; 46th Infantry 166
Voltaire (horse) 181
von Blucher, Gustav 94, 140–141,
166
von Borcke, Johan August Heinrich
Heros 147, 158
von Fritsch, Frederick Otto 122
von Gilsa, Leopold 122
von Schaik, George W. 94, 130

Wade, Quartermaster 94, 152
Wagner, Gen. George D. 91
Waif (horse) 181–182
Wails, William E. 142
Wainwright, Charles Sheils 116
Waiters, Mr. 125
Walker, Gen. John G. 43
Walker, Morgan 117
Walker, Dr. Nathaniel S. 37
Walker, Thomas 88
Wallace, George 162
Wallace, Gen. Lewis "Lew" 146
Wallace, Gen. William Harvey
Lamb 36, 165
Waltermire, William 136
Walters, Hugh T. 113
Walton, Thomas 155
War Eagle (horse) 182
The War Horse (statue) *ii*, 102
Ware, Charles Alexander 173
Waring, George W., Jr. 139, 147–
148, 153, 170
Warren (horses) 182
Warrenton (VA) Battle 123
Washington (horse) *see* Reno
(horse)

Washington & Lee University (Lexington, VA) 101, 102, 108, 131, 180
Washington College 178, 179; *see also* Washington & Lee University
Washington Quartermaster Depot 15
Watkins, Col. 109, 184
Watson, William 7
Watts, Gov. Thomas H. 20
Waud, A.R. *57*
Wauhatchee (TN) Battle 42, 69–71
Webby (horse) 182
Webster, Frederic S. 131
Weed, Gen. Stephen H. 47
Weldon Railroad, VA 110
Weller, Benjamin Franklin 135, 186
Wellington (horse) 104, 182
Welsh, Thomas 117
Western Reserve Historical Society (Cleveland, OH) 88
Westport (MO) Battle 114, 134
Wettstein, Peter 147–148
Wheeler, James Russell 112
Wheeler, Gen. Joseph 5, 20, 42, 46–47, 104, 141–142
whinny 30
Whipple, George M. 121
White, Benjamin Stephen 152
White, John 25
White Bull (horse) *see* Jerome (horse)
White Eye (horse) 182
White Oak Creek/Swamp (VA) Battle 67, 169
White Surrey (horse) 182
Whitefield, Capt. 94, 156
Whitesides, E.G. 116
Whitey (horse) 107, 182–183
Whitie (horses) 183
Whiting, Gen. William Henry Chase 134
Whitlow, Wright 44

Whittington, J.F. 87
Wickerham, Adam 121
Wikipedia 103
Wild Bill (horse) 183
Wild Bill of the Woods (horse) 183
Wilder, Burt Green 116
the Wilderness (VA) Battle 10, 11, 44, 63–64, 90, 115, 118, 120, 128, 135, 140, 144, 154, 164, 173–174, 176
Wilkinson, Bayard 43
Willcox, Gen. Orlando Bolivar 122, 126, 140, 152, 167, 170
Williams, Gen. Alpheus Starkey 32, 51, 52, 54, 55, 56, 61, 116, 154, 164
Williams, Martha "Markie" Custis 178
Williams, Noble C. 65
Williams, Robert 125–126
Williams, Toddy 127
Williams, W.T. 160
Williamsburg (VA) Battle 40, 56, 126, 155
Willits, Dr. 35
Wills, Charles W. 25, 172–173
Wilmington (DE) Cavalry Depot 17
Wilson, Gordon 122
Wilson, Gen. James Harrison 5, 21, 24, 34, 96, 172, 181–182
Wilson, Jeremiah DeBell "Jerry" 144
Wilson, Robert A. 111
Wilson, Thomas 88
Wilson's Raid 24, 65, 134, 181–182
Winchester (VA) Campaigns & Battles 54, 97, 162, 164, 177
Winchester (horse) *see* Rienzi
Winslow, Edward F. 114
Wisconsin Units (US): 5th Infantry 146; 6th Infantry 161; 21st In-

fantry 84, 85; 24th Infantry 119; 36th Infantry 127
Wisdom, John H. 79
"Wisdom's Ride" 79
Wise, Gen. Henry Alexander 91, 166
Wise, John Sergeant 151, 164
Wise, Obadiah Jennings 166
Wolseley, Gen. Lord Garnett 81
Wonka (horse) 183
Wood, Gen. Thomas J. 72, 91
Woodruff, Hiram 185
Woods, Joseph Jackson 145
Woodstock (VA) Battle 110
Woolly-Horse (horse) 186
Wright, Howard D. 86
Wright, John C. 139
Wright, William 139
Wright, William W. 43
Wyeth, John Allan 72, *76*, 132
Wyman, Henry 183
The Wyman Horse (horse) 183

Yancey (horse) 183–184
Yankee (horse) 184
Yates, Gov. Richard 80
Yeatman, Thomas R. 131
Yellow Horse (horse) 184
Yellow Tavern (VA) Battle 34, 47, 121
Yorktown (horse) 184
Young Giffords (horse) 184
Young Salem (horse) 184
Yountz, James W. 183

Zella (horse) 94, 184
Zollicoffer (horse) 184
Zollicoffer, Gen. Felix 47
Zook, Gen. Samuel Z. 47
Zoozoo (horse) 184